Elsevier *Global Energy Policy and Economics* Series

Agile Energy Systems:
Global Lessons from
the California Energy Crisis

Woodrow W. Clark II

and

Ted K. Bradshaw

Elsevier Internet Homepage - http://www.elsevier.com
Consult the Elsevier homepage for full catalogue information on all books, journals and electronic products and services.

Elsevier Titles of Related Interest in this series

ARENTSEN and KÜNNEKE
National Reforms in European Gas
ISBN: 008-043687-0

MIDTTUN
European Electricity Systems in Transition
ISBN: 008-042994-7

MIDTTUN
European Energy Industry Business Strategies
ISBN: 008-043631-5

WANG
China's Oil Industry and Market
ISBN: 008-043005-8

Related Journals:
A sample journal issue is available online by visiting the homepage of the journal (homepage details at the top of this page). Free specimen copy gladly sent on request. Elsevier Ltd, The Boulevard, Langford Lane, Kidlington, Oxford, OX5 1GB, UK

Energy
Energy Economics
Energy Policy
Resources and Energy Economics
Resources Policy
Utilities Policy
The Electricity Journal

To Contact the Publisher
Elsevier welcomes enquiries concerning publishing proposals: books, journal special issues, conference proceedings, etc. All formats and media can be considered. Should you have a publishing proposal you wish to discuss, please contact, without obligation, the publisher responsible for Elsevier's Energy and Power programme:

Tony Roche
Senior Publishing Editor
Elsevier Ltd
The Boulevard, Langford Lane   Phone: +44 1865 843887
Kidlington, Oxford   Fax: +44 1865 843931
OX5 1GB, UK   E.mail: t.roche@elsevier.com

General enquiries, including placing orders, should be directed to Elsevier's Regional Sales Offices – please access the Elsevier homepage for full contact details (homepage details at the top of this page).

Elsevier *Global Energy Policy and Economics* Series

Agile Energy Systems: Global Lessons from the California Energy Crisis

Woodrow W. Clark II

Clark Communications LLC, P.O. Box #17975, Beverly Hills, California, USA, and Senior Fellow, Sustainable Development, The Milken Institute, Santa Monica, California, USA

and

Ted K. Bradshaw

Human and Community Development Department, University of California, Davis, California, USA

2004

ELSEVIER

AMSTERDAM – BOSTON – HEIDELBERG – LONDON – NEW YORK – OXFORD
PARIS – SAN DIEGO – SAN FRANCISCO – SINGAPORE – SYDNEY – TOKYO

ELSEVIER B.V.
Sara Burgerhartstraat 25
P.O.Box 211, 1000 AE
Amsterdam,
The Netherlands

ELSEVIER Inc.
525 B Street, Suite 1900
San Diego,
CA 92101-4495
USA

ELSEVIER Ltd
The Boulevard,
Langford Lane,
Kidlington,
Oxford OX5 1GB, UK

ELSEVIER Ltd
84 Theobalds Road
London WC1X 8RR
UK

First edition 2004.

Library of Congress Cataloging in Publication Data
A catalog record is available from the Library of Congress.

British Library Cataloguing in Publication Data

Agile energy systems: global lessons from the California
  energy crisis. - (Elsevier global energy policy and
  economics series)
  1. Energy policy - California 2. Sustainable development -
  Government policy - California 3. California - Economic
  policy
  I. Clark, Woodrow W. II. Bradshaw, Ted K.
  333.7'915'09794

ISBN: 0-08-044448-2
ISSN: 1571-4985

⊚ The paper used in this publication meets the requirements of ANSI/NISO Z39.48-1992 (Permanence of Paper).
Printed in The Netherlands.

Contents

Foreword

The future of energy has become a critical question in public policy debate around the world. Increasing political instability in the Middle East, the high price of oil on world markets, global warming, and escalating first and third world debt are forcing the nations of the world to ask a fundamental question. How do we begin preparing for a post-fossil fuel era?

What we so desperately need is a roadmap to a renewable energy future and a hydrogen-based economy. Woody Clark and Ted Bradshaw have spent more than two decades each at the center of public policy with Clark asking the technological and economic questions and Bradshaw the community context around America's energy options. At a time when few individuals have been willing to suggest a way out of the old energy regime, they have stepped forward with real solutions that can be implemented in America and around the world.

This book is a promissory note for a global clean energy future. It should be widely read, discussed, and be made part of the ongoing public debate. A roadmap indeed, this work provides policy makers with insightful directions and the private sector with near-term and future markets. In the end, the book defines what the practical world of energy is today and can be in the future. More importantly, that New World energy order is not isolated, but inextricably linked to other infrastructure sectors such as water, waste, climate, transportation and most importantly, education. After all, the future of the world is in the hands of our children. It is our responsibility to make them participants and owners of the new clean peaceful world order today.

Jeremy Rifkin is the Founder and President of the Foundation on Economic Trends in Washington, DC and author of numerous trend-setting books on environmental issues. His latest work is *The Hydrogen Economy* (2003).

Jeremy Rifkin

Preface

In early 2001 when the lights were flickering and blinking on and off throughout California, we conceived of this book as a report on the California experience. We envisioned a volume that would go behind misleading news stories and examine how the disaster could turn into an opportunity for California. The State had a history and tradition of making gold out of physical and economic disasters, so we envisioned the same public attitude for California as it rebounded from the deregulation debacle. This is our first collaboration, and we expect to continue working on these issues in the future. A word on authorship. The order of authorship does not reflect contribution or input, because the whole book was jointly written. Lead authorship will be alternated in subsequent publications.

At the time we started this book, Professor Clark had just taken a position in California State Government as Deputy Director/Senior Policy Advisor to Governor Gray Davis for "energy reliability." He quickly became aware of the need to develop alternative initiatives than those urgent and emergency ones that were being proposed to solve California's blackout threats. He worked publicly and increasingly behind the scenes to try to find long-term and clean environmental solutions that would benefit the entire population by making California a sustainable nation-state.

Dr. Clark brought to the book real-time experience and knowledge of how state government was responding to the energy crisis with hands-on experience. He formed collaboratives and forums on renewable energy and hydrogen, developed partnerships with private industry, held meetings, negotiated strategies among political and industry leaders, and mobilized the brightest staff he could find within and without government to rethink deregulation and its consequences. Clark was fond of saying that he taught policy makers how to spell "energy" and then to understand its important link to "environment" and "climate change." Of course, he was not alone in these teaching lessons. However, he often delivered and led the dissemination about renewable energy which was needed to inform decision makers. All the while, Clark documented, wrote, published, and gave hundreds of speeches internationally on the solutions to the energy crisis.

Professor Bradshaw had rekindled his interest in the California electricity industry after having published articles on the state energy system following the first State energy crises in the late 1970s and on the response to PURPA in the 1980s. He had done this work while at the Institute of Governmental Studies at University of California, Berkeley. Now, with his position teaching Community Development and Economic Development at University of California, Davis, he brought to the book the long-term perspective that is so sadly missing in many of the "crisis studies" being published on California.

In addition, Dr. Bradshaw added a useful theoretical/analytical perspective from his ongoing scholarly work in community and economic development. Based on his understanding of the role of technology in development, the interplay between business and government in developing industries, the way universities are key players in technology transfer, and the way complexity alters the ability of policy makers to reach civic goals, he was able to shape and guide the volume into a record of the past that is clearly a pathway to the future to energy public policy worldwide.

Both authors bring an international perspective to the work. For example, Clark, in 1994, had been teaching and conducting research on renewable energy generation systems as a Fulbright Scholar at Aalborg University in Denmark as well as teaching entrepreneurship in several other countries throughout Europe. He had returned to a full-time Visiting Professor at Aalborg in the summer of 1999, before the California crisis had occurred. Bradshaw, as well, had a Fulbright grant to study the Swedish electrical system in 1991, and had explored some developments in the rest of Europe. However, the international perspective was given a boost from our invitation to participate in the UN Environmental Program in Paris (May 2002) as well as numerous other speaking and lecturing invitations worldwide. We thank our colleagues at that meeting for helping us understand the global dynamics, concerns and impact of electricity restructuring and sustainability.

We appreciate the help and input from our editors at Elsevier. They pushed us to add the international perspective to the book, recognizing that the deregulation issue in California was a tip of the iceberg of restructuring in Europe, as well as the rest of the developed and developing world. Subsequent events in Europe over the summer of 2003 certainly proved the point. But even more significantly, many of the solutions to energy policy and technical issues are derived, as the volume continually references, from international, not either California or USA sources.

Bradshaw appreciates support from the University of California Davis. He was given a three-month Sabbatical in 2002 to work on the book which was also supported by his appointment with the University Agricultural Experiment Station over the last two years. The AES appointment provided a fantastic opportunity to do research in the public interest on issues of importance to the State, and this project exemplifies the way the University enables faculty to do research critically important to public policy.

In particular, Department Chair Michael Smith and Associate Dean Lovell Jarvis have been particularly helpful in making this effort possible. I appreciate how Noemi Danao, Managing Editor of the *Journal of the Community Development Society*, kept me from being overwhelmed as Editor of the Journal while writing about energy policy. My colleagues and students in the Community Development Program at UC Davis provided a supportive intellectual environment. In particular, Vlad Stasuc helped to find data and literature, while Nathan Brightbill worked on issues of housing energy efficiency. Doug Svensson, Steve Wahlstrom, Jim King, and colleagues at Applied Development Economics in Berkeley have also contributed more than they know by providing office space and doing the nation's best economic development research by which communities and the state of California can link technology and economic change.

Clark's appreciation list and support network is extensive as well, but must start with this bride, Andrea Kune, who as a newly wed saw her husband countless hours working and writing on his Mac laptop. Andrea indeed is Clark's "My Girl" through the adjustments of a marriage of two "type As" in context of California's historical events from 2001 to 2003 including not just the energy crisis, but also the recall of Governor Davis himself.

Clark was challenged, after only two week in taking his position, at a Local Government Commission dinner meeting to write the book, by then California Resources Secretary, Mary Nichols who heard him talk. However, there were countless others in California government to numerous to name here who contributed to this volume. Some will see their names in the Reference list and others will see their contributions in the text.

Forming teams and attacking problems directly and collaboratively were the key to solving problems in "civic markets." Clark did just that for three years. He was hired, not by governor Davis directly but by Steve Nissen, Kari Dohn and John Stevens whom he owes much to in their support of this volume and the applied work for couping with the energy crisis. Clark identified the able expert advise from a diverse group within and outside government spearheaded by Dr. Don Schultz, Arnie Sowell, Professor Bryan Jenkins, Dr. Greg Morris, Doug Grandy, Steve Prey, Gary Mattinson, Panama Bartholomy, Amanda Eichel Dan Adler, Jonathan Teague, Anna Ferrara, Nick Bollman, Judy Corbett, Pat Stoner, Bud Bebe, and many others. Much, of course, is due to Clark's former colleagues, too numerous to name, from Lawrence Livermore National Laboratory, University of California system especially Berkeley and Davis and certainly Aalborg University in Denmark who remained both knowledgeable and inspirational while he worked on the energy crisis and this volume.

Clark recruited interns globally, first in the summer of 2001 with Magnus Johansson from Iceland, but was a former student of his from Aalborg, Denmark and Adam Dondro who went on to be elected the President of the Student Association at Chico State University and a leader in the California State System for "greening" its 24 campuses. When Clark moved from University of California, Los Angeles in 2003, Seth Jacobson, Russell Vare, Rob Tai from UCLA, and Evan Forrest from Pepperdine University. Each of them on their individual pathways to be future leaders in energy and environmental public policy.

Dedication

Woody Clark dedicates this volume to his wife, Andrea, and his two loving children, Woody III and Andrea. This book represents the reason why I came to California — to start a cleaner and healthier world for my parents, brothers, family, children and future generations.

Ted Bradshaw dedicates this book to his wife, Betty Lou, whose love and help made this possible, and to our sons, Niels and Liam, that their world may be agile and their power from hydrogen.

Chapter 1
The End of the Old Order: The Roots of Reorganization

1.1. Introduction

Beginning in Southern California during June 2000 and then throughout the whole state during the Winter of 2001, rolling electricity blackouts darkened California. The power outages were the most visible part of an energy crisis that shocked the world. California's recently deregulated utilities saw wholesale electricity rates skyrocket from their typical $30 per MWh to over $750, Pacific Gas and Electric (PG&E), the State's largest private utility, ended in bankruptcy, and the State had to step in to buy power to avoid a total energy collapse. The crisis created an economic downturn which is still unraveling years later. Moreover, what happened in California during 2000–2001 portended energy, economic, and environmental problems around the nation and the world.

Electrons are the raw material of the "next economy," the medium for conveying information, computing data, mapping gnomes, calculating biomedical information, and driving the development of an affluent society. How is it possible, many asked, that California, the world's fifth largest (and probably the richest) economy was facing a "Third World" problem of power shortages and blackouts? Even more pronounced was the realization that a sophisticated industrial nation-state could be subject to private industry manipulation of power supplies. If California was afflicted by such a crisis, could the rest of the USA and the world soon follow? Indeed, they did.

This book is historical, contemporary, and futuristic. We look at the California energy crisis not so much to find its complex historical roots, but to explore the nuances of the crisis, which gripped California from 2000 to 2002. We do not seek to assign blame for the crisis. Instead, we use the California energy crisis as a case to show how the State is hardly unique in coming face-to-face with the changing realities of a large electrical grid. We seek to distill from the California case lessons that can be applied throughout the world.

Moreover, the fundamental lesson of the California case is that continuing business as usual by centralizing the electrical system will fail in large part because of the limited premises on which the current system was built over its 100-year evolution. We will argue in this book that change is inevitable in energy systems around the world, but that the moves to privatize, deregulate, or liberalize not only have a low chance of success but are doomed to failure. This is because power systems and their grids are inherently interconnected in ways that tend toward monopoly or integrated control without continuing public oversight.

There is no political, social, and especially economic justification for eliminating the public regulation of the energy sector for private market forces that do not have the public interest foremost. As we conclude, continued public oversight of market forces is needed. We agree that the concept of a centralized vertically integrated utility managing its own grid is no longer viable in the next economy of the 21st century. However, we think that the future for the energy infrastructure is not to give control to what will be a small number of "competing" corporate producers. Nor is it to have longer-linked supply, transmission, and distribution systems. To deregulate responsibility to a fragile open but not free market is a bad public policy. Reregulation is equally a bad policy. And no change should rely primarily upon economists and energy system engineers, also including experts, without looking out for long-term civic benefits in terms of the environment, community values, public health, and economic development.

Recent events surrounding 911 and its aftermath dictate that the public sector must be concerned for the protection, security, and reliability of critical infrastructures: energy along with waste, water, and the air quality. Now after 911, issues of public security over critical national systems have increased public responsibility for governmental oversight, investment, and regulation. In addition, public responsibility has increased at the state, regional, and local levels to assure that system reliability and security are pursued, even at the expense of short-term market decisions that are made daily in competitive private power markets.

Clearly, we do not argue for a return to the public-regulated (and sometimes publicly owned) system of the past, but instead we present the case for the creation of a truly agile and sustainable energy system. We will analyze the current system and distill from it an understanding of the pressures on the system to change as well as the indicators of the potential for a new type of electrical system. We will show how in the current turmoil of energy crises, reversing policy directions, bankruptcies, and legal intervention there are nonetheless potentially successful strategies being developed that are increasing flexibility. These innovative efforts are being pursued by the main utilities, by local communities and individuals as well as progressive "third party" firms, in small places and innovative communities throughout the world.

We will show how powerful market forces are building dispersed systems that rely on renewable technologies, locate generation closer to demand, use technologies that have a vastly simpler infrastructure, and reshape the government's role as the public interest "watchdog" for the new system. The role of government can also go much further as it can seek to form public–private "business partnerships" on the regional and local levels. The public sector must be a partner in order to insure that there is continuous protection of the ratepayers and promotion of investment for the public good and technological change.

Our model is to propose a viable model for that future. The agile energy system we detail will meet the growing energy needs of an increasingly interdependent world, not by deregulating existing utility systems, but by promoting civic capitalism and utilization of renewable, distributed, and hybrid technologies that are just now becoming available. We outline steps that lead to this future. Some of the steps are proactive such as concentrating or competitively aggregating government energy purchases for state buildings, or college and university campuses, and supporting programs to create a market for emerging technologies and systems.

Other public sector steps facilitate collaboration to commercialize technologies such as the fuel cell collaborative organizations that advance forward fuel cell research, development, and commercialization. Public-focused expenditures also help conservation, energy efficiency, and other public good programs, which compete with centralized wasteful traditional energy generation. However, some steps are preemptive such as suggesting that the rapid construction of many natural gas fired power plants or the building of liquefied natural gas facilities will cause huge spikes in the price of natural gas that can be avoided by relying on renewable energy sources. Moreover, expanding the number of natural gas power plants fails to halt continued greenhouse emissions problems, causes a glut on the market which will close off opportunities for new innovative solutions, and increases dependency on foreign fossil fuel supplies. These programs decrease the flexibility and robustness of the power system rather than making it more diverse and distributed. The alternative is to build an agile energy system that uses flexible technologies and adaptive social systems.

The purpose of this book is to understand what happened in the California energy crisis and to apply the lessons learned to issues relevant to the restructuring of the California system following the crisis. Our goal is to anticipate how new technologies, organizational structures, and analytical frameworks can create systems that are much more robust, environmentally sustainable, and cheaper than anything found in the arcane energy infrastructure of most existing counties. If we do this well we will show how California, and electrical systems around the world, can get out of the mess that they currently find themselves in and thereby create a new equitable future for all their citizens.

1.2. Overview

This book is organized into three sections. The first section looks at the California energy crisis of 2000–2001 in the context of global restructuring of the electricity industry. Five core concepts explain what changed leading to the problems that disrupted the electrical system in California (and to some degree in other states and nations). These five core concepts also provide a perspective on alternatives for crisis resolution, which will be developed in the second section where we set out the criteria for a sustainable energy system and show how the network of suppliers, transmitters, and distributors can create a viable alternative system while meeting the public good.

The theme of this book is that electrical power systems in advanced countries are in transition. We would argue that these transitional energy systems foretell the future for developed as well as developing countries. Furthermore, the problems with power systems need to be understood by the social and financial institutions who are asked to support the people and organizations or companies responsible for the reliable distribution of power to all citizens. Multinational banks and organizations must create policies and programs for energy systems in developing and third world nations which are based upon the learned successes of the industrial nations. For ease of analysis, the transition in the energy sector can be divided into three stages:

1. *Vertically integrated utility systems.* The model electrical utility that evolved from the first development of electrical systems around the end of the 19th century until the first major energy crises of the early 1970s was the self-contained, vertically integrated utility

that included generation, transmission, and final distribution to consumers. In this system the larger producers had efficiencies of scale that led to consolidations, and long-distance transmission grids were established to balance loads and sources of energy in large regions. In the traditional vertically integrated utility, demand continued to grow, and technological improvements meant that new larger power plants were more efficient and cost effective than the average installed capacity of the utility. The system was controlled and planned within a single company which had responsibility for assuring adequate supply for all needs in its service area, and it was subject to state regulation on a "return on investment" basis which assured private investors reasonable returns with relatively small risk.

2. *The transition phase.* Beginning in the early 1970s the vertically integrated system started to meet its limits and a new model started unfolding in an uncertain manner. For a number of reasons during the 1970s costs of generation no longer were lower on new power plants, fuel costs rose, and alternative generation technologies including conservation became more competitive. During this period environmental regulations more strongly determined technology, cost, and location of power plants. The system became more complex and out of control, with deregulation coming as an experiment to manage the uncertainty. We are currently in the transition phase in America and Europe, with the old system being dismantled to different degrees depending on local conditions and policy environments.

3. *Agile energy system.* The third stage is what we are calling *Agile Energy* because it responds to the challenges of the new economy in both a sustainable and civic-minded way. The agile energy stage is emerging, though it is not fully developed nor understood. Moreover, its implementation is not likely to proceed quickly, in spite of its logical validity and its inevitability in the long run. The foundations of the emerging system are technological and economic, and supported by a growing political and civic concern for more accountability of the power system. The components of agile energy systems are greater reliance on dispersed and renewable sources of energy, using new technologies and recognizing the civic role in promoting them. It is based on conservation and power management, with greater options for closer linkages of producers and consumers, with open access through a regulated grid. Complexity of the system is seen as an asset rather than a limitation, and neoclassical economic models are replaced with new models that look at community markets and impacts. In the agile energy model,

environmental and economic development agendas are consistent with efficient power production, not the cost.

Two chapters introduce the first section. This chapter looks at the roots of the California power crisis in order to show how the traditional model ended and to show that what went wrong as an example of what is challenging electricity systems elsewhere. The second chapter examines these same tensions in the other states of USA and Europe to show how traditional utility structures in other places are experiencing the end of the traditional model. The purpose of these chapters is not to point blame (there is plenty to go around), but to learn the lessons of the past and to put in perspective the fact that while predictable, the current crisis: (a) has deep economic and ideological roots; and (b) has resulted in a rapidly changing energy infrastructure system.

The five overlapping core ideas that will be introduced in the first section get interwoven as both an explanation of what went wrong, a framework for understanding the complexities of one of the largest and most critical technical systems developed by any society, and a roadmap to the future. The five core ideas are essential tools for understanding the transition in the electrical system and building an alternative. They are:

1. The technology for generation, transmission, and distribution of electricity has changed.
2. The regulatory system needs to keep profits reasonable given the monopoly power of utilities.
3. Economic theory suggests that competition in parts of the system will lead to lower prices, but an uncritical acceptance of the competitive premise led to market manipulation.
4. Planning for change is increasingly difficult because of the complexity of the system.
5. The consequences of changing energy systems have implications for economic development—paying for the crisis and opportunities for rebuilding.

These five core ideas are the building blocks for understanding system change in California and around the world, initially in terms of how we arrived at the current crisis, and later in terms of how we can resolve the problem.

The first core idea presented in Chapter 3 is the changing technology used in electric utilities. We will distinguish a concentrated energy infrastructure from a dispersed system, showing how California's early experiments with dispersed production opened the system to pressures by large users to reduce rates by bypassing the utility monopoly. Not only was some sort of restructuring of the utility inevitable, the system had a level of vulnerability that made system security nearly impossible to assure.

Regulatory options are the next core idea to be examined in Chapter 4 where we look at the interdependent roles of public regulation and private economies, and how the misguided efforts at deregulation led to the violation of the public trust. This chapter is critical because the new structure set up by deregulation was the precipitating cause of the crisis, but as we will show deregulation was actually a faulty response to pressures on the electrical system from changing technology and markets that got manipulated into an unworkable system. A comparison with the municipal utilities in the State which did not deregulate provides an appropriate perspective.

Chapter 5 introduces the limitations to the conventional neoclassical economic model, and how its promise of the benefits from competition dominated the policy process, blinding corporate officials and government leaders to an accurate assessment of their actions as well as causing them to miss obvious positive opportunities.

The core idea in Chapter 6 draws on complexity theory to help us understand how information was vulnerable to unprecedented misinterpretation, how rapid swings in energy availability and price caused large effects from small changes, how undeterminable forces led to surprising outcomes, and how rapidly changing political agendas aggravated the conditions they were supposed to stabilize.

Finally, the fifth core idea (Chapter 7) is that the electrical system has a powerful role in economic development, and the $40 billion cost of the California power crisis has huge multiplying consequences for different industries.

Once these core ideas are presented the case will have been made that the misguided effort to introduce competition into the California energy system had disastrous consequences because of the broad premise that competition over price would work in electricity where its technical properties lead to potential abuse of market power. The remaining task which is taken up in the second section is to explain what options are available to make the system viable. To do this we revisit these five core ideas from the perspective of the agile energy system, learning the lessons of the current crises in the electrical grids in England, Italy, and many other countries. Using what we learn from the past, we then build an emerging vision that will lead toward a sustainable future.

First, in Chapter 8, we examine technology again, looking at dispersed production, the expanded use of renewable energy sources, conservation, and alternative energy technologies. These technologies can help to create a more robust set of technologies capable of building a fully functioning system.

In Chapter 9 our focus shifts to a consideration of the regulatory system that is needed to support a new energy system. We reject the premise that the problem is that California just did not deregulate fully enough, as well as the premise that we should return to the old "return on investment" model. Instead, we articulate a model based on oversight and partnership, offering five premises for a civic market.

In Chapter 10 we return to the economic critiques of the competitive model that was at the core of the deregulation model that first led to the crisis. Here we build a new foundation of civic capitalism for balancing private markets with public interests in an agile energy system.

Chapter 11 continues this analysis to consider planning under conditions of increased complexity. The goal in this chapter is to demonstrate the structure and logic of an agile system, showing the many ways in which agility is increased by accentuating the civic market.

Chapter 12 revisits the last of the core ideas where we look at the economic development implications of the future development of an agile power system. We use an example of how new power systems can increase local control over their economic well-being.

To conclude the book we consolidate some of the potential of the hydrogen economy and provide a roadmap to a hydrogen future. This is accomplished in Chapter 13.

Then in Chapter 14 we end the book, presenting an argument for the agile energy system that balances public and private ownership and control while also balancing public oversight or regulation with competitive forces. This is what we call the "civic middle" an alternative to the clear model of many energy economists who see the ideal model to be privatization and competition.

The outline of the book is represented by the following matrix. In the matrix we outline not only the themes discussed in each chapter but also the core ideas. We see a significant link between these themes and core ideas. Our purpose in diagramming the book in this manner is to both exhibit to the reader a very straightforward way to understand our approach, and even more importantly to demonstrate the way in which a future energy market can be created on the supply side that has diverse clean fuel, environmentally sound robust systems, distributed networks, and is economically profitable. To accomplish the transformation of the energy systems in any society requires public and private competitive collaborations. The entire volume is dedicated to that end.

1.3. Matrix of Chapters: The Core Concepts of an Agile Energy System

Chapter 1. The End of the Old Order: The Roots of Reorganization
Chapter 2. Energy System Change in a Global Context

	Vertically integrated 1900–1972	Transition and deregulation (1973–2002)	Agile energy system 2003–
Technological basis		Technological factors leading the change from centralized generation with transmission to the breaking up of the system (Chapter 3)	Dispersed production and new technologies can lead to implementation of renewable standards and alternative technologies (Chapter 8)
Regulatory scheme		From return on investment regulation to the deregulation debacle; myths, experimentation (Chapter 4)	New framework for civic markets and oversight to replace old regulatory scheme; focus on investment for public good and civic choice (Chapter 9)
Economic basis		The problem of neoclassical economic models in energy systems, which give rise to market manipulation; the role of economic thinking in the California deregulation scheme (Chapter 5)	New economic models better model's appropriate role of energy in new economy— networks replace neoclassical competitive model (Chapter 10)
Planning complexity		The impact of growing system complexity and the problem of mistakes and lack of knowledge in making trend forecasts. Miscalculations and market manipulation includes considerations of environment and most of the story of what happened during the crisis (Chapter 6)	System analysis and state planning based on better understanding of complexity of system; public–private partnerships support renewable energy; advanced integrated technologies make agile power realistic (Chapter 11)
Economic development		Understanding the role of electrical systems in the economy and the way large users manage policy. The deepening understanding of the implications of the $40 billion cost of the crisis to the economy (Chapter 7)	Partnership between economy and energy system. This chapter looks at the benefits to the economy from flexible energy systems in the future and ideas about how this will benefit the State (Chapter 12)

Chapter 13. The Hydrogen Economy
Chapter 14. Conclusions for the Road Ahead

1.4. California's Vertically Integrated Utility System

Several basic structural features of the California energy system distinguish it from other state and national systems. First, California has a combination of three major investor-owned utilities that supply most of the State, including Pacific Gas and Electric and Southern California Edison, both among the nation's largest utilities, and the smaller San Diego Gas and Electric. Several smaller private utilities serve some rural parts of the State. In addition, the State is served by 33 public or municipal utilities, mostly owned by small and medium size cities, but also including two very large municipal utilities in Los Angeles and Sacramento.

The private utilities are regulated by the California Public Utilities Commission, which does not have jurisdiction over the public utilities. Prior to the mid-1980s the utilities were monopolies with fully integrated services—they generated most of their own power, had long-distance transmission lines to link their service area to production sources, and controlled final distribution to customers, and with the exception of Southern California Edison, they also supplied gas for generation (and residential and industrial consumption) within their service area.

California was an early participant in the growing electricity industry shortly after systems were first developed in the late 1800s. At that time a number of innovators and entrepreneurs demonstrated electricity to an amazed population. One of the first demonstrations of electricity was a single electric light bulb Father Neri of San Francisco's Saint Ignatius College placed in his office window in 1871. A decade later San Jose built a 237-foot tall light tower with six arc lamps in order to light the entire community. While it was a failure as a lighting project, it succeeded in publicizing the potential of electricity and cities rapidly followed with increasingly large and sophisticated demonstration systems (Williams, 1997: 170).

The first real commercialization of electricity in California, however, grew out of gold mining, where large hydro works had been built to conduct hydraulic mining and to process timber. As the gold fields became depleted, entrepreneurs tapped the water flows throughout the Sierra mountains to generate electricity, first for nearby towns and for the remaining mining operations. With the invention of alternating power and the construction of high-voltage power lines that minimized transmission losses, electricity from the mountains was brought to cities along the coast, at distances of up to 100 miles or more. These projects were virtually all investor owned and succeeded because of the high cost of alternative fuels for boilers, as California had no local coal.

The key at this time was that the early system was privately owned, and firms rapidly merged or were bought up so that the remaining large utilities achieved economies of scale. A few cities either had access to cheap hydro power or sought to eliminate corruption, and became municipal utilities. State regulation of utilities was initiated early to prevent abuse of monopoly power, but the utilities pursued strategies of consolidation and growth in an era with rapidly growing generation efficiencies and declining real prices. By the 1930s Pacific Gas and Electric and Southern California Edison dominated in the State and they were well-established vertically integrated utilities with generation, transmission, and distribution tightly coordinated to serve the State. Los Angeles, with access to hydro power from tapping the eastern Sierra water flowing into Owens Valley built its municipally owned electrical system as part of its water project (Brigham, 1998).

This system, privately owned, large, and vertically integrated, is a prototype traditional utility for the mid-20th century. For the most part it worked well, especially considering the growth pressures that California was having. California electricity systems expanded rapidly during a period of unprecedented population and economic growth. For example, from just after statehood until 1970, when the population in the State reached 20 million persons, the State's long-term population growth was the fastest sustained population growth in the world. The population doubled every 20 years for a 120-year period, with the consequence that during each 20 years there were twice as many people, twice as many houses, and more than twice as many jobs (Bradshaw, 1976).

A doubling of the electrical infrastructure every 20 years could be expected simply based on population, and more could be expected due to increasing per capita demand. New plants could be built with little risk since the population and economy were growing so fast, and due to the technological advances in this period, new plants were larger and more economical than older ones, which were reserved as peaking plants to be run only on hottest summer days. After 1970, the rate of growth decreased (because of the large base) but the people continued to come to the Golden State; the population grew by 10 million persons in the next two decades to reach 30 million persons by 1990, largely migrants from other states and around the world. Williams (1997) describes the background and history of the California power industry. There is no need to review that background herein.

At the start of the 1970s most electricity in the State was generated from hydro and oil combustion, and many utilities were proposing construction of large nuclear power plants because of supposed cost savings. But oil shortages due to the OPEC embargo necessitated conversion of the oil plants to natural gas and a growing interest in renewable sources in the 1980s. While few blackouts were experienced then, the "first" energy crisis set the context for the current crisis. Like the current situation, the perception in the mid-1970s was that there was a significant undersupply of electricity generation capacity, and expansion was limited by regulation. Expanding the supply of electricity through the 1970s was perceived as a regulatory problem, with siting delays slowing construction of needed power plants.

The era of the concentrated vertically integrated utility was well established into the 21st century. The significance of the oil embargoes in the early 1970s and 1980s was felt in California as elsewhere.

1.4.1. Nuclear concerns

Nuclear plants were widely considered to be cost-effective sources of power during the post-oil crisis period. However, in California siting nuclear plants had run into a number of regulatory barriers, starting in 1961 with a proposed nuclear power plant on Bodega Head, just north of San Francisco (Williams, 1997: 305–307). Unfortunately for PG&E, this site was just off the San Andreas Fault and posed unknown seismic problems. By 1976 the Nuclear Regulatory Commission ordered PG&E's small power plant on Humboldt Bay to close over nuclear safety issues, and earthquake concerns were responsible for rejection of applications to build three additional plants. In the mid-1970s an active fault was also discovered just offshore from the PG&E Diablo Canyon nuclear plant, which was nearing completion. These problems were serious setbacks for nuclear power, and diverted much planning by utilities for expanded supply. However, nuclear remained the technology of choice for most utilities.

Concerns over nuclear safety at plants and unresolved issues with the disposal of nuclear waste led to public concerns, however, and a number of environmental organizations placed Proposition 15 on the statewide ballot in 1976 that would increase safety standards and require a safe disposal of nuclear wastes. The standards were strong enough that if it passed it would have effectively stopped nuclear plant construction for some time. This proposition was hotly debated, and raised issues of cost, safety, need, and alternatives, in what was an emotional but highly educative campaign. In the end, the proposition lost by a two-to-one margin, but the debate (and preemptive state laws) effectively raised the bar on nuclear plant construction, without banning it directly. A preemptive policy impact prior to the election was taken by the legislature, with support from all sides, and three nuclear safety bills were passed that were "less draconian," placing a moratorium on state approval of nuclear plants until there was a federal solution to the nuclear waste disposal problem. As of today, there is no such solution, and consequently the State law had the same effect as if the proposition passed, effectively barring new nuclear power plant construction (Williams, 1997: 307).

1.4.2. Growing concern: institutional and regulatory issues

The scrutiny initiated by the nuclear referendum opened other parts of the vertically integrated utility to public information and concern. It is impossible to identify one event that triggered the breakdown of the traditional utility model, a transformation that is still ongoing. But during this period, the problems of the size and scale of the electrical system led to both further growth and increasing conflicts within a growing affluent and environmentally conscious population.

As a consequence of increasing regulation of environmental impacts of power plant construction, utilities resorted to innovative solutions that linked utilities into joint ventures to construct plants where regulations were weaker, typically out of state. The utilities during the 1970s took advantage of new higher-voltage transmission technologies that allowed longer distances between supply and final demand. The large utilities expanded interconnections with other utilities within California and out of state in order to achieve some economies by transferring power north and south depending on season, weather, and emergencies. Transfers with the Pacific-Northwest (Bonneville Power primarily) occurred for the same reasons.

But as environmental regulations were becoming more strict during the 1970s, all utilities in California looked to obtain larger shares of power from plants sited out of state, often Nevada and Arizona, but also as far away as the Four-Corners region (Utah and Colorado). The utilities would purchase shares in new coal and nuclear power plants able to be built in these areas, and they would collaborate on building transmission lines to bring the power to urban areas where it was needed. Transmission became a more significant part of each utility's operations.

At the same time, utilities continued trying to speed their siting of power plants which were being held up by regulatory barriers. Utilities complained that they had to get too many permits from different agencies to build a plant, and they were looking to consolidate and simplify regulatory approvals. On the other hand, the environmental movement was fortified by successful legislation such as the California Environmental Quality Act (CEQA) which was passed in response to the Santa Barbara oil spill (an offshore drilling catastrophe). Environmentalists were seeking stronger legislative and regulatory control over power plants, especially nuclear, as well as plants that would reduce dependence on fossil fuels.

Between 1970 and 1973 legislative action around power plants reflected these tensions and generated a number of important studies, plans, and commissions. Based on one study, the Public Utilities Commission (PUC) urged rapid expansion of the State's generating capacity, especially through nuclear plants. Eleven proposed sites had state approval by the early 1970s, and others were being proposed by the utilities. The PUC generally approved utility long-range generation need forecasts that would increase generating capacity from 35,000 MW to about 105,000 MW by 1993, nearly a tripling of capacity, and the PUC assumed that half would come from nuclear. On the other side, a Rand study (Mooz *et al.*, 1972 as quoted in Williams, 1997: 429) showed that steps could be taken to reduce the rate of electricity demand growth and that conservation measures would reduce the need for more power plants. Moreover, the Rand study advocated renewable resources such as geothermal and solar.

With energy as an increasing concern in the State, Senator Alfred Alquist and Assemblyman Charles Warren proposed legislation to resolve the conflict between energy development and environmental protection (Williams, 1997: 310). However, their initial bills, which passed through their respective state legislative houses, were sharply divided along utility-environmental lines. Eventually, Alquist changed his bill to the environmentalist friendly version sponsored by Warren, and in the process created the California Energy Resources Conservation and Development Commission (CEC) with responsibility for siting, forecasting, conservation, and development of alternative electricity technologies. The Arab oil embargo added pressure for a solution as this bill was being negotiated, but it did little to assure that it had a clear mandate.

Thus, the CEC was born with conflicting agendas. Warren wanted the CEC to slow the growth in state energy consumption while utilities hoped it would be the one-stop power plant siting authority they wanted. During its first few years, the CEC was involved in issues over nuclear power and Proposition 15, but gradually started focusing on supply and demand forecasts. Williams concludes that this leadership quickly altered the regulatory environment.

A new energy paradigm began to emerge in California. Energy industries found themselves confronted and embarrassed by a dedicated and organized activist population. With the prodding of environmental organizations, the regulatory persuasion of the PUC and CEC, and legislative insistence from the state and federal governments, California energy providers began to respond to the interrelationship between energy and the environment in new ways. The integration of energy conservation techniques and alternative energy resources into the existing energy systems began to alter California's energy landscape in earnest during the 1980s, revealing radical new possibilities for meeting energy needs (Williams 1997: 319).

1.4.3. Revised electricity demand estimates

The shortages and fuel changes necessitated by the oil embargo led to some technological changes, but the most significant thing to come out of the oil embargo period was new state roles in oversight of the energy industry and especially electricity. The creation of the California Energy Commission (CEC) supplemented the PUC in regulating energy in the State, and the presence of the two organizations in dynamic tension led to results that were not predictable. Unlike the PUC, the new Energy Commission was not limited in its oversight to just investor-owned utilities; it looked at municipal utilities as well. But its powers were significantly different, as it did not have authority over prices, profits, or business operations as did the PUC or the municipal governments which ran public utilities.

What the Energy Commission was established to do included four things: First, to regulate siting of power plants, including simplifying the multiple permits required to build a plant, promoting locating plants where they are needed, and coordinating the siting of multiple plants. Second, the CEC was to get better estimates of the demand forecasts of the different utilities and to develop a consistent method-ology so that demand estimates of the different utilities could be reconciled. Third, the CEC was to evaluate and promote to the extent feasible alternative technologies such as wind and geothermal, including mapping the availability of resources. Finally, the CEC handled conservation and demand management.

At the time the CEC was founded, the regulated utilities operated on a return on investment basis, with their rates being set to assure investors a fair (and not excessive) profit. Power generation efficiencies were increasing dramatically during this period, with new plants generating electricity at a much lower cost than old plants. For the most part utilities' earnings were calculated on the basis of their investment in generation, transmission, and distribution, so increased profit came from expanding their system and selling more electricity. Since demand had historically been increasing rapidly, they looked to expand their production as a given, and not expanding rapidly enough as a business liability. This model more or less characterized the operation of private utilities throughout the United States and most of Europe. Consequently, few questioned utility projections of rapidly increasing demand.

However, utilities in the late 1970s and early 1980s failed to recognize that demand was not increasing along the geometrical curve that they had been assuming. Instead, demand was flattening and would continue to do so. Self-interest and a failure to observe a break in trends led to too high estimates of demand, and the proposal at this time was to construct at least 12 major nuclear power plants at an investment cost of billions of dollars.

The CEC in one of its first significant contributions undertook a biennial energy report that included questions about the continuation of this demand curve, and they developed a consistent methodology for forecasting electrical demand. Gradually, the utilities accepted the methodology and the much lower-estimated demand forecast by the new methodologies. The utilities as a consequence of the new forecasting methodology relaxed pressure to complete installation of new power plants, including the nuclear plants on the drawing board. The overestimation of demand in the late 1970s was perhaps the most serious of the essential information miscalculations that threatened the viability of the utilities.

The fact that the overestimation of demand was "caught" is an enormous public policy success for the new CEC, and it can be credited with saving the State from building a huge supply excess. However, the old demand forecast methodology still had long-run consequences for California leading to the current crisis because throughout the rest of the nation plants were being constructed based on inflated demand estimates that were not caught. This led to eventual financial disaster for many utilities, especially WPPSS in Washington state that embarked on a program to construct five nuclear power plants. Only one of these plants was completed, with a default of $2.5 billion, and the admission that the Pacific Northwest had such a sizeable surplus of power to last for 10 years (Anderson, 1985: 138). This surplus actually ended in 2001, after supplying California for the intervening period. Around the country nuclear plants were abandoned, including Portland's Pebble Springs plant. Others produced power that essentially had no market.

Thus, in the 1970s the CEC rethinking of the utility electricity demand led to reductions in the estimated need for new power plants. Ironically, state creation of the Energy Commission was designed to help facilitate the siting of power plants, but its largest accomplishment was to help the utilities to realize that investment in any power plants was unnecessary and to abandon plans for at least 12 nuclear plants. These reduced demand forecasts turned out to be right, saving California utilities from billions of investments in unnecessary power plants through the late 1970s and early 1980s.

The size of the investment avoided by the revised demand forecasts would also prove significant because of escalating nuclear plant construction costs, as illustrated by the Diablo Canyon nuclear power plant on the coast near the southern end of the PGE service area. This plant, initially estimated to cost $300 million,[1] ended up costing $5.6 billion after the discovery of an earthquake fault undersea a few miles from the plant. In December 2003 the Paso Robles earthquake measuring 6.5 on the Richter scale was near Diablo Canyon, but did no damage. Mistakes in retrofitting the plant also escalated costs, but the whole experience showed that the nuclear facilities were greatly more expensive than initially believed.

However, while California utilities were lucky that they aborted construction of their 12 plants, other utilities throughout the nation forged ahead with construction at this time. Throughout the 1980s, then, plants were being built to meet demand that did not materialize, especially Bonneville and other western state utilities. The same happened throughout the east. Several utilities went bankrupt over these plants, and others were in weak financial shape. The result of these mistakes was that a huge surplus of electricity was available through the 1990s at very low rates.

1.4.4. PURPA history and contracts

Another development during the 1980s contributed to the background for the 2001 electricity crisis in California, this time involving the federal government. In 1978 the Federal government passed legislation known as the Public Utilities Regulatory Policies Act (PURPA), as part of the President Carter's energy plan. A small part of this legislation

---

[1] Estimates of $162 million for Unit 1 in November 1966 to be completed by May 1972; Unit 2 estimated to cost $157 million and be completed by July 1974 (www.energy-net.org/diablo1.htm).

became significant in California (Summerton and Bradshaw, 1991: 26). The overall plan aimed to reduce dependence on fossil fuels by stimulating conservation and promoting new technologies for electricity generation. PURPA guidelines set favorable conditions for new suppliers, especially small producers, to enter utility markets with new technologies. Under PURPA the utilities were required to (a) purchase available power from small (less than 50 MW) "qualifying facilities" that were not subject to oversight by regulators, and to (b) pay the provider an amount called the "avoided cost."

The avoided cost is the price that the utility would have to pay for the next increment of power if it were to build it itself. Avoided costs are the "anticipated marginal cost" of energy or capacity or both that the utility would have had to pay if it built a plant to generate that much power. Avoided costs at this period generally exceeded average costs because many of the existing utility plants were paid for or used hydro or other cheap energy sources. Theoretically, this pricing framework supported the principle that the consumer would be indifferent to the fact that some electricity would be supplied by independent producers.

California, by the late 1980s, needed additional power. State regulators were interested in expanding the potential of many alternative power generation sources because they realized that nuclear options were unlikely. PURPA was an attractive solution. Since each state was given latitude in interpreting how to implement the broad policies set out in PURPA, California regulators took an innovative and more vigorous approach to implement PURPA than most other states. In doing market research, they discovered that alternative producers needed contracts that established a steady market for their power over a long enough term to enable them to obtain financing. The State had tried to negotiate individual contracts with producers and quickly discovered that a consistent definition of what constituted "avoided cost" for different technologies could be fashioned. These were set out as a series of "interim standard offer" contracts that covered payments for capital expenditures and for fuels or their alternative (Summerton and Bradshaw, 1991).

The available contracts with the independent producers led to both a quick solution to the supply problem the State was facing, and to long-term problems because of mistakes in the way the avoided costs were calculated and administered. Three problems emerged with the implementation of the PURPA programs in California.

First, the concept of avoided cost ended up being calculated in a way that in retrospect was too high. It may be debatable how high it was, but there is little doubt that the prices calculated led to large amounts of independent power being built under contract with the utilities and over the long run this turned out to be very expensive power that the utilities wanted to dump later, and much of it did not meet the objective that the ratepayer would be neutral. The prices included in the standard offer contract were reasonably based on a proxy new gas combustion turbine, which was the new plant of choice for the utilities at the time and these plants were more efficient and cost effective than other options.

The standard offers included payments to the independent producers for return on capital in the form of capacity payments, and secondly included energy production payments to cover costs of fuel and operations. The State made a forecast of future fuel prices that caused a lot of the problem. The expectation was that oil and gas would be in continuing short supply and that prices would continue to rise. However, after rates were set, oil and gas prices fell instead. Thus, wind power and cogeneration alike received higher payments than what the utilities would have had to pay, though these estimates were based on the projections to which utilities agreed.

Second, the process failed to limit the number of offers that were made to the utilities, and it resulted in too many contracts for too much generating capacity. The three major private utilities in the State signed contracts with 1428 projects by 1988 that would generate a total of 15,881 MW. By 1990 a total of 8817 MW had come on-line and another 5000 were still committed to be built. The total supply through the dispersed production of the independent suppliers added or promised to add about one-third of the total 41,000 MW demand in the State at that time. While much of this was needed, consensus was that it was excessive and expensive (Summerton and Bradshaw, 1991).

The excess number of offers that the utilities and regulators had to work with created a problem and discussion of breaking contracts. What happened informally however seems to have solved most of the problem with regulators and utilities discouraging some projects by enforcing deadlines and other contract conditions that forced projects off the books. Several thousands of MW were not constructed. For several years, no new contracts were offered and in the early 1990s San Diego Gas and Electric first needed additional power. A revised "auction" procedure was established by the PUC and additional independent producer power was brought under contract, but by then utilities utilized cheap spot markets to add supply.

Third, the sizable incentives for renewable power at the time led to construction of some projects to maximize tax benefits rather than to contribute power. Some of the early wind farms got the reputation as being "tax break farms" with low productivity, unreliability, and extremely beneficial financing. However, with many projects costing a lot and lacking efficiency, especially using newer technologies, the program got saddled with problem projects and a growing bad reputation.

On average, however, the California PURPA process created the world's largest experiment in alternative energy construction, a highly diversified mix of supplies, demand that stimulated technological innovation in geothermal, solar, and wind, and extensive use of cogeneration throughout the State. The independent producers became a viable industrial force and produced what became a fifth of the State's power (see Chart 1.1). Thus, institutionally and technologically, PURPA contracts were successful, though miscalculations on the price and policy implementation tarnished an otherwise valuable experiment.

1.4.5. Conservation

While increasing supply was attractive, the regulators recognized in the energy crisis years of the 1970s and 1980s that conservation was cheaper than new generation capacity. Through state leadership and programs, utilities offered a combination of audits, technical assistance, and financial incentives aimed at reducing demand. The logic was attractive for the utilities, in that demand side reductions cost less

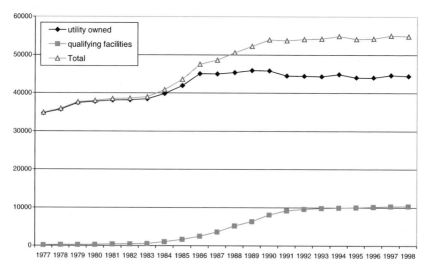

Chart 1.1. California electricity-generating capacity, 1977–1998.
Source: California Energy Commission.

than the marginal price they were paying for power and so it helped solve utility problems, and the regulators assured that they got a return on investment in conservation. Conservation since the 1970s in California has produced about 9500 MW peak savings through efficiency programs. Included in this estimate is about 2000 MW from market-driven benefits, 4000 MW from building and appliance standards, and 3500 from utility programs (estimated from graph, see CEC April 2000: 12). This is about a quarter of total capacity in the State, and without it generation capacity would have had to be considerably greater.

Incentives were offered for businesses and residential consumers to receive free or low-cost energy audits, to subsidize insulation and installation of more energy-efficient machinery, to replace home appliances with ones that met higher standards, and to increase public education. These strategies were very effective in reducing demand and proved quicker and more certain than construction of new power plants. The size of the savings initiated by these programs was nearly equal to nine large 1000 MW nuclear power plant units (almost what was desired in the 1970s). This program is broadly considered a success for demand side management technologies. Interestingly, the State estimates that by 2015 energy-efficiency peak savings could be double what they are in 2001 (CEC April 2000: 12).

On balance, up to this point California was the world's largest experiment in dispersed production and it was working. The big change instituted at this time was that utilities gave up their monopoly on electricity generation to nonutility producers and developed an effective demand side management program. This was an enormous change. Moreover, alternative and many renewable technologies were implemented in the State at a level not seen anywhere else. However, even in this successful implementation of electricity policy, the information system failed to forecast what was happening and as will be shown below, once a mistake was perceived, it failed to have any self-correction built in.

1.5. The Emergence of the Transition Phase: The Tensions that Led to Crisis

Following the PURPA years, the California electrical system seemed to be balanced, with the extensive network of dispersed suppliers meeting demand, and concern at the energy commission diminished so much that forecasts and analyses stopped. Most of the fears of system control problems resulting from dispersed operation did not materialize (lots of small producers not under direct control of the utilities did not create management problems). However, on the horizon were the immediate seeds of the current crisis. This series of events placed the California system clearly in the transitional phase, with the traditional vertically integrated utility no longer viable but the alternative not yet envisioned or formed. At least seven system tensions were operating at this time.

1.5.1. Self-generation and nonutility supplier pressure from large consumers

The lucrative contracts for independent producers who had cogeneration opportunities created an explosion in the knowledge and awareness of cogeneration opportunities. For example, The Chevron refinery in Richmond used about 5% of the total PGE capacity, and they planned to systematically add cogeneration capacity with a well-publicized plan of self-sufficiency. Moreover, the cost and efficiency of small gas turbine generators became so attractive that most large users of electricity at this time considered significant amounts of self-generation to be in their economic interest.

The utilities panicked that their most lucrative market would vanish, and with PUC blessing instituted huge connection and backup power fees that by themselves largely removed the financial incentives for self-generation. However, the large users publicly and forcefully opposed these fees and immediately saw that the rates they were paying the utilities were much more than their nonutility options. Moreover, the large users saw that wholesale prices out of state were low and they tried to find a way to get the power transmitted (wheeled) to them, but because of the utility monopoly on transmission these efforts were temporarily blocked.

During the energy crisis of the 1970s California regulators used price signals to ensure conservation, instituting an inverse-sliding scale of prices. Homeowners were given a low-price base and then if they used above this the rate increased. Large users and businesses were perceived to have considerable conservation potential and were given the highest prices, in contrast to bulk discounts which were in operation in other parts of the economy. These higher prices also created an incentive for large users to increase conservation efforts and to pursue ways to decouple themselves from the high-priced utility grid.

In a regulated system the large users have significant political power, and in this case their interests were backed up by strong economic incentives to disconnect from the grid. However, the utilities now awash in dispersed power and an inverted rate schedule needed the large users to help pay their costs. The utilities entered into a series of negotiations with the large users, and the regulators held hearings to try to resolve the potentially damaging crisis. Users pointed out the vastly lower electricity prices that their competition was paying out of state, and argued that the true cost of supplying them was greatly inflated in order to subsidize residential base lines.

The resolution came in the form of lower specially negotiated rates between the large users and the utilities on the promise that they would stay on the grid. Some customers developed cogeneration plants as well, but the threat of massive migration of large customers from the grid was effectively mitigated by sharply lower rates. More than anything else, the threat of self-generation and the political power of the large users created a price pressure. The utilities needed to respond competitively in order to avoid loss of these customers entirely.

1.5.2. Out-of-state surplus

While California carefully scaled back its construction of new generation plants based on CEC-initiated forecasting methodologies, other states continued to build excess capacity. By the mid-1980s California had a reasonable balance of supply and demand, while throughout the rest of the nation and west there was an enormous glut of electricity, and this had to be sold at bargain rates. California was a good market. Seeing the price pressure, California utilities quickly expanded their long-distance transmission lines to bring this power into the State, and in a series of projects expanded links to Oregon/Washington and the Southwest. The out-of-state power was coming in at 1 and 2 cents per kWh where instate generation was costing 2–3 cents and independent qualifying facilities had contracts from 5 to 20 cents, depending on peak load. Diablo Canyon cost at least 15 cents, though that did not fully cover the utility costs. In short, out-of-state power was a means by which the utilities could reduce their costs to meet the price pressure from the large users.

The surplus also contributed to the fact that during the early 1990s California had a large reserve margin due to contracts and high prices with qualifying facilities which translated into retail electricity rates that were up to 50% above nearby competing states (Faruqi *et al.*, 2001: 24). This became an economic development problem, especially as the State tried to pull itself out of the persistent recession that plagued it during the early 1990s.

1.5.3. Fuel costs fall

The PURPA contracts were calculated on the basis of steadily rising oil and natural gas prices in keeping with post-oil embargo experience. However, fuel prices fell instead, making the calculations in the standard offers seriously high.

While utilities and all producers needed to make estimates of fuel prices under different scenarios, and the utilities participated in the calculation of fuel prices for the standard offers, the result was locked in for qualifying facilities that resulted in disproportionate costs. Moreover, there were no links to fuel prices for producers using wind and other renewable technologies. Thus, when fuel prices fell for gas-fired utility plants, consumers benefited. But as fuel prices fell, contracts with many independent producers did not fall as well.

1.5.4. Nuclear plant issues: Diablo Canyon

The Diablo Canyon nuclear plant was proposed by Pacific Gas and Electric as an attempt to produce low-cost power. What started as a $300 million plant to generate 2000 MW turned into a $5.6 billion project. Upon completion, it became apparent that even under the most optimistic price forecasts this plant would not be able to compete with other options, but PGE was assured financial returns under return on investment regulation. After a series of regulatory hearings, PG&E was allowed to recover most of their costs and blend high-priced power into their rate base for many years. While the issue of blame has not been fully resolved even yet, the cost implications for the state system remained and finding a way to merge high-priced Diablo Canyon power into a system already perceived to be too expensive drove many policy decisions leading to deregulation.

It is fair to say that the enormous investment of capital in Diablo Canyon predisposed the California system to rely even more on low-price out-of-state power to dilute prices, and finding a way to pay off debt from Diablo Canyon became a priority in the transition to deregulation. It was also the last major power plant constructed by the large California utilities, and its problems signaled to the utilities that the generation part of their operations would likely cease in the future and that their operations would be limited to transmission and distribution.

1.5.5. Dispersed system solutions abandoned

An immediate result of expanded power lines that could access very cheap power from out of state was that the marginal price for additional power now was lower than the average cost, while during the period when PURPA contracts were negotiated the opposite was the case—the marginal price for new production was higher than the average. As a result, conservation which had been a key piece of the California energy strategy no longer was as cost effective for the utilities who now needed sales volume to reduce costs. Not only did utilities pay more than 1–2 cents for conservation, they could not dilute high-price power from the independent producers and Diablo Canyon with the cheaper out-of-state power unless they increased demand.

Thus, the dispersed and renewable power which had become an hallmark of the California energy system quickly vanished under the pressure of deeply discounted out-of-state power. Instead of an increasingly robust system instate, the utilities became dependent on short-term opportunistic prices created by the out-of-state glut, and conservation started to make no sense.

1.5.6. Deregulation debacle

The botched deregulation of California's electrical system that went into effect in 1998 is a large and long story reserved for Chapter 4, but for now the key is to recognize that the preceding conditions led to many pressures on the California electric system that deregulation was thought able to resolve. While many contemporary critics argued that there was no reason to consider deregulation because the system was not broken, in fact, there were so many pressures on the regulated electric system that some kind of change was inevitable, deregulation being just one option.

Based on local experiences at the time deregulation was proposed and on projections about what was likely to happen, deregulation seemed like a solution that would resolve a cascade of problems including the tensions of high prices, inability to recapture the costs of Diablo Canyon, pressures from large users, and need to better capture low out-of-state prices. The deregulation strategy generated widespread support and AB1890 passed with unprecedented support from the industry and politicians who all believed that prices would fall rapidly.

Deregulation was first proposed by the Public Utilities Commission in 1994 and approved by the legislature in August 1996. The plan had the following characteristics, fully endorsed by all parties in state government. As Governor Wilson said at the time of this "landmark legislation," it was "A major step in our efforts to guarantee lower rates, provide customer choice and offer reliable service, so no one is literally left in the dark" (September 23, 1996 Press Release). The elements of the deregulation plan were:

• Consumers were free to choose their electricity supply company.
• Utilities would freeze their 1996 prices at 10% below previous levels for 4 years, through 2002. The rate reduction was paid for by the sale of bonds that will be repaid.
• Utilities would be reimbursed for "stranded assets" of plants that would not be competitive, such as Diablo Canyon and high-cost PURPA contracts through higher retail prices. Once stranded assets had been recovered, the price freeze would end.
• Incentives would entice utilities to sell half or more of their generation capacity to assure competition among suppliers. By May 1999 utilities had sold 17,683 MW capacity, or about 40% of total generation of 55,000 MW (Woo, 2001: 752).
• The state would set up an Independent System Operator (ISO) who would manage the high-voltage transmission grid, and the California Power Exchange (PX) that would operate the wholesale market.
• Power purchases would not be from long-term contracts but would be limited to the spot market (hour and day ahead markets). Generators would bid power to be sold in these markets, but all suppliers would be paid the price of highest accepted bid—the Market Clearing Price.
• Renewable energy and demand side management (conservation) were to be subsidized until 2002, at which time all technologies were to compete on the open market.

However, after two years of working as predicted, the blackouts of 2000–2001 have led to a new consensus that it is seriously flawed and that deregulation is the immediate cause of the problems facing the State (Faruqui *et al.*, 2001). During the first two years when supply was ample, utilities made money buying power on the low-price spot market, and they sold their power plants for more than expected to companies interested in operating them, often headquartered out of state. They set up independent companies to own some of their assets, independent of their power distribution companies.

Prices stayed low during these first years of deregulation, but consumers did not see price competition through this transitional period because the wholesale market was consolidated statewide, and all retail suppliers had to purchase power through the same pool and at the same price. Some supply companies signed up customers based on "green production," but these customers had to pay a premium. Most customers remained happy with the mandated 10% rate reduction.

By the end of 1999 some of the flaws in the California deregulation scheme began to be visible. San Diego was the first utility to recover costs of stranded assets, and their price cap was removed, but instead of offering lower prices, they started having trouble buying low-price power and passed the increases to customers. Eventually wholesale price would increase everywhere causing problems unable to be fixed within the State's regulatory scheme. Deregulation in other states has not had the serious problems that developed in California, but the consensus is that these other states are having problems and that they are taking strong steps to assure that they do not repeat what has happened on the West coast.

1.5.7. End of out-of-state surplus by 2000

Deregulation worked successfully for the first two years simply because the utilities were able to buy great amounts of out-of-state power at very low rates that kept other rates low. However, the surplus ended by 2000, and with the utilities owning very little instate capacity, they could not respond. The immediate end of surplus was a record dry year in the Pacific Northwest. With snowpack water content as low as 35% of normal, the State lost up to 3000 MW of power, equal to three nuclear plants. High gas prices also drove up prices and restricted supply from some plants in the southwest (see Chart 1.2).

Rapid economic growth in California and other western states combined to increase demand. While the increased demand was gradual, and construction of new supply was stagnant, the late 1990s saw a general tightening of supply throughout the west. Interestingly, the first blackout actually occurred in Nevada (Las Vegas) rather than California.

Moreover, this end of surplus was not undetected. Many analysts worried that the low prices associated with excess supply would create shortages, and the data were widely available to support these

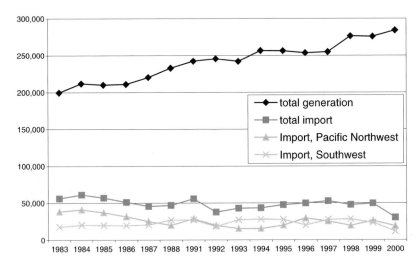

Chart 1.2. California electrical generation million kWh 1983–1988; 1991–2000.
Source: California Energy Commission, data missing 1989–1990.

concerns. However, in the deregulated environment, no entity had responsibility for assuring adequate supply because the market was supposed to take care of it. Moreover, in deregulation with its reliance on short-term spot markets for supply, there were no viable systems for assuring that reserve margins were maintained because they are not adequately valued in a system that only pays for power delivered. (An ancillary services market handled reserves and capacity to balance voltage and frequency bid separately on a short-term basis.)

However, it is the end of the surplus that enabled new players, such as Enron, to enter the market as brokers in what turned out to be both an unregulated and a scandalous strategy that manipulated shortages into crisis. The full story of the role that Enron and other large energy traders played in California is just now being told, and the role that they played in manipulating the market increasingly seems to be a role that they helped to create in shaping both the actual structure of the deregulation legislation in California, but also the federal role and response.

1.5.8. The crisis

Starting in the summer of 2000 deregulation became a problem rather than a solution. Hot weather, drought in the Pacific Northwest, and population and economic growth in states that previously supplied California with surplus power reduced supply to narrow

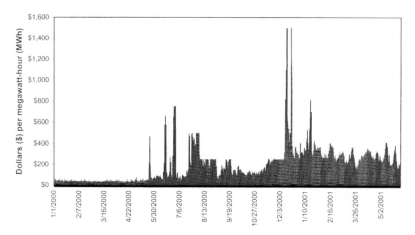

Fig. 1.1. California electricity prices rose starting in May 2000.
Source: CPUC (2002: 12).

margins. With shortages and escalating prices, generators and brokers discovered that they could drive up prices by withholding some supply, and in documented but still being litigated moves, took power plants out of service for unscheduled maintenance or other reasons, exacerbating the shortages. Prices which had been 1–3 cents per kWh rose to 15 cents, and then climbed to 30 cents or more during January to March 2001, peaking at 75 cents during the top emergency hours (see Fig. 1.1).

While prices toward the end of 2000 had been high, by early 2001 they had increased even more, which proved catastrophic and set in motion a system breakdown. Utilities had agreed to the cap on prices at the retail level, which on the one hand protected consumers from a pass-though of escalating prices paid to generators, and on the other hand, the price cap reduced the utility ability to recover funds to purchase power. As the utilities defaulted on paying electricity producers, some independent suppliers withheld sales and others only continued selling because of court orders. The utility financial crisis then became a reason for suppliers to reduce generation, leading to a spiral of even higher prices.

Governor Davis ordered the State's Department of Water Resources to purchase electricity on behalf of the utilities, using the State's credit, to avoid total collapse of the electricity industry. However, even with these efforts supply did not match demand, and the utilities were ordered to institute rolling blackouts in order to shed enough load to avoid system failure. By late Spring 2001 one cycle of blackouts had affected virtually every customer on 38 different days, and forecasts were for frequent recurring blackouts all summer. In addition, the State ISO was forced to declare 82 stage 2 and 39 stage 3 emergencies[2] during the period from November 2000 and May 2001. (In the previous 2½ years of ISO operation, they only declared one stage 2 emergency during the November to May period. See California PUC, September 2002, 11.) California had never before experienced a similar challenge to the reliability of its energy system, and this occurred during the winter when the system has lowest demand; summer peaks typically have much higher demand.

On April 6, 2001 the State's largest private utility, Pacific Gas and Electric—one of the largest in the nation, declared Chapter 11 bankruptcy. Southern California Edison was negotiating with the State to buy some assets, postponing similar insolvency. The State, in order to maintain power supplies had in a series of steps purchased $7.6 billion of power with state funds that were to be repaid to the State by a bond offering that customers would then repay. By 2003, PG&E was still emerging from bankruptcy and Edison was still deeply in debt. But further blackouts were avoided and the supply has stabilized so that the system is operating with standard levels of reserves. Moreover, the State is finally ending its role as power purchaser. The bonds which were to cover the costs of the crisis paid by the State Treasurer or the California Power Authority have become problematic due to the weakening economy, large state deficits, political changes (results of the California Recall), and disagreements over how the bonds will be repaid.

Transmission bottlenecks also emerged. The need to shift power from one part of the State to another and to tap out-of-state sources strained a number of sections of the grid, and in several cases power available in one part of the State could not get to people who were having blackouts. During February 2001 the PX ended its role as wholesale purchasing agent, and changes took place in the market for wholesale power. In response to the crisis, a number of efforts were instituted in order to avoid a total crisis during the approaching summer with its peak demand.

- Governor Davis and his staff negotiated long-term contracts with many producers for significant amounts of power at

---

[2]A stage 2 emergency is declared when the ISO anticipates reserve margins below 5%, and stage 3 emergencies are when reserve margins are anticipated below 2%. Blackouts are scheduled when reserves are less than this.

around 6–7 cents per kWh, well below spot-market prices of 15–75 cents (but well above the earlier spot-market prices of 2–3 cents).

- Legal and press scrutiny of producer and marketing companies increased, with concern over alleged unnecessary plant outages for repair or other reasons. Consequently, plants came back on line and fewer outages were experienced.
- Construction was completed on several major new power plants as well as peaking plants.
- Construction was started on many new plants expected to provide capacity over the next few years.
- The price cap was removed and consumer rates went up with surcharges, with large users having the highest increases.
- Consumers who conserved more than 20% compared to the same month in the previous year received 20% rebates on their electricity bills, and these price signals served to increase conservation. Estimates are that conservation reduced demand between 10 and 15%, with more during peak periods.

The claim has been made that California had not built enough new power plants since the early 1990s to meet demand. The State only added 672 MW in the last five years, compared to Texas which added 5700 MW over the same time period (Woo quoted from Newsweek January 22, 2001). While this indicates some lack of responsibility, it is important to keep in mind that the average retail price of power during the last five years was lower than utilities could build plants for, given the surplus power available. In other words, there was little need to build new capacity, and the fact that some plants were under construction indicates that planners recognized that supply may be getting tight. No one correctly estimated the extent to which weather, drought, mechanical problems, and the booming economy and population growth throughout the entire West would make the system vulnerable so quickly, but this was not a simple problem of not building enough power plants. The point is simply that there had been so much surplus capacity that plant construction was delayed too long because of poor estimates.

The good news coming out of the crisis, if any, is that during the summer of 2001 supply was generally adequate and forecasts of hundreds of hours of blackouts were wrong. Mild summer weather can be credited for helping avoid a summer crisis, but evidence is accumulating that the system is regaining stability because the many emergency responses instituted by state and local agencies succeeded in restoring stability to the system. For example, prices on the wholesale spot market have fallen to near what they had previously been, and power seems generally available at lower prices.

Yet the long-term contracts negotiated with producers during the peak of the crisis now are higher than the average spot-market prices, leading to criticism of these long-term contracts. The contracts, which are still not fully available to the public, are supposedly being renegotiated, though it is not clear whether this is either possible or feasible. While the legal issues raised by the crisis period of 2000–2001 will take years to resolve, it is becoming clear that California's electricity system has come back from the brink and is now entering a new rebuilding phase. Nonetheless, the energy sector remains fragile and desperately in need of change and reorganization.

1.6. Sustainability and the Future of the California Electrical Crisis

The goal for avoiding electricity crises in the future and for resolving current problems is to forge a system that avoids the brittleness of the current system. If we are right that the problem in California is that the system became uncompetitive and distorted because it was too concentrated, too tightly tied to long-linked supply networks, and without anyone looking out for the public interest, then solutions must look for dispersed and proximate solutions that assure public goods are adequately provided.

From a system point of view, the electrical generation and transmission network had become vulnerable to pressures which deregulation only exacerbated. Key breakdowns were caused by miscalculations and inadequate information, as well as poor future projections about things that were essential to the management of the whole electrical system. The reason the information was so inadequate and miscalculations so critical was that the system was just so complex that it became fragile and had few self-correcting mechanisms.

The information needed to make the complex electrical system reliable and cost effective, unfortunately is inadequate. For example, in a recent report on the implications of efficiency programs and distributed generating, the CEC reported that their models lack necessary "locational data to translate its analytic database to the disaggregated size required by transmission planning" (CEC April 2000: 40). The electricity data system in California is significantly hampered by the fact that the State's electricity report was not published by the CEC for a five-year period while deregulation was being implemented. But at a more consequential level, there is a serious question about whether the data are available to enable a large technical system like the California's electricity system to be reliably managed when facing the competing pressures that shaped the system over the last two decades. This means that data miscalculations and load estimates, transmission capacities, and other issues are going to be hard to manage reliably. Alternative sustainable "internet-like" systems may be more robust because they do not depend on centralized information-controlled systems.

Fortunately, technological options for a sustainable system are increasingly attractive. Energy-efficiency programs that remain cost effective could reduce peak demand by another 10,000 MW (CEC April 2000: 12) in residential and commercial programs alone, and if the voluntary consumption savings during the summer energy crisis averaging 10–15% can be sustained, the demand could be further shrunk. Most of these programs cost 2–3 cents per kWh, compared to new generation which is at least 5–6 cents. The State programs in conservation clearly paid off during the summer of 2001 and many are expanding because they are cheaper than new plants.

Dispersed technologies that are located near demand are complicated because of air pollution problems in many California areas, but when coupled with cogeneration, heat and electricity production may actually reduce pollution with very efficient systems. Another item that is emerging is the fact that many power plants in areas near population centers are old and not very efficient. New plants generate about 25% more electricity for the same amount of fuel, and their exhaust is even cleaner. It is argued that replacing many of the old power plants with new ones would generate more power without creating shortages of natural gas and the new plants might actually reduce pollution.

Perhaps the greatest potential lies in renewable energy sources and technologies. These not only solve some of the state supply problems at competitive costs, but they also assist the state and nation in solving some of the carbon emission problems associated with global warming. Renewable and dispersed options are available, many with extensive capacity. These typically are near or below the cost of new generating facilities. In fact, a recent article in EPRI review suggests that photovoltaic panels have now fallen in price another increment and are more cost effective than new power plants. While these findings may still be premature to the creation of a solar future, we can assume that it is not far away. In general, however, recent estimates by the PIERS program at the CEC of the cost of dispersed and renewable sources are shown in Table 1.1.

Table 1.1.   Alternative and renewable sources of electricity and cost per kWh.

Hydro	(cheap, already developed)
Conservation incentives	2–3 cents
Cogeneration	2–3 cents
Wind	4–5 cents
Geothermal	5 cents
Solar thermal	(18 cents now, 6 long term)
Biomass	7 cents
Photovoltaic systems	15 cents—3 cents midterm

Source: CEC PIERS program.

The conservation and cogeneration options stand out, along with wind, as being more competitive than new gas-fueled power plants, and they are cheaper than the long-term contracts signed by the Governor. While these options need an institutional structure to get implemented, and in the case of cogeneration, environmental, and air quality qualification, it is clear that renewable and dispersed production can be achieved with little financial shortfall and perhaps considerable benefit.

In addition, these technologies are suitable to being located near users which reduce the demands on the long-distance transmission system. While some additions and relocation of the grid would be necessitated, the long-distance transmission lines would shift from being a key part of the base load of the State's electrical system to returning to their historical function of shifting power depending on seasonal efficiencies and to provide more robustness to the system.

However, the largest sources of renewable power, wind and photovoltaic-generated electricity, still have the problem that they are intermittent and cannot be brought on line when demand increases unless the wind is blowing or the sun is shining. This intermittency problem is serious but not catastrophic because of hybrid technologies which can store some of the advantages of intermittent power through pumped hydro or eventually hydrogen. Following Rifkin (2002), we believe that coupling photovoltaic and to some extent wind power to "Green Hydrogen" through electrolysis is a cost-effective step in providing hydrogen for fuel cells, which are already proving to be cost effective in general applications. New generation photovoltaic cells are already available for 10 cents per kWh, and Sharp hints that this will fall to half that much within a year. Electrolysis that generates hydrogen when the power is not directly needed will make even this a cost-effective solution for all public buildings, businesses, and residences. (We will elaborate on the economic calculations in Chapter 13.)

In sum, the potential for a dispersed production system that avoids the problems of concentrated power generation in the hands of few utilities or companies is within reach. We see the transition as a mix of central grid and traditional utilities that also accommodates a growing independent renewable and distributed sector that generates electricity as in PURPA days by stimulating and assuring the market for independent and alternative power producers using cost-effective technologies. Second, location near to demand will reduce the proportion of power that has to go long distance through interstate transmission lines. Finally, ample supply of power close to users will create the competition that deregulation was intended to stimulate, and it will leave the regulators with the task of assuring public good concerns such as maintaining adequate peak power and spinning reserve or mandating (and finding ways to pay for) demand side management programs.

1.7. Conclusion

The California energy crisis has multiple roots that are specific to the California experiment. The deregulation debacle in California set in motion a series of events that have been avoided in degrees elsewhere, and other nations and states should surely learn the lessons from California. However, the California energy crisis is about the electricity system everywhere not in the specifics but in the fact that California was the first to face a number of serious challenges. Several of these lessons are important.

First, the electrical system has depended on policies using accurate information and models, but miscalculations have been at the root of the many crises shaping the system. Demand miscalculations were recognized that helped avoid overbuilding during the 1970s, but failure to sustain analysis led to miscalculation of the demand after deregulation. Miscalculation of the interest in independent producers to respond to qualifying offers led to too much power being contracted, a problem compounded by miscalculations in the cost of oil and gas fuels for power generation, prices that were expected to rise and they fell instead. And lack of adequate information on transmission bottlenecks for both gas and electricity led to system problems. Most recently, the miscalculation of what utilities would do under deregulation led to a financial crisis for the utilities and the State, along with serious economic crises.

Of course better models and data, as well as better policy leadership in identifying important trends and pending problems which are not "politically correct," are essential to avoid future crises. However, analysts are increasingly recognizing that no matter how optimistic one is about getting and analyzing data on a system as large and complex as the electricity system, our ability to know what is going on seems inadequate to the needs of managing such a system.

The thesis of this book is that an alternative exists, and that when the system worked most effectively it was by being more dispersed and sustainable, avoiding the catastrophic problems that result from miscalculations inherent in complex systems.

Chapter 2
The Global Context of Changes in the Energy System

2.1. Introduction

Energy system change is pervasive around the world. However, the issue of reorganizing the electrical industry takes on different manifestations depending on where one looks. In different countries, energy infrastructure changes are at different stages of development and under different economic and political conditions. In this chapter, we place the process of energy system change in a global context— showing the range of ways power systems are being transformed and the types of problems encountered along the way. While there is no one approach to energy reorganization, there are clearly patterns driven in large part by developed industrial world economic ideologies and agendas.

From the global perspective, the lessons learned about the consequences of reorganization are uniformly bleak. Around the world pressures for restructuring and reorganizing—privatization, liberalization, and deregulation—lead to changes in the generation, transmission, and distribution components of electrical systems. But instead of enthusiasm and a vision of better service and lower prices, country representatives are trying to control damage from blackouts, avoid price spikes, resolve shortages, reduce risk and uncertainty, and manage grid overloads. It appears to us at this point in time that nowhere in the world has restructuring proven to be a total success due to the changes from privatization and deregulation.

The California energy crisis has influenced and was part of the global trend to reorganize the power industry around the world. For example, in May 2002, scholars, analysts, and representatives of many regulatory and industry groups met at UNEP Headquarters in Paris to consider the process of energy restructuring and the potential for sustainable development (see Wamukonya, 2002).

By early September 2002, another international meeting was held at Electric Power Research Institute (EPRI) in Palo Alto, California to consider how to bring electricity to the approximately 2 billion people who had none in order to update the International Energy Road Map (EPRI, 1999 and now revised, 2003).

In addition, among the many countries initiating change in their electrical industry, the issues surrounding these changing systems needed to focus on the fuels and operations in order to assure environmental and economic sustainability. Heretofore, international energy system changes were oblivious to and placed at relatively low priority on environmental impact because of the many competing financial and profit demands on the power system. Programs designed to provide affordable power to poor people or those unable to afford electricity were stymied. Corporations that were supposed to lower prices and increase supply did the opposite. Sometimes these firms came back to the government wanting guarantees to be able to continue in business. In addition, the power system was no longer a rational economic institution, but had become so politicized that decision makers had personal agendas for providing or withholding power.

The California crisis is thus just the tip of a global iceberg of the reorganizing crises itself. Bad news continues to accumulate from every corner of the world about how these efforts to institute change lead to economic, social, and political disaster. Since California has often played a global role in creating change for good or bad, when deregulation went bad in California, it caused a shockwave that spread to virtually every national capital and state house, causing a rethinking of deregulation. For example, Rudnick and Montaro (2002: 170) conclude their review of Latin American electricity reform:

> *There is no doubt that the California (energy) crisis has reshaped reform programs across Latin American countries. In the case of Argentina and Chile, the authority has been persuaded, at least temporarily, to postpone liberalization reform and apparently has desisted from using a decentralized approach like the one in California . . .*

Regardless of their level of development and the progress they made in energy system reorganization, an increasing number of reports suggest that governments have slowed down their process of reform until leaders better understand what happened in California in order to make sure that it does not affect them. One of the purposes of this book is to help these decision makers and other countries learn from the mistakes in California so that they can solve and plan their energy systems without falling into the problems experienced in the Golden State.

2.2. Perspectives on Energy System Change

The process of energy system change is truly a global process. Virtually all countries have either changed the structure of their electricity system or have been discussing it. Pressure from multi-national organization is often the catalyst, such as the World Bank, International Monetary Fund, and European Union. In fact, the EU requires privatization or liberalization of electric systems for member nations and as a criteria for new member states. A Minister of Competition is in charge of monitoring and "enforcing liberalization." Nonetheless, the privatization takes different forms in different nations, much to the chagrin of others. As we shall see below, the actual form of privatization in many EU member states needs to be examined much closely. Some experiences led to problems, while others are viable organizational structures that could be adopted by other nations and regions, especially where the public power system sold shares to private owners but retained public or government shareholder control.

We discuss the power sector process under the term energy system change, restructuring, or reorganization, while most of the literature calls it power sector reform or labels it as privatization, liberalization, or deregulation. We think that the term "reform" is value-laden, and it implies that the process of reform is to fix something that is clearly broken or wrong, while in the power sector case the changes that are being made are open to question whether they are fixing problems, or whether they are just simply transferring the problem from the public to the private sector.

While our California experience clearly shows how reorganization made the energy and environmental situation worse rather than better, we can hardly call it reform. On the other hand, we are not ready to say that all the power sector changes around the globe are part of the failed reorganization movement. Our point is simply that there is no necessity, inevitability, or inherent good in all the comprehensive set of changes bandied about under the terminology of "reform."

Instead, energy system change is actually two different processes taking place in tandem, but analytically different. The first trend is for the government to divest ownership of the power system. In the US the power system has largely been private since the first power systems were developed (Hughes, 1983; Williams, 1997), with private companies owning vertically integrated utilities that serve regional customers on a regulated monopoly basis. A portion (about 25%) of the American system is owned by municipalities who are strong advocates of public ownership of the power system; municipal utilities can take advantage of government provided tax breaks, but in fact they operate much like private utilities regulated by their local government rather than the State (Brigham, 1998; Bradshaw *et al.*, 2003).

However, in most developing countries, the former Soviet Union block, and much of Europe, the power system had been owned and developed by the government with public ownership, and private companies as either a minority or not allowed at all. Today, in these same regions, privatization differs in each nation. Meanwhile in Asia, South Korea borrowed funds from international financial markets in order to provide the capital for its rapid industrialization. As a condition of these loans, it had to convert public companies to private ones. Now South Korea is moving toward full privatization (Pineau, 2002: 1008).

The second trend in power system change is to lighten regulatory controls and let "market forces" compete by setting prices, attracting investors, and planning for system growth. The potential for monopoly control of power systems over geographical areas is inherent in both competition (low-price winner gains control over the market) and technology (ability to dominate with advanced technologies and know how). To control these monopoly abuses, public utilities commissions or other governmental oversight organizations were created to control prices and assure stable supply.

In cases of public ownership, the government and its agencies supposedly manage the system for public good. In contrast, private firms would be expected to try to maximize profits for their owners, restrained only by regulatory power. This led to ongoing struggles between public utilities commissions to keep prices as low as possible and their regulated firms who aimed to increase profits. The art of regulation, however, as will be pointed out later in the book, is an inexact science, contrary to its economic proponents. The market prices are widely perceived to be inefficient, at least compared to market competition which has proven effective in setting reasonable prices in some other industrial sectors. It is this tension between perceived regulatory ineptitude and belief in the benefits of competition that generally is at the root of international pressures to change power systems. In the USA, this change is called "deregulation" but varies from state to state in both degree and mechanisms for operations.

The California experience is about deregulation and creating mechanisms for competitive markets to replace regulated monopolies. California does not have an issue of privatization because the State's power system has long been dominated by private power companies under public regulatory regimes. However, in most countries the process of privatization takes place either prior to or concurrent with deregulation and establishing competitive markets. Various forms of privatization and deregulation are being addressed by policy "reformers" seeking improved efficiency, lower prices, and more public benefits, depending on the level of development in the countries and the politics involved.

Hunt and Shuttleworth (1996: 14) laid out the basic reform model which is shown in Fig. 2.1. In their model, countries and their power systems move from government ownership and complete monopoly through the matrix to private corporation ownership with full retail and wholesale competition. They note that the majority of countries are moving toward both private ownership and competition, though few are there already. With California's retreat from this same sort of target, it becomes unclear if and how this objective is ideal for all countries, as had been suggested.

The Hunt and Shuttleworth ideal model is the classic formulation for deregulation. It has been adopted by many of the analysts looking at what they often label "restructuring the power industry." Given the debacle of the California deregulation, few economists or policy experts want to call it more than "restructuring," since they consider the California deregulation an incomplete and flawed market system, although most of them played key roles in designing and implementing it. A skeptic might call these policy makers "revisionist"

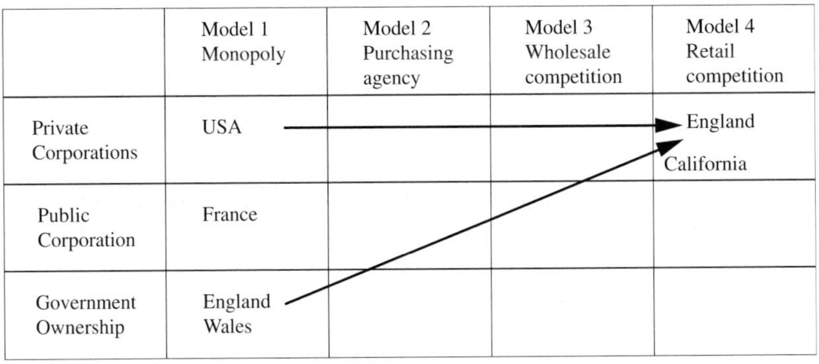

	Model 1 Monopoly	Model 2 Purchasing agency	Model 3 Wholesale competition	Model 4 Retail competition
Private Corporations	USA			England California
Public Corporation	France			
Government Ownership	England Wales			

Fig. 2.1. Basic ideal energy reform model.
Source: Adapted from Hunt and Shuttleworth (1966: 14).

since they do not want to acknowledge that their original proposals, programs, and hands-on advice to decision makers were in large part responsible for the California energy crisis.

Privatization according to the ideal model, on the other hand, proceeds along the vertical axis from government ownership to private ownership, while increasing competition and deregulation proceeds along the horizontal axis, in a cumulative way to full retail and wholesale competition. The arrows show England and Wales moving from government ownership to private ownership, while also going from monopoly to full retail competition. The US, on the other hand, was already private, and it, according to the model only, is moving to include retail competition experiments, led by California. Variations of this chart (Fig. 2.1) have been widely used in the literature.

However, the restructuring or reorganizing process is being driven by a number of different forces relative to the area in which it is taking place. Moen (2002) notes the following drivers of the restructuring process that serve as the primary incentives for change and examples of where these processes have been central:

- Privatization (reduce government role and investment) in England and Wales
- Innovation and reconditioning (Chile)
- Efficiency (Scandinavia)
- A single integrated market (EU)
- Financial issues—sell assets for immediate income (developing countries)
- Infrastructure development (World Bank)

Bachrach (2002) identified 11 factors when comparing the restructuring of energy systems in the United States: time (passed on legislation) when competition begins, regional transmission organization, energy market structure, capacity in gigawatts (GW), retail choice, stranded assets and transitional costs, divestiture, renewables, demand side management (DSM), low-income families, and green power market. The analysis was also broadened to select countries in the European Union. The conclusions made in the early spring of 2001 were startling given what happened in California and they foresaw the quick halt to restructuring in almost all other American states.

For example, twenty-four (24 of 50) American states (including D.C.) who had enacted electricity restructuring legislation by 2001: Arizona, Arkansas, California, Connecticut, Delaware, District of Columbia, Illinois, Maine, Maryland, Massachusetts, Michigan, Montana, Nevada, New Hampshire, New Jersey, New Mexico, Ohio,

Oklahoma, Oregon, Pennsylvania, Rhode Island, Texas, Virginia, West Virginia and sixteen (16) other states had commissions or legislative investigations into deregulation going on by the spring of 2001. Only eight (8) states had no activity. By early summer of 2001, almost all USA states stopped deregulation. Since then most have either halted or reversed deregulation.

Most significantly, Bachrach (2001) states that, "In general, the states that have restructured were the same states that had high electricity prices, often due to poor investments in nuclear power." This same conclusion was echoed in the United Kingdom (Kapner, August 2002) over the British Energy Company which is primarily a nuclear power generator with 20% market share, when it sought bankruptcy protection in early September 2002. The universal issue appeared to be the nuclear power generation companies who had high stranded costs that could not be recovered at competitive rates (Pool, 1997).

A similar situation occurred in California where nuclear energy was very high cost. The alternative, however, was natural gas fuel source, as was the many other states and nations. By early 2001, natural gas accounted for 52% of the California fuel source for electricity. After new power plants were sited and approved for peak and emergency power, the percentage of fuel from natural gas increased to even higher levels. The exact percentage is unknown as of the fall 2002 since the final long-term contracts for power contracts were under review and renegotiation in the State. However, the number of power plants approved for new generation was significant.

The problem in California and elsewhere is that when nation-state or regional energy plans no longer exist, as was one result of the California deregulation legislation (the market, not state, would plan for future power needs), there is little or no coordination between power generation needs and type of fuel supply. California is now heavily dependent on natural gas with only three major gas transmission lines into the State. Threats from terrorist, natural disaster, maintenance, or other problems cause price spikes and power outages. This is exactly what happened in the summer of 2002 with several energy alerts and a few sporadic brownouts.

2.2.1. Privatization and liberalization

The task of building energy systems in most countries fell upon the government. Historically this was due, in part, to the enormous capital investment in large power-generating plants that was necessary as power systems went from their initial introduction in Europe and the

US to other countries. Public ownership in developing power was considered an infrastructure investment, a part of nation-building (Mez *et al.*, 1997: 4). Often using large hydro projects to start the electrification process, countries would create integrated systems of transmission and distribution that were funded out of government revenues, often with international loan assistance. These programs created government utilities that were owned, operated, managed, and regulated by the State, often including other objectives as well. Government ownership may have been necessary to initially establish a power system, but it is beset with problems in most cases.

The most common problem, according to advocates of privatization, is that government-owned power systems are run inefficiently due to lack of incentives and poor management skills among the civil service. It is widely perceived that the lack of competitive discipline leads to uncontrolled spending, poor judgment in investment decisions, and tolerance of poor business practices. Government regulation is unable to enforce improvements and cost reductions because clear alternatives are not known, cronyism and corruption are prevalent, and funding is not available. Often employee numbers are out of line with real needs and employees are not adequately trained. However, poor management is only part of the problem.

- In some cases the government utility can recover only a small part of its costs due to political barriers such as in India where farmers benefit from virtually free power—now seen as an entitlement given in exchange for political support for the Congress party (Dubash and Rajan, 2001).
- In other countries the system is so insecure that half or more of the power is taken illegally before it is metered.
- In a number of countries the power sector is closely tied to government interests in supporting other industries, especially coal mining. Both England and Germany have shaped their electricity policies around support for coal because of the powerful political interests of the industry and its unionized workers.
- Perhaps the greatest incentive for developing countries to privatize their power systems is the need for governments to raise cash by selling assets and to reduce its debt load. The assets in the power system are seen as resources that can be used for other purposes by the government, and the sale of power systems has been relatively easy since global corporations have been interested in investing in them. Private ownership, however, has not always raised expected revenues and many times has led to higher power rates for

consumers. Nonetheless, for many poor countries their power system is their one asset that can be sold.

In order for change of these real and perceived problems, international aid organizations and business advocates are pursuing a policy of privatization. However, variation in the needs and constraints on national power systems makes the conditions and the process unique to each country. Hunt and Shuttleworth argue that the first step from direct government ownership is the establishment of a government-owned corporation. In this case the direct operation of the utility is separated from government agencies and the government is "one step removed from day-to-day control" (Hunt and Shuttleworth, 1966: 15). The board of the corporation is appointed by the government, and it sets policy and objectives, and hires the staff who run the corporation. The corporation receives money (or credit) from the government, and profits, if any, are returned to the government. This model is characteristic of Electricite de France and most of the municipal utilities in the United States.

The second step from a government-owned corporation is full private ownership, either regulated monopoly utilities as has been the case in the United States, or competitive ownership by private companies which is the eventual goal of the reformers. In private firms the owners make all the decisions about investments. Private ownership of monopolies involves regulation to assure fair prices and efficient operations. Below we explore various kinds of energy corporation structure and organization. Competition among several companies is supposed to achieve the same purpose. Key issues in privatization include assuring that proper regulation or dispersal of assets prevents exercise of market power to distort prices. Privatization has been promoted by the World Bank, IMF, and other agencies to increase funding for utilities in developing countries.

Privatization may or may not include all vertically integrated components of the power system. In some cases the generation system alone is privatized, with the government retaining ownership of the transmission grid and distribution system. In other cases the government may retain only the transmission system, as in many Scandinavian countries. The unbundling of the system is a component of privatization that can proceed at different paces.

Three cautions about the benefits of privatization need to be made at this point. One is that privatization was never successful in the energy sector in developed countries. As evidence mounts about how corrupt private energy companies manipulated supply and thus prices in California and elsewhere in the USA, the assumption that private business could manage energy markets better than government or publicly controlled companies was false. Cavanagh (2001), for example, notes that "Regulators cannot leave this function (privatization or deregulation) exclusively to unregulated participants in wholesale markets. Without designated portfolio managers operating under incentives to promote long-term public interests, deregulation of wholesale electric markets is unlikely to succeed." (Cavanagh, 2001: 1). He argues that to do so means that resources for new research and development as well as renewable or green energy systems will not be developed. Energy is not the same as other goods or services that can be accounted for by traditional neoclassical economics. Energy (as water, environment, waste, etc.) must be part of the public trust administrated by government. Similarly, Byrne and Mun (2003) argue that electricity should be handled as an "energy commons" where public ownership and public good goals dominate any individual or corporate interest.

A second point concerns the role of energy systems themselves in any society. As Hvelplund (1999a,b) argued, before the crisis occurred in California (2000–2001), the issue was political and not just business or economics. In examining energy systems in Denmark, Hvelplund found that politics played a key if not the sole role in determining the plans for privatization. Often these plans were based upon the political decision makers having biased and ideological goals for creating or enhancing private sector profit-making businesses, more concerned with profits than public good in providing electrons for all citizens.

The third point is a simple economic reality. The evidence is mounting that the logic of privatization to reduce prices by increasing efficiency has failed. For example, Kwoka (cited in Pineau 2002) offers mixed evidence and Steiner shows that in a number of cases privatization results in higher prices. In another example, Pineau suggests that some of the realistic goals of electrical sector reform may be accomplished by other strategies than privatization.

The results of privatization include, by chance or design, international assistance in softening the strain of macroeconomic fluctuations on governments with large debt, finding solutions to organizational problems in state-owned electricity companies rather than assuming that simply changing ownership will solve the organizational problems. In addition, some of the IMF–World Bank reform strategies need to be refined to take better advantage of local capacities without privatization. Pineau (2002: 1010) concludes that the "IMF and World Bank policy seems to be inappropriate medicine for a difficult situation."

2.2.2. Consolidation and global electric companies

An aspect of privatization is the consolidation of smaller energy companies into larger firms, and eventually into global companies. Philipson and Willis (1999) make the case that aspects of the private electric system around the world have continued to consolidate as private companies increase in size and capacity. For example, the largest company involved in electric power is claimed to be the firm Asea Brown Boveri (ABB) which has manufacturing and service businesses in 160 countries, and their generators, transformers, switch gear, power lines, and other essential components of the electricity industry are in use virtually everywhere.

ABB is a private firm, largely unregulated at any level, and their global capacity came from mergers including Asea (Swedish firm), Brown Boiveri (Swiss German manufacturer), parts of Westinghouse Electric (American), and Combustion Engineering (global power plant manufacturer). While generation, transmission, and distribution are still largely decentralized, the equipment that is purchased by utilities is increasingly reliant on ABB, Siemens, and other large equipment manufacturers who operate on a private global scale (Philipson and Willis, 1999: 314–315). Given the uncertainties of deregulation and privatization, however, ABB and other large firms still exercise enormous power and influence.

In addition, privatization has opened up the national electrical systems of many countries to foreign investment. The purchasers of power systems in developing countries around the world are rarely firms from that country, but are international conglomerates or existing utilities such as Electricite de France, Enron (before it collapsed), PG&E, and similar firms. One clear trend has been the corporate strategy of many Western European energy companies purchasing the public energy companies in the new applicant members to the EU. In Hungary, for example, the purchase of the former energy generation suppliers has been by either Western European countries or American energy firms. The results have been questionable in terms of ownership, reliability, and safety (as in the case of a nuclear plant).

In sum, privatization has the clear advantage for developed and developing countries that it raises cash for the state treasury. However, it is also based on a deep-seated premise (largely untested, but increasingly challenged) that private ownership and the discipline of the stock-holder value and the market will lead to greater efficiencies, lower prices, and better service. As was seen in California, this premise that private firms would, through market competition, lower energy prices was false. Furthermore, the notion that private energy companies would have better management without regulation that would improve reliability, investment, and service also proved a false economic and business premise.

The failures of these private energy companies have resulted in declining valuation on the stock market and executives going to jail. Moreover, reform in the Securities and Exchange Commission as well as in corporate governance are underway worldwide. US legislation (Sarbanes-Oxley Bill, 2002) was passed to help assure investors that company executives did not manipulate markets with false or inflated accounting practices. However, most observers feel the reforms did not go far enough (Clark and Demirig, 2003). And as this volume states, the reforms are based on faulted economic theory in the first instance—privatization is not inherently good for all members in any nation-state.

2.2.3. Competitiveness in the energy system

Along with turning the control of power companies from govern-ments to private investors who expect dividends, the other major economic premise in the deregulated power industry is to increase competition between companies. Hunt and Shuttleworth track four stages of increasing competition. In the first stage, monopoly, there is no competition among generators, wholesalers, or final customers.

The second stage allows competition among generators who sell to a single purchaser who is the local wholesaler or distribution company, but the generator cannot compete outside their local area in part because they cannot gain access to transmission lines. This is the model created under PURPA in the United States where independent power producers (IPP) could sell to the local utility which had to buy the power, but the IPPs could not sell it to other utilities or to final customers.

The third stage promotes competition among wholesalers and generators, with opened transmission lines, so that generators can sell to any wholesaler. The wholesaler still maintains monopoly over distribution to final demand at this stage, but they can obtain power from many different competing sources wherever they may be located.

The final phase is to open the market to retail competition, where individual customers can choose their power company based on price and service. In the ideal open competitive market, individual consumers exercise demand for quality service and low prices on their distribution company, which in turn purchases only the most economical power from competing generators, all accessed by an open transmission system. The British privatization as well as the attempted deregulation in California anticipated that private companies would be engaged in retail competition in the hope of neoclassic economics to make the system more efficient and hence prices lower.

2.2.4. The transmission system in a competitive system

There is general agreement that the physical characteristics of electricity flows mean that transmission systems are a special business and hence economic case. With transmission systems interconnecting countries and spanning continents, the management of power is increasingly difficult, as evidence in the preliminary reports from the Great Blackout in Northeastern America (August 2003) and the distributions throughout the summer of 2003 in Europe.

The physical characteristics of electricity flows are that the power follows paths of least resistance, but not necessarily the shortest line, nor can the flows be directed very easily. Circuits can easily become overloaded when multiple generators try to meet load connected by several paths. In some cases cheaper generators that may even be closer to the load need to be curtailed because their generation might cause electricity flows to increase to dangerous levels elsewhere on the grid. High-voltage electricity can also loop and cause other problems for grid managers.

Over time the physics of these power management issues have become better understood, but they do require close oversight and management. Thus, electricity transmission is not like water or even natural gas, where suppliers can purchase capacity on sections of the transmission system and then they can follow their product as it goes through the system. In electricity, the electrons go where they want to go according to laws of physics, and an individual customer actually uses power from many sources that gets mixed in the transmission grid itself.

Internationally, the transmission system has tended to remain under either government ownership or strict regulatory control by regional entities. Even in cases where multiple entities own all or part of the transmission system, there is no real competition envisioned because of the desire to avoid costly duplication of power line construction and the fact that management of the complex flows of electrons requires sophisticated control. In transmission, competition cannot provide this control, though one can imagine isolated branches of a transmission system feeding the grid close to demand in order to compete for specific business.

2.2.5. Sustainable technologies and environmental issues

In addition to the concerns over cost and efficiencies, energy system change has parallel consequences for a broad range of issues which are relevant to flexible power models and sustainable developments. The United States has not taken steps to join the world by reducing carbon emissions or pollution according to the Kyoto treaty, though California passed and Governor Davis signed legislation committing the State to strict pollution reductions and conservation goals.

However, change in power system design and investment may have a large effect on pollution levels. A major concern in developing countries is older and dirty power plants which are also inefficient. Modern power plant technology has increased efficiency while reducing emissions, but many countries continue with old plants that lack even minimal pollution reduction technologies. For example, the very dirty power plants in Eastern Germany have been a source of concern, and most had to be shut down after reunification. Some developing countries have many dirty and inefficient plants, which would benefit from being replaced.

A second change is the greater availability of cogeneration (combined heat and power) units and the use of small gas-powered generation for distributed power production. Cogeneration units have been widely used in Europe and elsewhere, and their role as a growing source of supply seems dependent on market conditions and political will. With the growing number of dispersed production facilities, as in Denmark, transmission capacity has not had to grow as rapidly.

Renewable sources of energy are attractive in all parts of the world, especially in developing countries. According to Martinot *et al.* (2002), about 48,000 MW of small-scale renewable power is grid connected in developing countries, along with some 260,000 MW in large hydro projects. The restructuring of power systems could emphasize and value sustainable systems to replace inefficient and dirty ones, though that would require innovation to break the common wisdom of typical utility engineers and accountants. We hope that the response to California's crisis will be a global awareness that change to renewable and dispersed electricity systems not only are economically attractive but environmentally friendly. (This is the type of reform that would have truly been beneficial.)

2.3. Regional and Nation-State Experiences

The global experience with energy system reorganization and change has been largely an unhappy experience. Although, there are many examples of changes that have not turned into crises—YET. Lund and Clark in 1998 and 1999 (2002) cochaired two international energy conferences focused on these issues: one held in Denmark and the other, ironically, in the California State Capital building in Sacramento. Both conferences were cosponsored by the Danish (Ministry of Energy and Environment) and American Governments (US Department of Energy) and involved participants from all over the world who were studying energy and environmental planning. The conclusions from almost all paper presentations were very much the same: privatization or leaving energy to the private sector was froth with potential problems ranging from market manipulation to lack of investment in upgraded systems and advanced cleaner technologies.

The conclusion from this series of conferences and others such as the UNEP meetings in Paris in May 2002, all appear more true than ever. In the electrical power sector, including generation, transmission, and distribution, there remains an unresolved tension among government, regulatory agencies, and public interests on the one hand, and the private business interests of investors and shareholders for providing a commercial profitable service on the other. Searching the globe for an unquestionable model of good practice has turned up empty. Every nation-state appears to be polarized between either privatization or not-to-privatize (substitute deregulation or liberalization). Consider some noteworthy cases below.

2.3.1. Canada

Canada shares grid interties with the United States, and in many ways Canada is part of the same power system as its southern neighbor. On the other hand, Canada has long had a stronger public sector than the US, and Canada has been willing to publicly invest in health care and to participate in some manufacturing sectors to a greater degree than in the States. Canadian companies have become large suppliers of power to both New England on the East Coast and California on the West Coast from Hydro Quebec and British Columbia firms. While Quebec is a major supplier of power to New York, all along the border Canadian and US utilities share power, backup each other, and seek efficiencies of operation. However, these utilities also shared price spikes during the energy crisis and they suffered simultaneous blackouts when the grid collapsed in August of 2003. Blame continues to be made at all levels, yet never addressing the basic premises that created the problems in the first place.

Ontario Hydro had its own power crisis in 2002 provoked by privatization and deregulation. A privatized power market was initiated with competition among generators to supply a centralized power pool. While prices fell the first couple of months after the system started in May, by mid-July prices had doubled from their low point and by mid-September prices reached 8.7 cents (Canadian dollar) per kWh, more than double the benchmark prices based on previous year's prices of 4.3 cents (Hampton, 2003: 206). These prices were passed on to consumers, but it created a massive public outcry. In response, the government used reserve funds and tax revenue to rebate the difference and calm the political crisis.

Power programs in Canada are largely under provincial jurisdiction and several power systems have been hotly contested. The Ontario program is a clear case of the negative impact of uncertainties of privatization and deregulation. While the control of the electric system has shifted between the New Democratic Party (liberal) and the Conservative party, there is no doubt that deregulation has caused turmoil in a power-rich region whose Niagara falls power station is a major resource. Like California, Ontario's power was hurt by high nuclear power costs when they tried to increase capacity, and by a dream that by privatizing they would somehow solve their problems through competition.

Alberta, a Plains state had the lowest power prices in Canada as well as North America, at about $14 per MWh. After deregulation prices soared to 10 times that much, reaching California prices of $500 at the peak. The Alberta Power pool, facing limited local generating capacity, had to compete with California for limited excess British Columbia power. Again, the free enterprise market did not deliver the stability and capacity that was expected. Even fuel-rich areas were hurt by deregulation.

2.3.2. Latin America

If there is a set of success stories for privatization and deregulation, the Latin American case could be it. Chile was one of the first countries to embark on deregulation experiments starting in the 1980s. Its national power system was privatized and sold to a Spanish company (Endesa) as well as other utilities such as Pennsylvania Power and Light (USA) which has been relatively successful in providing power in a growing economy. Argentina followed shortly after and assured that generation capacity was fragmented into many companies. The privatization process enabled international capital to come into the countries and relieved national governments of managing debt (Philipson and Willis, 1999: 317–319).

The initial experience of Chile has stimulated proposals for reform across Latin America. According to Bouille and Wamukonya (2003), reforms were proposed but without evaluation or review since the early 1980s:

1982   Chile
1992   Argentina
1993   Peru
1994   Bolivia, Columbia
1996   Guatemala
1997   Panama, El Salvador
1998   Nicaragua
2001   Jamaica

As in most countries, time will tell in terms of how successful the deregulation schemes are. By late 2003, there were no apparent problems with the deregulation to date. However, political turmoil in most of the Latin American countries continues to undermine the reorganization efforts. Mexico under President Fox, for example, has attempted during 2002–2003 to reform the power industry but this will take considerable amounts of investment and coordination especially since the government controls the oil and gas supplies in the country.

2.3.3. Great Britain

England and Wales were the first European regions or nation-states to embark on a major reorganization of the power industry. Both energy systems underwent privatization and market competition (Thomas, 1997). In many respects, the British experience was promoted by conservative political philosophy of Margaret Thatcher based on neoclassical economics. Thatcher had been a leader in helping shape the privatization or deregulation debate around the world. Prior to reorganizing, the British system had a number of distribution companies or Area Boards with one generation and transmission system, the Central Electricity Generating Board (CEGB). The Area Boards provided distribution to customers, but they were supplied by the single CEGB.

The British system was plagued first by underestimation of demand leading to shortages in the early 1960s and later by overestimation of

Agile Energy Systems

demand, which exceeded 35% in the mid-1960s. The planning problems were compounded with other management problems, leading to significant inefficiencies. In addition, political agendas of breaking the high dependency on coal (mostly associated with union busting) and the wish to develop nuclear power also led to technological problems (Thomas, 1997: 46). The nuclear program, for example, was criticized for poor technological choices and for favoritism in making investments. The energy generators, furthermore, were unable to counter the pressures from coal interests, and one of the implicit goals of the restructuring was to reduce the power of coal union interests to dominate power production.

The first phase of the British privatization was to divide the CEGB into three companies, one generating company with 70% of the capacity including nuclear would compete with a second generating company having the remaining 30%. Transmission would be a third company. A power pool was established but it did not become very important. One of the big problems was that the British nuclear power ended up being much more expensive than any of the other options, and for the most part, British coal was more expensive than other sources. On the other hand, flexibility was gained from the new availability of natural gas that could be used in combined cycle turbines, an alterative that reduced initial capital costs, introduced more siting flexibility, reduced emissions, and had lower operator skill requirements. However, the government also imposed a 10% fee on electric bills to subsidize nuclear and alternative power, most of which has gone to nuclear (Thomas, 1997).

Retail competition was gradually phased in over a period of time starting in 1990, first with the large industrial users choosing their suppliers. By 1999, all customers had the option of choosing suppliers, and the results are generally favorable, with prices falling up to 30%. However, as noted, previous prices were inflated by nuclear and coal policies.

The slow introduction of competition in Britain has allowed response to problems as they are discovered. For example, in late 1997 regulators saw some evidence of price manipulation during peak periods, and as a consequence new rules were introduced in March 2001 that increased trading outside of the pool, reducing manipulation. The British also have instituted a price cap regulation scheme which enforces productivity gains (Brennan *et al.*, 2002: 35–37).

By 2003, a significant portion of the United Kingdom energy system appeared near to collapse as British Energy neared bankruptcy. As Kapner (2002) noted of British Energy, but also extrapolated to other ventures into privatization, rail, telecom among others, including higher education and universities:

In the 1980's, under Prime Minister Margaret Thatcher, Britain started turning state-owned entities into private companies, often by selling shares to the public. Private business, the thinking went, would be more efficient than the government at running businesses and providing services, and opening industries to competition seemed like the ideal way to pass savings on to consumers.

After British Energy was "privatized" in 1996, problems emerged in its major business, nuclear energy. A number of reasons have been given, but the basic result by mid-2003, was that the company needed a partner. The Government was actively considered to be both a partner and also a lender. Companies in France and the USA were also suitors but in the end, the British Government appears to be central to solving the financial solutions for the company.

Another recent change in the UK deregulation strategy is that they have decided that their reliance on market-clearing prices in their power exchange has been a failure. The UK pool model was to have firms bid to supply power at a given price and the power would be available to the utilities from the central pool. In this scheme all suppliers receive the same price regardless of their bid, with the price being the top price of the last bid accepted. This model has been used in many commodity auctions, and the British model was one that was adopted in California and the hope was to keep prices lower that way. In the UK this pool model has recently been scrapped with a return to the pay as bid system where all bidders get just the price they bid. The changes were instituted to prevent market manipulation as in California, and to make the system more transparent (Crow, 2002: 48)

The irony is that Thatcher, once considered the most forward thinking political leader by pushing privatization in the public sector, has now become the focus of serious reconsideration. By the middle of 2003, California and a number of other states and nations had totally reconsidered and even reversed deregulation and privatization laws. What appears critical is that the reversals in public policy need also to advocate new approaches that are neither just public nor private firms. These new public and private companies are just that—a combination of both, and several examples exist in Scandinavia.

Canadian politician Howard Hampton (2003: 160) sums up the UK experience which has generally been used to document the success of system change:

> *What does the UK have to show for more than ten years of privatization and deregulation? A bankrupt nuclear company kept from sinking by the taxpayers. A non-nuclear power generation sector that is largely foreign controlled. A number of foreign controlled distribution companies. A transmission company that was built by public enterprise but is now owned by private shareholders who use their UK generated profits to invest elsewhere. Lower wholesale prices, for a while at least, but not meaningful retail prices . . .*

2.3.4. European Union

The European Union has absorbed the variety of national systems of its member countries and is working to achieve both uniformity and coordination, as well as to pursue a gradual introduction of competition in the generation and market sectors, while continuing to integrate the grid across all countries. Inspired by the privatization in the UK, this is an ongoing process with a number of countries such as France, Germany, and most of Scandinavia more reluctant than others. Integration of the national power systems and the provision for trade and competition across borders are at the top of the EU agenda, though the reorganizing of many national systems to hopefully increase efficiency is ever present.

In general, the EU under Directive 96/92 aims to introduce competition among suppliers and marketing companies, while keeping transmission regulated. However, before this is possible the EU considers several steps essential.

- Create an integrated internal market instead of 15 individual national markets by 2003–2005. Nondiscriminatory access to the transmission and distribution grid is essential to this.
- Adoption of rules on cross-border tariff setting and congestion management of electricity based on simplicity, nondiscrimination, and cost reflection.
- Development of European infrastructure plan to remove barriers.
- Negotiation of reciprocal electricity market agreements with EU neighbors, including issues of environment and safety.

The problems with deregulation or privatization, however, have given some concern to policy makers and even industry within the EU. Nonetheless, official policy and requirements for countries considering membership (soon to be over 10 nations) promote privatization policies. Little consideration is given to assisting these nations or providing assistance gained from the bad experiences in California and the UK. New public–private models are needed as discussed elsewhere in this volume.

In a comprehensive overview of the European efforts to respond to the challenges of both an integrated European market and the technological and organizational changes that are altering utilities everywhere, Midttun (1997) and his colleagues have traced changes occurring in different countries. They conclude that there are changes in virtually every country, and that the changes reflect the complexity of the power systems as well as the political and economic structures of the countries contemplating change.

We agree with this analysis and that it is difficult to predict the outcome of initiatives being proposed by the different countries to obtain advantages as they might be found. In general, however, it appears that the restructuring that has been most successful in Europe has been gradual and incremental, responding to opportunities where they emerge. On the other hand, the changes that have taken place in Europe seem not to have led to major shifts in ownership or greatly reduced prices of power. The lesson seems to be that the gradual transitions taking place on the continent and Scandinavia are incremental, and that this may be a much better approach than the comprehensive restructuring characteristic of California.

The changes in Europe have not been without glitches. For example, the blackouts during the summer 2003 demonstrated how grid failures could hit Italy and many other countries. France, for example, while supplying substantial amounts of energy generated from its nuclear power plants had transmission failures to northern Italy. While the economic results in the EU have not been fully accounted for, the French counted at least 14,000 deaths directly attributed to the energy outages during the summer of 2003.

What is interesting to notice in Europe are two conflicting themes. One is that major western European power companies are investing heavily to purchase the once state-owned generation from former Soviet Block countries who are now seeking membership in the EU. Ten new members are to be admitted in 2004. Most of them under the requirement to sell or privatize their energy sector. There are mixed reviews on the successes and failures of this effort throughout central and eastern Europe.

The second theme is far more interesting and reflects both national and economic concerns. For example, when government and private industry executives are asked how is privatization defined in practice in their countries, the answers are not what it means in the UK or USA. In those countries, privatization or even deregulation mean that the state-controlled energy sector has sold all its control to private companies or investors. Not true in Germany or Scandinavia.

In the northern European countries, significant corporate control after privatization remains with the state or even regional governments. This is both the result of national laws and also practical experiences. For example, when the Norwegians considered selling their once national power company to Sweden, they discovered that about 30% of the Swedish company was owned by a German power generation company. The Norwegians did not like that and withdrew the offer until it was renegotiated. A similar occurrence happened with Norway's state-owned telecom company. When the actual control appeared to be either too nationally centric or lacking enough local ownership, the deals fell through.

In Germany, meanwhile, national laws insist that privatization remain but that the local governments or state hold sizable financial interests. Thus, when the German Bundespost privatized in the mid-1990s, 51% remained in control of the German national government assuring both oversight and control over prices. The same pattern but less than 50% exists in the energy sector. What is critical in these cases is the direct and constant involvement of the government in these "privatized" companies. Hence, public or government officials sit on the Boards and make "public good" decisions rather than those strictly for shareholders.

2.3.5. Scandinavia and the Nordic countries

The goal in Scandinavia has been to make a relatively low-cost system more efficient by reducing the centralization of government planning. Government ownership is still considered important, and privatization is not on the agenda. In contrast to Great Britain, the Nordic changes are attempting to create "competitive public capitalism" (Midttun, 1997: Chapter IV). While public capitalism may appear to be a contradiction in terms, it reflects a particular Scandinavian perspective of strong governmental participation in all aspects of the society. It also reflects the fact that Finland, Sweden, and Norway are all rich in hydrological resources which have been exploited for inexpensive and abundant power. The cheap power attracted heavy industry including electricity-intensive aluminum manufacturers in Norway, while the paper/pulp industry in Finland has contributed considerable power through cogeneration. Sweden chose to supplement its hydro resources with nuclear, a decision that has been politically contentious for over three decades.

Norway was the first of the Scandinavian countries to reorganize in the early 1990s (Midttun, 1997: 100–106). First, the grid was separated from the state power company, Statkraft, and open access was introduced. Then, suppliers and local distribution utilities were freed from exclusive contract and had to compete for electricity supply. Then, a joint spot-market was established with Sweden that gradually signaled the end to decades of national self-sufficiency. Retail sales were opened to spot market purchases by both industry and residents, but residents were initially reluctant to participate. Overall residential participation in the new structure has been slight and prices have not changed much.

Sweden and Finland restructured their electrical system after Norway, noting some benefits from the Norwegian experience. Sweden separated its transmission system from the state power company, providing open access. Finland made provision for public–private ownership of their grid. Also, electricity has been used for many purposes that would be too expensive elsewhere such as residential and business space heating. Both countries moved in a gradual and measured way to increase competition among their many producers, giving them more independence. Several mergers have strengthened and expanded various companies so they could compete better (some claim they will reduce competition). One of the areas that has expanded is export of power to Denmark and Europe. Since the early 1990s, a number of lines have been laid beneath the Baltic to link Sweden and Norway to Denmark and Germany, but also the Netherlands and Poland. Finland is primarily trading power with Russia.

Denmark, with few traditional fossil fuel sources from which to generate electricity, has both been open to importing more power and has pursued a strategy of alternative sources with vigor, especially wind. The Danish electrical system is a nonprofit one, with the sector not being able to build up surpluses or use electricity funds for other public purposes (see Hvelplund, 1997). Any excess earnings are returned to consumers the following year in the form of lower prices. In addition, the system does not borrow money for expansion, collecting funds in advance for any new plants. This has led to conservative structure protecting against change, but also considerable latitude to pursue innovation in the form of green power such as wind. Pressures for changes in the Danish system appear to be less intense than in other countries because of prior strategies of public involvement and ownership.

In sum, the Scandinavian countries have formed international pools to provide more balanced and competitive arrangements between them, and they have sought markets for power in Europe. Residential and industrial customers in Scandinavia seem not to be hurt or to benefit greatly from the changes, but national trade had helped generate revenues and system stability. An interesting twist has emerged in Sweden and Norway throughout 2003. Norway, due to a shortage of rain and hence water for its hydroelectric plants, has been seriously reconsidering its reorganization plans for power generation.

Sweden, on the other hand, generates most of its power from nuclear plants. In 2002, the Government decided to close half of its nuclear power plants. Hence, Sweden needed to create and generate more energy from other sources. The most critical pathway appears to be through the increased use of renewable energy sources including wind, biomass, and hydroelectric resources. Finland, to the contrary and in part to offset its growing dependency upon Russia for energy, has decided to build a nuclear power plant. Thus, a political conflict has emerged now not only with Russia but also with Sweden.

Iceland has gained a worldwide reputation for declaring itself the first national "hydrogen economy." With its large geothermal energy production and renewable resources from wind and biomass, Iceland political decision makers are certain that they will achieve the hydrogen economy within a few years. Major oil, gas, and auto makers agree. Diamler-Chrysler along with Shell Oil and Norsk Hydro have invested heavily in a hydrogen refueling station as well as committing to supply basic supplies and vehicles.

Now the EU under a new program has expanded the Icelandic experiment to 10 cities throughout Europe for the distribution of 30 Diamler-Chrysler hydrogen-powered buses. The second hydrogen refueling station will be a team effort and installed in Hamburg, Germany during 2004. Under the leadership of EU President Prodi, the hydrogen economy has been launched in Europe. Chapter 13 explores more details. But suffice it to note here that the EU approach to hydrogen is vastly different than the American: the EU has committed to "green hydrogen" based on renewable energy generation whereas the USA (Bush administration) has committed primarily to "dark hydrogen" generated from fossil fuels and nuclear energy.

2.3.6. Russia

Amidst the many economic woes facing Russia, restructuring of the power sector seems essential. While some progress has been made, it appears that a widespread rush to competition is underway with potentially harsh results.

According to Bashmakov (2002), the accomplishment so far has been to cure a long-standing problem of not being able to collect payments due. Progress is being made with payment collection rising from a low of only 35% in 1999 to 84% cash collection in 2001. However, employment has increased and productivity has fallen, with the utilities reporting large excess capacity.

Restructuring is proceeding in Russia, a process that will take at least 8–10 years. The wholesale market will first be opened up, but significant problems are foreseen. For example, restructuring of the gas industry will quadruple gas prices, which are a significant input to the power sector, but the electricity sector has promised to reduce prices in spite of this forthcoming price shock.

2.3.7. Developing countries

The key driving force in developing countries is the overall need for economic growth, which also includes reform of national budgets, managing external debt, stabilizing currency and interest rates, and restructuring many key industries such as agriculture and key industrial sectors. Many of these countries need to attract foreign investment, while others need to control the exploitation and negative consequences of the foreign firms that dominate their economy. In other countries corruption and the lack of a stable political–legal system mean that economic activity is insecure. Public infrastructure investment in systems such as highways, telephones, water, and health compete with electricity, though each competing demand is interconnected as a precursor of development. Many of the poorest countries lack infrastructure to collect taxes and payments due for power, which makes public or private investments risky. Consumer dissatisfaction in many systems that are corrupt, inefficient, or inadequate contributes to the pressure to change.

The key problem in the poorest countries, especially Africa, is that any development of the electrical system is still primitive. In Central and East Africa access rates (percent of population with access to electricity) are below 10%, while West and Southern Africa averages below 20%, with the exception of South Africa and Mauritius which are 66 and 50%, respectively (Redwood-Seyer, 2002).

It is in this context that most developing countries have little flexibility to control any system, and they are highly dependent on loans and investments by outside organizations such as the World Bank, International Monetary Fund (IMF), United Nations, and others.

Wamukonya (2003) quotes a London *Observer* article saying, "although Thatcher's private power market scheme was a poor idea that proved worse in practice, the IMF and World Bank adopted it as a requirement of every single structural assistance programme worldwide."

India has had a difficult time with its power system. Although progress in developing capacity proceeded well during the1960s and 1970s, by the late 1970s political candidates promised to offer flat rate and subsidized power prices to farmers for their water pumps. Over time these subsidies have been interpreted as entitlements and change are unlikely in the short run. However, the reliability of the subsidized power is so low that more reliable metered power may be attractive to enough farmers so that they can plan their watering.

India also experimented with independent power production starting in the early 1990s. In spite of signing many agreements with foreign investors, most plants were never finalized or put into operation. After this policy failure, under urging of the World Bank, the Orissa project was initiated to restructure the sector in one state. The principles were the common ones of unbundling transmission, generation, and distribution, private sector participation and ownership, competitive bidding on new generation, establishment of an autonomous regulatory mechanism, and reform of tariffs. Overall, this experiment seems to have been partially positive, especially given the serious problems in India. Wider restructuring was envisioned in extension of the process to other states and then a national program envisioned in the Electricity Bill of 2000. However, this was put on hold when California ran into trouble.

In her review of the conditions leading to power system reform, Wamukonya notes that there are many issues leading countries to restructure their power system. A critical issue in some developing countries prompting reforms is inability to meet soaring demand for power. If systems could not invest in adequate supply, such as Guatemala and Columbia, initial reforms were proposed to allow independent power producers contribute supplies under contract. China and several Asian Pacific countries changed their power system in order to gain access to more capital.

Wamukonya (2003) is highly critical of restructuring efforts around the world. Based on extensive research, she notes that there has been extensive private participation in the construction of power projects in developing countries since the wave of restructuring began. A total of over 600 projects were implemented from 1990 to 1999 representing investment of $160 billion in 70 countries. However, the vast majority of these were built by multinational megacompanies. The largest investors were AES and Enron from the United States, Electricite de France, and Edndesa from Spain.

In addition, these private investors secured government guarantees which limited the country's ability to invest in other projects. In return the governments of developing countries were expected to reap high returns from their utility investment, but it is believed that the governments had to invest in the restructuring, and sales of the assets have fallen short of the expected revenues. Moreover, the new owners cut jobs and improved reliability, but this came without significantly lower prices to consumers.

The future remains uncertain in most of these countries because the companies involved in competition are consolidating, and there is a great fear that a monopoly or an effective monopoly will result. In sum, the results of nearly a decade of restructuring in the power industry in developing countries appear to have minimal benefit, while struggling governments have fewer assets and less control over the important power sector (see also Bouille *et al.*, 2001).

2.3.8. Energy corporate governance

The key to successful, sustainable, and reliable energy systems appears to be public–private collaborations usually in the form of a business structure (Clark and Jensen, 2001). Ownership of power companies is a key aspect in the deregulation or privatization of the energy sector (Savitski, 2003). Consider how some regions are organizing their restructured energy sectors. Malmö, Sweden, for example, across the Baltic Sea from Copenhagen, has developed a number of dispersed energy systems and corporate governance structures between the public and private sectors. Sydkraft, the western Sweden public power utility went through privatization in the late 1990s.

However, when privatization of Sydkraft was defined by executives in the firm during interviews in the spring 2001 (Clark, 2001), the new company was composed of public and private entities. Sydkraft like many energy companies was not formed along the lines of the pure privatization (neoclassical economics) model. In fact, a large share-holder ownership (over 20%) of the new company was controlled by a large Norwegian power company as well as another large percentage by a German power company. The remaining shares were owned by individuals, investment funds, and the local city government.

Local government or community control and hence choice of power is critical in the restructuring of the energy sector (Lund, 2000). Examples exist throughout northern Europe and in some areas of the USA.

Again in Malmo, Sweden, the local city has created ownership over its power needs. For example, the Harbour District in Malmo has a projected residential population: 2–3000 with over 1000 homes, offices, shops, nurseries, cafes, restaurants, schools, libraries, and more. The goal is to make the community within Malmo, "sustainable." Hence partners in energy, environment, waste, water, and other public needs include: City of Malmo; Sydkraft Power Company, BoO1 City of Tomorrow (European Housing); Lund University and Swedish National Energy Administration (BoO1, 2001).

Examples of public–private corporations in the energy sector and elsewhere are growing worldwide (Clark and Jensen, 2002). What appears to be a pattern is the composition of the company itself. Elsewhere, the discussion about Enron concerning its finance and accounting problems focus on the issue of corporate governance. In America, the issue in terms of due diligence along with corporate checks and balances has now been uncovered as a significant issue in other corporations.

Basically, the issue focuses on the officers of a corporation and how funds are administered. For example, one American nonenergy company had two of its top executives indicted for fraud. The federal prosecutors noted that these two executives treated the company as if it was their own "piggy bank." The allegations included the accountants and finance department reporting directly to the two executives rather than the Board of Directors. Clearly, corporate governance for the responsibility of shareholders was compromised if these charges are true. Similar patterns existed in Enron and apparently other American energy sector companies.

The argument to include public and government representatives on Corporate Boards does not assure either compliance to the law or fiduciary duty to shareholders. This problem can be seen in California again when the State created its California Independent System Operators (CAISO) corporation under deregulation. The original Board was composed of "stakeholders" (not "shareholders") who were dominated by private sector energy companies and those who firmly believed that a totally "open market" would work in the energy sector.

Governor Davis had to reconstitute and replace that Board of the CAISO with five people selected who ascribed to his political–economic view that the CAISO had to control the market rather than the other way around. By July 2002, the Governor's decision resulted in a American Constitutional confrontation between the Federal Energy Regulatory Commission (FERC) who had ordered the removal of the CAISO Board to be replaced by a "regional Western State ISO" and the State of California. By the fall of 2002 this matter was still being adjudicated.

In short, governance of power corporations is critical in any consideration of restructuring the energy sector. There appears to be no direct pattern or formula for the organization and control of companies, but in sectors that have direct impact on the public there is a need for public–private partnerships that are legally institutionalized in the companies themselves. Civic markets can only be achieved when responsible elected officials are engaged in infrastructure sector decision making.

2.4. Perspectives for the Future of Agile Energy Systems

The global movement toward more agile and flexible power systems is still emerging, but if the Johannesberg summit was any indication, it is a movement which has a chance to move from talk to action around the world. Global concern with renewable energy lends itself to more dispersed power. What is important for governments is to achieve energy independence, much like California sought as a result of its energy crisis (Governor Davis, 2001). Dependency on one fuel source or a few private corporations or merchant marketeers leads to market manipulation. California and other states and nations have experienced the same situation. Dispersed power in the form of flexible systems controlled by public–private corporations would prevent future market manipulation.

Probably the most important competition now is for dominance in production of photovoltaic systems. The EU White Paper on "Energy for the Future: Renewable Sources of Energy" (1997) noted the competition between Europe, Japan, and the United States for leadership in photovoltaic panels, with huge markets forecast. The EU proposal called for a million photovoltaic systems, half in the EU and half in developing countries. At an average size of 1 kW, it would provide a considerable share of the renewable goal for the EU, and it would provide enough market to have substantial economic development impacts. Germany already is investing heavily in photovoltaic systems.

Wind is the other highly visible target for renewable power in the EU. With leadership from Denmark, Germany, and Britain have followed with ambitious wind programs that support the expectation of at least 10,000 MW of large wind farms (European Commission, 1997: 29). Some public subsidy of the early and remote locations are expected, especially for offshore wind turbines. Biomass is considered to be a third component of the European model, using farm and urban waste, as well as constructing facilities for transport fuels.

2.5. Conclusion

The various political and economic reasons given for restructuring the electricity system around the world must be seen in the context of local situations and dynamics. As pointed out in the first chapter, there are strong and pervasive pressures for change in the electrical system coming from political and business entities who claim that a new generation in technologies and a changing economy warrant dismantling the publicly controlled energy sectors in favor of private business competition. However, both developed and developing countries appear not to benefit in the same way from restructuring, if at all.

The key to understanding energy restructuring is that it by itself does not produce benefits. In some areas the goal of restructuring is the sale of public assets to improve government revenues as in developing countries and transitional economies of eastern and central europe, while in other countries it is to achieve efficiencies such as in western Europe, America, and Scandinavia. In other cases it is a structural change that can enforce social change such as the breaking of contracts with the British coal unions. In some countries, the claim has been made that energy sector government bureaucracies are corrupt and restructuring is the only way to correct that problem.

Energy companies, in other cases as seen herein, seek to influence national political policies and then world stock market valuations. Reforms in revenue collection, accounting, and market prices, however, have indicated that many private energy companies have used "suspicious" legal and financial practices. The economic impact in the USA has been enormous as companies declare bankruptcy, their bankers and investment bankers come under scrutiny and investigation, and stockholders watch their savings and retirement funds disappear. The financial impact in many developing countries has yet to be realized, but strong indicators are emerging that suggest the situation could be far worse. Hence in both developed and developing countries, it is less clear what the objective is for restructuring.

Around the world, it seems that hasty and ill-conceived structural reform of the power sector leads to chaos and catastrophe. Such situations internationally echo what happened in California. What can be done is not clear. Privatized power systems cannot be returned to public ownership since their governments lack funds with which to purchase them. A return to full public regulation in the developed world is no longer a viable option either. Too much has occurred and new forms of structures and markets have already appeared for this to take place. In developing countries and the financial institutions that support them, the message is even clearer: stop privatization and carefully consider what kind of public–private civic market system is desirable to meet local needs and concerns.

PART I
Roots of the Crisis

Chapter 3
Technological Change and Impact: From Vertically Integrated to Dispersed Energy Systems

The pace of change will be influenced by the fact that the most important new energy technologies are relatively small devices that can be mass-produced in factories—a stark contrast to the huge oil refineries and power plants that dominate the energy economy today. (Flavin and Lenssen, 1994: 23–24)

Technological change has been pervasive in the electricity industry, and this has had persistent impact on the structure of utilities and the cost of energy for homes and vehicles. Historically, technological change has been the catalyst for change. We think that advanced and emerging technologies have been primary drivers for the transformation of the energy sectors, be it transportation or for buildings. To a certain extent, the lack of technological innovation and change led to societal changes which helped to create the conditions that led to deregulation and the catastrophic energy crisis that created energy disruptions in California from 2000 to 2001, and seen since then in the Eastern USA and Southern Canada as well as most of Western Europe during the summer of 2003. In this chapter we discuss shifts in the technological base of the energy industries that led to pressures which impacted the market, organizational, and regulatory structures.

This chapter will present the first of the five core ideas that helps explain the transformation of the rigid vertically integrated regulated utility systems of the past into a new transitional structure that is becoming the "agile energy system" of the future. We make the case that California is experiencing the transition from the old centralized power supply system to the new dispersed agile energy system. New advanced technologies necessitate a new approach to regulation, economics, planning, and economic development. As we will discuss in detail in Chapter 13, we argue that the "hydrogen economy," in fact, demonstrates a "paradigm shift" from not only the central power system to an agile one, but also the fossil fueled energy supply to a renewable—clean energy system.

We do not argue that technological change alone is driving system change, but technology is at least a catalyst for it. Thus, we will argue that California's early experiments with dispersed production by independent generators using small-scale technologies including renewable technologies such as wind and cogeneration (Summerton and Bradshaw, 1991) necessitated major organizational restructuring as major consumers gained new access to attractive market niches.

While the pattern of deregulation chosen by California was not inevitable, we argue that some change was essential. Given the choices made by California policy makers, the State created a level of vulnerability that made the 2000–2001 crisis nearly inevitable. However, our purpose here is not to point blame but to outline the lessons to be learned from the responses to technological change that led to organizational and policy failure. After all, the policy and decision makers who deregulated the state electricity system were bipartisan and of a single mind, "the system had to change."

3.1. Historical Overview

Thomas Hughes in *Networks of Power* (1983) shows how the early development of the technical system, which is the basis of the electrical industry, was socially shaped and that the same technology was adopted in different ways in different cities and countries as the technology was first deployed. In other words, Hughes shows how the technological system coevolves with a social or organizational system that implements the technology. This historical lesson continues to be true as new technologies are starting to replace and alter the current technological basis of power in the advanced industrial economy.

Furthermore, Pool (1997) documents how "social construction" or the growing consensus of public opinion finally stopped the expansion and use of nuclear energy worldwide in the 1990s. Until the late 1970s, nuclear energy production was the most notable and dramatic technological development in the last half of the 20th century, in almost every industrialized country. What Pool identified was the fossil fuel energy production with technologies in the nuclear sector that were part of what can be labeled "fossil fuel paradigm" that dominated the production and supply of all fuels since the mid-19th century.

Electrical systems developed around the start of the 20th century, and perhaps no other technological innovation requiring public infrastructure was as broadly influential in shaping the century. In the late 1800s electrical lights and motors were novelties that cities used to attract interest. San Jose, California, for example, erected a 200-foot tower on which four arc lights were a proud statement of modernization. The early power systems developed technologies that took advantage of local fuel resources. In California, at the turn of the century, fuel for powering electrical generation was generally scarce, with no significant reserves of coal in the State. On the other hand, gold mining had established a broad network of dams and flumes, and the use of water power was at the core of much innovation in the years immediately following the initial gold rush, including hydraulic mining projects that washed whole mountains away and clogged rivers and the San Francisco Bay with mud.

As the gold fields became depleted and electricity demand increased in urban California, the miner's technologies for harnessing hydropower were easily converted to generation of hydroelectricity (see McWilliams, 1949; Williams, 1997). However, these sources of power were in the Sierra Nevada foothills, a hundred miles or more from coastal cities, and it was the development of high-voltage alternating current that allowed long-distance transmission of power from the mountains to urban populations. Because the transmission systems developed greater capacity, efficiency, and reliability, electricity reached further into the coastal region and prices fell. By the 1930s the discovery of oil in California (as well as several drought years) helped stimulate thermal plants in that state (Williams, 1997: 278–279).

For the most part, the systems throughout the Western states were conceived of and built by investor-owners and entrepreneurs who experimented with technologies and in many cases competed vigorously with each other to gain the franchise to supply power to cities and towns. By the 1920s and 1930s firms consolidated and prices dropped, but scandals were frequent, leading to local, state, and national regulatory structures. Only a few communities chose to take over as municipal utilities in the Western states, but in the 1930s public oversight became mandatory in order to assure reliable electricity as a reasonable or just price (see Berman and O'Connor, 1996; Bradshaw *et al.*, 2003).

Throughout the American Midwest and East, the early development of steam-driven turbines had the same general effect of expanding early access to electricity, though turbines were located closer to urban areas and there was greater prevalence of municipal ownership. The gradual increase in technological efficiency led to more widespread availability and declining prices. Turbine design improved rapidly, and thermal efficiency increased with size and scale of units. Throughout much of the country municipalities were deeply involved as early investors in power technologies. This was the logical extension of public water and transportation systems. With increased efficiencies of scale, many of the early public utilities were converted to investor-owned utilities, and interconnections increased so that power was carried to larger and larger service areas. With these systems, regulatory responsibilities grew in order to assure reliable energy and reasonable prices.

Changing electrical technologies reflected changes in the primary fuels for the energy system. Dorf (1982), for example, has traced this trajectory, forecasting changes that are now emerging. During the mid-1800s fuel wood was the primary source of energy, followed by coal peaking after the turn of the century. By 1940 oil and natural gas had exceeded coal, and these technologies were expected to peak before the end of the 20th century (see Fig. 3.1).

In Fig. 3.1 Dorf also projects a future replacing oil and gas starting in the 1980s. He includes in this unnamed alternative, solar, nuclear

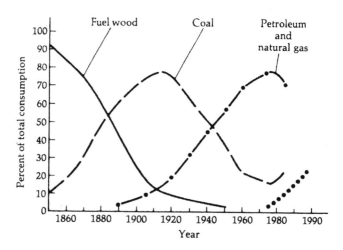

Fig. 3.1. Changing primary fuels over time.
Source: Dorf (1982: 9).

fusion, and conservation, projections that are remarkably prescient given the fact that this analysis was written near the start of the first energy crisis. While no one seriously thinks that fusion will be a source of power any time soon, the rise of solar (including wind) as a cost competitive technology has occurred and we think solar will shortly become the dominant technology coupled with hydrogen storage.

There are many reasons why the power system in all major developed countries through the 20th century consolidated and utilized a growing interconnected transmission system. The fact that separate systems in so many different countries evolved in similar concentrated ways suggests that the technology choices set in motion early had something to do with a trajectory of consolidation that dominated the first eight decades of the century. The key force was improving technology which increasingly favored larger power plants which were more thermally efficient and cost effective, and could be located far from their final load because of increasingly efficient long-distance transmission and interconnections among suppliers. In addition, the history of electrical system consolidation is lubricated by politics and political favors, scandal, corporate bullying, and an inadequate vision on the part of alternative power suppliers.

The technological foundation of power plant concentration through the 1980s is pointedly demonstrated in Fig. 3.2. The optimal plant size

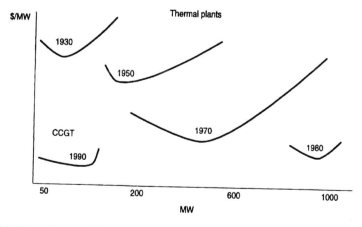

Fig. 3.2. Size and cost of electricity-generating plants.
Source: Hunt and Shuttleworth (1996).

for each decade is shown based on the cost in constant dollars per MW. Optimal price in the 1930s was for plants just over 50 MW. By 1950 optimal size was 200 MW and by 1970 it was around 500 MW. While there were diminishing returns to larger scale (see the high cost of 1000 MW plants [presumably nuclear] in the 1970s), by the 1980s virtually all large plants in the 1000 MW range were more cost effective than the best a decade earlier. However, the big surprise comes in 1990 when the new technologies of that decade are decisively smaller and more efficient. The curve for 1990 shows that 100 MW plants, reflecting new dual cycle gas-fired turbines, reversed a century-long trend, and larger was no longer cheaper. In spite of protests by nuclear and coal advocates, the new technology reflected by this trend so dramatically has transformed the economics of the power industry that concentration and consolidation are no longer driven by cost factors.

3.1.1. Theoretical underpinnings of dispersed systems

The notion that an electrical system could be based on alternatives to the integrated utility was most pointedly argued by Amory Lovins. In a paradigm-breaking paper published in *Foreign Affairs*, Lovins (1976) laid out the difference between "hard" and "soft" paths for supplying electricity. The hard path involves increasingly large centralized power plants connected by an elaborate long-distance high-voltage grid, and supported by the assumption of increased demand.

The soft path, in contrast, involved alternative technologies for the generation of power, shortening the lines in the grid with more production closer to where it is needed, the exploitation of con-servation to reduce demand instead of assuming growing demand, and the pursuit of environmentally friendly renewable sources of power. He called attention to the waste system of burning oil or coal to make heat that generates electricity with only 30% efficiency, transmitting that electricity hundreds or more miles at high voltage with more loss, and then using it to heat air or water, typical uses of large proportion of our electric demand. He argues that electricity should be reserved for uses of high quality and highly refined power such as motors or computers.

While the transition to a mature soft path energy economy has not happened for many reasons that will be explored in this book, Lovins' contribution was to put into perspective two alternatives that in one way or another have shaped the direction of change. The hard path finally became so brittle that it broke in California during 2000, and across the globe hard-path power generation has become so polluting that the electrical system is the major contributor to acid rain, ozone depletion, carbon dioxide buildup causing global warming, and international tensions around primary energy supplies. Its size and interconnectedness makes it vulnerable to terrorism.

Nonetheless, much has been accomplished in the transition to a soft path. The slow development of an adequate market for alternative power has sustained considerable technological development which will be outlined in the last half of this book, and it has made several technological options competitive on a price basis. These technologies promise other benefits in environmental pollution reduction, economics, and diversification. Holdren states well the transition that the world is facing in terms of energy:

> *The transition is from convenient but ultimately scarce energy resources to less convenient but more abundant ones, from a direct and positive connection between energy and economic well being to a complicated and multidimensional one, and from localized pockets of pollution and hazard to impacts that are regional and even global in scope. (1992: 379)*

Holdren (1992: 389) goes on to argue that the future should be looked at in terms of "no regrets" and "insurance policy" elements. The no regrets strategies are ones that are beneficial even if the future demands and technologies turn out different than we expect. Conservation and reduction of environmental deterioration have strong no regrets elements. New technologies may be low-investment options that might be critical, though perhaps unnecessary. The insurance policy elements are choices that have costs and may not pay off unless the unexpected happens, and in that case it is well worth to cover the risk.

Flavin and Lenssen in their book, *Power Surge*, argue for a global technological change based both on the limitations of the past system which pollutes, has global political risks, and is inefficient. They foresee a future of increasing demand that must be met by a changed paradigm that disavows small adjustments to today's fossil fuel-based systems:

> *To meet the needs of poor nations and of the global environment, incremental change in today's energy systems is clearly not enough. Instead, the world will need to forge a new energy path, making a gradual transition to an entirely different energy system—one that ultimately relies on renewable sources of energy. (1992: 25)*

Flavin and Lenssen predict a chaotic transition from the 1980s through the turn of the century as large energy companies and utilities try to maintain the old system, while newer firms innovate and seek new political support. They warn that, "the investments required for achieving a sustainable energy system are sizable, the economic forces to be overcome well organized, and the challenges to human ingenuity enormous" (1992: 310). However, they are optimistic that the social responsibility of creating a less environmentally destructive energy system and the economic opportunities of a new system combine to create new opportunities that in their view are nearly inevitable.

The case study of California is a good place to identify the central driving force for the transition from a centralized system to a new and dispersed one. A dispersed system builds on the logic that a loosely coupled system made up of many efficient and diverse parts is superior at scale to a tightly coupled system of few critical and nearly identical components. The dispersed system gains reliability, agility, and efficiency, as well as the capacity to respond to unknown and complex futures.

A number of academic studies on a form of dispersed systems were conducted throughout the 1990s. One by Isherwood *et al.* (2000) made the point that in remote isolated communities, renewable energy with fuel cell storage technologies made a closed energy system that was totally self-reliant and cost effective. Work in Northern Europe (Lund *et al.*, 1996; Clark and Lund, 1999) came to the same conclusions. These "distributed energy systems" or for the Europeans, "combined heat and power," since that was the main end-use of the energy produced, began to be commercialized by advanced technology companies producing microturbines and other companies (Lagier, 2003) promoting a dispersed energy system for regions and communities based on local energy supply factors rather than reliance on grid-connected power supplies.

Here the case is made that the electricity system is a "system" that is interconnected with other infrastructure and that the type of system makes a difference. Moreover, we argue that the system is not just driven by technical and economic forces that shape the direction it will take, but by environmental and socio-political forces that may be more important than the comparative costs of different technologies (see Tatum, 1995: 33–59). In short, the changed milieu that we now find ourselves in creates tensions between technologies and the social and organizational system of utilities, political interest groups, regulatory bodies that will reshape both the choice of technology and its costs well into the future.

The basic reason why hydrogen is a paradigm change rests with the fact that it can be produced and used for power in vehicles and buildings with no environmental impact and little waste other than water vapor. While researchers will argue and conduct studies into the costs of hydrogen from various sources, it is now able to be produced from renewable resources, as well as from fossil fuels including nuclear. Social constructionism enters the political arena as nation-states must choose how they want to produce and use hydrogen without impacting their neighbors.

In Europe, the decision appears to be "clean hydrogen" (renewables primarily) while in the USA, hydrogen will be both clean and dirty (fossil and nuclear). The USA with a wide range of renewable and fossil fuel sources may well have hydrogen produced from a variety of sources, creating dispersed energy systems at the regional and local levels. Technological advances play a key role as government, incentives, and infrastructure needs are based on public policy and decision makers. Large sums of money can be spent by industry, especially if encouraged by government, that may be stranded in the long term in order to meet short-term power demands (CEC, Integreated Resource Plan, December 2003).

3.2. The Concentrated or Central Grid System Challenged

Throughout the developed world, as we have seen in Chapters 1 and 2, change in the technological system for producing electricity and the social organization of the electrical system has brought persistent and convulsive change to the traditional concentrated electrical utility model. Understanding this basic issue is important for developed countries and especially developing countries which seek reliable energy systems (UNEP and IEA, 2002). The concentrated system may have been reasonable as it developed during the first three quarters of the 20th century, but its limitations started to be seen. We think that there are five essential attributes of the concentrated system characteristic of traditional vertically integrated utilities that proved to be challenged by the potentials of a dispersed system. The limitations to these characteristics of the traditional system are at the core of change that is taking place worldwide.

3.2.1. Transitions in key technologies created alternatives to the old model

The core technology of integrated electric utilities has been characterized by increasing scale and some new sources of power since early

20th century, when central power plants were established to provide power inexpensively to customers in a monopoly franchise geographical area. This model involves a small number of generation plants linked by high-voltage transmission lines to distribution systems that supply residents. The local utility generally owns most of its generation capacity and optimizes its generation to supply its load. This integrated model is more or less the same regardless of whether the utility is a public or private owned entity, or if it serves a very large city or a small rural region. While there has always been some flexibility in the model, most utilities have aimed to control generation, transmission, and distribution within their service area, and to make it more efficient they have tried to grow larger through mergers and acquisitions.

Large and centralized generators and utilities became less competitive

The technology during this period supported the logic of large integrated utilities. Larger power plants were more efficient and cost less than smaller ones, both to operate and to install per MW. Moreover, the large integrated utility could balance fluctuations in demand for electricity due to seasonal and time of day peaks and valleys with several plants that could backup each other. Additionally, old and less-efficient plants could be used to provide peaking power which was more expensive but used only occasionally. In short, during most of the 20th century the technology favored increased scale and systems that allowed managers of each utility to plan for their short-term and long-term needs. They had a monopoly on the customers, and electrical use was steadily increasing so that there was little risk in expanding with new plants because demand could be expected to buy whatever power was produced.

The advantages of concentration were established on a number of premises. First that new larger plants were cheaper, and that with nearly assured growth in demand that the continuing construction of more plants would reduce the average cost of power. Utility plant construction also favored large plants because the process of siting and getting permits became a high proportion of the costs. Getting permits and finding a site for a plant was somewhat a fixed cost, regardless of size.

However, during the last decades of the 20th century these premises changed. Large power plants were no longer cheaper and easier to build. First, new large power plants just increased in cost. In part this was because the large plants had to meet environmental and multiple fuel demands so that expanded facilities ended up costing much more than similarly sized plants a few decades earlier. In addition, public opposition to large power plants increased the risk in finding a site and getting the necessary permits, leading to long delays, public outcry, and expensive mitigation fees. These higher-priced plants caused utility executives to rethink their previous expansion plans because new plants would increase rather than decrease average system costs. Some of the older resources were now the cheapest and this included in California the hydro system and some thermal plants.

As pointed out earlier, new technologies using dual cycle natural gas turbines became widely available and they had advantages of being smaller, more easily sited, and the most cost effective of the new technologies. Because their scale and time for construction was less, the era of ever increasing size of power plants slowed.

Renewable and "alternative" technologies became cost competitive

Under pressure to reduce dependence on foreign oil for electricity generation, to reduce pollution especially in the atmosphere, and to conserve power, research and development in renewable sources of electricity have become a viable alternative to large centralized power plants. Over the last 25 years prices have fallen and policies have overcome many of the institutional barriers that blocked more widespread technological adoption. While the strategies to increase the use of these technologies is the topic of the second half of this book, the current availability of renewable and alternative technologies is starting a massive technological change that will reshape utilities as we know them.

Turner (1999) writing in the journal, *Science*, has argued that renewable energy is widely available and technologically feasible. For example, assuming 10% efficiency in solar collectors, an area only 100 square miles could produce each year energy equivalent to all the energy used in the entire United States. Furthermore, wind power could supply a substantial portion of the national power needs. But the issue is not what one technology could do—instead it is what a combination of renewable technologies can do, in part helping to overcome the problem of intermittent power generation from wind and solar sources. However, at the present time we are seeing applications where renewable technologies are fitting into the grid in an effort to supply a portion of the portfolio that avoids the problems of hydrocarbon-based generation.

Even these initial efforts to tap renewable technologies is having a significant impact on transforming the electrical utility system because in California and elsewhere these new technologies are proving that

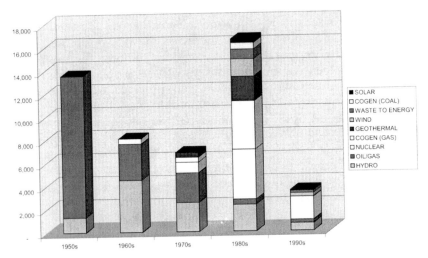

Fig. 3.3. Generating capacity additions in California by decade and primary energy type, in megawatts.
Source: Griffin (2001: 12).

they can be cost effective and fit into the existing system without a complete restructuring of the power system (see Fig. 3.3).

Figure 3.3 shows the role that alterative technologies have played in California. The 1980s showed that there was 2000 MW new nuclear (Diablo Canyon) and the rest of the major contribution was cogeneration and other technologies. Previously, the vast majority was oil/gas in the 1950s and 1960s with some contribution from hydro. However, the large hydro projects were completed by the 1990s and there are few additional options in the State. The other interesting feature of this chart is that in the 1990s all technologies had stopped being introduced.

Mandates to use renewable energy have helped stimulate investment in wind and other technologies. In Europe the mandate from the European Commission is for 12% renewable energy within eight years. In fact, some countries such as Denmark already are getting around a quarter of their power from wind and renewable sources. In Denmark, Germany, Spain, and India wind power has become the technology of choice because of low cost, and even in the United States it is the fastest growing power source (Markels, 2002: 40). In addition, major multinational companies such as Shell, General Electric are involved, as well as some large European companies.

The United States has a total of 1.7 billion dollars invested on wind projects, below several European countries. Several new wind farm projects have been installed in California, using advanced technologies

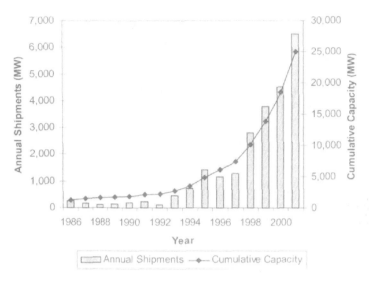

Fig. 3.4. Increase in global wind power.

and often replacing older and less-efficient machines. In total the cost of wind is now competitive with gas-fired plants, and wind is not subject to anticipated price spikes or regional shortages. Costs continue to fall as the newest machines now generate three times the power of state-of-the-art machines of 1995 and at half the cost per kWh (Markels, 2002). Global shipments of wind generation capacity are growing at an exponential rate as shown in Fig. 3.4.

3.2.2. The old utility model was unable to deal with externalities such as nuclear waste, air pollution, or global warming

In addition to changing technology that reduced the scale of power plants, the environmental movement started putting increased pressure on all utilities to reduce pollution and to consider the waste stream. The problem of nuclear waste became so politically important that it essentially halted construction of any new nuclear plants in California and to a large extent around the world; a number of power plants were closed due to rising concern over safety, such as the Sacramento, California, Rancho Seco reactor. The issue of pollution had several effects. It increased costs and reduced options for expanding low-cost power.

Environmental concerns over energy peaked in 1969, perhaps, with a catastrophic offshore oil spill opposite Santa Barbara. Some 235,000 gallons of crude oil leaked from the ocean floor, creating an 800-mile long oil slick and killing over 3000 birds (Williams, 1997: 300). With this oil spill, environmentalists were mobilized in opposition to the entire energy industry, and increased scrutiny was given to the direct and indirect consequences of energy issues, intended or not. In many ways the realization that the energy industry was the cause of considerable environmental problems gave way to an ongoing search for alternative solutions that would reduce the impact of energy expansion on the natural environment.

In California, pollution led to siting plants outside urban areas and to assuring that most plants used natural gas instead of oil or imported coal. By the end of the 20th century, this issue became known as "environmental justice" and tended to impact poor ethnic communities. However, the energy crisis in California and the need to site new power plants as well as power peakers began to move these plants into middle and upper middle class neighborhoods. The issues of air pollution and health problem knew no class or ethnic boundaries. Numerous studies by the UN on climate change began to emerge from the Rio Summit in 1992 that documented the need for global action but also the focus on the solutions (UN and IPCC, 1999; UN, 1998), many of them in the energy sector (UN and FCCC, 2000).

A second impact was to shift some generation out of state where environmental rules were less rigid. The story of experiments with nuclear power are a clear example of the tradeoff of new technologies that promised significant cost savings versus externalities of the technologies as perceived by the public. In the years after the end of World War II, nuclear technology was promised to be utilized for peaceful purposes and at a price that would be "too low to meter." The promise of cheap and unlimited power from nuclear fission was supported by the University and the US Department of Energy Laboratories such as the Los Alamos National Laboratory, Lawrence Livermore and Lawrence Berkeley National Laboratory, all managed by the University of California. In 1954 PG&E teamed with General Electric and built the State's first nuclear plant near Livermore, and in 1958 built another in the northern corner of the State, near Eureka. Larger-scale plants started in 1968 with a Southern California Edison plant at San Onofre, between Los Angeles and San Diego. By 1970 nearly 100 nuclear power plants were operating, under construction, or on order in the United States, and France and Sweden in Europe were pursuing nuclear options. Thus, nuclear electrical technologies were becoming well established around the country and world.

The first problem nuclear power faced in California was not nuclear waste, but seismic hazards. The State's well-known propensity for devastating earthquakes became an increasingly serious concern.

Not forgetting the 1906 earthquake that destroyed San Francisco, the public became increasingly concerned when PG&E proposed a large nuclear plant at Bodega Head, just a few miles from the epicenter of the 1906 quake on the San Andreas fault. While the plant was being discussed, Anchorage Alaska was destroyed by a massive quake measuring 8.6 on the Richter Scale, emphasizing that no one knew how a reactor would stand up despite sincere efforts to make it safe (Williams, 1997: 306). In short, the potential for catastrophic failure during a quake led the Atomic Energy Commission to deny permits for the Bodega plant.

Nonetheless, during the 1960s and early 1970s utilities and regulators pushed proposals for nearly a dozen more nuclear power plants, based on projections that these plants would be safe and cheaper than other sources of power. The growing concern over air pollution and national optimism for nuclear power contributed to the sense that the State's growing and seemingly insatiable demand for electricity could be met by atomic power was broadly embraced by technical experts and politicians.

These dozen nuclear plants proposed in the early 1970s focused concern over safety and the permanent disposal of nuclear waste. As experts tried to figure out the waste disposal question, other experts stressed on protecting waste that would stay toxic for hundreds of thousands of years, longer than all recorded history so far. The technologies for containing waste for that period of time became a major concern and indeed they were unanswered. The safety and disposal issues came to a head in 1976 when voters were asked to approve a ballot referendum, Proposition 15, which would place strict safety and waste disposal rules in effect. In the extensive debate over Proposition 15 voters were asked to decide between competing experts, and the concerns were getting a strong reception. As the election neared, the legislature and pro-nuclear forces feared its passage and took steps to avoid its passage which would have most likely stopped nuclear plant construction in the State. These interests passed through the legislature a strong, but less severe, version of the Proposition that seemed more manageable. With this softer legislation, Proposition 15 was soundly defeated. However, the legislation turned out to have virtually the same effect as what it was feared for the Proposition—it effectively halted further nuclear plant construction (Williams, 1997: 307).

The end of nuclear power was occasioned simply by the requirement that the State would not approve additional nuclear power plants until the federal government certified that it could safely store nuclear waste and recycle spent fuels. While quick technological solutions to these problems were promised, in reality they have not been solved yet, some 25 years later.

Nuclear power also suffered from major and minor malfunctions that convinced many people of the danger of this technology. Three Mile Island and Chernobyl are the most severe of these nuclear catastrophes, but a number of near-meltdowns are also locally important. For example, Sacramento Municipal Utility District's Rancho Seco plant had a loss of coolant problem that narrowly avoided disaster in 1985 (Smeloff and Asmus, 1997: 25). This problem, and recurring unreliability and maintenance problems, led SMUD to decommission the plant in the early 1990s and pursue other sources of power.

Internationally, nuclear power now accounts for 421 plants in 26 countries. The United States has 110 plants, generating about 18% of the country's capacity, according to Hohenemser *et al.* (1992: 133). The prospects for nuclear power seem to be low around the world, though new technological breakthroughs continue to offer advocates encouragement. Even if cost and safety problems can be satisfactorily solved, the events of September 11 give added credibility to terrorism threats.

Air pollution proved to be nearly as significant a barrier for power plant expansion in the State as nuclear safety. The combination of industrial and automobile pollution created serious smog problems in Los Angeles. Environmental groups publicized pictures of the brown soup that engulfed the Los Angeles basin as seen from the mountains that ring the city, keeping pollutants trapped in the warm air for weeks at a time. Power plant air pollution control became a necessity both as retrofits for existing plants and as a precondition for new ones. As a consequence, many plants had to be located in further remote places, including out of state.

Today California has a complex system of emission credits that permit certain amounts of emissions and these credits are traded and purchased. During the 2000–2001 energy crisis the lack of pollution permits and their escalating price contributed to power shortages.

In sum, large centralized power generation became inexorably linked to uncontrollable externalities that required public response. Largely the public response has been to try to reduce the impact of the environmental problems created by the energy sector—control unwanted emissions, improve safety, or anticipate problems so that impacts can be mitigated. These mitigations added to the cost of energy, but for the most part policy makers did not tax energy to the degree that European countries did, to provide incentives against consumption.

3.2.3. Diversification—the uneven commitment to diverse supply

A key issue here is the fact that most utilities were highly dependent on fossil fuels and when they tried to diversify with nuclear they still remained vulnerable. While hydro had been a large part of the State's power supply, as the State grew and consumption increased, hydro resources remained constant.

By the end of the 1980s California had the most diverse mix of electrical generation sources in the world, and was recognized globally for the innovative inclusion of renewables, cogeneration, and other independent nonutility sources of power that were integrated into its supply system. The foundation for diversity in power supply was established early with the hydroelectric development along with oil and nuclear. Innovative strategies to tap geothermal steam fields in Northern California's coastal mountains contributed to diversification even before the first energy crisis. However, it was the impetus of the search for alternatives that started with the establishment of the Energy Commission and the development of the qualifying facility niche in the market that developed the true diversity that was key. During the 1980s diversification was a state goal and it was part of the principles behind the State's energy policies at that time.

The energy crisis of the 1970s and the enactment of PURPA led to a rapid diversification of the State's power sources in the 1980s that stagnated by the end of the 1990s. Figure 3.5 shows new generation capacity by decade. The 1980s were a period of extensive new generation capacity added in the State, and it was an extremely diverse mix. A total of some 16,000 MW were added in the State during this decade, with cogeneration from gas and other fuels as well as wind helping to assure diversity. This was a period of experimentation as well as the establishment of public programs to stimulate new technologies in order to avoid catastrophic shortages such as were faced during the oil embargos.

Moreover, the shift in emphasis to alternative and decentralized generators stopped the construction of new capacity in California because so much came from qualified facilities. Figure 3.5 shows the new utility capacity from 1977 to 1997 and the abrupt slow down of new capacity starting in 1988, about the time the alternative suppliers became active.

Figure 3.5 shows another very important factor about the California energy crisis in that the end of utility capacity expansion ended around 1987 not only in California but in all the states in the West. While many claim that the reason California did not have adequate capacity which led to the energy crisis of 2000–2001, it is clear that

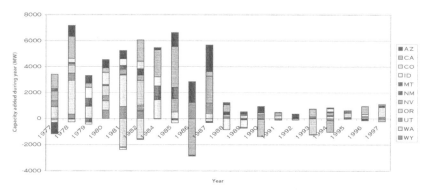

Fig. 3.5. New utility capacity by state, 1977–1997.
Source: Fisher and Duane, 2001.

the State was responding to external forces nearly the same in all of its neighboring states, and deregulation simply left the State too vulnerable to market manipulation. However, the story is much more complicated in that two things were going on. First, the excess nuclear and other capacity in the rest of the region provided a surplus that none of the states responded to by continuing construction—in fact they did the smart thing and halted additional construction. Second, California continued expansion through the continued implementation of nonutility capacity as mandated by PURPA. This is shown in Table 3.1. By 1998 California had a total of 10,386 MW capacity from qualifying facilities, whereas the rest of the region had a negligible amount. However, it is clear that even by 1995 the expansion of QF capacity virtually stopped as deregulation started being discussed and implemented.

The public role during the buildup of diverse electrical generation capacity involved extensive contributions to analysis of options and the identification of resources and support for private experimentation that was critical to the exploitation of diverse options. The Energy Commission, for example, identified natural resources such as wind, untapped hydro potential, and geothermal resources that could be used for generation. Most of these resources had not been mapped before and little was known about them. For example, wind resources in the more populated areas were well known, but it turned out that they were not as strong as in several mountain passes surrounding the central valley. It also turned out that the researchers discovered higher average wind speed closer to the ground in some areas, counter to other resource inventories which documented higher speeds at higher elevations.

Table 3.1. Capacity in California (megawatts).

	Utility owned	Qualifying facilities	Total
1977	34,724	163	34,887
1978	35,716	237	35,953
1979	37,425	237	37,662
1980	37,760	269	38,028
1981	38,120	407	38,527
1982	38,176	433	38,609
1983	38,456	545	39,001
1984	39,847	1030	40,877
1985	41,942	1645	43,587
1986	45,107	2487	47,594
1987	45,045	3599	48,644
1988	45,405	5198	50,603
1989	45,944	6336	52,280
1990	45,876	8109	53,985
1991	44,548	9203	53,751
1992	44,473	9631	54,104
1993	44,370	9859	54,229
1994	44,957	9967	54,924
1995	44,073	10,067	54,140
1996	44,071	10,196	54,267
1997	44,699	10,344	55,043
1998	44,493	10,386	54,879
Total increase			
Percent	28.1%	6287.0%	57.3%
Absolute	9769	10,223	19,992

Source: Fisher and Duane (2001: Table E-3).

Cogeneration was a central piece of diversification. Before 1978 California had only nine cogeneration plants, but with the incentives and opening of the market with PURPA contracts, cogenerators in California had installed 380 more plants, and by 1997 an additional 270 were added. While the construction of cogeneration plants slowed or stopped by the mid-1990s due to reduced regulatory pressure and the potential loss of markets due to deregulation, the size and scale of the cogeneration capacity in California remains outstanding. For example, today the State has a total of 6457 MW of cogeneration installed, and this is nearly six and a half times the capacity of a typical large nuclear reactor. In short, with very little additional use of fuel and in a very short period of time, the State constructed at low cost an additional 12% of the power consumed in the State (California Energy Commission, Oct 2000: 2–4).

However, the early 1990s saw the price structure which supported cogeneration get severely disrupted. The cogeneration capacity was initially installed under PURPA agreements in California based on the utilities "avoided costs," that is the price the utilities expected to pay for additional energy, and the contracts were structured so that the customer would be indifferent whether the utility purchased power from cogenerators or other diversified suppliers, or from the standard lowest cost options that the utilities had available to them at the time.

At the time the contracts were signed the avoided costs were anticipated to continue increasing, but in fact they fell as natural gas prices declined and as dual-cycle generation systems became more widely available. Consequently, the price advantage shared by cogenerators declined and when contracts came up for renewal at the end of the first 10 years, the price dropped and many could no longer continue. For example, initial contracts were for between 4 and 7 cents per kWh, and these fell to near 2.5 cents. At the same time, low utility rates led industrial and other users with potential cogeneration to abandon their construction plans because they could negotiate preferable rates with the utilities.

In short, falling prices led to a temporary decline in cogeneration. However, the basic economics of cogeneration remain attractive with new technological improvements allowing businesses with need for process heating or with considerable waste heat to generate electricity. The 2000–2001 energy crisis showed that the cogeneration technology is a fast and effective solution to providing power, and at a cost lower than that negotiated on behalf of the State's utilities.

The barriers to greater use of cogeneration are largely policy and political, and not so much cost or technological. One of the largest concerns is the interconnection system, where the existing power system and grid are designed to take power only one way from centralized generation plants to customers, and the cogenerator sends it partially the other way. While this requires greater planning and control on the part of the operators of the distribution system, experience has shown it as a manageable problem. Better state-of-the-art control technologies are available, and favorable regulatory standards have shown to be effective in spite of the fact that many rules are unnecessary (CEC, Oct 2000: 5). In addition, utilities are anxious to obtain the power when prices are right, but they have charged producers who use some or all of their generated power internally high standby or backup charges. These fees amount to the backup capacity the utilities have to maintain if the system were to fail. But critics of utility pricing systems argue that the likelihood of all the cogeneration systems needing backup at the same time is so slight that they should only have to pay for a small additional capacity used as insurance for the random outage of plants. Since there are now a large number of these cogenerators, reduced capacity charges would make sense. Finally, some barriers are land use zoning and permit problems. While some additional land use impacts are clearly undesirable, many potential cogenerators have problems getting permits.

Wind programs had a similar emergence during the 1980s. From early technological development that promoted demonstration of large wind machines, early innovators chose to invest in smaller wind farms of hundreds or thousands of small wind machines that cumulatively had a significant contribution. This is an interesting case in that the first machines were relatively small and available technologies, but over time larger and larger machines were installed with greater efficiency.

Another interesting feature of the wind programs was that many of the operators and machines were inadequate and as a consequence failed to perform well. Tax incentives that stimulated their initial construction and lucrative capacity payments ended up overriding the power generation benefits of the wind farms, to the extent that they were called "tax farms."

Solar energy programs also contributed to the diversification of the State's energy system in the 1980s, with both solar and thermal towers in the Mojave desert, as well as early applications of photovoltaic panels. Most of these plants were heavily subsidized demonstration plants, which have had the effect of promoting technological development, a process that continues to pay off.

Finally, an aspect of the diversity in power system that is now being recognized as a problem is the fact that in spite of the surge of construction during the 1980s, the relatively flat demand and low level of construction in the 1990s has led to an aging generation system. With the leveling of demand for electricity, California and other states have seen their generation capacity get older, with less replacement with newer, cleaner, and more efficient plants. Leading to the California crisis, 55% of the State's generation facilities are over 30 years old, and as a result these plants have higher maintenance requirements and lower reliability.

The overall conclusion to this issue of diversification is that the renewable and alternative technologies continued to increase in efficiency and their cost continued to fall during the 1980s and 1990s. However, the price of other fossil fuels also fell. For example, Darmstadter reports that an estimate by the Department of Energy had forecast that energy prices would increase about 5% from the early 1980s to the mid-1990s. Instead, new generation plants saw a decline of 40% largely due to the fall in the price of fuels used for conventional generation—natural gas for example. The promise of alternative technologies had been that they would become more cost competitive because their price per kWh was falling, whereas traditional sources would increase. It is now clear that alternative technologies met their expected price goals, but planners failed to correctly estimate that fuel prices would also fall.

In addition, utilities have not embraced alternative technologies, which have limited their potential expansion. Berman and O'Connor (1996), for example, note that utilities view photovoltaic and other technologies as potentially disruptive to their control of the electricity market, and they have used their political power to be the conduits for solar innovation and marketing. This has slowed its introduction and has created a tension with public power and grass roots groups who see solar power as an opportunity for citizen control.

3.2.4. Shaping demand and flexibility in meeting supply; integrated planning and demand side management

The classical vertically integrated utility thrived on growth and it assumed that it needed to find supply to match whatever demand it could generate or expect. In fact, utilities attempted to balance their load by stimulating demand when use was low, for example, with promotion of household appliances and air conditioning. However, the possibility of demand side management was not explored.

Peak demand is a global challenge for electrical systems. California experiences peaks on hot summer days, with lower electricity use during winter periods. Heating is largely done by natural gas while air conditioning is largely from electricity. Figure 3.6 shows typical power sources for hot days, with the peak of nearly 55,000 MW, nearly double the lowest nighttime demand of about 28 MW. The base of nuclear, renewables, and imports changes little with time of day, while hydro doubles or triples its contribution and gas and coal plants ramp up to cover the increased load. On the hottest days a small number of peaker plants start up and demand side programs remove load from the system.

Reducing that peak is a serious challenge for utilities, since when demand arises power must be available or blackouts or catastrophic failure will result. The problem of peaking is that the capacity to meet that peak is used only a few days a year, and in some cases for only a few hours. Utilities have traditionally responded to the challenge of the peak demand in a number of ways. The most common way was to retain some of the oldest, dirtiest, least efficient plants, which were

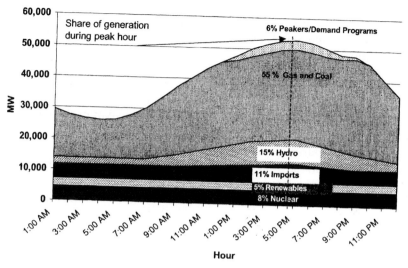

Fig. 3.6. The electricity supply and demand profile for a typical hot summer day. *Source*: CEC 2002–2012 electricity outlook report: I-11.

about to be retired, to push into service on those few occasions when needed.

During the transitional period, demand side management was utilized to help reduce the peak. Utilities (encouraged by the PUC) lowered rates overall for some customers who would agree to reduce their load when peak demand was high. Some industries had processes that could be cut back for selected hours, and they were willing to do so in return for lower rates during the rest of the year. In other cases, general efforts to insulate and install more efficient air-conditioning equipment allowed load reductions.

Conservation programs are perhaps the most significant feature of the transition programs that undermine the classic formula of large centralized plants that meet continuously growing demand. Under the notion of providing "nega-watts" conservation has reduced the total demand and need for new generation facilities in the State. The size of this effort is considerable, which has been both economical and environmentally beneficial.

3.2.5. Transmission issues: grid expanded to include wheeling

During this period the transmission grid expanded, and utilities started being part of regional grids for security and backup, as well as sharing excess power to meet seasonal or time of day peaks. Today the State has about 40,000 miles of power lines that connect utilities to the national and international power grid (Kahn and Lynch, Report to Gov: 12).

Grids cross states and nations like giant highways. States are linked to other states and nations, and this density of interconnection has both costs and benefits for participants. The benefits are enormous, in providing reliability and the ability for areas to benefit from cheaper power far from themselves. California gets power from Canada and Mexico, and a significant part from other states. About one-third of the power used in California comes from out of state, as shown below in Table 3.2. Interestingly, California utilities have located about 14% of their capacity out of state, mostly in Arizona and the four corners region where access to coal and less-stringent regulations allowed more economical construction of plants.

California has the second largest grid in the US and the fifth largest in the world, handling at peak 45,000 MW (Dennis Silverman, www.physics.uci.edu).

Grids are interconnected in highly complex ways that make whole regions vulnerable when disaster strikes. On November 9, 1965, a single short circuit caused a cascade of outages that blacked out nearly the entire New England region, and about 30 million people were without power for as long as 13 hours. New York City, especially, was hard hit and suffered great economic and social damage. In the wake of the blackout, the North American Electricity Reliability Councils were established to coordinate grid operation across regions of the US, Canada, and Mexico. In spite of their best efforts, the grid has become so complex that failures still cascade out of control, as happened in the summer of 2003 when a series of line failures set a cascading set of failures that blacked out a substantial portion of New England and Ontario.

Table 3.2. Source of power imported into California.

Northwest	10%
Southwest, import	8
Southwest, owned by utility	14
Instate	68

Source: California Energy Commission Electricity Analysis Office, July 2001.

Grids are largely owned by utilities for the purpose of supplying their customers with power generated elsewhere. As such utilities own lines that go long distances, and often share ownership of these lines with others whose power needs to be delivered along some leg of the distance. To maintain control over their lines and protect their investment, the FERC has allowed utilities to negotiate access to their lines by other companies.

3.3. Conclusion

This chapter has traced the ways the changing technological system has undermined the traditional structure of electric utilities, substituting instead a smaller scale, dispersed, and generally more environmentally sound set of technologies. Today, we are experiencing a "paradigm change" from a fossil fuel energy system to a hydrogen economy. The advanced technologies are reshaping the social and political system surrounding the electrical industry, and they led to a number of changes in federal law that sets the context for state-level changes.

The first major policy level change was the 1978 Public Utilities Regulatory Act which required utilities to purchase power produced by independent "qualifying facilities" which opened the closed utility system to outside generators for the first significant time. The qualifying facilities were largely renewable or cogeneration plants, which helped diversify the organizational and fuel mix of the electricity system. Then, the Energy Policy Act of 1992 authorized independent power producers to have access to the transmission network and to be able to sell to municipal and cooperative utilities.

In addition, the Clean Air Act of 1977 forced electricity generators to reduce emissions, which gave an advantage to natural gas technologies (Cavazos and Buss, 2003: 203–204). Now North America, Europe, and Asian nations are facing choices for the future of their regions. The choices will be political but there are certain areas that tend to be politically neutral—one is hydrogen and the other are advanced technologies and the positive economic impact in the communities.

The key point is that the technological developments in the last decades of the 20th century were reversals of long-standing trends. The switch from ever declining power prices to situations where new power coming on line was more expensive due to nuclear and environmental issues was perhaps the most significant. Then when dual-cycle turbines were commercially available, the price fell again, but through the use of small-scale plants that were dependent on natural gas. However, the simplest and easiest resource became conservation and cogeneration, ushering in a new paradigm of distributed energy production.

Chapter 4
The Deregulation Tragedy: When Theory Meets the Real World

4.1. Introduction

The interdependent roles of public regulation and private electricity service evolved as a best case solution to the historical early development of private investor owned electricity generating and distribution firms, and the realization that these firms inevitably had a monopoly in their service area. Regulation by publicly appointed public utilities commissions was initiated in order to control monopoly exercise of market power which could lead to unrestrained price increases and profits for the private firms.

Network industries including railroads, electricity, telephone service, and airlines along with trucking were the major industries to be subjected to state and national regulation. Gradually all these industries except electricity became deregulated, and by the mid-1990s pressure mounted for a variety of reasons to deregulate electricity as well. This chapter is about how public policy for electricity deregulation tried to renegotiate the regulatory compact between the public- and private-owned utilities, leading to the catastrophic deregulation scheme tried in California starting in 1998.

Interestingly, deregulation in other industries has not eliminated the public interest and oversight, and the ability of unconstrained market forces to reduce prices, increase innovation, and serve the public interest is contested at best. For example, prices fell when airlines were deregulated, but complaints about service, safety, and other factors increased. This led to new rules about airport access, reliability, and other factors that are evidence of the retention of some oversight, and the threat of additional rules if corrective actions are necessary.

Even in one of the most competitive deregulated industries, telecommunications, the regulatory role remains important as evidenced by the recent requirements that providers allow subscribers to maintain their cell phone numbers when moving from one firm to another. In short, the issue should not be framed as an all or nothing issue of regulation versus no regulation, but the question of how much oversight over what functions.

Since we started this volume, much has transpired that verified and proved our original thesis that electricity deregulation was not only a bad ideological idea but that electricity is the network industry most subject to market manipulation without regulatory oversight. Moreover, our original premise for this chapter remains valid today: that the energy sector, perhaps like many others, should not be left to "open or free trade" in the neoclassical economic paradigm where market competition exerts control on prices and is the incentive for efficiency, rather than public regulation.

In this chapter, we start with an understanding of the historical role of regulation in the power industry. We then trace the origins of return on investment regulatory logic. We will look at the strengths and weaknesses of this type of approach, and will look at how the technological changes noted in the previous chapter made changes in the regulatory scheme inevitable. However, when it was deregulated as in California it has led to widespread market abuse and blackouts in spite of efforts to make the power system fit the model of a self-regulating competitive industry.

4.1.1. Historical overview

The electric utility industry started during the late 19th century as a set of opportunistic capitalist ventures by entrepreneurial inventors and financial investors who aimed to sell a service to private parties. The service was initially to provide incandescent lighting, but soon included motors for transportation and other infrastructure functions (Hughes, 1983; Williams, 1997). Combining daytime use of electricity for powering trolley lines and nighttime lighting increased the market for electricity. Expanding uses of electricity in industrial as well as residential locations helped to usher in the age of electricity, but this was never simply private firms implementing better technology because from the early stages of the history of electricity, private firms pursued their own best interests rather than seeking the overall public good.

Electricity firms early in the history of the industry realized the advantages of exclusive service licenses to provide energy to cities and regions. The potential waste from duplication of lines and transmission systems made direct competition unfeasible at the local level, and consequently in order to attract private investment municipalities were willing to issue licenses with some conditions attached. The profound benefits of economies of scale in all parts of energy generation, transmission and distribution of electricity drove fierce battles among competing companies for the right to serve geographically bound communities. And, of course, the winners were able to exercise near monopoly control.

Municipal governments by the end of the 19th century tried to regulate the power utilities granted exclusive rights to serve the customers within their city limits as a condition of their charter. This led to the early Public Utilities Commissions, and eventually to state and national control. In some cases cities early got involved and started their own municipal utility, and in other cases, often where the private utility proved particularly corrupt, the municipality took over and ran the utility. These public investments controlled by the elected government led to a thriving public power sector in the United States. In some countries that developed their power at a later time, the public had to assume the primary role as investor and owner of the electricity system at the national level. Hence throughout the USA and around the world, thousands of power utilities were created with a variety of ownership and government oversight responsibilities.

Regulation advanced by 1907, just 25 years after Edison's Pearl Street Station in New York City first started delivering power. New York and Wisconsin became the first states to establish rules and institutions for the regulation of the electric utilities. Samuel Insull, who initially advanced state regulation of electricity, argued that instead of local governments running electric utilities, more profit could be made by allowing larger companies to become a regulated natural monopolies. Insull and J. P. Morgan called for exclusive franchises for power companies to be regulated by state public utility commissions (Smeloff and Asmus, 1997; Brennan *et al.*, 2002). The initial public utility commissions in New York and Wisconsin became models for other states as they too became regulators. Their main objective was to assure "reasonable" rates and reduce the effects of inefficiencies and corruption.

Regulation of utilities has been a reluctant obligation of government from the start, though citizens have generally been supportive of efforts to control costs and programs through the legal process. In California, government regulation started with the Railroad commission, initially formed to deal with transportation abuses. In 1911 the Public Utilities Commission was granted power to regulate electric utilities, though this was not a central concern until later.

The collapse of many utilities during the depression was related to the fact that many holding companies operated in several states. As a major part of the New Deal response to restructuring the economy, the Public Utilities Holding Companies Act (1935) expanded federal power over the geographical reach of the holding companies and their functions. The act served to assure that companies were broken into state entities, and it created the structure of utilities linking generation, transmission, and distribution as a vertically integrated utility.

Thus, single companies were formed during the late 1930s that are the structure found today, replacing overlapping and confusing initial structure. The Federal Power Commission was also formed in the 1930s to regulate wholesale power and interstate transmission of power. The initial powers of these Federal regulatory bodies have remained largely set with the renaming of the power commission to be the Federal Energy Regulatory Commission (FERC), an organization that has increasing significance now with restructuring.

Brennan and his colleagues (1996: 25) argued that the structure of regulation set in motion during this period enjoyed considerable success. From the 1930 through the decade of the 1950s, regulation provided a very satisfactory and calm period. The rate of growth in demand for electricity was very high, and the technological improvements to all aspects of the electrical system were keeping prices down. The industry was satisfied with the regulatory system because it allowed it to expand with relatively few impediments, and it assured a constant flow of revenues to fund expansion. The population and industry were pleased because power was available at generally falling rates, and reliability was increasing.

The logic of most of the electricity regulatory programs was to be certain that the companies have a return on their investment (ROI). This premise held that the utilities would be permitted rates that provided them with a reasonable profit to share with stockholders based on their investment in the electrical system. This framework was a compromise because it provided a predictable and justifiable basis on which to regulate utilities. However, it was very poor at penalizing utilities for poor investments or at forcing the utilities to run their business in a cost-effective manner. Nonetheless, shareholders (at the time, wealthy individuals rather than pension funds, middle-class employees or retirees of today) had a safe and consistent investment basically guaranteed ROI by federal and state governments.

When utilities set rates they would show the state public utility commissions their costs and investments. Based on that, they would suggest a retail rate that would cover their costs plus a profit. For the most part around the world, these regulatory proceedings were about these costs and the calculation of these figures as they translated into rates. Little discussion was over the competitiveness of the final rate or whether the development plans were either necessary or wise. It is important that in this period rates were generally falling and it was easy to satisfy a post-World War II population with expanded power at lower rates.

The mid-1960s saw this guaranteed economic euphoria unwind. A major catastrophic grid overload in 1965 in the Northeast blacked out 30 million people. Concerns over increased pollution demands were voiced and heard in Washington DC and state capitals. Grid management became a larger issue, and the North American Reliability Council was formed.

Three large interconnected networks were set up—eastern, western, and Texas. Regulators began to worry about public outcries over pollution, nuclear dangers, waste, and other factors. In fact the whole resource capacity of the utilities started to be part of the regulatory battle. As competition by qualified facilities under the Public Utilities Regulatory Policy Act (PURPA) were mandated by Congress, the regulators stated having to balance competition among generators. Later as the large users wanted to contract directly with independent producers, the regulators realized that they not only had to set rates, but also had to keep the industry from decomposing.

One of the decisive steps that FERC took at this time was to open up the transmission system so that generators could "wheel" power across other utility transmission lines. Wheeling had been done between utilities. FERC did not permit other parties such as the independent generators to use the transmission lines of firms located between them and a customer to conduct a sale of electricity that bypassed normal utilities along the way. By the 1990s, as part of the Energy Policy Act of 1992, FERC was given expanded authority to order transmitting utilities to provide wholesale wheeling services rather than just between buying and selling utilities. Later two new rules (Orders 888 and 889 in 1996) set fair pricing and open information systems to accommodate growing numbers of nonutility wheelers.

Thus, the deregulation move was set up by a number of federal changes that needed to be integrated into a system that had remained somewhat stable in its organization structure and operations since the 1930s. Yet Joskow notes that the move to deregulate was not based on the system being in crisis. Instead he writes that,

> *The traditional system (in the US) was efficient and reliable in dispatching generating plants; making cost-reducing short-term energy trades between generating utilities; maintaining network reliability; and dealing with*

congestion, unplanned outages, and system emergencies. This record contrasts sharply with the performance of the electricity sectors in many other countries, especially developing countries and many developed countries that rely on state-owned utilities. (Joskow, 2000: 119)

However, Joskow goes on to say that there was room for improvement in the operation of the regulated utilities. He claimed that the *short-run* benefits from deregulation are expected to be small, while the *long-run* benefits are expected to be large due to,

lower construction and operating costs overall in the supply of generation over time, improved incentives to close inefficient plants, better investment decisions, improved retail price signals, and so forth ... that can offset some additional imperfections in generator dispatch, network coordination, and constraint management that may accompany horizontal and vertical decentralization. (Joskow 2000: 124)

Like most analysts and economist at the time, Joskow does not substantiate these long-term benefits. Nor does he show how they would truly overcome the imperfections that eventually brought deregulation down.

On the other hand, critics of deregulation have estimated that the costs associated with deregulation greatly exceed the benefits. For example, J. A. Casazza (2001) in an admittedly rough estimation suggests that across the USA, the costs associated with deregulation total $27.8 billion more than benefits. Hence this leads to a 13% increase in national electricity prices. Included in Caszza's estimates are about $6 billion to acquire generation assets at above book prices which was common when states like California were required to deregulate in part by the same of most power generation assets.

Additionally, deregulation led to higher prices due to a number of factors including bid payments at clearing price, larger transmission line loss, costs of operating power exchanges, ISOs, etc, new costs for billing complexities, new coordination expenses, costs of interruptions, and power curtailments. In contrast, some savings did come from mergers, lower operating costs, and other factors.

4.2. Theoretical Perspectives

Electricity had been inherently a publicly regulated monopoly service because of the physical requirement that it must be generated as needed (since it can not be easily stored) to all citizens. The duplication of energy systems for transmission and distribution would be grossly inefficient, as early 20th century entrepreneurs found. Moreover, customers have little opportunity to directly choose providers since electrons flow through the entire grid regardless of who produced them or who will use them.

Regulators have two concerns: one is assuring that the utilities can supply the power that is needed; and the other is limiting the utility rates for that power to just and reasonable levels for the service provided. The business model for return on investment was designed simply to assure that the rate setting task provided the utilities with the capacity to supply the power that was projected to be needed. However, regulators are not always able to set rates fairly and to assure that the system will have the capacity it needs. Five issues inherent in the concept of regulation are of significance:

1. Regulators do not always have the information they need to do their job well. Regulation is a complex task and when costs are rapidly changing, determining what is a reasonable basis on which to set rates becomes hypothetical. Moreover, it is in the interest of the utility to only give the regulator the information that is most favorable to their interest of setting the highest rate they can get away with, while the regulators will try to develop models, estimators, and arguments that will counter the information provided. The utilities often are claimed to have the upper hand in this process because they have not only access to all the raw data, but they have resources by which to hire more lawyers, economists, and public relations firms to manage the flow of information to their regulators.
2. Regulators are in an inherently political environment, and they respond to political pressure and interests more than to popular will. The large power consumers and interest groups with a stake in the outcome such as power plant construction firms or other industries have the ability to focus pressure on the regulators for their interests, whereas small consumers lack the organization and resources to effectively advocate for their interests. In recent years, nonprofit advocacy groups have become increasingly effective in providing a voice for these groups who had been excluded from the process.
3. The needs of regulators for information and understanding of the complex system means that many regulators are recruited from the regulated industry because they have the necessary understanding and expertise. The issue regulatory bodies must face is to define boundary between having regulators with expertise to effectively ask the right questions and analyze the information

provided, and having regulators with a conflict of interest because of their experience prior to becoming a regulator. This has been a problem in most regulated industries, and in some cases has diminished the legitimacy and effectiveness of regulation.

4. Regulators work in environments where the boundary between the controlled part of the technical system and the firms in it blur with the market or uncontrolled part. Even in a traditionally tightly regulated industry such as electricity, much was not regulated. For example, the major cost for most utilities is the fuel that powers their generators, and that comes from an industry, which has deregulated most of its essential parts. The price of oil, gas, coal, or other inputs has been subject to considerable market forces which leaves the regulated part to anticipate or readjust revenues depending on costs that are not within their control. Similarly, the regulators do not control the providers of technology and the rate with which efficiencies increase. Market demand can be estimated, but utilities have few contracts for firm demand while most demand must be met as it occurs.

5. In spite of the Federal role, state and local regulators work in a complex world of competing regulatory interests. None is more pressing than the role of state regulators with their respective Public Utilities Commissions and the Federal regulatory effort through FERC. Increasingly, interstate transmission and production link utilities under one regulator with regulators in another state. FERC has jurisdiction over all interstate transmission, and since virtually all states are connected the role of FERC has become enormous, as California found out in trying to control the crisis in 2001. In addition, the electrical production system is so interlinked with air quality regulation, water regulation, safety and financial regulations that it is more accurate to describe a network of regulation than single organization doing it.

These characteristics of electricity regulation mean that the current energy system is no longer regulated in the traditional simplified manner, but by a hugely complex set of competing and collaborating interests. The regulator no longer is just a legal entity that makes a decision where there is the rule of law forcing compliance, but the regulator becomes a proactive part of a complex rapidly evolving set of interdependent relations.

As evidenced in the California energy crisis, regulators are people who come to their appointed government positions with both experiences and a history. The regulator often is appointed for just that reason—they have a particular public policy agenda reflecting the current government in power. Thus, at one end of a continuum of public action, the public interest can be achieved by the public organization directly doing what needs to be done, by investing public funds, owning and operating services, and asking for public payment. But at the other end, as in deregulation rules and boundaries, the regulators were to let the market be open, free, and compete without government interference.

Moving in the direction of less direct involvement, the regulators can use its "police powers" or rule-making to force firms to do what it wants through regulations, laws, and rules about rates and other items. Less direct involvement by the public involves public actions that offer incentives and other rewards for compliance, but the public is not in the business of setting the way its interests will be achieved.

Finally, at the least direct end of the continuum, the public works by setting the context in which common interests are found that will lead to publicly advantageous outcomes. Some of the best examples of the fourth level come from environmental mediation where interested parties discover that their common interests also benefit the public. These four forms of public action form a continuum as shown as a continuum of public action.

1. Direct public action, where public investment does some or all of the task being desired.
2. Regulation by law and rules about rates and action
3. Incentives, where payments and other desired rewards are given for desired outcomes
4. Coordination and collaboration, where common interests are discovered

All four of these types of action take place at the same time in a regulatory environment. Nonetheless, it is generally agreed that the use of law and rules in regulation is the least effective approach in any public sector. With the exception of the State taking over infrastructures and systems in which it has a civic interest, it is best to move up the ladder of public action and find ways in which private and public interests are best maximized with the minimum of rule making.

Traditional regulation has been litigious and confrontational. All to often, it is referred to as using the "bully pulpit" meaning that government forces industry and local governments to take actions based on threats or "deals." Sometimes these actions lead to calls for municipalization in which the public would assume ownership.

The assumption is that local public officials can operate the utility more efficiently than the private firms, while meeting public needs.

Historically this has been the origin of many municipal utilities in the US where they constitute about 25% of the utility sector. However, there is no widespread evidence that most municipalities currently served by private utilities can afford to acquire or operate their utilities more efficiently than a well-regulated private utility (Bradshaw *et al.*, 2003).

The other option presented later herein is for regulation to move up the continuum of public action and use partnerships, coordination, and collaboration to achieve the public interest. Government can therefore minimize its reliance on rules, standards, and regulations as public legal and legislative authority. With coordination on projects between the utilities and the regulators based on sharing a common interest, win–win solutions rather than impasses would surely occur.

4.3. Pressures for Deregulation

Pressures for deregulation mounted in the 1990s as the structure of the electricity industry changed due to the new smaller size distributed technologies championed by independent producers and due to the greater interest of customers in obtaining lower-price power available out of state and far from their end use. Thus, the pressures for deregulation would have come to electric utilities in the 1990s regardless of the political influence of the Enron or other large advocates, in spite of utility management, and even if many of the governmental regulators were differently inclined. The fact that deregulation occurred in so many different states and countries at about the same time suggests powerful forces for deregulation that could not be discounted easily.

Many of these "forces" led to deregulation pressure at this period of time, and not all of them were present to the same degree in all places that moved to deregulate. Probably the most significant "real force" was simply the realization that modern technology and management would allow utilities to run effectively if they were not vertically integrated. The belief in vertical integration was unquestioned until it was challenged in a number of places by policies whose implications were not fully understood.

The most prominent of these policies were the implementation of PURPA in the United States and the deregulation of aspects of the electricity market in Great Britain. While the changing belief that something previously unthinkable is indeed possible is hardly demonstrable as cause of something as major as the wave of deregulation that is sweeping the world, it was a necessary first step. Experience with a growing number of options and alternatives that broke the traditional mold was clearly at the root of changing the thinking of leaders, advocacy groups, and citizens.

Global pressures in the economy also motivated interested parties to look for options to utility generated power. Firms, especially in energy intensive industries, have long sought cheap power and have moved or threatened to move to locations where power is cheaper. With global competition among firms increasing in the last part of the century, the pressure on local communities and their utility to provide lower rates became closely tied to economic development, as we will explore in more depth in a later chapter. However, with evidence that cheaper power was possible especially in areas where utility rates were high, pressure mounted to do something.

In California, for example, it was widely believed by policy makers and many independent analysts that the state utility rates were too high and that the regulatory system was unable to control them. The wholesale market for years was accused of passing on excessive costs to consumers because production costs had fallen and spot market prices were even lower. It was the belief of those looking to deregulation that these low production costs were benefiting producers too much. The evidence tended to support this position as well.

Joskow (2000) notes that California and several East Coast states had average power rates way above the national average. For example, in 1997 the average residential rate in the US was 8.43 cents per kWh and was 4.53 cents for industrial users. In California the same year the average residential rate was 11.5 cents and the industrial rate was 6.95 cents, both about 50% above the average.

In contrast the state of Washington had average residential rates of only 4.95 cents per kWh and 2.59 cents for industrial users. Rates in New England were even higher than in California. While there are reasons for rate differences, including access to low-cost hydro versus having high-priced nuclear generation sources, these differences in consumer price led to pressures to find ways to reduce prices in states with high rates. In addition, spot-market prices where surpluses were available were often well below average state prices even at peak.

From the California regulator side of the picture and the political leadership, they saw that businesses were threatening to leave the State because of high electricity rates. The early 1990s saw California mired in a depression due in part to the end of the Cold War. The State had 19 bases closed with over 100,000 losing their jobs while major defense contractors downsized or reinvented themselves from 1990 to 1995.

Some of the largest and most vocal consumers formed a powerful interest organization called the California Large Energy Users Association, with only 11 members who nonetheless represented much of the industrial energy use (cement, steel, and a gold-mining firm). These users were threatening to find ways to bypass the local utilities to purchase power on the open wholesale and spot markets where costs were less. In a sense they wanted to take advantage of the lower prices while leaving the residential market and other consumers with higher cost options that would remain after the low-price sources had been plucked off. The economies of cogeneration confirmed this option because many firms thought they might self-produce or even become suppliers to the grid.

From the power industry point of view, they saw very uneven opportunities. Some of their plants and contracts were not competitive and had to be subsidized by other sources, which were more efficient. Many of the renewable source contracts signed under PURPA and expensive plants such as Diablo Canyon nuclear power plant were obtained either with the regulators blessing or by mandate, and the utilities wanted to get rid of these expensive components. If competition was to come to utilities, the power producers wanted to be able to transition from regulation where they had some high costs to an advantageous set of facilities.

At the same time, the utilities were transforming their structure by splitting their corporate structure so that generation was organizationally separated from distribution and transmission. With different companies under the same corporate umbrella, the utilities' overall operation remained, but they legally isolated different risk and profit centers. Well before the deregulation debate got strong, many utilities such as PG&E started separate companies to construct dispersed plants and renewable projects, selling power to their parent company as would any qualifying facility.

Smeloff and Asmus report an astonishing finding that drove much of the pressure for deregulation. The electric utility industry as a whole uses only about half of the constructed generating capacity that has been built in the United States. Power plants on average sit idle half the time and as a consequence there is a substantial surplus of power. Of course some of this excess capacity is used to meet peak needs for which capacity must be available. But more troubling is the fact that a lot of capacity was built for which a market did not materialize. As we claimed in Chapter 1, individual states such as California, which did not overbuild were nonetheless affected by the low rates and excess capacity in neighboring states.

The regulators noted these changes in the industry, and they tried to respond. However, their response was perceived by the legislature and the public to be ineffective because while costs for power from new plants was falling, enormous surpluses existed, and yet the utility generating capacity was fixed by cost plus regulations.

Deregulation in electricity is not a new idea. California followed other nations and states. Maine had begun its deregulation process four years earlier. In addition there is a substantial literature on electricity deregulation and privatization from the mid-1980s, with roots that preceded this period. For example, Michael Crew and his colleagues had published a series of books on regulation and deregulation of utilities since the early 1980s (see Crew 1989). Moreover, in 1969 Richard Posner wrote an article on natural monopolies such as utilities, now reprinted by the Cato Institute, that concluded,

> there are different degrees of justification for the various regulatory controls, but in no case do the benefits clearly outweigh the costs. There is no persuasive case for the regulation of specific rates in, or of any entity into, natural monopoly markets; yet these have been important areas of regulatory activity, whose principle result has been to promote inefficient pricing and to create unjustified barriers to entry and competition. (1999: 85)

The move to deregulate was also based on widespread belief that it had been successful elsewhere. The California PUC and some legislators traveled to England to observe the first hand operation of deregulation there, and several other states had preceded California in the process of deregulation. The early experience of these efforts was positive (anticipating the early success of the plan in California). By the time of the California energy crisis a number of states had also initiated deregulation, with less disastrous consequences.

4.4. The California Deregulation Debacle

California electricity deregulation has become one of the most extensively discussed public policy failures in modern times. While it is unique in its early impact and the types of mistakes made, other states have similar deregulation processes in place and may be vulnerable to some of the same problems that hurt California. See Appendix 1. In spite of the analytical attention, the enthusiasm of virtually all parties at the time that deregulation was enacted is now hard to reconstruct. It is one of those rare policy initiatives to pass unanimously by both houses of California state government. Then it went to Congress where the enabling legislation passed with the same margin: No significant opposition.

The deregulation plan itself was formulated by the California Public Utilities Commission (CPUC) and drafted into legislation as Assembly Bill 1890 (AB1890) in 1996. It "built upon a very open, very public process led by the CPUC" (Sweeney, 2002: 33), though the basic premises were not deeply questioned. There was some debate, but the supporters virtually everywhere it was discussed overwhelmed the doubters. The hearings involved hundreds of participants from both political parties. The bill was adopted unanimously by both houses of the legislature, a rare show of bipartisan support. It was signed into law by Governor Pete Wilson in September 1996 and was to take effect in 1998.

The history of how such a disastrous piece of legislation got passed and the arguments that carried it and whose interests dominated is too long of a story for this book (see Smeloff and Asmus, 1997; Sweeney, 2002; Weare, 2002). But several historical points are important.

First, the turbulent period of the early 1990s in California was one of economic recovery and growing optimism after a long and deep recession. However, the growing sense of stability did not carry over into the utility sector. The CPUC proposed a dramatic reorganization of the electric industry in the State by publishing in 1994 a Report "A Vision for the Future of California Electric Services Industry." Locally, the Report was called the "Blue book" because of the color of its cover. It called for competition in electricity, and ventured into a number of areas, in order to support the redevelopment of the State's vibrant economy.

Smeloff and Asmus (1997: 75) summarize the contribution of this Report: it called for ending the monopoly power of the investor owned utilities in their service area, it eliminated government supervision of resource planning for new power supplies, and it gave consumers a choice of electricity suppliers. These steps were directed toward lowering rates to consumers. The PUC seemed incapable of doing this through regulation, perhaps due to such regulatory actions being abhorrent to its mandate or philosophy at the time. What decision makers and policy makers did not know at the time, or failed to acknowledge, was the political and financial influence of corporations like Enron on the "experts" promoting deregulation (HarvardWatch, 2002).

The CPUC produced plan based on this report was contentious and divided, not the picture of harmony that characterized the legislature. It passed by a 3 to 2 vote, and blended a power pool system similar to that used in England with direct access to be phased in gradually as the transmission system proved capable to handle the direct transactions. Direct access customers could be aggregated by suppliers and third parties for marketing purposes—something municipalities found potentially beneficial (Bradshaw and Lee, 2003).

The California deregulation proposal had the goal of allowing competition among power providers on the basis of price in an unregulated marketplace. It was assumed that consumers, first industrial consumers and then residential, would have information on their choices and could choose the supplier that provided electricity at the lowest possible price. However, in order to reach this simple self-regulating free market, many problems had to be solved that stood in the way of competitiveness. The transition to a free market required dismantling the regulated system where the utilities were responsible for meeting all the challenges of providing power to customers and the regulators had a small number of utilities they could monitor and force to do things for the public good.

It is essential to keep in mind that deregulation was not snuck upon the public, though in hindsight it was clearly not debated enough. The opposition to the plans was generally stifled, and warnings about potential problems were ignored. For example, San Diego Gas and Electric filed a brief with FERC explaining that it was opposed to the new structure and open markets, but the report was never considered and it was finally withdrawn under pressure from Governor Wilson and others (Stanton, 2001).

In addition, the Municipal Utilities Association warned legislators that the new market could lead to higher prices if there were power shortages, but their concerns were quickly dismissed. The details of the plan were worked out in relatively public meetings, though the meetings were held in a series of airport hotels from San Francisco to Riverside, and Stanton suggests that they were hard to keep track of. Moreover, a consumer critic, Eric Woychik, was barred from some meetings. He persisted in trying to make his concerns heard and finally published some of his critique in a trade magazine on ways the California market could be gamed. However, the regulators would not listen.

4.4.1. Understanding the deregulation plan

The deregulation plan passed for California had a number of key parts. (The most complete analysis of these parts is in Sweeney 2002.) First it would quickly open the utility system to both wholesale and retail competitions. Second, the vertically integrated utilities would be broken into functional parts—generation, transmission, and distribution. To run the system, all power would be purchased statewide by a Power Exchange (PX) and the grid would be managed by the California Independent system Operator (CISO). Utilities would receive compensation by ratepayers for their unprofitable generation plants (stranded assets) so that they could compete with other power providers. In addition, the utilities would sell their gas-fired plants to other firms who would operate them in competition with the utilities.

The most useful way to understand the deregulation strategy adopted in California is to examine the problems that were faced by the advocates of deregulation and the solutions that they adopted. Incidentally, these are the same problems that all states or countries must face. Consider these core questions:

What part of the system should be deregulated?

Unbundling complex vertically integrated industries is not an easy task. In electricity the overlapping service areas of the providers in the early days of electricity led to huge inefficiencies, solved by assignment of exclusive franchises to power companies. However as options were explored for deregulation, it was not deemed feasible to have competing companies string new sets of wires around town. In virtually all deregulation schemes, distribution systems remain a monopoly. Long-distance transmission, also, remained less likely to be divested for many of the same reasons. However the option was to allow competing generators and their marketing companies to sell directly to the consumer over the wires of the existing utility. This decision led to many other decisions.

Deregulation of the generation industry was a typical first step in most deregulation schemes. The competition by producers of electricity is typically the easiest to stimulate and to accommodate, and it requires no action by consumers. The PURPA model effectively opened the California system to multiple generators in the 1980s and by the mid-1990s this was not considered problematic. However, the question was whether to open the system to more than just utility customers were, and how to do this.

As noted before, a major issue is allowing alternative suppliers sell directly to consumers of power. This required ending the vertically integrated utility monopoly that excluded customers from buying power from anyone other than the utility that served them by regulations that controlled the transmission lines. While wholesale wheeling among utilities was common practice, retail customers were excluded from wheeling.

Reinforced by rules from FERC until the mid-1990s, large users who wanted cheaper out of area power were denied, and even firms that self-generated power were restricted from wheeling their excess power to a nearby facility they owned if the power had to go over utility lines. And because of the monopoly granted to the utilities, private power lines were prohibited except on single parcels of private property.

The CPUC proposal in the blue book surprised people by advocating *retail wheeling*. Under their proposal, customers could arrange to purchase power from any supplier or from their own existing utility, and it would be delivered through existing utility lines. This arrangement solved the problems that the regulators were having trouble with—and they believed that competition among suppliers would drive down prices.

In the California case the regulators and legislation attempted to unbundle service with different rates and competitive structures for generation, transmission, and distribution. Different components of the rate appear on utility bills, though most consumers did not notice the difference.

How can you assure fair competition after deregulation
especially for existing utilities with stranded assets?

The second problem advocates of deregulation faced was dealing with stranded assets. Restructuring a regulated system into a competitive one means that ways must be found to make the transition from a system that is inefficient because it has a lot of poor performing parts into a fairly competitive one in which the existing utilities are not saddled with all the inefficiencies which were built with approval of the regulators. If the inefficient parts of the system were to be just allowed to falter, that either would lead to unreliability for the entire system or the playing field, would not be level. The problem of transition to fair competition has been labeled one of "stranded assets" because some parts of the system would not be competitive (too expensive) without subsidy from the rest of the system which is not reasonable under the logic of competition.

Agile Energy Systems

The regulated utilities claimed that they would be at a disadvantage because they invested in some uncompetitive projects under regulation and the Public Utilities Commission assured them the ability to pay for these projects by approval of their plans. Moreover, some of the uncompetitiveness was due to contracts with qualified facilities for power under PURPA. These contracts miscalculated energy prices and were often for a higher rate than the utility average. However, the largest problem for the utilities was their nuclear plants, which had real prices much higher than average system costs.

For example, Diablo Canyon cost about 12 cents per kWh while low-cost suppliers were offering power on the spot market at around 2 cents. Solving this *stranded assets* problem became a system problem for the officials advocating utility deregulation, because in a competitive marketplace these power plants would not be competitive and would have to be abandoned as consumers chose lower priced power (leading to shortages).

The utilities and ratepayers argued that the expensive QF contracts were stranded and that the utilities needed assistance in getting out of these contracts. However, Smeloff and Asmus show the cost of the high-priced QF contracts becomes smaller over time, while nuclear has the largest long-term rate implications. In Fig. 4.1 Smeloff and Asmus show the prices in the PG&E and Southern California Edison

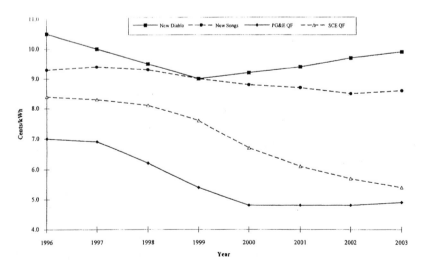

Fig. 4.1. Nuclear is much more expensive than QF contracts.
Source: Smeloff and Asmus (1997: 81).

service areas for the Diablo Canyon (PG&E) and Songs. (SCE) nuclear plants, and their QF contracts.

While the nuclear prices remain in the 9–10.5 cent range, the QF contracts fall from the 7 to 8 cent range to only 5 or slightly over 5 cents. This is because the QF contracts were largely set for 10 years based on faulty price estimates that assumed shortages of oil and natural gas that would result in escalating fuel costs that would be avoided by the QFs. The 10-year contracts started expiring by the late 1990s; after the start of year 11 the independent power producers would receive the utility short-term marginal cost of electricity—the wholesale price (Smeloff and Asmus, 1997: 80). By 2000 the bulk of the QF contracts had reached the 11-year mark and was no longer exceptionally expensive.

The deregulation solution advanced by the PUC was a complicated one. The proposal was to impose a "Competitive Transition Charge" (CTC) on all electricity sold. This fee on all power consumed would go to the regulated utilities to subsidize the sale of these stranded assets or to reduce debt on them so as to make them fiscally attractive. The major beneficiary of these CTCs was the nuclear power plants, and to some extent overpriced contracts with QFs.

Some additional plants and transmission facilities were also included in the stranded assets calculations. The CTC was to be collected until the stranded assets were paid for, and then it would be removed from the rates and utilities would purchase power on the open market. The CTC would be collected as the difference between power costs and a price cap that was set 10% below previous rates.

Another strategy the California legislature took to assure competition was to require the two largest utilities to divest at least 50% of their fossil fuel generation capacity. This strategy of forcing the large utilities to get out of the generation business (at least partially) was driven by what was perceived to be two equally attractive forces. On the one hand the utilities liked the divestiture because they thought that being in the generation business was too risky with low returns for the effort.

Starting with being forced to share the generation market with qualified producers, the large utilities envisioned a future where their profit could be in other aspects of the market. They saw this having a number of advantages, including that the divesture process attracted a lot of attention and they were able to sell many of their plants for much more than their book value, meaning that they made a huge opportunistic profit. Another advantage was that they could set up subsidiaries to which they transferred some of the plants, and these were essentially outside the integrated regulatory structure. This left the original utility to handle transmission and distribution while the squeeze was on the generators to reduce costs.

The divesture was also intended to spread competitiveness around so that viable firms could compete with the existing utilities. Already before deregulation, utilities had started selling some of their assets and out-of-state brokers were assembling power supplies to sell to utilities based on availability and cost. With more power in the hands of competing firms, it was thought that lower prices would surely result.

However, the prices at which the utilities sold their power plants and the high investment by the competing utilities led to a situation in which the old utilities were relatively rich and the price charged by the purchasing entity could not fall because of the high costs they had invested in acquiring the plants. The utilities assets from the sales were in different parts of the company than the distribution utility, which protected these assets from the cost overruns during the energy crisis. Thus, instead of reducing costs by creating competitive conditions, divesture led to stable high costs and enormous utility profits from the sale of their plants. The comparison of book value and sale price illustrates this in Table 4.1.

The divestiture of plants was supposed to cover stranded costs, but Joskow (2000: 146–147) shows that the sale of most of the plants was well above their book value. In other words, the major buyers of the stranded plants placed a higher value on acquiring the plants than the regulators who forced their sale. He suggests that either the regulatory system obtained too low of a value for these plants (which would benefit consumers) or that the new operators intend to operate the plants more efficiently. In retrospect, they may have intended to operate them in the unregulated market in ways that could eventually drive up prices, which is what actually happened.

The divesture had unanticipated consequences as will be described below, including the fact that many of the plants were purchased by just four large generation companies. The fact that the large utilities essentially got out of the fossil fuel plant business meant that the competitiveness of the market was not much better off than before when there were the three major utilities.

How do you protect conservation and other public benefit programs such as innovation and renewable sources?
The third issue that deregulation advocates had to solve was to assure that public benefit programs continue because of their value

Table 4.1.   Sales of generating plants in California.

Power plant	Purchaser	Nameplate capacity (MW)	Book value $million	Sales price $million
Divestiture of IOU generating assets in California				
Morro Bay, Moss Landing, Oakland	Duke Energy Corp.	2881	390.2	501.0
Contra Costa, Pittsburg, Potrero	Southern Energy	3166	318.3	801.0
Geysers (Sonoma and Lake Countries)	Calpine Corp.	1353	273.1	212.8
	PG&E Subtotal	*7401*	*981.6*	*1514.8*
Alamitos, Huntington Breach, Redondo Beach	AES Corp.	4706	224.1	781.0
Cool Water, Etiwanda, Ellwood, Mandalay, Ormond Beach	Houston Industries	4019	288.3	277.0
El Segundo, Long Beach	NRG Energy and Destec	1583	168.8	116.6
San Bernadino, Highgrove	Thermo Ecotek	300	(4.3)	9.5
	SCE Subtotal	*10,607*	*676.9*	*1184.1*
Encina, Kearny, and other Peakers	NRG Energy and Dynegy	1347	94.8	365.0
South Bay	San Diego Unified Port District	833	64.4	110.0
	SDG&E Subtotal	2180	159.2	475.0
	Total	*20,187*	*1818*	*3174*

Sources: California Energy Commission, www.energy.ca.gov/electricity/divestiture.html.
Sweeney (2002: 63).

to the overall power system and to customers. The value of conservation, energy efficiency, development of renewable power sources, and load management was to be protected in the deregulated environment, acknowledging that each of these major public interest goals was counter to the interest of competitive utilities without some form of public requirement that these goals be pursued. The contribution of conservation has exceeded most estimates and more potential seems to be discovered daily. For example, through conservation measures and programs that yielded from 10 to 12% conservation reductions in demand was credited with enough to avoid blackouts in California during the summer of 2001 in spite of short supplies. The backbone of conservation and public benefit programs are:

- Public information and incentive programs to help all classes of consumer install cost effective energy saving devices. The logic of these programs is that most users of electricity have a trade off between initial investment in energy conservation and long-term payback on investment through lower expenditure for power. In many cases the payback is very quick—a matter of months or years. In other cases the payback may be 7–10 years or longer, a period in which the savings would pay the capital costs of installing the energy saving item. The savings for better lighting and appliances are often in the former category whereas new windows might be in the latter. Effective public information programs have shown the public that there is much they can do that will have a short payback, such as turning off computers and office machines while one is not at work, and the information from these programs has helped individuals make decisions to change behavior and install things like compact florescent light bulbs. In other cases, the public programs have used incentives such as rebates on refrigerators or even free caulking to help reduce the cost and give consumers more incentive to purchase the most energy-efficient things.
- Load management programs whereby consumers agree to reduce load by a certain amount at certain peak times, often when dispatched by utilities or grid managers. These programs often provide lower rates all year in return for the company being willing to reduce load a certain amount of the time.
- Promotion of new technologies such as wind and photovoltaics. The public interest in the environment leads to advocacy for technologies, which have fewer environmental impacts.
- Special industry projects such as improvement of water pumps in agriculture and time of day programs that slow water pumping during peak demand periods; similar programs in many industries help to shape the load and reduce overall demand.
- Public advocacy and regulation programs in zoning, residential construction, and community programs such as shade trees, building codes, etc.
- Self-generation and cogeneration programs at public buildings, colleges and universities, etc. that help stimulate demand reduction
- Alternative and renewable resource programs that develop alternative technologies and ones that are more environmentally

friendly. These programs at both state and utility levels are very effective in supporting new technologies and efficiency.

It should be noted that public interest programs including demand reduction were warmly embraced by the utilities prior to deregulation because of market characteristics. These programs were able to be used because of two interrelated factors. First, the growing electricity market led the vertically integrated utilities to need to expand their capacity and because of the cost of constructing new power plants, the marginal cost of adding capacity was greater than the average cost of power from the plants already constructed. This meant that at a fixed rate for electricity, the expansion of capacity would not mean more profit but less.

Second, with activist regulators, the utilities could not just pass the additional costs of marginal power on to consumers, they were required to find the lowest cost means of achieving supply. This meant that the utilities were all forced to do conservation to reduce demand and protect profits. The joining of public and corporate interests supported vast programs in the 1980s supporting conservation, and it led to savings of at least 12,000 MW or about 12 nuclear power plants.

Under the logic of deregulation, conservation and public benefit programs would not be continued by the utilities and so the deregulation proposal needed to take these programs outside the competitive arena of the utilities. Since power companies are in competition to provide electricity at the lowest possible price to customers, companies make more money by selling more power, not less. Prior to deregulation, and partially because deregulation was being discussed, the regulators relaxed conservation measures through most of the late 1990s. Without pressure from legislature and regulators, and with conservative governments in Sacramento, the conservation programs dwindled and by the time deregulation started, conservation programs had declined significantly, enough that the blackouts might have been avoided if they continued.

To handle this situation, the deregulators wanted to find a funding mechanism to assure maintenance of some amount of public good programs. This also was important to garner the necessary public support. The solution reached was to impost a public goods benefit charge on all electricity sold in the State, a fee that could not be bypassed by customers choosing a new retail provider. This fee calculated at 1.3 mills per kWh is estimated to generate $275 million per year that would be administered as part of the CPUC responsibility and it would be used to create long-term conservation. Following the energy crisis this fund has been channeled to the three large private utilities in the State, though there is a threat of funding nonutilities to do the conservation programs if the utilities do not meet goals.

The character of public interest programs has changed in California. Initially the programs provided incentives for conservation to avoid further blackouts during the summers of 2001 and 2002. More recent efforts have focused on longer-term benefits, though long-term programs have not been possible because the utilities only have a short-term mandate to administer the programs (Blumstein *et al.*, 2003).

Who assures that enough power is in the system to meet
all demand at the moment it is needed, especially at peak times?

The problem of balancing supply and demand in a competitive market led to the creation of two new organizations charged with this responsibility. The first, the California Power Exchange (PX) linked the distribution utilities to the generators, and all the previously regulated investor owned utilities were required to purchase their power from the PX, which would buy from suppliers by bid and sell to all at the same rate.

The difference between the frozen rate and the PX rate would provide funds to purchase stranded assets. The Independent System Operator, another new organization, was charged with operating the grid. They had responsibility for controlling load and balancing generation with demand in specific places. Initially it was thought that the Power exchange would purchase the power and deliver it to the distribution utilities, and the PX would simply pass on the costs.

The logic of deregulation is that the supply and demand in peak times will balance according to market forces. On the supply side, the generators will know that when there is peak demand that prices will rise, and they will try to build capacity to take advantage of these spikes. However, the time when there is high demand and prices rise are also by definition a limited number of hours a year, and it is costly and risky for producers to have capacity that is reserved for only a few hours a year.

The market for top peak capacity is thus limited, and to a large extent producers may not want to gamble by holding capacity for peaking. Under the regulated economy, the ability to meet peak demands was a top priority of the regulators, and the utilities were strongly mandated to have enough power on reserve to meet these peak conditions. Under return on investment regulation, they were paid for this capacity whether they used it or not. However under deregulation there is no assurance that the utilities will choose to be in the market to provide the peak power that is needed. So far a number of solutions have been tried that address this problem, and as was shown in the California case, these solutions do not all work well.

One of the problems with assuring peak load power is that the incentives for providing it are weak. With inadequate peak power capacity, the price will go up very high for power that is available, providing a windfall profit. Regulators had been relatively successful in mandating that utilities provide adequate peak power, which has generally been part of the average rate base. However, under deregulation providers might calculate that they stand to profit more from the shortage during peak times, rather than from planning to meet the capacity.

Under the California model, where all bidders received the highest accepted bid price, this lack of incentive to provide peak power became one of the reasons prices escalated. Especially during the summer of 2000, the lesson learned from the shortages during this period was replicated again during early 2001 when most of the blackouts occurred. The critical issue of providing enough incentives to cover peak periods has not been resolved in deregulated systems.

The provision of backup and spinning reserve used to be included in the regulated structure of the utilities, but these "ancillary services" were not purchased as part of the California procurement process. Power capacity in these categories is used to maintain grid stability and it is often not needed, but it has to be available or the grid will fail. In other deregulated systems, the ancillary services are purchased on an hour-by-hour basis when supplies are purchased, usually purchased from the next highest price supplier whose bid was not accepted for regular supply. In California the ancillary services were acquired through a separate auction and this often led to high prices and confusion.

The other side of the logic of deregulation and the market is that as prices rise, consumers will choose to use less power and will defer purchases until the price comes down. This reduces the incentive of the utilities to operate under-capacity systems. However, except for a few of the largest consumers, individuals and most businesses have flat power rates that do not reflect the peak costs, but are averaged. Moreover, there is no way that the average consumer knows what the actual time of day cost is of power.

This theme was strongly argued in the California energy crisis by Severin Borenstein (Borenstein *et al.*, 2002), who advocated switching large parts of the market into time of day metering. While thousands of large customers were switched to meters and information systems that allowed them to know marginal costs and to save money by switching their load to lower price times, the cost of new meters and the difficulty of installing them has limited this impact on the residential market. Thus, the lack of market signal undermines the ability of consumers to withhold consumption when prices rise.

How is the grid managed so overloads do not occur
on parts of the system?
When utilities were vertically integrated, each utility had responsibility for assuring the management of its grid, and they worked collaboratively with other connected utilities to assure that loads were properly balanced. To do this a number of dispatch arrangements were devised where organizations would have control for parts of the grid and would assure that their supply and demand were balanced. These dispatchers would be in close communication with other dispatchers to assure that the system as a whole was balanced and electricity would not circle to parts of the system where it might cause an overload on a transmission link. Under deregulation, the competitive nature of the electric supply and the unpredictability of demand led to the need for more centralized control. Thus, as the utility industry became more deregulated at one level, it needed more centralized control at another.

Load balancing is the term used to describe the strategies used by utilities to keep the supply of generated electricity in balance with the demand, since electricity can not be stored directly and most uses of electricity are instantaneous and must be met. A fundamental characteristic of electricity is that it travels from generation to distribution points over all the wires and all the paths connecting them. Unlike trucking where the traffic seeks the shortest distance between two points, electricity will run in parallel along both short and long paths. Load will take alternative routes depending on the capacity of each, but there is no way to direct certain electrons to go a certain way.

The challenge for deregulation policy has in most cases been to devise strategies for grid management. Some independent system operators have control over assuring that when the system load on particular lines gets too heavy, power will be supplied by generators which do not overload that part of the system. All these management decisions get more complicated as the voltage increases and very high voltage systems have behaviors that are complicated and sometimes counterintuitive to untrained system operators.

For these reasons the management of the grid in deregulated systems has been a considerable problem that has been addressed in a number of different ways. The California solution was to set up an "Independent System Operator" (ISO) whose task was to manage the grid and control generators so that problems do not occur, and to assure the efficient construction of links so that changing loads and sources of generation do not create catastrophic overloads. In California a board governed the ISO with officials of key utilities and they set rules for managing the load.

An alternative is to have the transmission system owned by a single entity, which would have common responsibility for all aspects of transmission, effectively bringing coordination within single ownership. The effect will be the same as far as the electrons are concerned.

The ISO also has some fiscal responsibility for assuring that transmission costs are allocated to the right parties and that different transmission lines are properly paid. FERC has ultimate authority over the transmission organizations.

How can new retail providers gain fair market share, including how many advantages can the State give to aggregators?

The opening of the market to "direct access" by the PUC was encouraged through media and other efforts. However, the alternatives for many of the smaller customers were few and the difference minimal, which led to only about 1.7% of the customers changing to alternative suppliers. In spite of extensive advertising campaigns, few individual homeowners switched, though there was more interest by the large industrial customers, where 13% switched, accounting for 28% of the load (Brennan, 2002: 41).

Among residential customers the only consistent attraction for switching from the existing supplier was a number of companies that promised all or a large part of the power they would deliver would come from renewable sources. These green suppliers, such as Green Mountain Power from Vermont, paid heavily in promotional campaigns to enter the California market, but with seemingly small accomplishment.

These providers were further hampered because their power was more expensive, and they had to buy the rest from the pool at the same rates as any other supplier does. In short, the complication of changing supplier, the uncertainty of the change, and the fact that alternative rates were if anything higher than their existing utility charged, provided scant incentive for most people to change from their traditional utility.

On the other hand, the prospect for aggregators to assist in the formation of markets was widely recognized. One of the most interesting options for aggregators is the municipality to become the aggregator for their residents. This would create a public utility that acquires power and sells it via the privately owned distribution lines. A number of municipalities have looked into this option.

How can you assure that rates will fall during
the expensive transition phase?
The problem most areas face when deregulating is that covering stranded assets and opening up the market is expensive, and customers may not see the financial benefits of deregulation at first. The California solution was to issue a state "rate reduction" bond that would buy down rates for an initial period and then once the transition is completed will repay these bonds with surcharges on the rates at that time, which are presumably to be lower.

California made a fateful decision with the rates in that it capped them at a 10% reduction below 1996 prices, which would remain frozen until December 2002, or whenever all the stranded costs were fully recovered. By itself, this rate was not very difficult to achieve as market prices were falling and for the first two years, excess revenues accumulated and utilities were able to pay off their stranded assets somewhat faster than anticipated. San Diego Gas and Electric was the first utility to pay off their stranded assets, and they experienced the first price spikes when the price cap was no longer in place. This may have alerted the electricity marketing companies of the potential to manipulate prices as they did later during the blackout periods.

What the bond did was to allow the stranded costs and high cost of transition to be deferred until the bonds get paid off rather than wait until money was available from rates to reduce costs during the transition. These bonds are a continuing problem because after the crisis payment of the bonds must continue.

How do you balance incentives and competitive power of
large users with residential users?
The final major issue to be considered by deregulation efforts is how to balance benefits to the large industrial user with benefits to the residential customer. The history of electrical regulation has swung between rate structures, which overcharged industrial consumers to protect individual residents, and rate structures that overcharge residents to offer competitive prices to large industrial users in order to attract and retain these firms and the jobs and tax base they

provide. Underlying these different rates is the fact that it is less costly to supply single large industrial customers because there is only one line needed, the usage of power is more consistent day and night since may plants operate 24 hours per day, and the load is more predictable.

During the first energy crisis in the 1970s the difference between the industrial and residential rates narrowed as policy tried to shift the burden felt by residential customers to larger firms because they were more capable of paying it. Moreover, appealing to voters led politically minded regulators to spare residential customers some of the price increases. On the other hand, it was acknowledged that with higher rates charged to industrial customers, they would have more incentive to conserve, and industrial conservation efforts were part of the package. These experiences for a while meant that industrial customers could protect themselves from some of the rate increases by long-term investments in conservation.

More recently, however, the emphasis has been on protecting the large industrial user from excessive rate increases and distributing increases more widely across the residential population. The justification has been that industrial power rates are already high and firms and jobs would leave the State if industrial rates rose.

There is perhaps no absolute framework for balancing incentives and competitive rates between user groups. The most logical framework under conditions of competitiveness is to try to determine actual costs to deliver power to different user classes. However, to do these calculations require ongoing regulation, which is counter to the objective. Pure market forces may create a stable condition, but even so the distribution utility is not in a competitive situation. Thus in California the deregulation scheme failed to really address this issue.

In sum, these points have shown that deregulation is very complex and that there are many policy issues which will be resolved differently by other states or nations embarking on deregulation. More significantly, deregulation or privatization is not good public policy. While the marketplace has been in turmoil, reregulation is not the solution either. Instead, our argument is that there needs to be a transition period, as is being experienced now, toward a "flexible energy system." This new approach is a mix of the old regulated and new deregulated energy sector in which the new energy sector marketplace will have a mix of public oversight and regulation while many private companies will compete independently and in many cases as partners with local communities and regions.

We will explore these possibilities for new energy systems in other chapters. Suffice it to say at this point, that leaving the energy sector or other key infrastructures to the private sector or "market forces" is detrimental to society and any community. History and now recent events in the California energy crisis prove that. What government must do is create policies and programs that provide clean and reliable energy to all its citizens.

4.5. Deregulation Led to the 2000–2002 California Energy Crisis

The California experience with deregulation started off very well. For two years the experiment seemed to be working better than the critics had imagined. Utilities had not only sold their generating assets for more than expected, but also the capacity payments had succeeded in making stranded assets competitive by paying off the bonds in a shorter period of time than expected. The euphoria of the early days lead directly to disaster and was an omen for other such public policies in other states and nations.

Deregulation led to the crisis because of a number of policy failures. In fact, lessons need to be learned from every one of the decision points that were outlined in the first part of this chapter.

Only part of the system was deregulated

In California the deregulation program chose to free generators and the wholesale price of electricity from regulation, while it fixed costs at the retail level during a period of time so it could pay for stranded costs. The decision to fix retail but not wholesale prices had two consequences.

First, because retail prices were set for all utilities who had to buy power at the same price from the PX and include the CTC charge that would pay for stranded costs, there was really no room for retail competition. Thus in spite of advertising that consumers could switch utilities, there was virtually no incentive to do so since the rates of all providers could not be below the fixed retail rate. A few "green power" firms that marketed a disproportionate share of wind and other renewable energy provided the only competition. These "green" providers captured a few percent of the market, a level of service that is rather amazing because they actually got consumers to pay a premium for their environmentally friendly power.

Secondly, the partial deregulation insulated customers from the spike in wholesale rates in 2000 and 2001 leaving the utilities with much higher costs than they could pass on to the consumer. This bankrupted the utilities and gave the wrong signals to the market in that there was no effective way to encourage conservation or shifting to other suppliers since the retail system was frozen. The large utilities who were in favor and sponsored the deregulation scheme, found that they had made a mistake and they quickly lost billions of dollars and stopped being able to purchase power because their credit and ability to pay bills ended.

Paying for stranded assets cost the consumer in the short run

The stranded asset solution in California neither leveled the playing field nor saved the consumer money. The solution in California shifted all the burden of covering stranded assets to the consumer and protected the utility stockholders. By protecting utilities from their less productive investments, these assets continued to be in the supply mix even when they should have been eliminated.

Conservation and public benefit programs were too little too late

The California energy crisis was in part a problem of an imbalance of supply and demand, in that demand had risen due to economic growth and population increases, while generation lagged. This would not have been a problem had adequate conservation programs remained in force. The public interest programs were largely dismantled by the Wilson administration and were deemed irrelevant to the competitive market. At least 1000 MW conservation effort was diminished after deregulation became a significant possibility, and this could have provided enough of a margin to avoid most of the blackouts.

Interestingly, conservation programs were a major part of the solution that is now widely credited with breaking the back of the high prices in the energy crisis and led to savings of up to 10%.

Supply for peak demands was not assured

When energy traders saw that the peak demand was tight, they realized that they could manipulate the market and did so. Initially, the peak fell under tight supply which drove up prices, but eventually the crisis hit during the winter and spring when there was a bit of extra demand because of fair weather. The fact was that by withholding capacity prices were able to rise.

Overall, however, the California deregulation scheme did not provide any incentive for a supplier to have capacity ready for peak times, and there were even no requirements for coupling supply bids and ancillary services such as spinning reserve, that is capacity by producers that can be added at a moment's notice. Typically large power plants take hours or even days to heat up to run at full capacity, though some of the newer gas turbines can be fired up quicker. In short, it is not in anyone's interest to provide peak capacity that will only be used a few hours a year, and California did not have any requirements in place to assure that the supplies would be available.

Grid management was unable to avoid bottlenecks

The California energy crisis was aggravated by bottlenecks in the transmission system. Most analysts now think that the merchant suppliers manipulated their supply outages to overload one major north–south section of the transmission system which had a limited capacity, known as block 15. This section of transmission in the central valley prohibited excess power from the southern part of the state going to the north when it was experiencing blackouts. Given the overall manipulation of the system going on at the time, it is not clear if greater capacity would have prevented more crisis, but the weak link in the grid certainly contributed to the crisis. The failure of the regulatory system to have adequate enforcement over supply coming into the grid led in part to the crisis.

New suppliers were offered opportunities to advertise, but they could not effectively compete on the price of power

The California deregulation scheme attracted a lot of attention from competing companies, but given the price structure none could compete on the basis of lower prices, which effectively meant that there was no competition. The only competing utilities were ones that offered high proportions of power from renewable or "green" sources, and for this customers paid a premium. As Heiman (2002) pointed out, the fact that they garnered about 2% of the business is a remarkable amount of interest in renewable alternatives, but it is hardly a policy success for deregulation.

Rates in California did not fall during the transition except for the mandated reductions

The fact that competition did not lead to lower rates made the whole deregulation process relatively obscure as far as most people were concerned. At its peak some of the largest consumers, representing about 14% of demand switched, but as the energy crisis worsened and the alternative suppliers went out of business, they switched back to the main suppliers.

Aggregation schemes also failed to get implemented. While there is currently some interest in municipalities aggregating their residential and business customers to provide power, so far these efforts have not been materialized.

Residential and commercial rates remain in tension

Deregulation did nothing to resolve the tension between residential and commercial rates, with the large users still in the system and not benefiting from competition. The transition to a deregulated structure, however, has pointed out that as customers and rates vary in a deregulated market, uncertainty about how many customers will switch to new suppliers and how long they will stay with the new supplier means that supply contracts are highly uncertain. While this type of uncertainty is always part of competitive business, the California mistake was not to allow for a gradual transitional period in which the adjustment could take place gradually. Rapid transitions made matters worse.

In the end, a number of studies provided various explanations as to why the predicted power shortages of the summer of 2001 did not happen. The California Energy Commission (February 2001) provide the standard explanation by the State government attributing the successful summer escape from a crisis to its own conservation and efficiency programs as well as to the Flex Your Power program from the State Consumer Affairs Agency.

Nonetheless the new California Consumer and Power Agency (March 2002) argued that new power generation reserves of 15–20% were needed. And more significantly these new sources of power should be renewable. Governor Davis agreed with that stand and issued a press statement and news conference in March 18, 2002 supporting a high Renewable Portfolio Standard (20% renewables by 2010) as reflected in legislation going through the State Legislature.

4.6. Deregulation Experiences Elsewhere

Deregulation as envisioned in California led to catastrophic blackouts, and the experiment was abandoned and to the extent possible reversed in mid-2001. Grid failures in New York and Toronto during the summer of 2003, failures in Great Britain and Italy, and generally disappointing results around the world have led to a conclusion that the move to deregulate has not been an unmitigated success anywhere that we know about. We do not argue that deregulation has had no positive results or that there are no benefits from some system changes in different countries. We simply argue that the more comprehensive the move from a regulated to deregulated private system, the greater the chance that the country will experience serious supply and reliability problems, that costs of power will either be stable or increase, and that political support for the experiment will be declining.

As of September 2001, Brennan *et al.* report that 23 states had encouraged comprehensive legislation to deregulate, and one additional state and the District of Columbia issued regulations to promote competition. As we write, these processes are on hold with only a few moving forward even though the California experience has provided a lesson of caution if not reverse public policy. Bachrach *et al.* (2002) outline the various programs throughout the US and compare deregulation in Europe and some countries in Asia.

The Europe Union and other countries are, however, even further along in this process under the leadership of the United Kingdom and the EU itself. Brennan *et al.* (2001) note that the US and other countries often face the challenge of restructuring from a different perspective since most electric systems throughout the world are dominantly publicly owned—usually national systems. This means that deregulation in most other countries is a process of state divesture and privatization so that the public entity sells its assets to private companies.

Chile privatized in the 1980s but most of the capacity rests within two large transmission grids and three generation companies. The solution by Chile is to split their market with the large users, mostly industrial and mining companies that have demand greater than 2 MW. These large customers negotiate directly with generation companies and distributors, with full retail competition. On the other hand, users with less than 2 MW demand remain regulated in a fairly traditional manner, with prices set to reflect power costs. A spot market helps to cover generators needing capacity, and these prices are based on generators marginal costs (Brennan, 2002: 34).

The United Kingdom restructuring began in the early 1980s with laws that granted independent power producers access to the transmission system and guaranteed that the Central Electricity Generating Board would buy power from the small producers. The plan was to divide the central system into three generating companies, 12 distribution companies, and a grid company to be owned by the distribution companies. The interesting strategy used in England was to phase in the deregulation, with only a few large consumers deregulated at first, and gradually the pool expanded to include all customers. As of March 2001 about 25% of residential customers had switched suppliers, driven by lower prices (Brennan, 2002: 36).

Also, the experience in the United Kingdom showed that a few large contributors to the grid were able to manipulate prices and so they were required to divest 15% of their capacity in 1993. In addition, in 1995 the ownership of the grid was taken from the regional distribution companies. The government retained control over the nuclear power plants, though recently some of the newest and most efficient nuclear plants were sold. The fact that the entire system was owned by the government let them be the buffer for stranded assets.

The UK system also is experimenting with several interesting optimism for solving the problems of deregulation. They are concerned over price manipulation at peak times, and consequently created a set of New Electricity Trading Arrangements to replace the traditional pool. These arrangements set up a forward and futures market where longer-term contracts work, comprising a large part of the supply. A short-term and spot market resolves gaps in these contracts. Price caps, which are adjusted to account for inflation provide some regulation of the whole system, while avoiding the details of monitoring actual expenses.

Within the United States, several other states have had successful starts to their deregulation. Table 4.2 shows the status of deregulation in five states.

Pennsylvania passed legislation to deregulate at about the same time as California, but their program did not run into the same difficulties as did California utilities. Some clear lessons can be learned from the Pennsylvania example. These include

- The program was implemented in phases, whereas the California deregulation was started immediately. The first pilot program included small efforts for each size class of customer. These pilot programs continued and provided working knowledge of how the program would work.
- Pennsylvania did not mandate an across the board rate decrease, but their rate decrease was set for each utility. The rate breaks were generally lower.
- Unlike California, the pilot programs in Pennsylvania attracted a lot of interest and customers had to be selected from a lottery. One reason this program is more successful is that a simplified cost comparison standard was set whereby the customer gets one price for generation, while transmission and distribution costs are held constant in that customers location.

Table 4.2. Comparison of electric industry restructuring across US states.

	California	Massachusetts	Pennsylvania	New York	Texas
Restructuring legislation or order passed	September 23, 1996 AB 1890	November 19, 1997 HB 5117	December 1996 HB 1509	May 1996 By PSC Order 96-12	1995 SB 373 wholesale market, June 1999 SB7 retail market
Competition begins	March 31, 1998 AB 1890 provided for phase-in, but PUC decided to have all retail competition begin at once	March 1, 1998	Phase in of customers to have full competition by Jan 2001 Later got accelerated (?)	Wholesale 1997 Retail 1998 Different phase-in schedule and rules for each utility	Wholesale first Retail by Jan 2002 with phase in
Regional transmission organization	CA ISO www.caiso.com Spot market	ISO New England www.iso-ne.com	PJM ISO www.pjm.com	NY ISO www.nyiso.com	ERCOT www.ercot.com
Energy market	PX www.calpx.com Day ahead and hour ahead markets FERC requires UDCs to bid and sell all power through the PX. (No longer-term or bilateral contracts)	ISO New England Monitored by Division of Energy Resources (DOER) Day-ahead market	PJM ISO Monitored by the PUC Hour ahead, spot market, and Capacity Credit Market (day-ahead and one- or multi-month contracts)	NY ISO Self-monitored Day ahead (95% of trading), hour ahead, real time markets	ERCOT (Electric Reliability Council of Texas)—was one of NERC's regional reliability councils, became ISO Day-ahead, hour-ahead, real-time markets
Capacity (GW)	ISO Control Area Capacity: 45 (75% of CA's demand) Total CA capacity: 55 Peak Demand: 54	ISO New England Peak Demand: 24	PJM Capacity: 56 PJM Peak Demand: 52	Capacity: 35	Capacity: 65 Peak Demand: 58

Retail choice				
Immediate 10% ratereduction, frozen rates until 4/2002 or until stranded costs were paid off Default provider = UDC Opt-in aggregation Switching rates Jan 2000: 14% of load 2% of customers Jan 2001: 11% of load 1.8% of customers UDC charges fee each time a customer switches to a competitor	UDC must provide service at the Standard Offer rate (10% reduction) to all customers who were in the service territory when restructuring started. Also must provide Default Service to others (including people who switched to a competitor and switch back), but not at the Standard Offer rate. Switching rates: Nov ~2% of residential load, <1% of residential customers Opt-Out Municipal Aggregation— Municipalities are allowed to aggregate their residents and be competitive suppliers and administer their customers' share of DSM money. Residents may opt-out. (A muni aggregator is not the same as a muni utility.)	Most UDCs had a small rate cut only for 1999, and then none after that. (UDCs cannot charge more than PUC rate cap while CTC is in effect.) PUC mailed an Electric Supplier Selection Form to all consumers, then mailed more info again to consumers who hadn't switched. Switching rates: 1999 28% of load Most active retail market	Most UDCs had a 5–10% rate cut. Starting 5/2000 no fixed rates through utilities (they pass on market rates)— had rates 40% higher than last year Recently, utilities started giving incentives to customers to switch to a competitive provider, has helped increase switching rates Switching rates Nov 2000: 3.5% of customers 11% of load	Rates frozen for 3 years until markets are opened to retail competition, then 6% reduction for next 5 years Default is UDC, but Provider of Last Resort is different. Provider of last resort will be required to provide to consumers no longer served by their provider of choice with service at a fixed price. A competitive bidding process will designate the last resort providers for each consumer class

(continued)

Table 4.2. Continued

	California	Massachusetts	Pennsylvania	New York	Texas
Stranded Assets/ Transition Costs	Non-bypassable charge to ratepayers Amount determined by PUC	Full recovery through non-bypassable charge to ratepayers	Non-bypassable charge to ratepayers Amount determined by PUC	Non-bypassable charge to ratepayers Amount determined by PUC	Full recovery through non-bypassable charge to ratepayers
Divestiture	PUC required UDCs to voluntarily divest themselves of at least 50% of their fossil generating assets, and gave them financial incentives to divest. PG&E and SCE sold all fossil-generating assets	UDCs sold off most (~90%) of plants, including some nuclear	Not required. Proceeds of sale applied to stranded costs. Many power plants sold	Utilities are selling most of their plants	Not required. However, no entity can own more than 20% of the installed generation capacity located in or capable of delivering electricity to a region
Renewables	No RPS $540 million per year collected through non-bypassable system benefits charge (Public Purpose Programs charge on the bill), to fund R&D and renewable generation in CA. Programs administered by the CEC	RPS—1% of sales from *new* renewables by 2003, increasing 1/2% each year after) Massachusetts Renewable Energy Trust Fund funded by a Renewables Charge on the bill, ~$40 million/year until 2002	RPS—minimum 2% of generation from renewables, increasing 1/2% each year) Charge on bill to go into each UDC's Sustainable Energy Fund (?)	No RPS RD&D funded by non-bypassable system benefits charge (~$70 million/year for all SBC programs, first three years) Administered by the NYSERDA	RPS—requires that the state have an additional 2000 MW of generating capacity from renewable technologies by January 1, 2009

DSM	Funds collected through the non-bypassable system benefits charge (Public Purpose Programs charge on the bill). Programs overseen by the CPUC, administered by the UDCs. Funding must be >$228 million/year	Funded by DSM Charge on bill until 2002, ~$150 million/year, programs overseen by Division of Energy Resources (DOER), carried out by UDC, or municipal aggregator	PUC required to ensure energy conservation activities are appropriately funded and available in each electric distribution territory. Funded by non-bypassable charge (might only be for low income?)	Funded by non-bypassable system benefits charge, DSM gets ~$40 million/year, for the first three years)	Each UDC required to reduce consumption by a min. of 10% of the utility's annual demand growth by January 04. Utilities should use third party contracting; utilities can apply to the PUC for cost-recovery
Low Income	Funds collected through the non-bypassable system benefits charge (Public Purpose Programs charge on the bill) Programs overseen by the CPUC	Low income customers get a discount on the distribution and transition charges	PUC required to ensure that universal service activities are appropriately funded and available in each electric distribution territory Funded by non-bypassable charge	Funded by non-bypassable system benefits charge (~$70 million/year for all SBC programs, first three years)	Rules set up by the PUC, funded by the system benefit fund
Green Power Market	Active, though shutting down now due to crisis	Not active (?)	Active	Not active (?)	Not yet active

(continued)

Table 4.2.   Continued

	California	Massachusetts	Pennsylvania	New York	Texas
Comments	Only state with PX separate from ISO California is the first state in the nation to offer large-scale retail choice and a competitive generation market Low default rate has prevented competition	Differentiating between Standard Offer and Default Service is an extra impediment to competition. RPS has not started yet Low default rate has prevented competition Also been having problems with rates capped below wholesale prices.	Phase in and telling each customer to choose a supplier helped competition.	NY has a large Public Power Authority Also been having tight supply and increasing demand … starting to rethink rules for the ISO	Retail competition has not begun yet. PUC is generally taking a slower and more cautious route to implementation
References	PUC www.cpuc.ca.gov http://www. cpuc.ca.gov/static/ electric/electric_ restructuring/ er_home_page.htm PUC Data on number who have switched suppliers http://www. cpuc.ca.gov/ static/electric/ Direct_Access/ DASR.htm CEC www.energy. ca.govhttp:// www.energy.ca. gov/electricity/ index.html	*DOER: http:// www.state.ma.us/ doer/utility/ utility.htm DTE: www.magnet.state. ma.us/dpu, DTE Order finalizing regulations under restructuring http://www.state. ma.us/dpu/restruct/ 96-100/cmr11-2.pdf	PUC http://puc. paonline.com/ electric/elect_ comp.asp Power Point Presentation comparing CA and Penn. http:// puc.paonline.com/ electric/competi- tion/calpael.ppt	PSC http://www. dps.state.ny.us/ yourenergy.htm NYSERDA http://www. nyserda.org/ programs.html	PUC—detailed information on implementation http://www.puc. state.tx.us/electric/ projects/20970/ 20970.cfm http://www.tex- aschoiceprogram. com Great guide to ERCOT http://www.tex aschoiceprogram. com/documenta- tion/MarkPart Docs/ERCOT_ Market_Guide.doc

All is not perfect in Pennsylvania, however. By 2002 interest in switching has declined, and some of the alternative providers have gone out of business. The cost of power in general has gotten to be very similar between the old utilities and alternative providers.

One of the most insightful comparisons of electricity deregulation efforts is provided by Crow (2002) who notes that areas initiating restructured electricity markets need to learn from the experiences of other areas and not make the same mistakes. He subtitles his paper, "Not invented here is a recipe for disaster."

This analysis compares the California's "unmitigated disaster" (Crow, 2002: 42) with more generally successful deregulation efforts in England, Argentina, Victoria (Australia), and Pennsylvania and the PJM interconnect, while Crow remains optimistic that restructured electricity markets can work well, he also shows that there is no one model for successful restructuring. He notes that some of the goals of change in electrical systems such as retail markets have not produced clear results yet, and that answers still need to be obtained.

4.7. Conclusions: Moving Forward into a New Energy Era

Deregulation failed in California. The State was experiencing rolling blackouts and soaring prices from 10 to 50 times normal for already high-priced electricity. Was deregulation the cause of these cost spikes, outages, and uncertainty? The State could not risk the unknown and put a stop to the experiment. The deregulation debacle is on hold. Governor Davis has been "recalled" or thrown out of office in part due to the public perception of how he handled or did not handle the energy crisis. California's energy sector is in "transition". Governor Schwarzenegger has not revealed his own vision or plans, but clearly returning to a regulated or furthering the deregulated system are not the options.

With "open" or "free market" competition largely dead, regulation is only partially in place and unfortunately distributed among too many state and local agencies, commissions, and departments. The State is heavily involved, and instead of a more competitive private energy sectors, California has ended up with a more publicly managed, albeit be conflicted energy infrastructure. The primary intention of deregulation to reduce government's role in the electricity system ended with just the opposite result.

California did some things that are particularly shortsighted even if one accepts the premise that deregulation is a sensible goal to replace utility regulation. Serious questions abound as to this wisdom. For example, it is foolish to fix retail prices when other parts of the industry are deregulated. Those crafting the deregulation policy expected only that rates would go down. Little did they think that if wholesale rates rose would there be a catastrophe, and so no thought was given to assurring that a mechanism was in place to deal with this problem.

Second, having the wholesale market be only day-ahead or spot-market prices led to a level of volatility that proved impossible to manage and easy to manipulate. Market forces soon came to be a few companies controlling supplies and hence retail prices. While the deregulation architects wanted to free the utilities to take advantage of unforeseen price declines, it was important to balance the risk against unforeseen price increases.

Third, the decoupling of the PX, which buys power for a pool, and the CAISO, which manages the grid, has proven unworkable. The former has gone bankrupt and the later has had to "redefine" itself and its role in the energy sector. Power purchases should be made with full consideration of expected transmission costs and constraints given the physical characteristics of electricity. This was never done and may never occur.

Fourth, California did not allow enough time for implementing the change in deregulation to allow all parties to make a successful transition into unregulated markets. Gradual implementation of regulatory changes seems as essential in deregulating industries as in making any changes in public or private sectors. The expectation and plans for backup options, in case something should go wrong as they occur in real time, is an important lesson from California. Reformers need time to respond quickly to problems, but also to think ahead and plan for future contingencies.

In spite of the premise that California could have deregulated more effectively if it had avoided making critical mistakes and had more carefully followed Sally Hunt's (2002) "Standard Prescription", the whole premise of seeking the magic bullet of "market competition" in electricity must be questioned. It is plain wrong to restructure regulation on the basis of naïve "faith" in the market forces and faith in corporations and business people whose personal and professional careers depended upon profits for shareholders. The traditional concerns for the public good and reliability of services for all citizens were placed in a secondary position.

The most significant lesson to be learned was that the entire deregulation scheme was based on the flawed assumption that infrastructure sectors like energy as well as water, waste, education, and the environment should be subject to pure business competition (see Sclar, 2000). In that paradigm, corporations win because of their market power and the public loses since whom they have to pay the bills.

This chapter examined the California deregulation scheme in some historical comparative detail. The hopes and impacts that deregulation were claimed to have were reviewed. Political and business interests played a significant role in formulating the California deregulation structures and mechanisms. Nevertheless, consumers, environmental groups, and the utilities all overwhelmingly were favorable to deregulation at the time. Such a consensus meant that the entire process and future outcomes were not evaluated carefully. And unfortunately compromises were made at the 11th hour.

In particular, the chapter questions the wisdom of deregulation, privatization, or liberalization or whatever label political–economists want to give it. Different definitions, revised historical events and theories along with subtle (and not so subtle) nuances prevail even now after the California debacle. The result is the same.

Moreover, the experiment has placed the entire energy sector, and even the entire state let alone nation, in chaos. Neither the old nor the new energy regulatory system is working well. The future shape and character of the California electricity sector remains uncertain. What promised economic rate relief to all Californian has resulted in a system that has responded with a 25% increase in costs. Politicians are struggling to reduce these costs, but no realistic prospect for significant reduction is in sight.

In sum, the competitive rate reductions that were the goal of deregulation led to increases instead. The State's largest utility still has not emerged fully from bankruptcy. The second largest utility has just now begun to recover. Moreover new gas-fired power plants have been constructed to supply more power just as reasonable estimates are forecasting natural gas shortages and spiking prices for the fuel. The State now has at least $20 billion in bonds to repay from the energy crisis. Meanwhile, the State exchanged stranded assets and PURPA contracts for long-term contracts with power brokers for power at rates well above what was expected.

The resolution of this debacle will require more than just a few new regulations and a restoration of the old regulatory scheme or furtherance of the deregulation debacle. California certainly does not require more deregulation. Other chapters provide some guidance and outlines opportunities that emerged from the energy crisis. The resolution requires more public participation in a civic market so that an "agile energy system" can operate based on a very different set of assumptions and principles.

Chapter 5
Economic Models
and Market Change

5.1. Introduction

The logic that led to deregulation needs to be understood. In 1994, the debate from all sides was becoming intense over how to respond to the pressures on the California electricity system. Industry power generators wanted to self-generate or get direct access to cheaper power. The public-regulated utilities were burdened by the high construction and operating costs of power from nuclear plants. The growing number of independent power generators were exerting increasing political and economic pressure to allow their role to expand.

Yet the system seemed to be awash in surplus capacity. California had some of the highest electricity rates in the nation, and most parties were looking for a way to bring rates down. There were no obvious solutions, however, as the California system was relatively well run, the utilities were efficient and diversified, and the regulatory system was perceived to be somewhat burdensome but fair. The regulators and policy makers started embracing the neoclassical economic theory that espoused a deregulated energy sector, opening electricity to the market force of competition and hence delivering lower costs and prices in the near future.

Few expected that the state political leadership would propose such a massive deregulation scheme that would open the vertically integrated utilities to both wholesale and retail competition. The issue now, years later after deregulation was made into law, is not to point blame for this failed scheme. The final vote in the State legislature was unanimous and all political perspectives and parties agreed to the adventuresome plan. The plan, now labeled by the economists and politicians as "restructuring," was adopted with such widespread support that virtually every governmental level, political group, private sector company, and environmental nonprofit was involved.

Less than two years later (2001), a cartoon at the time of the energy crisis asked, "How many Californians does it take to screw up a light bulb?" It showed a ladder with all the major players reaching to change the light bulb—PG&E, Southern California Edison, Energy Commission, PUC, Legislature, Governor, etc. The implication was that all had helped break the energy system down. Some revisionist economists call this "a perfect storm" or the result of a confluence of "natural forces" such as lack of rain (for hydroelectric power) generating plants in repair, market manipulation, growing demand, and others. However, if there is no one individual or group on whom the blame can be placed for fashioning the deregulation experiment, one key question is to understand the basis for the overwhelming bipartisan consensus that supported opening the system to market forces and competition on the belief that deregulation would reduce prices and increase efficiency. Because so much of the energy sector had to do with costs/prices and therefore economics, considerable amount of attention must be spent on business economics.

The logic of deregulation called for an open or free market competitive system in electricity, rather than the governmentally regulated system, on the premise that it would lead to lower prices and a more efficient choice of resources for consumers. Where did the concept that opening the electrical system to competition come from? Why did it emerge when it did? What made it so persuasive that it stifled virtually all dissenting views? A bipartisan consensus emerged. But from where? And why?

This chapter argues that the problem of deregulation lies in the theoretical assumptions of the neoclassical economic model that advocates less government interference (the "invisible hand" of Adam Smith) and competition among firms to control prices. Reinert (1996, 1997, 1998) does a comprehensive analysis of the key premises (example "raw materials") behind the neoclassical model's dominance in economics.

By the 1980s the model was being embraced by a number of conservative politicians. It was very effectively sold worldwide to political leaders with Prime Minister Margaret Thatcher in the

UK and her copolitical economic colleague in America, President Ronald Reagan leading the "market reform" movement. Both world leaders in the 1980s, based their political agenda on the neoclassic economists in the USA (many from the "Chicago School" at the University of Chicago) and in the UK (from Oxford and Cambridge). For some pundits, Thatcher and Reagan became the global "Queen and King" of neoclassic political economics.

This political economic agenda was felt not only by most American states, but also international institutions such as the UN, World Bank, and especially the European Union itself. This same neoclassical economic model is at the root of the privatization models being proposed in virtually all developed and developing countries around the world today (Clark and Fast, 2004). It is such a fundamental premise of modern society that it is rarely questioned (Lund, 1996, 2000).

However, when the model is used as a justification for political agendas and actions, the model is able to convince businesses, regulators, politicians, and the public that competition, rather than government regulation, can magically provide lower prices and a better electrical system. Just the opposite happened in California and globally (Clark, 2001). Moreover, deregulation or privatization in other sectors had led to similar consequences of market manipulation by market forces.

The widespread adoption of a competitive or market framework for both wholesale and retail power in California led to many unanticipated consequences that resulted in blackouts and price spikes throughout 2000 and 2001. The relentless drive for competition without questioning the benefits of a fully competitive market was at the root of the policy mistakes in 1996. While the system needed to be opened to more options, the competitive neoclassical economic model was oversold to the legislature and public with little discussion, debate, and close examination. For example, economist Sally Hunt, who understands the process of restructuring power systems as well as anyone, concluded her book on competitive models in electricity by stating that the problem was how generation was deregulated. She did not question the soundness of the fundamental premises about creating a competitive production market for electricity or considering the transmission issues:

It is the deregulation of generation, not retail access per se, that has exposed customers to the risks we have seen in California. While we have argued that this is because it was done wrong—without demand response, with bad trading arrangements, and with a retail regime that was incompatible— it is quite simply true that if generation had not been deregulated, there would have been no problem. Yet there is no competition without deregulation of generation—it is the centerpiece of competitive production markets. (Hunt 2002: 53)

The purpose of this chapter is to examine the premises and assumptions of the neoclassical economic model as it applies to the electricity system and to ask why the drive to competition was so pervasive that it was worth risking the eventual problems that engulfed California. The drive to introduce competition was similar to an application of theoretical economic models without addressing why they were necessary in the first place. In many respects, unquestioning adoption of these models and their promised reduction in consumer prices for electricity predetermined the disastrous outcome in California and elsewhere (Lund and Clark, 1998, 1999).

5.2. Economic Models and Premises of Restructuring

Shortly after the Public Utilities Commission published their "blue book" in 1994, the California Energy Commission in its biannual Electricity Report addressed the viability and mechanisms of significant change in the structure of the utilities and how to introduce competition to the electricity industry. The report was optimistic, suggesting that the problems of restructuring the industry to be more competitive "will be straightforward to resolve" (California Energy Commission, 1994: 19). Deregulation was now being proposed by two State commissions with political appointees who subscribed to the political economic agenda of competitive market forces driving down costs and prices.

This move to restructure was driven by the economic model, not an outcry from the public. There is an interesting footnote in the Draft CEC 1994 Energy Report, a note that was eliminated in the final version. It said that the material in the report was based on extensive papers and analysis prepared by several well-known economists from out of state including William Hogan, Paul Joskow, Richard Tibors, and Sally Hunt, all of whom have published extensively on California's energy crisis. However, the most interesting part of the footnote has not been noted very much, and many revisionists today know why. The note included a thank you also to the firm, Enron (CEC, 1995).[1]

Today, of course, it is known that former Enron founder and President Kenneth Lay frequented California in the years leading up to the deregulation political decision, and that he and his corporate associates made large donations to politicians and their favorite "causes" from both parties. Hence, they had extensive access and influence in the proceedings leading to the final versions of AB1890 which made deregulation the law with its market mechanisms in California.

The alleged collaborations and lobbying of Enron executives predates and anticipates their much larger role in California which then shaped the future changes in the electrical system nationwide. Moreover, we know that Enron financed some part of the role played by William Hogan from Harvard through the Harvard Electricity Policy Group (HarvardWatch, 2002). Ex-CEO Jeffery Skilling, furthermore, partnered with Professor Hogan in California presentations on deregulation. Politically, Enron contributed over $2.4 million to federal political candidates, and another $4 million on its lobbying efforts in several states, including California, Montana, and regions such as New England which were all considering deregulation in the early and mid-1990s (HarvardWatch, 2002). By 2004, no one knows the full extent of the Enron role in funding other professional and academic papers, let alone politicians and special interest groups which helped shape the California deregulation proceedings.

The extraordinary role of economists (such as those noted in the 1994 Electricity Report) in defining the problem and the solutions to California's energy sector needs further discussion and analysis. To no small part the California energy crisis and the continued debate in the State reflect the limitations of the theoretical economic worldview as it got translated into public policy, or even pushed by the economists

---

[1] A footnote (#6) in the 1994 Electricity Report (California Energy Commission, 1995: 23) indicates the extent of the contribution of these authors. "Numerous papers have been prepared by Professor William Hogan (Harvard University), Larry Ruff (Putnam Hayes and Bartlett), Professor Paul Joskow (M.I.T.), Richard Tabors (M.I.T.), Sally Hunt, and others at National Economic Research Associates, as well as Charles Stalon and Eric Woychik, the New York Mercantile Exchange, the Enron Company, Commission staff, and others. Copies of these papers are available from the Commission." The authors have not been able to locate the California Energy Commission draft reports or final documents from this period as they are not in the Energy Commission Library.

themselves into the political decision-making process. This claim is not to denigrate all economics or economists, or even to point fingers at some such as Hogan, Joskow, Hunt, and others. However, the neoclassical economic model, which assumes a theoretical balance between supply and demand mediated by prices, has serious limitations in infrastructure systems such as electricity systems in which some part of a natural monopoly exists or should exist to assure the public good.

Of course, the issue of competition versus regulation in utility systems themselves, including telecom, transport, and environment have been well researched and studied by economists. Most, when pressed, are well aware of the potential problems. When the California crisis occurred economists were quick to assess what went wrong and to say that if the California system had been "restructured" properly the competitive model would have worked. Words like "dysfunctional" or "incomplete" or even "faulty" energy deregulation were attributed to the California experiment. Missing in most of the "revisionism" or hindsight analyses from the neoclassical economist tradition is a serious questioning of whether unregulated competition in the electricity industry is beneficial to anyone except those who can manipulate "market forces" for their own gains.

5.2.1. Neoclassical premises and assumptions

In order to understand the role of neoclassical or conventional economic model on the electricity crisis, consider the basic premise:

> *the electricity system would benefit from deregulation and competition among private companies and that such competition without government interference would in turn lower consumer prices, increase technological innovation, and improve service.*

While these ideas have a long history which will not be explored here (see Clark and Fast, 2004), a review of the literature, research work, and thought of the economists involved is useful. Restructuring the electricity system in California during the early 1990s was strongly advocated by economists such as Paul Joskow, William Hogan, and Sally Hunt. They had a deep involvement in the State and have recorded much of their respective thoughts in a number of easily available papers.

The attention to the work of the leading American energy economists are given in the following:

Open competitive markets

One of the most important foundations for understanding the role of "markets" in the electricity sector is Paul Joskow and Richard Schmalensee's book, *Markets For Power* (1983). Their analysis was cautious about the many difficulties and challenges that utility systems would face as they struggled with restructuring, but at the end they were supportive of early proposals such as those in England and the USA.

> *If important inefficiencies plague the current system, we are likely to be able to eliminate them fully only slowly over time, whatever reforms we put in place today. On the other hand, delaying decisions will perpetuate or increase performance failures for an even longer period. (Joskow and Schmalensee, 1983: 10)*

Correctly, Joskow and Schmalensee argue that before one can evaluate reform proposals, "one must have some idea of the problems they are designed to solve" (1983: 79). For them, the two problems are costs of producing electricity (are these costs as low as possible?) and the price that consumers are charged (are suppliers making excessive profits?). In short, these are the problems of production efficiency (quantity) and pricing which are the typical economic formulas.

In the early 1980s Joskow and his collaborators were cautious about the prospect of complete deregulation. They wrote that

> *any sensible deregulation scheme will require continuing economic regulation of some segments of the electric power system . . . Successfully managing a system that mixes competition and regulation is complex and requires that regulatory institutions, industry structure, and arenas of competition be designed carefully to complement each other. (1996: 212–3)*

A key point all the economic analysts of electricity deregulation took as a fundamental principle was that the electricity system needed to be split into competitive and monopoly services. Generation and retail sales were deemed to be competitive and different. Thus, transmission lines and distribution systems are a "natural monopoly" that should remain under regulatory control. Later, Joskow wrote that the

> *historical 'natural monopoly' industries are typically composed of both potentially competitive segments (eg, long distance telephone service, electricity*

generation, unbundled natural gas supplies, railroad rolling stock, etc.) and natural monopoly segments (eg, local telephone exchanges, electricity transmission and distribution networks, unbundled natural gas pipeline transportation, railroad track and switching networks). (1996: 345)

Vertical integration between them, it is argued, has led to an unnecessary expansion of monopoly from one horizontal level to another. Furthermore, vertical integration has extended inefficient regulation to segments where market forces can and should govern better. The perfect world of neoclassical economists is to have a perfect balance between the quantity and price of goods and services.

Sally Hunt also sets the stage for applying competitive principles to the electrical system. She argues that in spite of the California crisis, "we know what works and what does not," and that:

The industry is technically complex, and also institutionally complicated, but there is by now after a decade in international experience a "standard prescription" to deal with the complexities: a checklist of what is required for this industry to become competitive. The technical complexity can be solved: the institutional issues are at the root of the problem in the United States (Hunt 2002: 2).

To say that the "institutional issues are at the root of the problem" is a classic understatement. The institutional changes require revising the rules for the entire system and getting these right is indeed more difficult than solving the switching, balancing, and monitoring problems of the technical system.

For Hunt and other economists the goal of competitive markets is to increase efficiency. But none of the literature justifies how increased competition will increase efficiency more than in a well-regulated system. For example Hunt states that "... while it might be instructive to consider the problems of regulation and how competition will improve them, that is no longer the issue" (Hunt, 2002: 11). The decision of FERC in 1992 to permit open access on the interstate transmission system started a process that as we argued, put pressure on California regulators to fashion a changed system. While the system has changed as Hunt suggests, it is not clear that the issue of regulation and competition should *not* be examined, as the lack of examination is what led to the crisis in California.

In a contrasting perspective, Joskow noted that there are also efficiencies associated with the vertically integrated system that get lost with the neoclassical economic model for unbundling the utilities. With competition, he warns, the system for coordinating supply to instantly meet demand over constrained power transmission lines cannot be easily replaced with simple access rules or pricing schemes.

The competitive model did not fully evaluate the extent that the existing vertically integrated utility has system advantages instead of deregulation. For example virtually all integrated utilities control all the necessary components of the system and can make short-term and long-term decisions based on their supply and cost models. To the extent that a utility adopts best practice models, it remains unclear where cost and efficiency improvements will come from in a competitive environment. This point is crucial.

Risks and uncertainties

The neoclassical or conventional economic model suggests that the benefits of competition are in who assumes the risks in the power business, such as estimating price and demand, choosing technological options, planning effective management, and obtaining credit. Under regulation these risks are monitored by the regulators and passed on to the consumers. Under competition the risks are not monitored except by the owners of the system—"they will pay for mistakes or profit from good decisions and management" (Hunt, 2002: 29).

In a system with rich and robust competition, it is reasonable to assume that the private firms will have to absorb the losses from bad decisions, and similarly a smart firm will benefit when it makes good decisions. Moreover, in order to have improved efficiency in the system, we have to assume that over the long run the firm's gains from good decisions will be passed on to customers rather than used to escalate prices. However, in a less than perfectly competitive system (which has to be the starting assumption in electricity), efficiency gains will tend to be retained. Furthermore, in a less than perfectly competitive market, it is reasonable that the electric utilities will pass on the cost of their mistakes (or at least some of the costs) to consumers. If all the competing utilities make the same mistakes, there will be no price mechanism for firms to have to absorb the costs of being inefficient.

This unquestioned assumption that competition will shift the risk from consumers to the firms supplying power is very attractive to political leaders and to the consumers, as long as it works. Much of the theoretical premises have been modeled in what has become the field of "game theory" where the notion is that economics must be "played" on a level playing field between competing groups, companies, or teams.

The problem with game theory (aside from it being just a theory or, more recently, using computer models) is that there were always winners and losers. In short, one or two companies won the competition and hence controlled the market or playing field. The fact that the utilities supported deregulation indicates that they were not particularly worried that they were going to lose a lot of money by reducing rates. How wrong they were: Pacific Gas and Electric went into bankruptcy while Southern California Edison barely survived.

In addition, competition adds a number of layers of companies into the power industry. Each company has its management and overhead costs. The issue for increased efficiency and lower prices is to assure that the multiple firms do not add more costs to the system than an integrated utility under one management.

Even more destructive to the electricity sector in California from deregulation was the elimination of research and development (R&D) from within the energy utilities. Instead of innovation coming from the companies or vendors, the burden went to a government program, the Public Interest Energy Research (PIER) program in the CEC. This program while useful and strategic in some ways, is nonetheless hindered by bureaucracy and more significantly with an assumption that it will conduct R&D that is legislatively directed. The consequences over the last five years in California have been a lack of statewide energy planning, consideration of renewable energy generation, advancement of new technologies, or consideration of hydrogen. According to both CEC Commissioners and staff, "there had been no legislative mandate or authorization." Only due to the State energy crisis and the results of both legislation and Executive Orders did the CEC change its mission and role in the energy sector.

Market power and market forces

The limitation to a fair and efficient competitive market in network industries and regulated utilities is the potential for market power, the economist's term for abuse of monopoly or oligopoly power to raise rates to obtain unreasonable profits. As we write it is clear that Enron and other generators and electricity brokers manipulated the system and used their ability to withhold power from the grid, to create congestion on critical transmission lines, and to otherwise bypass competition in order to raise prices on the system. The presence of these market manipulations is relatively unquestioned, but there remains no clear resolution to the question of how much of the manipulation was due to criminal collusion and how much was an unfortunate confluence of circumstances.

Prior to passing the legislative plan to restructure the California electrical system in 1996, economists were concerned about creating a system that would not have the problems of market power that emerged. Joskow and Schmalensee noted this in 1983, recognizing that the amount of competition in generation would vary greatly from place to place and that without reducing the advantage of existing utilities the exercise of market power might not be avoided (2002: 199–202).

The solution in California and other deregulated industries has been to force the existing utilities to sell part or all of their generating capacity to other entities so that ownership is decentralized and a competitive market is fashioned. There remains a substantial debate in the literature about what measure of dispersion is adequate. The range extends from no firm having over 10% to no firm having more than 40% of the total ownership in a competitive market, and the means to achieving this goal is forced sale of generation assets. In California, existing utilities were given incentives to sell all their fossil fuel plants (mostly natural gas) and retain their nuclear and hydro resources.

In spite of quick divestment of power plants by the utilities, California's system did not really become competitive. The bulk of the power plants were owned by four companies. They were linked with brokers who marketed their power for them. Enron was the best known and most influential broker firm. The small number of competing firms made it easy for them to manipulate the system even without explicit collusion when supply was limited and huge profit could be made by driving prices even higher by strategic withdrawals of supply at critical times.

The real issue is whether neoclassical competition can solve the problems with the electric system or whether competition will aggravate or create new problems. The issue often painted by the advocates of competition who came to California is that competition is good and regulation is bad, and that policies that adopt competition and reject regulation are beneficial.

5.2.2. *Quantity: production efficiency issues*

From the conventional economic theory perspective, production efficiency is a process that is based upon balancing existing capital intensive generation and transmission capacity, fuel costs, and other inputs with optimal new investment and technological choices. When the system then meets the expected demand, but not more (achieving the classic economic need for a "balance"), the system leads to the lowest cost production over the life of the investment. However, there are many barriers to achieving production efficiency.

Planning and coordination of the power production system are complex and based on many unknowns and uncertainties that make these decisions risky. For example, fuel price forecasts have been notoriously off; forecasts in the early 1980s were for scarce natural gas at continually escalating prices, while in reality real prices for both gas and oil fell. In contrast, nuclear costs were consistently projected lower than they turned out to be. Demand forecasts have often been too high, which led to excess investment, though some areas were caught underestimating growth of demand. The economists would argue that there is no need in a deregulated market for state or federal planning as that process leads to government interference in "market forces" which by themselves are far better equipped and knowledgeable about what the market or consumer needs are.

Another production problem comes from the need to balance investment over the huge daily and annual cycles of market demand, which are unique to each area. Peak power demands based on weather, season, and other fluctuations are met by purchasing capacity not used but a few hours a year, while base load can be counted on day and night throughout the year. The energy load is further complicated by the need to have reserves in case of unexpected mechanical failure, transmission line breakage, or other problems.

The issue of reserves is one of the major policy decisions made by the new California Power Authority (CPA). For example, it has issued a report calling for 15–20% reserve capacity from new renewable energy suppliers to the system (CPA, 2002). Since load cannot be easily stored, a certain flexibility in generation needs to be built in—often as what is called spinning reserve—generating capacity that can be started or stopped at an instant's notice.

Given the technological complexity of power systems and the unpredictability of many components of the system, it is not surprising that local systems vary widely in their production efficiency. In some cases the power industry does not take advantage of operating efficiencies that are available. For example, in some cases individual utilities may operate their systems independently, whereas there would be benefits for them to pool resources with neighboring utilities and reduce costs to both systems. Over larger areas, regional differences in time of peak and weather patterns, winter and summer, allow for power flows that benefit both systems.

Long-run production inefficiencies include less than optimal investments. These show up in power plants that are poorly sized, especially with power plants that are too small to take advantage of some economies of scale. Recent advances in gas turbine technologies have displaced ever larger plants in efficiency, so this factor is not just one of getting larger plants.

Reliability issues are also important, because if capacity is not available and a utility has to purchase power from outside suppliers, these purchases may be very expensive if they are not planned in advance. Also inadequate transmission capacity limits production. Joskow notes that these inefficiencies have been long discussed in the literature (1983: 85), but he also notes that increased coordination has reduced the effect of these problems in the United States, though some productivity benefits remain to be captured. Gaming the market, as seen in the Enron case, was not considered.

In sum, production models under competition do not easily lead to optimal results and the belief that competition would do a better job of increasing efficiency and lowering prices than the regulated vertically integrated utility went unquestioned. Instead the argument can be made that the limitations of the competitive model should have led policy makers in California to seek partial and transitional solutions that would retain the advantages of the existing system and avoid the abrupt transition costs of making a transition to the competitive model.

Prices: pricing inefficiencies

Given the California energy crisis from 2000 to 2002, economists have been seriously concerned with the pricing problems inherent in the current regulated utility system. Most of the concern, according to the conventional economic argument, comes from the lack of "real-time pricing" and average costs which hide marginal prices. In other words, if the consumer (government, residential, or business) knew the actual costs of power immediately then they would cut consumption at the times when there were the greatest shortages and highest prices, thereby maximizing efficient system operation and minimizing total prices paid for power across the entire system. Hence, net-metering is the all too simplistic answer. But is it?

Nevertheless, like generation or production issues, pricing responds to very complex patterns and there are many barriers that stand in the way of utilities and consumers minimizing prices over the short and long term. The utilities must also deal with supply and transmission uncertainties as well as the problem of communicating all market issues to their consumers. While the gap between theoretically efficient pricing and the current regulated system is high, Joskow and Schmalensee (1983: 81) note that "the short term gain associated with moving from an inefficient set of prices to an efficient set of prices that appropriately reflect marginal costs may be relatively small." Market manipulation and gaming transformed the perfect energy market scheme from one that could minimize consumer prices to one that exposed customers and the State to high prices that would be unthinkable under a regulated system.

Pricing that is efficient and properly responsive must balance many factors that have emerged in recent years since deregulation. The main concern has been the realization that from a system perspective, conservation and public good programs may be a more cost-effective way to provide energy benefits to populations, without necessarily providing more power. Yet, utility price systems are poorly structured to reward investments that result in less power sold, even if it results in lower overall costs.

Marcus and Hamrin (2001), for example, conclude that "power markets such as in deregulated systems are not good at explicit tradeoffs between the present and the future or incorporating externalities such as environmental costs and benefits unless specifically designed to consider these elements." The key is that the tradeoffs for social goods must be specifically designed into the market and in most energy programs these considerations are not realized.

How, then, will the benefits of price competition be allocated? This question has not received much attention. The lessons in California suggest that profits soared among the generators and distributors, rather than the prices falling when they more than tripled in the winter of 2001. More and more research is now debunking the competitive economic theories whereby competition automatically results in lower electricity rates. For example, a study of the British version of deregulation (privatization or liberalization), Newbery and Pollitt (1997) show that overall prices fell by about 5%, while corporation profits rose 40% based on return on investment.

Transmission in a deregulated system: structuring of efficient and low-cost systems

A third neoclassical economic consideration emerges from the search for pure market competition to increase energy sector efficiency and reduce prices. The issue of operating an efficient transmission network under deregulation of suppliers has created almost a subspeciality among economists who need to also understand the complex physics and behavior of high-voltage electrical grids. William Hogan (1992: 213) wrote that

> economic dispatch of electric power plants connected through a transmission grid provides a natural starting point for discussion of efficient electricity markets.

Since electricity will follow paths of least resistance, and it will utilize all available paths to get to its destination, power cannot be directed from a generator to a consumer as a truck is directed over a single set of highways from one point to another. The analogy means that electricity will create loop flows that can overload segments of lines far from where the power enters the system. Hence, a critical issue for the competitive market is that sometimes the lowest cost generator may not be able to produce and deliver power because the supplier will overload a certain transmission line. The issue is what does this lack of transmission do to the price people are willing to pay? Similarly, when a generator contracts to send power to a customer, how is the cost of transmission figured since it covers many lines and may displace other lower price generation.

This point came up very clearly in the transmission failures that blacked out many parts of the Northeastern United States and several European cities during the summer of 2003. Reports coming from the early analysis of these failures indicated that utilities under the pressure of price competition cut investments in transmission capacity upgrades and extensions, while cutting maintenance budgets.

These same issues were imbedded in the vertically integrated utility where most of the transmission lines were owned by the utility and it could manage generators because they were all working together toward the same retail market. The problem under competition is that these functions are operated by different firms or agencies and each wants to maximize their own profit and an accounting system needs to be created that is fair and equitable under these constraints.

5.3. Deregulation Benefits? Seven Myths about Economic Efficiency

The key premise of the economics of utility deregulation is that market response will increase production efficiency and reduce prices to consumers. In short, customers benefit because of the neoclassical balance between production and demand. There are many economic arguments that became articles of faith supporting the premise that benefits would follow from deregulation and more competition in electricity. For the most part economists did not follow their own early warnings that it would be complex and difficult to actually deregulate the electricity sector. Instead, over the subsequent years economists started to believe that they could actually deregulate and that benefits would follow.

The following list of benefits are derived from Joskow's (2000: 119–124) examination of deregulation in the late 1990s in California and other states, though the article was written before the economic collapse in California. Joskow notes that in spite of general efficient operation of the electrical system and the comparative success of American efforts compared to those on most other countries, the pressures for deregulation increase. There are seven reasons with our analysis of each one.

5.3.1. Better investment decisions

First, deregulation in the long run will provide better guidance in deciding what generation plants to build and will exert pressures to control construction costs. The largest costs in utility industry are in capital expenditures and this fixed long-term investment is around half of the cost of generation of power. However, the cost of generation even with the same fuel and size of plant varies widely across regions of the nation and world, and the risk of bad decisions needs to be placed on the suppliers of these generation services. For economists this is a fundamental variable in all industries, where efficient capital investment provides competitive advantages. Can competition induce better investment decisions?

On the positive side, accountability for mistakes under the traditional system is largely shifted to rate payers with little recourse to investors. The example of Diablo Canyon nuclear plant is instructive. Cost overruns make the power too expensive to sell under normal expense recovery calculations, even though PG&E wanted to shift all the burden of cost to the rate payers. The regulator, the CPUC, wanted the utility to absorb most of the burden.

Finally, a compromise was reached in which the power was sold to customers at a rate well above the average of other sources of power (12 cents/kWh), based on performance criteria. If performance was below a set level the balance would be absorbed by the company. In practice, before deregulation, the plant performed reliably above the minimum, and costs were passed on to consumers. Under deregulation, presumably, cost overruns on plants like Diablo Canyon would not be competitive and would lead to huge financial losses to the utility.

From a conventional economic point of view, under regulation, the public regulator protects the utility from some risk for the investment decisions that are made. The fact that the utility can pass on costs shifts the risk and allows for poor investment decisions. Under deregulation, this risk buffering function will be removed, subjecting these decisions to competitive markets.

A counter argument is needed however. California's experience has shown over and over how private companies would have made horrible decisions if it were not for the regulatory system to enforce restraint. If Diablo Canyon was a problem one can only imagine the financial crisis of the utilities and the State if the 12 nuclear plants that were planned in the 1970s were actually built. While the regulatory system is not capable of micromanaging or of assuring that all investment decisions are wise, the fact that there is a second opinion may lead on average to fewer mistakes.

Good decisions are benefits for which there should be a public benefit, not just private gain, especially for those low-cost sources of power that result from the collaboration between the public through the regulator and the private utility. The benefits of the shared risk between the utility and the guaranteed pass through of the costs to the customer has made some projects feasible and has assured low costs of capital because investors sense a guaranteed return on their investment. Indeed the whole utility industry is more of a public trust than is an industry such as oil refining. Many of the resources used in the generation of power are derived from public lands especially hydroelectric. The power lines are typically acquired through the use of eminent domain proceedings to force access or sale of land.

5.3.2. Politicized priorities excluded

The economists point to the fact that regulation reflects politicized priorities that counter the best economic interests of efficiency and low costs. The economists do not like the fact that some of the decisions in the regulatory process reflect political priorities that turn out to have higher costs and add nonmarket factors into production decisions. This includes for California the contracts with QF producers which were priorities of the regulators and the QF industry, not the regulated utilities. The utilities would have preferred to remain in control of all of their generation, but PURPA opened up the supply to other providers, and this political decision led to inefficiencies.

Contracts based on faulty assumptions led to problems, but also to system advantages (Summerton and Bradshaw, 1991).

Clearly, the fact that regulatory commissions are public bodies means that they are under pressure from the public to reflect political priorities rather than just private priorities. From a regulatory perspective, one can see the danger that too many public good priorities for the power sector can divert from its primary mission and cause costly dysfunction. For example, in India, subsidies to farmers (virtually free power) was a political promise one political party offered to gain support for public investment in rural electrification, and now the farmers getting the subsidy are such a large political force that any reform of the power system is politically impossible. The goal of helping farmers at the expense of providing revenue to the electricity industry was a shortsighted solution to their real needs.

However, most regulatory bodies do not have as much of an overtly political aim that would undermine the electricity industry as they did in India. The examples of regulatory involvement generally have to do with natural resource issues such as air pollution, water management, nuclear waste, and other siting issues, or with equity issues such as assuring low rates for poor customers, reliable service in rural areas, and safety. In addition, regulators may be concerned with economic development and the use of power for public purposes such as street lighting and street car service in urban areas. In developed countries it is true that regulators have political agendas for shaping the efficiency and cost of power, and to some extent this is true in all countries.

Critics of the high price of power in California were unhappy with the decision of California following PURPA to open generation to small qualified producers by offering long-term Standard Offer contracts to facilitate new suppliers' entry into the power market. Without long-term contracts, QF producers could not get the long-term financing they required to enter the market. The opening of the closed vertically integrated utility system to other producers was a first break in the utility monopoly, and the utilities were distrustful. Although the QF contracts were supposed to be neutral to consumer and utility, all parties were involved in miscalculating fuel costs which led to overly expensive long-term contracts with the QF providers.

The QF standard offers were negotiated between the utilities and the independent producers, and the rates were based on data provided by the utilities, presumably the same data on which they would make internal facility siting decisions. In addition, none of the parties anticipated that there would be much interest by QF providers in the

Standard Offer contracts. While all parties may have been less than fully honest and cooperative, the process was designed with only one premise—that the consumer would be indifferent to the fact that power was generated by QFs and that this rate would be set to match the utilities avoided cost (Summerton and Bradshaw, 1991).

These contracts were not just created in a political process, they were based on utility provided numbers reflecting what the utility would have spent if it had gone ahead and built another plant— in this case a gas-fired steam plant which was the best technology at the time. Parenthetically, the problem with QF contracts came with technologies where there were no direct comparable fuel costs, such as wind, and so the contract negotiators took estimates for future oil and gas costs as a basis—but they made a mistake and calculated these costs way too high.

The real issue was not with the concept of avoided cost. Another problem came in that neither the regulators nor the utilities accurately estimated the amount of interest by independent producers, which turned out to be much more than expected. No cap or recalculation was included in the rate design to be instituted after a certain amount of power was contracted.

The problem from an economic point of view is that the system is regulated to achieve political goals, and the inclusion of these political goals into the rate system leads to inefficiencies that the market is supposed to correct. There are two sides to this argument. First, the regulated system is not perfect, and as Joskow points out, it can do better without being thrown out. Mistakes are made in the regulatory process, and neither party built in adequate protection in case the policy did not work out as well as desired. Two redundant voices in planning seem to be better than one and the benefits of the public input are not balanced against the losses.

The other side of this issue is that in the interest of the public good many of the values the economists define as political interference need to be included by regulation or else they would not be included at all. For example, increasing reliance on renewable sources of energy is a social value that would probably not be realized under pure market forces. Yet the development of adequate renewable industry is essential for reducing greenhouse gases, for promoting the technological innovation in solar and wind that will arguably be the technologies for the future. The capital intensive nature of the electricity industry means that long-term industrial values need to be introduced by regulation rather than the market, and it is good for the whole industry in the long run to enforce change. The economists miss the value of the latter.

5.3.3. End cost-plus rate setting that assures stable return on investment

The conventional economist points out that cost-plus regulation does not reward efficient operations and that a competitive market would enforce greater efficiency. Some regulatory experiments with incentive or performance regulation has been successful, but economists argue that regulation generally blunts performance. The reason is that under cost-plus regulation, returns increase as expenditures increase, whereas in the competitive market returns are reduced as costs go down.

From a simple logic point of view, the economists are right about the lack of performance incentives in simple cost-plus regulation. Indeed, the regulatory literature has considered this for years. However, Gilbert and Newbery (1994) point out that cost-plus regulation is itself relatively complex and depending on the rules used, it may lead to efficient outcomes.

The conventional economists are wrong however, to the extent that they assume there are no checks on utilities to improve performance and reduce costs and capital expenditures. Overall, there is a middle ground on this point, and efforts such as performance-based regulation are part of the key.

A second check on unfettered cost-plus regulation is comparisons with public utilities. Private investor-owned utilities have generally been very competitive with their public counter parts, and in most cases have delivered power at a comparable price and reliability compared to public utilities. Over time this balance changes somewhat, with California's two major public utilities (Los Angeles and Sacramento) performing better during the 1990s and through the energy crisis, but less well in the 1970–80 period.

If the private investor-owned utilities were to become grossly inefficient, municipalization is an ever present threat. Several cities such as San Francisco and Berkeley have each had recent elections threatening to buy out the private utilities, and in the aftermath of the 2000–2001 crisis many municipalities looked into municipalization (Bradshaw *et al.*, 2003). The competitive threat is fought in ballot boxes and public relation campaigns, but it is intensely real.

Another constraint on regulators passing excessive costs on to rate payers is that the regulators are under political pressure to reduce rates and thus they become very attentive to the justification for costs and capital expenditures. To the extent that the regulatory system is doing its job, unnecessary expenditures have a hard time getting into the rate base. The pressure of large power consumers with substantial political influence assures that regulators strive to reduce costs through the tools at their disposal, the force that led the California PUC to initiate deregulation in the first place.

According to utility managers and CPUC officials, rate hearings are not about the rate of return, which is independently set, but about what gets included in the rate base. The same point is made by Gilbert and Newbery (1994: 538) who note that "the focus of regulatory conflict has been on the assets that should be included in the rate base."

Hence, the utility tries to include as much as it thinks it can get away with, while the regulators see their job to detect and remove all these extras. While it is a bit of a game, the result is based on public hearings so that there is public oversight (often the public is represented by watchdog organizations such as TURN in California). When the regulatory system is working well, few excesses are allowed and utilities seek an understanding of what can be included in their cost-plus rates.

Again, the economic argument that regulation is a cause of excessive rates and operational inefficiencies seems at best mixed. The regulatory system on average has led to a relatively efficient system where there are still options to municipalize. On this, it seems that better performance regulation is the key, not doing away with regulation through competition.

5.3.4. More efficient operation of electrical system

Economists believe that with competition there will be more effective utilization of capital facilities. It is often noted that some utilities do not shut down old and inefficient plants in a timely manner, leading to higher costs. Joskow notes that some old plants keep operating in part because of the value given to them by regulatory agencies who will not let them be decommissioned, whereas competition would lead to retirement of inefficient plants and investment in more efficient ones. This argument seems to be the opposite of the first point above which suggests that under regulation utilities strive to overinvest to obtain greater returns.

The argument that competition can cure problems of the timely retirement of plants and replacing them with more efficient ones can be supported in some cases, but this is not necessarily large enough of a system's inefficiency to justify changing the structure of the electrical system. Even under competition, some companies operate at less than optimal efficiency, while others are more effective. Some regulatory agencies utilize the best strategies to support decisions about which plants to run and when to invest in new ones, while regulators may also pursue less-efficient allocation schemes. In general, there is no evidence that effective regulation cannot handle most facility utilization inefficiencies in a timely manner.

On the other hand, utilization of plants is a very complex decision matrix where factors such as availability of capacity for the highest peak demand needs to be balanced with solid capacity for base load, spinning reserve, and other operational issues. Anticipation of future fuel costs, willingness to risk investment when future demand is uncertain, and other issues need to be resolved by utilities in both regulated and competitive systems. On some of these details, competition may lead utility executives to make better decisions, to invest more in information and planning to support decisions, and to better communicate these decisions to customers.

The benefit of new plants over older plants also depends on the technologies available at the time the decision is made. During the 1970s the marginal cost of new plants was higher than the average utility load. While plant efficiency for decades increased as the scale of the plant increased, new plants are often more expensive because new plants require long and expensive permitting processes. They used expensive fuels, when interest rates were very high and pollution abatement requirements were more expensive for new plants than for existing ones. In addition, adding new large-scale plants would have to meet a significant increase in load which may not be available to the utility. The lumpy quality of plant additions, especially in small utilities, prevents much innovation that economists may seek. Competition would not alter these conditions.

Today, in contrast, combined cycle gas turbine technology allows utilities to install smaller plants that have the same or higher efficiencies, lower interest rates, and are inherently less polluting. Competitive and regulatory pressures to install a more efficient plant might be more efficient under these conditions.

Additionally, the problem of peak demand seems to be distinctly challenging to all systems. Peak demand in most industries is accomplished by storing capacity until it is needed; toys are made and warehoused to meet the Christmas rush, for example. But electrical power cannot be easily stored. In modern electrical systems peak demand is met by a number of management strategies that are not improved by competition.

First, hydro resources held behind dams in reservoirs are saved for use in peak situations, consistent with regulated releases to assure satisfactory river water flows that protect fish and aesthetic goals.

Second, a number of pumped storage systems use power during nights and cool periods to pump water to reservoirs at a high elevation, which may be released to generate electricity when needed for peak demand. The water is then stored at a low-elevation reservoir until it is pumped back up when there is excess cheap power. The pumping efficiency is reasonable given the higher value of peak electricity. Third, old and less efficient, usually more polluting plants are held in reserve to run at peak times. While these older plants are no longer cost effective as base load, they serve peaking demand well. Finally, price deals are set with large users who have variable demand to cut their use during peak times. In these cases peak load is shed to make sure the system does not overload.

The issue of peak demand illustrates the complexity of resource allocation in modern electrical systems. Single generators have little incentive to supply economical peaking power since they can sell the last increment of that power just a few hours a year. In fact, if demand is relatively inelastic at peak demand and there is a shortage of available peaking power, then prices will spike more than otherwise and more profit can be made. This is the experience of California utilities under competition during the 2000–2001 period. Under vertically integrated utilities, regulators assured reliability at the peak even though the costs may have been high. This system worked well, but the economic models suggest that competition may be less capable of assuring adequate peak supply.

5.3.5. Reducing payroll and ending unionization

Economists argue that employment costs can be reduced by eliminating unionization and hence putting firms under pressure to reduce the number of employees. In many developed and developing countries bloated utility payrolls undermine efficiency while increasing operating costs. Thus, one of the indicators of progress in deregulating the utility system was to improve worker productivity. However, in order to do that worker training and political issues need to be addressed. It is clear that price pressure may lead some utilities to trim payrolls and to disband unions, but neither will happen easily. The argument that competition will lead to loss of jobs and ending unionization would be a very unpopular justification for deregulation.

The prospects of changing employment was one of the most important motives for restructuring or privatizing in England. However, the new competitive structure was designed to break the coal miners union, which had forced the national power industry to buy primarily expensive domestic coal instead of cheaper alternatives from other countries or nonunion mines.

However, the counter argument to payroll cost savings is that more competitive firms may have to pay higher salaries to executives. Utility executives under regulated utilities have their salary set outside the regulatory framework, but it becomes public knowledge and executive compensation is mentioned in rate hearings. With competition, the little public scrutiny now given will not be available, and executives may just claim that they deserve more compensation since their tasks are greater and since they have to manage risk and competitive markets. Their success makes a greater difference to the company than under regulation, and executives will generally ask for more compensation if they are successful. In sum, the economists may be right that competition in an ideal world will reduce unionization and payroll, but in reality these gains will be hard to realize.

5.3.6. More efficient pricing options

Conventional economists also note that pricing efficiencies such as time of use pricing may be more easily implemented under competition. The key issue here is a valid one, and it suggests that under competition there will be more incentives for utilities to come up with different pricing schemes to attract customers who will better match their available generation capacity. This incentive may be delivered by regulators but it is more logical to see it evolves from a competitive environment.

In addition, pricing that varies according to season, time of day, and peaking needs remain important issues. Virtually all economic analysts such as Sally Hunt (2002), William Hogan, and Severin Borenstein of the University of California, Berkeley, Energy Institute have argued that "real-time signals" of price provided by new time-sensitive meters would cure many of the current system problems if they were first used for industrial customers and eventually all residents.

The economic argument goes that when demand exceeds available base capacity, prices would increase and customers would have immediate and direct incentives to stop using power because they would have to pay the high marginal price. Hence, consumers will be aware of their electricity use and conserve, but also consumer's will seek energy-saving technologies, devices, appliances, and companies that allow customers to manage their power costs at a lower rate.

5.3.7. Create competition by divesture and compensation for stranded assets

Finally, in order to assure a competitive market, economists have argued that utilities must be compensated for their "stranded assets," that is, those plants and facilities that are high priced compared to the average of the competition. This is seen as a one-time effort to level the playing field to assure competition. The economists also urged the regulated utilities to divest their generation assets so that there is more competition. In fact the incentive of getting paid for their stranded assets is what has led most utilities to support deregulation. They did not see long-term profitability in generation because of the risks and politics involved, and most California utilities were willing to let another company have that part of their business.

The notion of divesting generation assets has been based on the premise that competition requires that no supplier have more than about a quarter (25%) of market share to prevent exercise of market power in which a supplier can manipulate the market for monopoly style gains. In a competitive system prices are set by the balance between supply and demand and the economists suggest that the system needs to have enough players so that no one can manipulate prices by withholding power to drive up prices.

Today, it is widely known that this plan did not work. Even with multiple participants, brokers and generating firms knew that the supply was so tight that by withholding even a small amount of their power they could exercise market power and cause prices to spike, which would benefit them as well as everyone else. This is what led to the California crisis. In retrospect, divestiture turned the power plants into the hands of companies which had no regulatory responsibility to a customer base. Moreover, they lacked any interest in blending of resources including peaking.

The problem of stranded assets, which are overpriced resources, are considered a significant area for which action needs to be taken. While hard assets such as most hydroelectric facilities are very attractive resources which produce low-price power, most were not seen as overly beneficial corporate resources that could be balanced against the stranded assets. Hence, in deregulation, hydroelectric power plants and dams along with nuclear power plants were not sold off from the utilities.

Joskow (2000: 146) shows a chart with the book value and market value of divested assets. Many prices gained were well above the book value, which Joskow suggests either that they were undervalued by regulators or that the new operators think they can operate their plants more efficiently. But it may be that the buyers of the plants anticipated the potential for manipulation of the markets and higher profits.

5.4. Conclusion: The Failure of Neoclassical or Conventional Economies in Energy Planning for Complex Infrastructure Systems

The issue with which this chapter started was to understand the premises and assumptions of the neoclassical economic model that was advocated by Enron and show how it overwhelmed the concerns of critics and even other economists who thought that the market for electricity was not suitable for deregulation. The approach to the deregulation model was to rely on the generalized assumptions about the functioning of markets, not the particular realities of the energy sector. Moreover, the energy system was deregulated without the protections that a more skeptical analysis of the situation would suggest. The model was so pervasive that it blinded the response to the crisis as well.

For example, in the early winter of 2001, at the height of the crisis, a group of economists argued for quick action to allow "market forces" to operate. The economists, including several Nobel prize winners noted that "Electricity has now become a political commodity, not an economic one" (Manifesto, 2001: 1). Their solution as stated in the Summary of the last sentence to the Manifesto, "The laws of supply and demand cannot be ignored except at great peril." (Manifesto, 2001: 5).

In general the Manifesto argued, and has been often repeated since then, that the energy sector, under deregulation, must be allowed to function on its own. "Either retail prices go up, or the frequency of rolling blackouts will accelerate, absent even more costly and draconian governmental measures." (Manifesto, 2001: 1). In other words, the argument goes that the free market system will balance itself. And society, as popular economic journals and scholars consistently argue, should care for itself without government through its "invisible hand" (Economist, Sept. 20, 1997).

Not long after the Manifesto, several individual scholars modified their stance and noted that the California market was flawed and "dysfunctional" because it was not a true deregulated market. The "perfect storm" had struck California. This pronouncement in spite of several scholars having helped craft the California deregulation laws and those of other states (HarvardWatch, 2002). Nonetheless, as a whole, economists have vigorously supported competition, at all societal costs, although they quickly have disassociated themselves from California form of energy-deregulated markets.

Chapter 6
Complex Energy Systems: The Limits of Knowledge, Management and Planning

If the benefits (of deregulation) are nebulous and only marginal, then the status quo may be preferable—and certainly more predictable. (Sioshansi, 2001: 742)

It is clear that the experts, regulators, economists, environmental groups, elected and utility officials who deregulated the energy system in the early 1990s got it all wrong. The deregulation of the California power system did not make it more economical and efficient. There is no evidence that the failed policy was orchestrated through collusion of a small group for private gain. Nonetheless in the end, the chaos of the energy system in California certainly provided ample quick gains for the largely out-of-state power companies who gamed the system. While these market manipulators caused shortages in the short run, their impact would be felt in the long run. Many would argue that the energy crisis was the major factor leading to the Recall of Governor Davis in October 2003.

During the decade in which energy deregulation was considered, the State's investor-owned utilities were not the major proponents of the new policy. Basically, the deregulation plan legally forced dismantlement of the State's three large utilities with large parts of their generation business sold to competitors. Only hydroelectric and nuclear plants could remain under their ownership. Almost all the remaining power generation would be sold to out-of-state energy companies. The utilities did benefit greatly from the lucrative sale of their gas-fired plants. They also recovered costs associated with their expensive nuclear plants and other stranded assets. However, the utilities were reluctant participants from the beginning rather than champions of the changes initiated by the regulatory agencies and the economic market experts.

In fact, municipally owned utilities in two major regions of California remained outside the deregulated energy sector: the vast Los Angeles region in Southern California (Los Angeles Water and Power District) and the area surrounding the State Capital in Sacramento (Sacramento Municipal Utility District). During the energy crisis, starting in San Diego in the spring of 2000 through 2002, these two districts did not suffer from shortages in large part due to long-term guaranteed contracts.

As Norm Lior points out, many of the people with the knowledge about potential problems of deregulation were involved in the California policy, and though the knowledge was generated through publicly supported research it still was not taken seriously. In retrospect, it is easy to join Lior (2001: 745), Editor of the journal, *Energy*, who offered the opinion that:

> ...there exists more than enough knowledge, and even common sense, rather readily available, in the possession of objective and peer recognized expert scientists, engineers, economists, and other energy specialists. To use this knowledge could have averted the poor decisions that led to this crisis and indeed to many others worldwide.

While politicians can be faulted for not listening, the other problem Lior (2001: 745) concludes with is that "the experts, as well as the voters in general, don't seem to care." This is really the key question in the California deregulation crisis—why did a policy that in retrospect seems to defy the common sense of Basic Business #101 get implemented anyway? From our perspective, the California crisis was not caused either by the lack of sensible knowledge or by leaders who "seemed not to care," but by an overwhelming belief that competition would both reduce prices and increase efficiency. When policy makers believe strongly enough that their policy goal is good, the details overwhelm a continued and objective application of knowledge to the initial question about whether the policy goal makes sense in the first place.

As the initial deregulation proposal worked its way through the regulatory and legislative processes, it got more complex. Sally Hunt (2002: 127) commented that the evolution in the California situation was like trying to build a bridge by voting where the girders should go. The analysis of the components of the solution are not thought out nor integrated together. The negotiations got so complex that the system perspective got lost in the blind effort to find bipartisan political solutions that would give some benefit to all the participants. In short, the final deal in California was so broadly approved that all the parties perceived the costs and benefits of the plan to be a reasonable compromise.

What went wrong? The argument can be made that the lesson from the failed California energy deregulation experiment is that modern power systems have become so complex that neither experts nor the public fully understand the way the system operates or its consequences. The purpose of this chapter is to explore the gulf between what was known and what needed to be known to have avoided the crisis in California. Most importantly, what needs to be learned from the California crisis so others can move forward. Clearly, the need for an "agile system" that reaches beyond centralized grids to predict, control, and diversify energy supply must be implemented.

6.1. The Issue of Deregulating any Complex Systems

The deregulation structure and mechanisms in California were designed by generally well meaning people. Most of the government officials and industry leaders who made decisions leading to the California crisis were not personally incompetent, malicious, or corrupt, but they simply designed a system that assumed idealistic market mechanisms based upon one set of economic theories. The basic problem with these theories is that they ignored reality and hence were so flawed that it led to a $40 billion catastrophe. The deregulated system left open opportunities for corporate officials and their companies, who were mostly out-of-state energy market players. California, as it has historically, beckoned to these companies and allowed them to engage in illegal and unethical behaviors. Without regulations and by manipulating a system that was more complex than the ability of those in charge to understand, monitor, control, or even dampen the extent and nature of the problems that would emerge, energy companies could make quick profits.

The deregulation plan more or less seemed reasonable at the time it was designed. The last piece of legislation, for example, needed to enact deregulation was approved without one negative vote. Bipartisan support was overwhelming, yet naïve. Woo (2001: 753) notes that this apparent reasonable quality among all the decision-makers was fairly persuasive:

> *A cursory review may lead one to believe that the California market reform should be able to provide reliable electricity at low and stable prices. After all, the PX-CAISO market design marries the economic model of market*

consumption and the engineering model of optimal dispatch. Competitive bidding among PX buyers and sellers should theoretically yield an efficient allocation of electrical energy. Competitive auctions of ancillary services should enable the CAISO to perform least cost dispatch. Zonal pricing of transmission should efficiently allocate the limited transmission capacity. Surging zonal MCP and the associated excess profits should attract new generation at the locations with dwindling supply or rising demand. But the reality of the events that have occurred since Summer 2000 obliterates such a belief.

The plan that was adopted in California had many flaws and pointing them out is easy picking for a critic. In fact, since late 2001, most experts and economists now refer to the deregulation public policy as "restructuring." Most analysts agree that aspects of the deregulation scheme have proven faulty and should not be repeated by any future deregulation scheme. However, it is far more compelling to question the very premise on which deregulation was proposed—the premise of competition. In the words of Governor Pete Wilson who pushed the policy and claimed at its signing that the policy would combat the 40% extra that consumers in California were paying every time they flicked on the light switch because competition and dismantling the electricity monopoly would "guarantee lower rates, provide customer choice and offer reliable service, so no one is literally left in the dark."

Of course, the public now knows more (but will probably never know all) about how brokers, traders, and generators used illegal and unconscionable gaming of the California electric system with such well-named schemes such as "Death Star, Get Shorty, Fat Boy, and Ricochet" to create artificial scarcity and to spike prices (see Bryce, 2002: 271; Cruver, 2002; Fusaro and Miller, 2002: 93). For example, it is now known how reluctant the Federal Energy Regulatory Commission (FERC) was to respond to price crises in California for largely political reasons (Dunn, 2002). However, most of the people initially responsible for making the decisions to deregulate believed the economic analysis and assumed these illegal schemes could not happen.

At the time of deregulation decisions, many analysts were concerned with the deregulation proposal and expressed concern that an unregulated market would not invest in enough generation capacity, or that competition would not be strong enough to control market power (Clark and Lund, 1999, 2001). Energy regulators were very familiar with schemes to manipulate the market, and they understood that the task of regulation is to control expected industry efforts to make more profit in monopoly industries than is fair and reasonable.

The problem was that the voices of caution and warning were not heeded, and the overwhelming enthusiasm for the deregulation experiment got out of control. When the prices for power were lower than expected for the first two years after the plan went into effect and stranded costs were being paid off at a faster rate than expected, the enthusiasts said "not to worry, we told you so." Eventually, however, controls on excessive prices simply did not work because gaming was perfected in a tight market and events happened that were not anticipated, though with hindsight they should have been expected. In spite of the vast amount of information that was available and that helped to run the state power system for several years, the planners forgot that large electricity grids are so complex that it is impossible to know enough in advance to avoid mistakes. It is expected that power providers have backup plans if a part of their system fails; policy makers had no backup plan in case deregulation did not work as expected.

The purpose of this chapter is to explore how power system information was used and misused. More importantly, complex systems have a language and organization all of their own. The electrical grid is no exception, and as subsequent events since 2000 have well-documented, public policy makers were sold a "bill of goods" that promised lower prices and efficiency from economic "mythical models" based on ideal types, situations, and market forces. Senator Dunn (2002: 8) who later headed the California Senate Investigation of the energy crisis tells what he thinks happened:

> *Everyone in Sacramento was driven by just one thing, across political lines. They were driven by the desire to deliver to their constituents lower prices; that's it. From that point on there was little additional analysis other than for a handful of folks like Steve Peace. Ninety-eight percent of the legislators just said: "Folks are telling me it's going to get lower prices . . ."*

The subsequent vulnerability of energy system decision makers to unprecedented misinterpretation and market manipulation cascaded into the energy crisis in California and subsequently into other regions of the world.

The rapidly changing political agendas aggravated the conditions that they were supposed to stabilize into competitive markets. The misinformation, the poor timing in which both public policy was made, and the market control exercised by private sector firms led to the rapid escalation of chaos and complex systems out of control. For example, the rapid increase and fluctuation in prices was nowhere near linear to the reduction in supply of energy. Furthermore, even when demand decreased, prices did not come down to previous levels. The political process necessary to control a complexity crisis in uncharted territory is different from what is needed to manage a system that is well understood.

In order not to loose sight of the scale of the problem in the electricity system, it is essential not to forget that the California price/cost problems were not experienced for the first time in the 2000–2001 energy crisis. Under the historical public-structured energy markets, the inability to handle information complexity had led to previous policy failures:

- The consensus was that nuclear power would be inexpensive, ultimately too cheap to even meter. The mistaken enthusiasm in the 1960–1970s over nuclear power led utilities to build some of the most expensive plants instead of the cheapest.
- Utility forecasts for power demand during the 1970s expected demand to increase, whereas per capita demand fell instead of increasing. As already noted, California avoided problems of over-construction of plants through a timely review of the methodology for demand projection.
- Prices for power paid to qualified facilities and independent producers under PURPA were appropriately linked to oil and gas prices, and projections of these prices were for rising prices and limited availability. Instead, prices fell and gas supplies were abundant during most of the 1980–1990s. Most of these contracts ended up being priced way too high because they were based on faulty price assumptions with no correction mechanism.
- Restructuring proponents assumed that spot-market prices would remain low and that they would provide the foundation for lowering prices following deregulation. Instead they became unstable.

In this chapter, complexity theory in public policy is discussed in order to offer a theoretical perspective on the information availability, influence, and problems for practical interpretation that affect the management of large technical systems. Then some examples as how these misinterpretations, miscalculations, and manipulation have plagued the electrical power system in California and elsewhere are discussed. In conclusion, suggestions are given for managing large complex technical systems under conditions of uncertainty and intense public interest stake in avoiding crises.

6.2. Complexity and Large Technical Systems: Theoretical Perspectives

The electrical energy system in most states and nations is one of the modern society's most technologically sophisticated systems because of the size and scale of generation technologies and the challenge of managing the grid where delivery of power must just balance generation with demand as electricity cannot be stored. From a theoretical perspective, the literature draws upon large technical systems such as airlines, steel production, automobile assembly, health care, or military operations with networks of organizations that combine to produce a product or service. While the term "large" is relative, the literature on large technical systems has focused on the interplay of technology and organization in order to provide services (LaPorte, 1991; Summerton, 1994). The interesting quality of large technical systems is that sophisticated technologies place extra-ordinary demands on the many components of the industry, including questions of reliability, communication, coordination, rapid change, and organizational flexibility. The literature in this field, over several decades, has documented the challenges of maintaining successful large technological systems, and how these organizations have managed to function in spite of the many challenges they face (Hughes, 1983).

Electrical systems are perhaps the most challenging of the large technical systems because they are grid systems that must operate within the constraints of electrical flow. However, electricity shares many characteristics with other network systems such as telephone, gas, district heating, the internet, railroads, water, and sewers in that transactions flow through physical networks of pipes, wires, or rails, and these connections are essential to the delivery of the good or service being provided. Summerton and Bradshaw (1991: 25) identify five characteristics of grid systems:

- *Long construction lead times* are needed to build the grid, both to plan and acquire right-of-way for unbroken system flows and long time to physically construct a system that covers large geographical areas.
- *Grid systems are capital intensive.* High fixed costs of investment in the network must be recovered over time and much of the investment has to be done to connect large numbers of suppliers and consumers before the system is particularly useful and marketable. Expansion of the system must be planned in advance, with changes often affecting parts of the system far from

where the change is introduced. In addition, because of these size issues, expansion usually must be done in chunks, providing excess capacity in some areas while other areas face limited capacity.

- *Grid systems are tightly coupled, both technologically and organizationally.* Changes in standards in one part of the system must be applied to most or all parts of the system, and failures in one part will have ramifications throughout the system. Redundancy and alternatives are necessary to keep tightly coupled systems from failing.
- *Monopoly* is especially attractive for grid systems because of capital intensive and tightly linked character of the network. While it is common for some overlap, grid systems make the case that they should have no or limited competition in order to justify the cost of installing the network.
- *Grid systems are public* systems, in societal function and accountability, if not legally public (e.g., public ownership). Grid systems, because of their broad connectivity and because they become essential to the communities they serve, have a public responsibility and interest that goes beyond simple industrial responsibility. Thus, grid systems have typically been regulated to assure both price and reliability.

Thus, the electrical system as a grid system is more complex than most large technical systems because its operation is constrained by the grid itself, and this limits options. On the other hand, it provides a certain amount of stability and guaranteed market within the system. Deregulation reduced this stability by limiting the monopoly to just the operation of the wires while letting inputs and outputs be decentralized, more like highway networks provide the pavement but have virtually no control over what goes onto or off the system.

Thus, a grid-based large technical system poses unique challenges in two areas. First, the management of the system requires technological and organizational arrangements that provide for the capital, reliability, and profitability of the system. These are the short-term operational issues that need to be met daily for the system to succeed. The second challenge is for long-term planning, strategy, and change. Given the size of the system and its grid character, operation based on proven techniques and protocols is easiest when following tested and proven protocols.

However attractive it would be for systems to remain static, technological change pressures the electrical system to innovate and change. Part of the pressure comes from its public quality and its need to be socially accountable. Some pressure to change comes internally from the awareness of the long lead time and capital intensivity of its operations.

Complexity theory provides assistance in understanding these pressures. While there are many competing definitions of complexity, Casti (1994), Waldorp (1992), and others suggest that complex systems have these defining components.

1. Complex systems are not easily described. They have many parts, complicated groupings of parts, interrelated linkages, and long lead times.
2. Complex systems are characterized by nonlinear effects. Small inputs lead to large consequences and vice versa. Catastrophe points are when big changes occur. This is the equivalent to the notion of increasing returns in economics, counter to the entropy principle in physics.
3. Complex systems are not decomposable. The system is not only greater than the sum of its parts, its individual parts are essential. To describe the system all must be included, and it would behave differently if something was missing.
4. Complex systems are compounded by feedback loops.

What do these complexity characteristics mean for energy systems? First, it means that energy systems are very hard to describe and the parts are often not fully understood. With complex systems our uncertainty about the system often exceeds what is known, and there are surprises because of parts that decision makers fail to understand. For example:

1. Energy systems have many parts, complex groupings of parts, interrelations, and long lead times. This is characteristic of most grid systems, but with deregulation the scope of the system expanded exponentially, with increasing ambiguity over who was responsible. Prior to deregulation, vertically integrated utilities gradually developed systems that balanced and gained experience managing all the different parts of their grid, but after deregulation new entities such as the PX and CISO were created to manage a system that they did not create.
2. Small differences in initial conditions lead to huge differences in outcomes, such as price spikes and system crashes. The relatively small shortages in power during the crisis of 5–10% led to price spikes of 100 or more times the precrisis price of power.

3. The interconnectedness of the whole energy system includes not only the grid but also the whole chain from source of power to waste. The complex interrelations between the price of natural gas and some of the initial increases in power prices illustrates the way electricity is embedded in a large and rapidly changing system where everything is related to everything else.
4. Feedback loops and responsiveness to changes led to the outcomes that are distant from the initial impact. For example, the feedback and responsiveness of the system permitted gaming of the system. The more we learn about the strategies used by Enron and other market manipulators to game the system, the more we understand that they worked not so much by conspiracy planned in advance, as by the fact that they had system information that allowed them immediate awareness that they could individually make small changes in behavior such as withholding some power that would benefit them individually as well as benefit others who were doing the same thing.

In sum, complexity theory helps us understand that policy makers often do not know how to manage the system and those in charge make mistakes, and that with such a complex system as the energy system one should expect that uncertainties will outweigh exact planning and predictability.

6.3. Knowledge Gaps and Management Problems

It is not hard to find gaps in knowledge and misinterpretations of complex sets of facts in the power crisis. Indeed, what is surprising is the success of the system overall in spite of the lack of ability to plan and manage the system. In this section, several major types of knowledge gaps are identified which lead to problems managing the electrical system.

6.3.1. Policy and planning problems

Of course the major knowledge gap in the California energy crisis was knowing the impact of the overall deregulatory steps taken. It is often claimed that the deregulation did not go far enough (Brennan, fall 2001: 64). Other economists have claimed that the policy failed because it went half way, using the image of jumping across a canyon. Clearly in this image half way is worse than doing nothing at all. This critique usually is applied to the fact that the wholesale market was deregulated while the retail market was under frozen prices that allowed utilities to recover stranded costs, but not to pass on rising retail prices. However, Brennan argues that these causes and solutions to the California crisis are not as simple as some say. Given the complexity of the electrical power market, any "flash-cut" deregulation that the critics propose with even more deregulation would have been even worse. Instead of jumping across the canyon, the sensible strategy is to build a bridge carefully and securely. In a complex policy and technical environment such as electricity the prudent approach is not to jump into the unknown.

Policy confusion created rapid escalation or problems as consumers tried to figure out what policy options were available and what they could do about them. For example, during the heat of the crisis the CPUC and CAISO prepared a set of new demand response programs to limit load during the summer of 2001 because their previous programs had been largely exhausted during the winter crisis period including January—firms contracted to voluntarily reduce their load had caps on the number of hours a year they would be asked to do so, and these hours had largely been used. In order to prevent problems during the summer of 2001, a series of new programs were designed usually offering incentives for reduction of demand on a day-ahead basis. These programs are shown in Table 6.1.

While the intent of the programs was to offer customers more choice among more flexible programs, Goldman *et al.* report that in practice this objective was diverted because

> customers got confused by the number of choices and frustrated by the ongoing changes to program design that occurred during and prior to summer 2001. For example, the CPUC initially approved a demand bidding program for summer 2001, the Voluntary Demand Response (DR) Program, but later cancelled this program and replaced it with the Demand Bidding Program which didn't become operational until July. As a result of confusion among customers, some utility DR programs fell short of their participation goals. (Goldman et al.: 11)

What this example shows is that there was policy confusion, and in the process of seeking to design a more effective program, confusion undermined the ultimate goal of the program. In 2001 the total demand reduction programs provided about 1900 MW load reduction, though in 2000 the simpler programs provided an additional 850 MW. Fortunately, the other programs in the State and better generator availability meant that the programs were called on only once during the summer to provide relief, and even then the total needed was only 800 MW, far from the maximum.

At a larger scale, the response to the energy crisis has been ad hoc largely because there is no clear consensus on what the problem was and

Table 6.1. Summary of California 2001 demand response programs.

Program name	Program administrator[a]	Description	Operational trigger	Incentive amount
Interruptible Rates and Base Interruptible Program	IOU	Participants commit to reduce to Firm Service Level (FSL) upon notification	Contingency	~$7000/MW-month
Direct Load Control (A/C Cycling and Agricultural Pumping)	SCE	Customer agrees to allow utility to interrupt air conditioning or agricultural and pumping loads	Contingency	$0.014–0.40/ton-day
Optional Binding Mandatory Curtailment (OBMC)	IOU	Participants commit to curtail at least 15% of the circuit load during every rotating outage	Contingency	–
Demand Bidding (DBP)	IOU	Participants bid load reductions day-ahead, through DBP Website	Market	$100–$750/MWh
Scheduled Load Reduction (SLRP)	IOU	Participants provide weekly load reductions in 4-h blocks on specific days	Prescheduled	$100/kWh
Rotating Blackout Reduction Program (RBRP)	SDG&E	Participants run Backup Generators during all rolling outages	Contingency	$200/MWh
Demand Relief Program (DRP)	CAISO	Participants provide a pre-specified load reduction upon notification by CAISO	Contingency	$20,000/MW-month and $500/MWh
Discretionary Load Curtailment Program (DCLP)	CAISO	Participants offer voluntary load reductions in response to requests by CAISO	Contingency	$350/MWh

[a]IOU, Investor-owned Utilities; CAISO, California Independent System Operator.
Source: Table #4 (Goldman *et al.*, 2002: 11).

how to try to solve it. When the PX stopped being able to purchase power the state turned it over to the Department of Water and Power, and then the state signed a large number of long-term contracts. None of these programs were based on a long-term strategy to bring health again to the electricity sector but were short-term responses to crisis. There were simply no previous models of response because no State had gotten into a similar mess. In addition, there was no time to figure out a solution analytically, developing the data and testing alternative solutions. Political values substituted for rationality.

To build or not to build?

The lack of a clear picture of the future leads to uncertainty in investment that is needed for a properly functioning electricity system. In November 2001 the newspaper headlines read, "Power glut may doom new plants: State says 31 proposed generators probably will not be needed." (Martin, 2001). This article came just months after the State survived the summer of 2001 without blackouts by massive conservation efforts.

The message went out that failure to construct power plants was largely responsible for the problem and that the State needed more generation capacity. Investors came forward with 3200 MW of natural gas-fired power plants, stimulated in part by the California Power Authority which could assist in funding through $5 billion in revenue bonds. However, the State countered the market manipulation of the existing producers with conservation and long-term contracts, and all of a sudden we had a glut. Rapid swings in capacity are expected when the complexity of the system exceeds policy ability to manage it.

Uncertain markets

This uncertainty manifests itself in another way. In a scathing analysis, Peter Asmus looks at the loss of leadership by California in the wind industry. Following the energy crisis, one would assume that new wind projects would make a lot of sense because wind is the cheapest source of new power. However, in the industry installing and manufacturing wind machines, the view is that the State is not viable. Asmus quotes some industry leaders:

> *California has become one of the most difficult power markets to develop wind projects from a financial point of view because of a lack of regulatory stability. Who is in charge? (Steve Ponder, FPL Energy)*

While business is inherently uncertain, business leaders try as hard as possible to reduce that uncertainty and to manage risks. This is essential for obtaining funding and for all types of planning.

6.3.2. Doing business in California is very, very complicated

Standards and procedures for purchasing
California still does not have any standard power purchasing contracts on the table. At present there is no government guidance on power purchases, with suppliers favoring plants that burn natural gas plants. This is setting the State up for future spikes in price when gas prices go up again. In addition the power market in California is complicated by the fact that there is no stable buyer that potential wind developers believe will pay for new wind power (Robert Gates, GE Wind Turbine). Another developer noted that the restructuring of California's electricity market created a new environment in which to do business in California. But this new environment created a number of barriers for developers to gain access to the electricity markets. "What we need today are power purchase agreements either with the State or with utilities so that we can finance long-term contracts and bring the price down." (Ed Maddox, personal discussion, SeaWest, Spring 2001).

These stories are not about one failed policy, nor are they just about political leadership. The market for power is complex and rapidly changing, but any solution needs to include some stability and certainty that new power supplies will have a market at a predictable price. For example, a quick infusion of wind projects does not require invention of whole new institutional structures to enable contracts to be fairly negotiated. While the State does not want to repeat offering overpriced PURPA contracts, investors in new capacity require some assurance that over the long term they will receive fair prices and access to markets in which to sell their power before investing in building new capacity in the State.

Duplicative programs and confusing responsibility
Finally, the programs dealing with energy in California have escalated as policy makers tried to solve real problems and make political capital by sponsoring legislation that does something. The problem is that the programs proliferated. A table of conservation programs listed over 80 programs or subprograms dealing with conservation and load reduction. The list expanded during the crisis to target funds to different groups. While 80 conservation programs is an accomplishment to be

proud of, it is also evidence of a lack of focus and policy confusion. Integration of programs could have a greater impact.

In addition, the energy crisis and deregulation recast the major regulatory bodies. As pointed out in Chapter 1, the creation of the California Energy Commission produced an effective tension between itself and the California Public Utilities Commission, where each had their area of responsibility, but the two commissions had a redundancy that led to error detection and conflicting innovation (Landau, 1969). However, the Energy Commission seemed to lose some of its functions and purpose as deregulation progressed. Many of the areas in which it excelled in the early 1990s were no longer needed or downplayed as deregulation was being debated and implemented, such as resource identification for renewable power. On the other hand, the transition from regulated utilities to competition placed the CPUC in a stronger leadership role and their relevance increased. The tension largely dissipated during this period.

Moreover, the State's response was not to further consolidate organizations in state government, but to create entirely new ones. The PX and CAISO are the most important prior to implementing deregulation, but later the Power Authority and a variety of minor organizations were created. The lines of authority among these organizations were often blurry and fluid, and critics have often mentioned that the State had confusing authority channels.

6.3.3. Information problems

Information and misinformation

While policy indecision and flux can create impossible conditions for the development of effective power systems, many times the reason policy making is difficult is that the information on which to make decisions is known to be so fluid and contingent that no reasonable person would rely on it. The response is no better than our understanding of the information on which we need to act. In many ways this is the dynamic that characterized California during most of the post-blackout period—what was known about the energy system was changing so rapidly that effective policy was nearly impossible. It is amazing that any positive results came out of the crisis, and these results are mainly documented in the second half of this book.

The fundamental imbalance

During the crisis it was widely believed that the power shortage was a "fundamental imbalance between the steadily growing demand for power and the limited increases in generation and transmission capacity during the 1990s" (Faruqui *et al.*, fall 2001). This imbalance was widely quoted and believed, and it seemed very plausible, because if there were more supply or less demand the lights would not be going out. However, in reality the supply situation had increased somewhat, plants were about to come on-line, and demand was essentially flat considering that the population had been growing rapidly and the economy was booming during this period. The shortage was indeed exacerbated by drought conditions in the Northwest which reduced imports from that sector, but these were long-term suppliers whose summer sales usually were surplus hydro and base load sold to California on a regular basis.

It was easy in the complexity of the crisis to state the obvious that there was a supply shortage, but it is hard to understand why. First, growth did exceed forecast rates of growth, but not by much. For example, from 1995 to 2000 according to the *1996 Electricity Report* (CEC 1996), total demand was estimated to increase to 11.7% but actual growth was 14.5%, an underestimation of 2.8%. While this underestimation is a problem, over a five-year period this amount of growth is much lower than the amount of reserve that is reasonable for a state energy system—typically reserves are 12–15% of total. The energy crisis was not a result of unanticipated growth in consumption, though consumption was a bit higher than expected.

Moreover, there is a lot of long-term uncertainty in the demand forecasts. While deregulation removed the forecasts from being important policy setting documents, they started out that way. It is interesting that the forecast 2000 demand declined from 1988 through 1996 forecasts which were produced as part of the Bi-annual Electricity Report cycles shown in Table 6.2. Total demand forecasts

Table 6.2. Energy commission forecast of peak demand for the year 2000.

Commission electricity report cycle (year)	Year 2000 peak demand forecast (MW)	Actual peak consumption
ER 88	56,673	
ER 90	58,873	
ER 92	58,684	
ER 94	55,819	
ER 96	55,422	1996 = 51,561
1998		1998 = 53,914
2000		2000 = 53,257 (actual use = 51,547 plus 1710 voluntary curtailments)

Source: California Energy Commission (2000).
www.energy.ca.gov/electricity/commission_demand_forecast.html.

actually decreased from 56,673 MW in 1988 to 55,422 MW in 1996, a decline of over 1200 MW forecasted 2000 demand, equal to two very large 600 MW power plants. In addition, one should note that the actual peak consumption also fell from 1998 to 2000 by about 1300 MW. (Data for 1999, not in the table, are 53,335 MW, nearly the same precrisis level as during 2000 during the crisis.) It is interesting to also note that voluntary curtailment programs contributed 1700 MW of demand reduction in 2000 that did not have to be met by new construction.

The data also show that California generation actually increased during the 1995–2000 period. Total generation increased by 2500 MW from 1997 to 1998, and by another 1000 MW between 1999 and 2000. Thus, the claim that California added no additional capacity was also wrong. Interestingly, the flow of applications for generation construction slowed to near zero during 1995 and 1996 during the planning for deregulation and then the applications for additional generation capacity increased to the highest level in two decades (see Fig. 6.1, from Sweeney).

Problems in calculations

So much of the dynamics of the restructuring in California has turned on the need for calculations of cost, demand, and other factors essential for the operation of a power system. Many of the problems of the California power system are the direct result of faulty

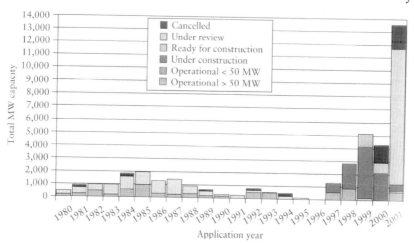

Fig. 6.1. Current status of new generating plants, applications since 1980.
Source: Sweeney (2002: 24).

calculations which were deemed the best possible at the time. Although debated and contested on both methodological and results basis, the problem with many of the policy-embedded calculations that formed the basis for the energy crisis is that the calculations were needed to enable projects to be funded, plans to be made, contracts to be signed, and power to flow. The conundrum faced by policy makers is that they need to have firm estimates for a future that is necessarily fluid and uncertain.

The most well-known miscalculation was in the price of avoided cost contracts under PURPA. The contracts for most renewable and alternative source power were based on high estimates of oil and natural gas in the 1980s, which led to overly generous prices paid for power compared to the price actually appropriate for conventionally powered electricity. For example, some renewable contracts were paying as much as 12 cents per kWh while regular power was dropping to 4–5 cents, and less on the spot market.

Another example of the problem of calculations shaping policy was the difficulty of establishing the value of "stranded investments." These were the power plants and contracts that were no longer economically viable. Sweeney (2002: 24) notes that, in addition, calculations of the magnitude of stranded costs by necessity include many subjective elements. No one could predict with any confidence future sales prices over time of wholesale electricity or future natural gas prices. Thus, issues of how to calculate stranded costs and how to reduce the need to calculate stranded costs also remained important. Once the crisis occurred, the theme returned.

In the policy process analysts often note the need to avoid calculating fixed prices and to remain flexible to the changes that are anticipated based on unknown and subjective factors. However, tools by which policies can remain flexible are limited. One of the attractive features of relying on spot-market prices, as the State did, is that they are perceived to be self-correcting and self-regulating. One does not have to calculate the expected fall in power prices when relying on the spot market because as power becomes available in greater quantity at lower price the cost will fall due to market forces. However, the opposite also happens, and prices rose.

6.3.4. Market signals

A continuing theme by economists since the energy crisis started has been the call for "real-time metering" and effective "time of day pricing." The economists argue that in order for a competitive market to work effectively, consumers should pay the real price for electricity at the time they use it. Not only would pricing-peak power higher than off-peak power better match revenues to costs for the utilities, the differential pricing would provide an incentive for consumers to switch their demand away from high-cost periods when there is high demand for available supplies. The current system in California has time of day pricing for large industrial customers, and following the energy crisis the time of day meters and pricing contracts have been extended to other users in California. However, the California power system still averages the cost of power for most users.

Knowing the differential price of power and communicating it to users is often seen as one of the most effective ways to make competition more effective. Faruqui *et al.* (2001: 48) estimate that the installation of real-time pricing (RTP) meters in industrial and commercial establishments would reduce peak demands by 2.5% resulting in a 24% reduction in wholesale prices during times of shortage. Their estimate is that RTP metering would reduce peak demand by at least 1000 MW. In addition, many other economists feel that the logic of RTP is essential to the competitive market.

The advantage of RTP is that it links price of power for the consumer with the price paid to generate it. Faruqui *et al.* (2001: 62) conclude that

> *by adopting RTP or other market based pricing programs, California would offer consumers considerable incentive to make more efficient use of electricity. That would enable the state and its residents to take fuller advantage of the benefits, and avoid the difficulties, of electricity market restructuring.*

This is a reasonable solution to the problem of the complexity of the power supply side which has, even in normal California markets, vastly different prices for power between hot summer afternoons at peak and mild winter late nights when demand falls to its lowest levels. However, it is not reasonable to suggest that RTP and metering for all businesses and residential customers will be a substantial long-term solution to balancing supply and demand. If industrial RTP meters can reduce peak demand by 2.5%, this is cost effective and should be done.

The attention given by economists to time of day pricing suggests that there are additional benefits because it would help send price signals to competitive suppliers to provide more capacity at peak. This suggests that there are greater benefits by extending the metering and pricing beyond the large industrial consumers. However, new pricing systems increase the complexity of billing and utility operations. It also increases the complexity of the information and decisions that consumers make. Will consumers buy appliances that delay operation until prices are lower? Are time of day pricing programs cost-effective demand side programs compared to other incentives such as better-insulated houses to cut air conditioning? These are questions for which there are only limited answers.

6.3.5. Uncertainty and risk management

Declining investment

A major source of uncertainty in the California system came from the National Energy Policy Act of 1992 which allowed states to start the process of deregulation and opened up wholesale power markets. During this period power companies and investors were appropriately cautious about investing in new generation capacity when they did not know the conditions under which the power they generated would be marketed (see Faruqui *et al.*, fall 2001: 59).

This sense of uncertainty increased when the PUC wrote the "blue book" suggesting that California might be one of the first states to deregulate and that the utilities would largely divest themselves of generation capacity. It only makes sense that existing power supply investors would cancel investments and that they would wait to see what changes in the market would be forced on them. Others took the role of trying to influence the changes but the most active companies in this were not investors but were power brokers. Many critics of California feel that it was irresponsible not to continue investments, but due to the regulatory uncertainty, partly from the Federal government, slower investment was a rational strategy. The problem was that during the change period, the state did not recognize the role of uncertainty to the investors, and something should have been done about it.

Another major risk factor in California that led to problems was the growing uncertainty about the availability and price of natural gas. While this tended to be minimized when utilities could pass through to consumers a fuel cost adjustment, but with prices fixed after deregulation this tool was minimized. Obviously in retrospect, this caused some of the problems (Fig. 6.2).

The weather is always unpredictable and drought conditions that limit hydroelectric power are a continuing source of uncertainty. California periodically experiences severe drought conditions that limit water for farming and urban uses, and also power generation. The real problem in California came during 2000 when drought conditions in the Northwest coupled with rising natural gas prices.

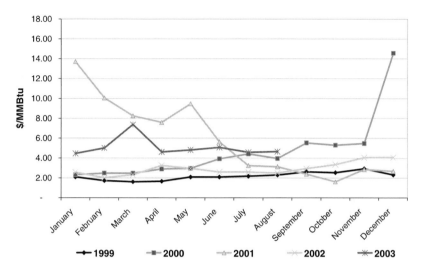

Fig. 6.2. Monthly average natural gas prices—Northern California.
Source: California Energy Commission.

Another unavoidable uncertainty is mechanical failure and taking generating capacity off-line. The goal is for utilities to do preventive maintenance during periods of low demand so that all units have the highest chance of operating during peak demand. However, once reliability issues for generation were not the responsibility of regulated utilities but of merchant generators, scheduling was based on their own agendas not on assuring that the whole system was operating with adequate capacity.

In addition, taking capacity off-line during times of demand to exercise market power clearly could benefit companies manipulating markets. The extent to which plants went off-line during the crisis shows that the maintenance during the summer which in 1999 was around 1000 MW, in 2000 it increased to 11,000 MW in May and between 6000 and 4000 from June through August (Sweeney, 2002: 158).

6.3.6. Complexity of definition of the problem

The political leadership in Sacramento defined the problem wrong as well. Republican Governor Wilson (1991–1999, and the democratically controlled Legislature) defined the problem as being a regulated utility problem. The reason rates in California were so high was perceived to be the fact that the utilities in California were not efficient and that the regulators had inadequate capacity to enforce greater efficiency. The reality of the problem in retrospect was not so clear.

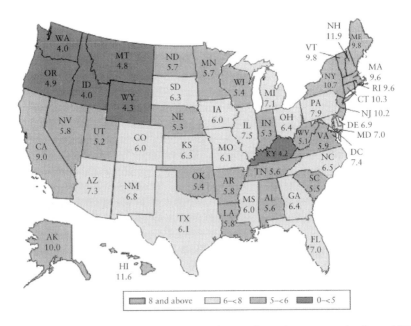

Fig. 6.3. Average revenue from electricity sales to all retail consumers by State, 1998 (cents per kilowatt-hour). US average = 6.7 cents per kilowatt-hour.
Source: Energy Information Administration, US Department of Energy.

First, the high power rates in California were indeed high as shown in Fig. 6.3.

However, the problem is not really as simple as that comparison. The most important alternative set of data show that in spite of higher price per kWh, the average cost to consumers for power in California was lower than in most of all other states. This can be attributed to several factors. First, the conservation programs in the State, as well as larger number and higher percentage of new buildings and businesses because of recent population growth, led to much lower needs per person. As Faruqui *et al.* (2001: 34–35) report, California had been the US leader in demand side programs. With rigorous codes and standards as well as incentive programs, the State had reduced the electricity load by about 10,000 MW, equivalent to 20 medium size power plants. This permitted much less investment in new capacity and fewer opportunities to spread high costs (of nuclear for example) across larger loads, resulting in higher unit costs. Second, the State has more temperate weather than many other states because of its location near the Pacific Ocean, and thus the electricity demands for heating and air conditioning are lower along the coast than in other states. While the State faces very high peak cooling needs in Southern California and the

Central Valley, the reality is that these are not as high as in other states and the heat is not humid like in most of the US Southern and Midwestern states. Third, the economy of the State of California is more knowledge and service based rather than manufacturing or other energy intensive industries. While this is true in broad categories of industry, it is also true that because of the high technology and rapid growth of industry in California, the industries in the State tend to have much higher productivity per unit of energy than other states. Finally, California electricity generation has to meet extremely high standards for air pollution controls, which rises prices for electricity as it does for most other activities in the State. In total, electricity may cost more in California, but industry and residential consumers in California are less energy intensive, and this translates into lower total costs even though the cost per kWh is higher (Fig. 6.4).

Thus, the initial definition of the problem was wrong. Instead of focusing on unit costs, regulators, politicians, and businesses, California should have compared their total costs for electricity to the total costs of electricity paid by their competition in other states. On this basis California had an advantage and the solution should have been to do more of what led to that advantage rather than trying to find a way to get the per kWh costs down. The widespread discussion of the relative per-capita costs of electricity in California would have immediately diverted some of the anxiety over kWh prices and led to a less frantic search for deregulation.

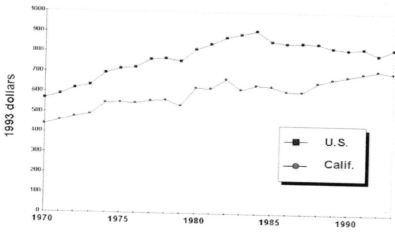

Fig. 6.4. Comparison of California and US system average anual residential electicity bills: 1970 to 1993.
Source: CEC; 1994 Electricity Report.

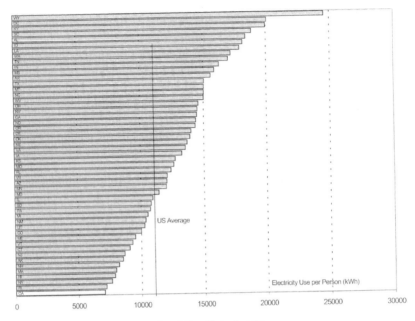

Fig. 6.5. California is the most electricity-efficient state.
Source: CEC 2002–2012 Electricity Outlook Report, p. II-1-8.

The inadequate definition of the problem was also seen during the peak of the energy crisis. Governor Davis, to his credit, was one of the first leaders to define the problem as one of market manipulation by outside power brokers. Since the first shortages and spiking prices in 2000, most editorials and initial analyses pointed to a shortage of generating power as the source of the problem. There is little doubt that the State was slow in adding capacity as shown in Chapter 3. However, the willingness to believe that it was the lack of capacity to generate power rather than a manipulation of the market seems silly in retrospect.

The poor definition of the problem during the crisis led to some wrong decisions that allowed market manipulation and the inadequate financial capacity of the utilities to continue disorienting the market. At the time of the crisis and afterward, the under-analyzed reason for the blackouts was purported to be increased demand and shortage of generating capacity. For example, Sioshansi (2001: 739) stated that "before one can solve a problem, one must define it." His definition was the following three causes:

- High energy prices due to a serious supply and demand imbalance in both generation and transmission that had been festering for years.

- Unusual price volatility due to the absence of incentives to hedge the risks and offer fixed prices.
- Lack of appropriate incentives for demand to respond to variable prices.

Sioshansi and other economists did not distinguish short-term shortages that drove up prices from the long-term supply shortages. On the assumption that most of the problem were long-term supply shortages, the solution is to build more supply and transmission lines. However, the State had some capacity under construction and the shortage was not as large as many thought. There is no question that the supply picture was tight during the summer of 2000, coupled with shortages of imported power from the Northwest due to limited hydro power because of exceptionally light winter rain and snow. The bulk of the blackouts, however, did not occur during the summer but during the late winter and spring 2001, when California has its greatest excess capacity since summer air conditioning, is not needed and virtually no power is used for winter heating. The generators claimed (falsely) that their power plants were not available because of scheduled maintenance or unscheduled mechanical failures. What this means is that the definition of the problem as a supply problem reinforced the belief that more generators needed to be built and not that plants were being artificially withheld from service to drive up prices.

Finally, with the use of long-term contracts the critics of California's failed policy are suggesting that the competitive model be significantly dampened because short-term competition is too volatile. If competition has this serious problem one needs to ask if the problem is not with the competitive model rather than the failure to create ways to buffer consumers from its inherent volatility. Another aspect of the definition of the problem that the demand needs to be more responsive to high prices supports the solution of installation of time of day meters (see below).

However, the Governor and other leaders during the crisis were reluctant to change the cap on retail prices as a short-term solution. The Governor emphatically said that he was determined not to increase retail rates to consumers. This sense that the problem could be solved without having the consumer pay for it persisted through the early part of the energy crisis, and it had several implications. First, it postponed the successful implementation of the conservation programs that eventually stopped the market manipulations. Since the problem was not costing the consumers anything, the majority of the public attention was on blackout schedules and the rules for rotating blackouts, rather than on widespread participation by the public in both reducing demand and increasing supply. The political decision to hold rates was widely popular at the time, though in retrospect the several increases that were eventually added to the price customers paid is credited with helping to encourage conservation during the summer of 2001.

The lack of revenue to the utilities led to another cascading problem that was identified later than it should have been. In a recent paper, James Bushnell (2003) argues that the evolution of the crisis resulted from the early hits that the utilities took from spiking prices that made power more expensive to supply than the revenue received under the retail price cap, and this led to utility credit problems that eventually drove many independent suppliers to stop providing power because there was little chance they would get paid. Bushnell (2003: 7) shows the complexity of the situation:

> The crisis, if defined more broadly to include both economic upheaval as well as physical supply shortages, was caused by a lack of competition that was exacerbated by inconsistent Federal and State regulatory policies. In short, the lack of competition led to high prices when the market got tight. The inflexibility of regulators led to the insolvency of the utilities, which in turn led to the blackouts. Accusations of "withholding" during the blackout periods are probably overstated, but also besides the point. It was the market power exercised earlier, during the summer of 2000, that produced the financial conditions that led to the supply crisis.

While this issue of paying suppliers was well known and eventually led to the state using its credit through the Department of Water and Power to arrange for the purchase of power, the fact that the utilities became financially limited led to a further reduction of supply to the state at the time it needed the most. This allowed more market manipulation and the prices of power to rise to the benefit of the large out-of-state aggregators without their additional market manipulation.

Thus, once the crisis got into blackouts and skyrocketing prices, the initial mechanisms that started it were supported by this new condition of financial crisis that complemented the market gaming strategies of the large power brokers. The fact that both processes were operating made it harder to identify what was causing the crisis at the time and still is making it hard for legal staff to prosecute those who made the greatest gains from the crisis.

6.4. Unanticipated Events that Should have been Expected

The problem in California at one level is that many of the situations that led to a crisis were not anticipated. However, we argue that the policy change proponents should not have been so optimistic that their changes would overcome the complexity of the system they were trying to reform, but that they should have adopted the Murphy's Law theme, that if anything can go wrong, it will. In short with a realistic look at some of the simple issues, policy makers should have expected some problems.

6.4.1. *California's significant reliance on natural gas*

California imports 23% of its electricity and 83% of its natural gas. Because natural gas-fired generation dominates California's electricity mix, increased prices for natural gas get directly translated to higher electricity prices. End-use gas demand peaks in winter and is lowest in summer, which is the opposite of the seasonal pattern of gas demand used for electricity generation. This creates a double peak for natural gas, with the summer peak coming when gas is traditionally being pumped into storage. In short, the State is too dependent on natural gas as its primary source for energy.

The CEC Integrated Energy Policy Report (December 2003) argues that the significant increase in natural gas demand warrants an increase in natural gas supply. Specifically, the increase forecasted demands require the importation of liquified natural gas. As the CEC Executive Summary (2003: 3) puts it:

> *California's unique location at the end of the West Coast natural gas pipeline network makes it particularly vulnerable to supply disruptions and price volatility. Adding a liquefied natural gas (LNG) terminal on the West Coast will help reduce the state's vulnerability by adding another source of natural gas.*

Under State law, the California Energy Commission (Bowen, SB 1389) in 2002, must develop an Integrated Energy Policy Report. As part of this mandate, the CEC has the "responsibility for developing energy policies for California that conserve resources, protect the environment, ensure energy reliability, enhance the State's economy, and protect public health and safety. Public Resource Code section 25301(a)" (2003: 5). If the Governor of California takes no action in regard to the Report, it becomes law at the end of December 2003. If the recommendations become law, the LNG initiative will be dangerous for the future of the State in both environmental and economic contexts since the costs for building LNG facilities are estimated in the billions of dollars. Additional transmission, transportation, and pipeline costs along with projected limitations in natural gas supplies worldwide place LNG in the middle of international security and terrorist threats.

The electricity crisis was stimulated by spikes in the price of natural gas, which could not be passed on to consumers of electricity because of the deregulation format. In 1999, gas prices rose from a normal $2 per MMBtu in January to $4.50 in May and $10 in December in Louisiana. Because of a pipeline fire in New Mexico, prices rose even faster in California, reaching $50 per MMBtu in late fall. This 25-fold increase in the price of gas helped set up the shortages and financial crisis that eventually caused blackouts. The small event of a pipeline fire and rising demand for gas ended up with much more significant consequences. The policy system was not robust enough to deal with the extent of this externally forced impact on the system.

As natural gas demands grow and storage capacity remains limited, natural gas markets become more volatile that result in higher prices in both the natural gas and electricity markets. This was exactly one of the key elements in the scenario that caused the California Energy Crisis (2000–2001). One strategy for California to gain more control over the price of electricity is to invest more heavily in renewable generation technologies which diversifies the State's energy generation portfolio.

California's energy system is also constrained by the delivery systems for natural gas. Recent new natural gas pipeline projects have reduced pipeline capacity constraints to California. But there will never be enough. According to industry interests and the analyses of the California Energy Commission, it is inevitable that LNG is the only viable solution (see Table 6.3). For electricity, these regional limits on gas used for power generation mean that generation in areas with ample gas cannot always supply other parts of the State. Insufficient transmission capacity may also limit delivery of potential renewable and cogeneration options.

While the deliverability issue has decreased, the increasing cost of natural gas continues to be a concern even in the near term. Finally,

Table 6.3. Companies actively seeking permits for LNG in Calif.

Project (update July 2002)	Location	Capacity (MMcfd)	Projected on-line date
Baja California, Mexico			
EL Paso & Phillips Co.	Rosarito	600	(on hold)
Marathon Oil Co.	Tijuana	750	2005
Shell Group	Ensenada	1300	2006
Sempra/CMS	Ensenada	800	2006
Sound energy solutions	Long Beach Harbor	750	∼2007
Crystal energy, small Ventures, *et al.*	Offshore near Oxnard	550	2006

Source: California Energy Commission.

industry estimates of future natural gas supply range from only 20 to 30 years. Some countries like Norway, the world's second largest exporter of oil and natural gas see only a 20-year supply and are already making plans for a post-oil and gas society. The simple conventional energy fuel supply solution for natural gas supply, that is to increase both exploration and drilling along with investment in facilities for importing and transportation of the natural gas, are absolutely wrong, let alone the environmental impacts to the ports, pipelines, and roadways.

Meeting California's electricity and heating needs

Meeting peak demands for electricity and natural gas, and creating reliable, affordable, and environmentally acceptable energy systems, requires measure and public policies well beyond supply and demand side conventional answers.

On the supply side, the challenge is to install additional capacity (emphasizing renewable generation, while moderating the costs for new natural gas-fired electricity generation, gas supplies, gas storage, gas pipelines, and electricity transmission) sufficient to meet expected peaks. On the demand side, the challenge is to implement strategies that give residential and business customers the tools, appliances, education, and incentives to manage their annual and peak energy demands, through the support of cost-effective energy efficiency investments by all electricity consumers.

Transportation fuels

Nonetheless, demand for transportation fuels is steadily increasing. The CEC projects that the number of vehicles on our roads will reach over 33 million in California by 2023, up from about 24.4 million in 2002. Meanwhile, vehicle miles traveled will increase from 313 billion miles in 2002 to over 440 billion in 2023.

This increasing demand for petroleum fuels presents two serious supply challenges. First, California's production of petroleum has been declining by about 2% a year and increasingly California must rely upon imports (53% in 2002). In addition, the State's crude oil refining capacity and marine terminal infrastructure are becoming insufficient to handle our growing need for imports.

6.4.2. Complex systems need complex analysis

The conventional complex system approach to energy—that is, increased demand means simply increased supply of fuels—is not only economically flawed but also violates public policy set in California. Elsewhere, a discussion on the Integrated Resource Management tools for energy systems is explored that demonstrates how it is flawed as a standard engineering set of mechanisms for designing and implementing power systems. Without getting into volumes of details, however, about the dependence upon natural gas as the "base load" fuel for complex power systems, the issues can be basically outlined as follows.

The most critical point is that the dependence on one fuel supply is both a dangerous public policy and bad economics. As noted earlier, California depends on over 55% of its fuel supply on natural gas by the beginning of 2003. CEC analyses and projections estimate that the need for natural gas will rise substantially (ranging from 20 to 25% depending on the scenarios) due to increased demand. The demand is led not only by the increased number of power plants built in the State for power peaking during the Energy Crisis but also from other sectors including transportation that now uses increasing levels of natural gas and certainly the introduction of hydrogen production from reforming natural gas for both energy power in buildings and as a transportation fuel.

The second point is that the then Governor Davis declared (Davis, 2001) that California seeks "energy independence." The only way to achieve that goal is from a diversified energy portfolio of supply. Increased dependency on one fuel source, such as natural gas, violates that goal. While during the Energy Crisis, natural gas power peakers were needed to control for market-manipulated storages of natural gas, the objectives now need to be to diversify those supplies. Hence, the Governor's Renewable Portfolio Standard for renewable energy supplies must be sought.

The initial costs for these renewable energy sources might be higher than natural gas, but when historical costs are compared (e.g., the introduction of natural gas 20 years ago to solar systems today), there is parity. Moreover, the costs for wind are competitive today with natural gas and solar systems appearing, according to some leading industry sources, to be on a parity by 2004 or 2005. The "intermittent" nature of wind and solar have been addressed as well, both in terms of public policy (see CAISO Rules, January 2002 and later FERC Tariffs, March 2002) along with technical advancements and reduced costs on new, often "hybrid" systems for energy storage (see Chapters 12 and 13).

In short, increasing the use of natural gas, its transportation, storage, and delivery are all fundamentally wrong in both economic and public policy. Diversified fuel and energy supplies are needed from sources more available and under local (regional or state) control and oversight. Complex systems for power, otherwise, can easily be manipulated.

6.4.3. Collapse of the PX: the end of a "market mechanism"

One of the first casualties of the shortage of supply and the escalating prices during 2000 was the California Power Exchange, a recent invention of deregulation policy to purchase power on the open market on behalf of the utilities, and to set a blended price for the power. Generators were to make bids to the PX for the amount of power they would sell and the price by hour for the day ahead. The PX looks at the bids, and chooses suppliers based on availability and price, but also location of the supply relative to forecast demand.

One of the common features of commodity exchanges is that the marginal or clearing price is the price paid to all lower bidders. There were several flaws in the system that allowed strategic action on the part of the generators. For example, they could bid most of their power at a reasonable price and bid the remainder at much higher prices. If the market cleared at the lower price, they did not loose much, but if demand increased to the higher price they got the higher price for all their power.

The PX purchased power on behalf of the utilities and billed them for it. However, as the prices paid by the utilities for power exceeded what was being billed to customers by the utilities, they proved unable to pay their suppliers. This catastrophic condition led suppliers to withhold power unless they could be guaranteed payment, which of course the PX became unable to do. As the financial condition of the PX deteriorated, it became unable to continue since it had no other resources to secure funding.

As prices escalated during the crisis, the PX needed more assistance to assure that power continued flowing. The State stepped in through the State Resources' Agency, Department of Water Resources to purchase power for the state utilities, using the State's overall financial security and credit as backing. This allowed power to continue to be supplied, but it also left the PX with no role so it was disbanded in late January 2001. The Department of Water Resources had expertise and capacity in dealing with power because it is itself a large generator and consumer of power to provide the irrigation water for state farms.

The PX seemed like a good "market" idea at the time it was invented. It was modeled after other power pool arrangements in

Britain and elsewhere, and its advantage was that it provided an impartial auction for power when there were multiple suppliers selling to a variety of end users who needed some flexible power.

Relying on short-term rather than long-term contracts

This is a serious problem in the California deregulation. It should have been expected that suppliers would be very reluctant to get into long-term investments without long-term contracts for the power produced, especially in an uncertain market.

Withholding capacity to generate

The state CPUC (September 2002) conducted an investigation into the availability of power to satisfy the shortages on days when blackouts occurred. The conclusion to this study was that the generators did not supply all available power when they could have prevented some or all of the blackouts. This study is limited in many ways, including that they used data provided by the generators to the California ISO and these data were not verified. It also relied only on data provided by the five largest generator companies supplying the state grid at the time: AES-Williams, Mirant, Reliant, Dynergy, and Duke.

The CPUC concluded that "on most of the 32 days of statewide blackouts or service interruptions between November 2000 and May 2001 the five generators had sufficient available unused capacity to prevent or substantially alleviate these blackouts and service interruptions." (p. 21). The excess capacity calculated by the CPUC report was power that was not bid into the system and that was not removed by any known explanation, though the generators have criticized the report by saying that their reports were misunderstood. The price spikes that resulted from withholding this power were more than enough to repay any one of the companies, and they did not have to operate in collusion in order for shortages to occur.

For example, during the blackouts of May 8, 9, and 10, 2001, Duke alone had enough available and unused power to meet the needs of the nonfirm customers those days, a total of between 574 and 974 MW, depending on the hour. On other days Duke had between 200 and 400 MW unused power, which alone would have reduced or substantially alleviated service interruptions (Fig. 6.6).

Dynergy had nearly 1000 MW available on November 13, 2000, the first day of blackouts. Dynergy alone could have supplied half

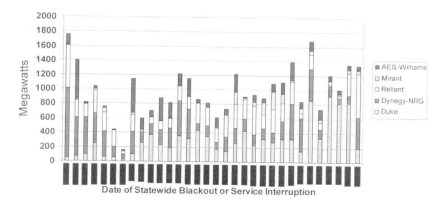

Fig. 6.6. Average of power available, but not supplied, during blackout and service interruption hours.
Source: CPUC Report on wholesale generation... (September 2002: 2).

the gap that day. On 11 other days Dynergy had enough available power to significantly alleviate blackouts. Mirant had small amounts of available capacity most days, but on March 28, 2001 they could have avoided blackouts to nonfirm customers. Reliant, similarly contributed 600 MW of unbid capacity on November 13 that combined with Dynergy to account for most of that day's gap. Reliant could have avoided blackouts with its excess capacity on 15 days. Williams had over 500 MW out on November 14, the second day of the blackouts that combined with almost the same from Dynergy to create blackouts that day.

The key to large parts of the blackout experience was that the generators had capacity but did not bid it into the power pool, and by withholding a share of their capacity they could drive prices up leading to greater profits than if they had fully participated in the market. Other system problems accounted for capacity that was not used. For example, as prices spiked independent producers and renewable resource firms such as biomasss stopped producing because payments were not guaranteed and their contracts did not cover fuel costs. However, increasing evidence supports the conclusion that withholding capacity, rather than the lack of construction of new generation plants, was the cause of the blackouts.

6.4.4. Abandonment of conservation

Modern energy conservation programs grew out of public response to shortages caused by the OPEC Oil Embargo in the early '70s. The Oil

Embargo of 1973 and OPEC control of the petroleum market brought about long lines at the gas pump and eventually abrupt rises in electricity prices. These price rises in the mid-1970s jolted and angered consumers who had grown used to low-energy bills and decades of falling electricity prices. The Public Utilities Commission (PUC) ordered California's investor-owned utilities to offer energy efficiency programs in the late '70s that could reduce customer high-electric bills and assure adequate power supplies.

Early utility efficiency programs offered consumers suggestions such as turning off the lights in unoccupied rooms or turning down the thermostat in winter and putting on a sweater. Quickly, however, the programs focused on longer-term solutions such as adding insulation and weatherization based on professional energy consumption audits and improving commercial and industrial efficiencies. One of the first efforts in the mid-1970s by the California Energy Commission (CEC) was to develop comprehensive energy codes for new commercial and residential buildings, as well as programs to promote design and sales of more efficient household appliances such as refrigerators and air conditioners. These standards led the nation, and they paved the way for similar standards to be adopted by other states.

In the early '80s energy conservation programs evolved into more comprehensive demand side management programs. The term demand side management was coined by the Electric Power Research Institute in 1983 to describe a broad range of programmatic efforts by utilities to shape total customer demand to better match system-generating requirements and system costs. In California, three different types of demand side management programs have been implemented by state agencies and the utilities. They include:

- Energy-efficiency programs
- Building standards
- Appliance standards

The historical contribution of these three programs is to save an estimated 35,000 GWh per year and over 10,000 MW peak demand, or about 20% of the states current 55,000 MW peak demand (see Fig. 6.7, *source*: Hewlett Foundation). The various programs each contributed to the 10,000 MW savings. The largest share was conservation and energy-efficiency programs, followed by building standards (see Fig. 6.7). Appliance standards also contributed, though less. The savings amount to about 20 large 500 MW power plants and they have significantly reduced pollution and carbon dioxide in the

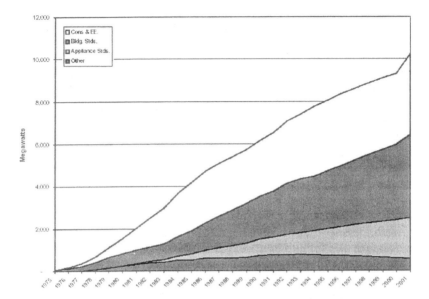

Fig. 6.7. Peak demand impacts of energy-efficiency programs and standards.
Source: California Energy Commission (February 2002), p. 5.

atmosphere. Data show that these programs have helped California to be more energy efficient than the rest of the nation.

While the demand side management programs were important, California would be somewhat more energy efficient even without the utility incentives. For example, the state economy is more knowledge intensive and service oriented than other industrial economies, and proximity to the ocean helps keep summer cooling demands lower than in other inland states. However, the conservation programs have encouraged business and residential customers to invest in more energy conservation than most other states which show up in the aggregate efficiency statistics.

As demand side management concepts and programs grew in popularity, statewide utility spending grew from $100 million a year in 1980 to $230 million in 1984. However, the fall of oil and gas prices in 1985 triggered a downturn in program funding. In 1989, total demand side management funding dipped below $100 million a year.

In the early '90s a group of government, utility, and public interest groups met to discuss ways to rekindle utility interest in demand side management and to encourage utility management to promote energy efficient programs. The group was called the California Collaborative. They came up with the notion of paying utilities for every kilowatt hour saved. This led to action by the PUC which authorized the utilities to collect ratepayer funds to buy what was now called conservation resources. As a result, the utilities found energy efficiency programs profitable and initiated massive energy efficiency programs statewide. The funding for those programs rose to $350 million a year in 1994.

During the mid-90s with the uncertainty that developed around utility restructuring, investment in conservation fell once again, but public mandates retained the program around $200 million.

In February 1997, the PUC, directed by Assembly Bill 1890, issued Decision 97-02-014 to create new structure to implement public purpose energy efficiency under a restructured utility industry. PUC stated that its goal for energy-efficiency programs had changed from trying to influence utility decision makers to trying to improve the functioning of the market so that individual customers and suppliers would make informed energy service choices.

One of the hallmarks of the restructuring process was to formalize and increase public funding of conservation and demand side efforts under the broad umbrella of public goods programs. These are administered by the PUC based on a surcharge on all customers. They fund programs now estimated at $273 million. Another component of the publicly funded effort is the Public Interest Energy Research (PIER) program. This effort annually awards $62 million to conduct research on energy issues.

It is interesting to note that several municipal utilities developed extensive conservation programs during this period. SMUD used conservation and distributed generation efforts successfully to compensate for the closure of their Rancho Seco nuclear plant. The key to this effort was the conceptualization of a "conservation power plant" which resulted in 372 MW peak demand reduction, or 40% of the closed Rancho Seco plant (Smeloff and Asmus, 1997: 54).

The lack of awareness of the pending shortage of power in California in the late 1990s coupled with the cuts in conservation set-up conditions that aggravated the energy crisis. From 1995 to 2000 peak first year power savings averaged about 200 MW per year, half of the peak first year savings of 400 MW in 1994 before deregulation started. If the program had continued at the 400 MW level, an additional 1000 MW would have been saved in the five years leading up to the start of the energy crisis, possibly enough to have reduced the supply–demand gap enough to have avoided most of the blackouts entirely. While the State has been criticized for not building enough power plants to respond to the growth in population and the economy, it would have been easier and more cost effective to have continued the proven conservation programs as an effective way to better utilize available supply until new power plants came on-line.

6.5. The Enron Case: A Study in Market Forces at Work

All the facts in the Enron bankruptcy will not be known for many years due to extensive legal and accounting litigation that surrounds this case. As we write in late 2003, a third top official in Enron has just been convicted of wrongdoing. The fall of Enron brought with it the huge Anderson accounting firm that certified many of the fraudulent schemes. Based on public information, however, a picture has unfolded about Enron that symbolizes the problems with deregulation and privatization. While the Economist (various articles in 2002) and Fortune, January 16, 2002, focus only on the accounting errors of Andersen, the basic fact remains that Enron executives instructed and managed Andersen's activities. In other words, the collapse of Enron is not only an accounting firm gone wrong, but also the core issue of unfettered free market economics in the energy sector.

Enron is (was) a merchant energy company that represented the myth of neoclassical economics at its best: a "market force" (e.g., private firm) unencumbered in its business activities due to its competition in the market. What became apparent later was that competition meant influencing political decisions, taking a strong role and hence having an impact in forming the deregulated market, manipulating prices (due to supply), and finally directing the spurious accounting of its cash funds.

As a point of departure for the Enron case, consider an outline prepared by the staff for the Governor of California (Staff, 02) as they prepared to address the impact of the Enron bankruptcy on the State. Many of the points, later that became public, are outlined in this internal overview including the market manipulation by some energy companies, illegal trades, and federal regulatory compliance. For a good overview of the Enron case, consult McGraw Hill PowerWeb (2002).

6.5.1. Lessons must be learnt from America's largest corporate bankruptcy

"The end was not unexpected, but it was still spectacular. On December 2nd Enron, once America's seventh-biggest company, filed for Chapter 11

bankruptcy. Only days earlier, its bonds had been downgraded to junk and Dynergy, a smaller energy-trading rival, had pulled out of a planned takeover. Enron is the largest company ever to go bankrupt. Disentangling the resultant mess (and lawsuits) will keep legions of lawyers employed for years to come." (Economist, December 6, 2001)

The monetary impact in California in terms of long-term contracts was relatively low. For example, about $84 million in contracts was obligated by the University of California system alone. Nevertheless, the prices paid for the supply of energy to the State were controlled by "market" companies or "merchant firms" like Enron so that about $9 billion in additional costs for energy were paid by the State to ensure power in the winter of 2000–2001 (see Fig. 6.8).

In 2000 and the first half of 2001, Enron, among other market force suppliers, reaped enormous profits from California's deregulated energy market. Governor Davis stated in a letter to the FERC Chairman, "Since the summer of 2000, I have on numerous occasions demanded that the FERC investigate allegations of market manipulation by power generators and marketers, including Enron. In my testimony before the FERC on November 9, 2000, I urged the FERC to investigate and remedy California's dysfunctional electricity market. Last June I called upon the FERC to investigate and refund the detailed overpayment by California consumers and businesses." (Davis, January 31, 2002).

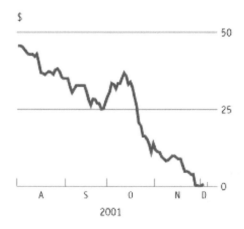

Fig. 6.8. Enron share price.
Source: Economist, December 6, 2001.

FERC did finally take action in the late spring of 2001 as Governor Davis acknowledged in a Press Release and noted the actions taken by the State and its citizens to curb the immediate energy crisis: "I appreciate the action taken by you and your fellow FERC commissioners to finally reinstate price caps last June. Your action, combined with California's successful conservation efforts, our construction of 11 new power plants, and long-term contracts, caused energy prices to decline." (January 31, 2002).

Subsequent reports and studies have verified the State of California's analysis of how a far more devastating energy crisis was averted over the summer of 2001 with these and other policies (California Energy Commission, February 2002). While acknowledging the role of more rain in the winter of 2001 (hence supplying more water for hydroelectric power), the fact was that the summer of 2001 was one of the 25 hottest in California history.

The California government programs and citizens conserved over 12% throughout the summer of 2001. And the market suppliers were forced to keep prices reasonable through price caps at the State from the California Public Utility Commission (CPUC) and Federal (FERC) levels. Long-term contracts further assured a constant supply of power, rather than relying upon market manipulation in the spot market.

Yet public records confirm that on April 17, 2001, for example, then Enron-CEO Kenneth Lay made eight recommendations to Vice-President Cheney regarding federal energy policy. One of those recommendations was continued opposition to price caps. A memo containing those recommendations was released in the week,

Table 6.4. Power profits—megawatts, mega profits.

Company	Headquarter	No. of large plants in CA	Megawatts	2000 Profits (in millions)	Profits increase— since 1999 (%)
AES Corp	Arlington, VA	3	4076	$641	+181
Duke Energy	Charlotte, NC	2	2092	$1178	+18
Dynergy/NRG	Houston, TX	4	3208	$452	+210
Mirant (Southern)	Atlanta, GA	2	2702	$366	+36
Reliant	Houston, TX	4	3474	$838	+65
Total		15	15,552	$3475	+510

Source: Sacramento Bee (California Energy Commission), April 2001.

March 20, 2002. On April 18, 2001—the very next day—Vice-President Cheney told the *Los Angeles Times* that the White House emphatically opposed price caps.

When the White House released the final report of its energy task force, seven of Enron's eight recommendations had been fully adopted by the report. But this was not unusual. Further documentation reveals that Enron staff and senior officers as well as members of its Board had tried to influence the White House during the Clinton administration and systematically pursued its self-interests in states like California who were considering deregulation. As Kuttner (March 25, 2002) notes "Perhaps the most damaging effect of all is the eclipse of an opposition politics. Embrace of deregulation by 'pro-business' Democrats is more than a mistaken philosophical conversion."

The White House's energy policy, as enforced by the FERC, particularly its opposition to price caps, helped to sustain the outrageous prices of the wholesale energy market. "This prolonged California's energy crisis and continued the massive transfer of wealth from our state to out-of-state energy companies such as Enron." (Staff, 02).

As of mid-2002, it is still unclear how much direct influence Enron had over the White House. What is clear, however, is that the White House's energy policy was nearly a mirror image of Enron's energy policy. It is also clear that that policy was detrimental to California and the wholesale energy market throughout the West. If Enron was able to use its market power and public influence to unfairly manipulate the California energy market, then FERC must take action (Staff, 02). Here is a checklist (Kuttner, 2002) of the several icons that collapsed with the fall of Enron:

A pension double standard. *Enron's retirement plan was heavily invested in its own stock. Executives cashed out over a billion dollars, while ordinary employees were locked in. Janice Farmer, who retired with $700,000 in Enron, told a Senate hearing last week that she is left with a $63 monthly Social Security check.*

Bogus accounting. *Since the Great Depression, the one form of regulation that even Wall Street has supported is the regulation of stock trades and corporate accounting . . . (when) once asked an ultra-Chicago economist if there was any regulatory agency that he endorsed. "The SEC," he said instantly, explaining that capitalism itself depends on honest information. Enron's entire game was to make its business plan so complex that neither investors nor regulators nor even its own auditors could penetrate it. While its core energy business made money (at the expense of consumers), it had speculative* *off-the-books subsidiaries. These borrowed heavily to make risky investments and eventually took the whole company down.*

The business press. *Enron's breathless cheerleaders included not only its own insiders and stock touts but also a business press that pronounced it the epitome of the new economy. It surely was that—epitomizing all the smoke and mirrors. In the wake of its collapse, Enron's former sycophants have turned on it, with Forbes and Fortune running scathing denunciations. BusinessWeek asked giddy Enron boosters what they thought now. (Gary Hamel, chairman of Strategos, before the collapse: "Enron isn't in the business of eking the last penny out of a dying business but of continuously creating radical new business concepts with huge upside." After: "Do I feel like an idiot? No, but if I misread this company in some way, I was one of a hell of a lot of people.") Well, yes.*

Deregulation generally. *Enron's collapse impeaches the conceit that a market economy can be efficiently self-policing. Enron fleeced consumers by manipulating prices of electricity and gas; it fleeced investors and its own employees. Tycoons do this because they can. Enron should signal a whole new era of re-regulation—of everything from electricity to pensions to accounting standards. And it is another warning that Social Security pensioners cannot trust Wall Street.*

Nevertheless, the Economist (December 6, 2001) and economists in general continue the same theme today as it did when the Enron bankruptcy began: The company's opaque accounting makes it hard even now to understand why it got into trouble, and whether the cause was bad luck or worse. The close links between Enron's chairman, Kenneth Lay, and George Bush will keep the affair in the political limelight. And Enron's staff, whose retirement fund was, at the company's urging, mostly invested in Enron shares that they, unlike the company's bosses, were then unable to sell, deserve public sympathy. But if America's capital markets are to stay the cynosure of the world, some quick lessons need to be drawn.

The bottom line to the neoclassical economic community whose unflagging support of market power contends that "proper" deregulation or privatization will sort out the Enrons and other companies. Some will survive and others will disappear. Business as usual is the economic creed. Or as the Economist concludes one article "In the drama of capitalism, bankruptcy plays an essential part—until the next boom." (Economist, December 6, 2001). However, in the Enron case, the culprit is the accounting firm that ventured from its traditional and honorable function in the audits to the consulting role now seen in all accountancy firms. As the Economist wrongly puts it

> *The most important concern is auditing. Enron has restated its profits for the past five years, chopping $600m off its earlier numbers. The company's auditor was Andersen, now a target of many lawsuits. Last year Enron paid Andersen a fat audit fee of $25m; it also paid the firm $27m for consulting services. (Economist, December 6, 2001)*

However there are many regulatory issues, according to the Economist.

> *There is a risk of turning any bankruptcy into an excuse for massive new regulation. Some have argued that energy is too important to be left to markets of the sort that Enron pioneered; or that, since it was engaged in financial speculation, Enron should have been regulated like a bank. Neither conclusion is justified. Energy deregulation has brought huge benefits in lower prices and more secure supplies: energy trading will continue to grow regardless of Enron's collapse. Nor would it be wise to subject all companies with financial arms to stifling bank regulation. Enron's energy exchange was, however, explicitly exempted from oversight by financial regulators: that should be changed. (Economist, December 6, 2001)*

The Enron scandal shows that America can no longer take the pre-eminence of its accounting for granted, that is, a far bigger concern than any number of congressional investigations (Economist, January 19, 2002). Again the same issue of the Economist (January 19, 2002), as well as Fortune (January 16, 2002), other international business journals, and most economists worldwide come to same conclusion: Enron was a case of bad accounting (or at least mixing accounting and consulting) rather than a mistake to deregulate public good markets like energy. The culprit here is the mythology of neoclassic economics that fosters and encourages market forces to manipulate.

6.6. Conclusion

It is no wonder that the public policy for the electricity industry has problems given the complexity of the electrical power system and the number of issues that affect it. The power industry is indebted to the public since it is so capital intensive and its product cannot be conveniently stored. In the process of deregulating the electricity industry in California, the State envisioned changing the foundation of a publicly regulated industry that had been operating quite well for many years. The industry faced a number of significant new challenges due to technological change and the availability of many independent power producers both in the State and out of state. The massive changes introduced into the California system were catastrophic because they were not simple and they led to unanticipated and unprecedented conclusions, based entirely on false assumptions about the market. While some analysts recognized the danger of the scale of changes proposed in California, and while in retrospect almost everyone should have been more cautious, no one person or group is in a position to point fingers at others.

The system complexity is not a cause of the failure in California, because everyone knew that the system was complex. What caused the failure was that the solution drove the problem. The myth of competition was the solution to a very complex problem that was not fully discussed, analyzed, and considered independent of the proposed solution. A simple solution required a complex implementation, and the complex policy that resulted worsened the problem rather than fix it.

Complex problems can be addressed by effective policy, but the more complex the problem the more attention needs to be given to finding agile solutions where the benefits outweigh the costs. J. A. Casazza (2001: 42) proposes that the costs and benefits be assessed:

> *The entire restructuring process failed to investigate the costs and benefits resulting from the policies being adopted. Unlike our environmental procedures, an impact statement was not required from those proposing major changes in how electricity was to be produced, distributed, bought, sold, and priced.*

The California crisis suggests that the failure to understand the complex economic and technical character of the electrical system has potentially catastrophic consequences. The fact that the California policy failed was not an accident, but was largely predetermined. When public policy is made over vital societal infrastructure sectors through political compromise, the end result will be failed mechanism for implementation. This is especially true when the political basis for decision making rests with economic theory rather than business realities.

Chapter 7
Economic Development and the Energy Challenge

7.1. Introduction

The complex cascade of economic effects of the energy crisis throughout California and the world has major consequences for firms and communities. Thus, the energy crisis is not just about electricity, but it is about national, state, and local economies. On the one hand, blackouts and high prices have cost firms business and profits, leading some firms to leave the state or close for good. In addition, the overall economic shock of the electricity crisis is at least $40 billion, and this is one of the leading factors responsible for the State's economic downturn starting in 2001 as well as subsequent Recall of Governor Davis in October 2003. Furthermore, there is also a human side to the crisis. In California alone, there are over 500,000 ill people dependent upon electricity to operate their respirators, breathing, and dialysis devices. They need—in fact their lives depend upon—reliable electricity.

On the other hand, changes in the energy system resulting from the energy crises appear to have positive economic benefits. For example, energy conservation and energy-efficient investments over a relatively short time period have large cost–benefit paybacks and end up making firms more competitive. Advanced technologies, generation, and clean energy investments have created new jobs and businesses as well as help reduce environmental degradation including reducing greenhouse gases leading to climate change. Regions and communities embracing alternative technologies are at the cutting edge of sustainable development and are more economically active in smart growth as well as physically more attractive. California has already experienced some of these "positive" economic outcomes as a result from its energy crisis. More sustainable business development is anticipated and clearly expanding rapidly.

From a local economic development perspective, electricity supply and price has become increasingly central to state, regional, and community "smart" growth. As noted in Chapter 1, large energy users pressured state and federal regulators to provide lower-priced power in California, which helped to open the power grid and reduce industrial rates. However, during the energy crisis large users were called upon to play a very important role in stemming and preventing further blackouts. For example, large energy users have the potential to save or conserve enough (overall and especially at peak times) to be targets by regulators for load reduction. Consequently many have shifted to time-of-use or "net" metering, so their power costs are reduced when they shift load to off-peak times.

Most energy users of any size must have highly reliable power because of their sensitive manufacturing, data processing needs, or general electronic computational needs. In fact, California's "new economy" from the "dot.com" era was predicated and assumed to have consistent price and reliable electricity. Many consumers, both businesses and residents, therefore, have had to install "on-site" backup systems so that their activities will not be interrupted by system failures. Hence, the demand for reliable backup power generation has stimulated the demand for stationary fuel cells, microturbines, and other advanced technologies. These more "localized" or "on-site" forms of energy generation are known as "distributed generation" (Isherwood *et al.*, 2000; Clark and Isherwood, 2004).

All these changes in the power supply and demand systems have direct implications for economic development. In this chapter, regional, state, and local efforts are considered in order to assure that changes in the electricity system will have positive impacts on the growth of jobs and well-being, including business attraction, retention, expansion, and creation (Blakely and Bradshaw, 2002). From an economic development perspective, issues of cost and reliability are dual issues that link energy with economic well-being. Furthermore, the rapid development of new energy and environmental technologies can be enhanced through government incentives, investments, and partnerships in industries seeking to create the products needed to solve the long-term energy crisis.

Electricity is a large sector of any economy. The reason the energy crisis severely impacts any nation-state, such as California, is that electricity is on an economic par with total revenues generated from other major sectors such as automobile sales, higher education, and telecommunications (Brennan *et al.*, 1996). Total sales of electricity in California were

1990 $22.6 billion
1994 $22.8 billion
1999 $19.8 billion

Of this total, residential electrical sales account for about 35–40%, commercial is 40% and industrial 20%. In all the talk about megawatts and generating capacity, it is important not to forget that electricity is an industry, and it is a large industry that accounts for a significant piece of the state economy, which in 1998 had total sales of $290 billion. This makes electricity about 7% of the California's retail economy, and utilities paid millions of dollars in state and local taxes. The fact that revenue fell in 1999 is due to the rate reduction as part of deregulation enacted in 1996.

In this chapter we first look at the way the energy crisis changed the relation between electric utilities and business, noting that utilities used to be very interested in economic development, but that deregulation has broken the mutual partnership between the power sector and economic development. Fragmentation of the utility–business partnership takes many forms and we outline these from an economic development perspective.

In the second half of the chapter we look at the economic development consequences of the energy crisis, tracing the impact that an estimated $40 billion loss due to the crisis has had on the regional economy(s), the bankruptcy of the State's largest utility—PG&E, the financial risk and insolvency of other utilities and the long-term reliability, cost, environmental, and business climate impacts. In conclusion, we suggest that an "agile energy system" will strengthen business partnerships using new technologies, creating new local economic opportunities.

7.2. Economic Development and Energy: Changing Perspectives

Energy consumption used to be a primary indicator of a nation's level of economic development. High levels of total energy use helped define societies as developed while low-energy societies were underdeveloped. The process of becoming developed has been assumed to require expansion of the per-capita use of energy. Energy consumption is seen as a measure of economic capacity almost as an end in itself, though of course it simply is the means to an end.

The correlation between gross national product per capita and electricity use per capita is very strong across nations (O'Toole, 1976).

A study by Ferguson *et al.* (2000) showed that energy and economy were particularly strongly correlated across the range of countries, but it did not hold among the very poorest countries. Among OECD countries from 1971 to 1995 the correlation between electricity use per capita and gross domestic product (GDP) was 0.998. These figures demonstrate the very strong relation between electricity use and growing economies, though it is not clear which causal direction is demonstrated—whether more electricity availability and use causes economic vitality or if economic vitality allows societies to afford more electricity. Clearly electricity goes hand-in-hand with any economy.

Advanced industrial societies, however, break this pattern. For example, the authors of this study note that in the "OECD post-industrial economies," improvements in energy efficiency and intensity uncoupled the relationship and these countries have lower correlations than less-developed countries. For example, in the ranking of 110 countries by their 1971–1995 electricity and GDP correlations, the United States correlation 0.984 is exceeded by 24 other countries. Other studies over the last 25 years or more have shown the same transformation where information economies and efficiency lead to lower energy and electricity use per dollar of economic output. (O'Toole (1976) suggested this but did not have data to substantiate it.)

The relation of energy and economic development is extremely complex as portrayed by an outstanding study by Sam Schurr and his colleagues (1990). The conclusion of their study is that in the United States electrification has progressed hand-in-hand with new techno-logical processes that not only increases electricity's share of total energy use in the economy, but in addition electrification leads to total savings in energy consumed, even accounting for the primary energy needed to generate electricity (Clark *et al.*, 2003b). The electricity-rich technologies also lead to greater productivity by workers. In short, this conclusion is replicated in developed countries around the world such that more electrification leads to less total energy use per unit of output. Two recent reports on technology diffusion confirm this hypothesis.

Price of electricity is relevant to the economic development of countries, according to Schurr *et al.* (1990: 12–13). The argument is that electricity is not just another substitutable form of raw energy, but the use and availability of electricity is coupled with productivity enhancing technologies. To the extent that electricity has a lower price, it stimulates technological development, productivity increases, and a wider dispersed geographical location of industries.

Development at the advanced industrial level brings with it the potential to have higher levels of well-being with lower amounts of energy consumed. The energy–economy relation has turned out to be a curve with energy use increasing with well-being among under-developed countries. Energy peaks in those countries in the middle range of development, while falling among the countries with advanced technology, where production comes increasingly from applications that use less energy.

In part, this phenomenon is a substitution of knowledge and efficiency for wasteful energy uses. Furthermore, it reflects a societal shift from agriculture and manufacturing to the service industries which are much less energy consuming and do not depend on large amounts of energy for output. Electricity is particularly essential in the service industries where its use in computers and communications equipment is comparatively low but where highly reliable service is essential (Bradshaw, 1976).

7.2.1. Economic development has new relation to electrical energy

As the California economy developed, electricity was taken for granted, but over the last decade of transition to deregulation that assurance no longer holds. The simplistic perspective on the relation-ship between energy and the economy is that ample power and low prices are good for the economy. Hence, anything a locality can do to assure that it has cheap power, the better. However, economic development is not so simple and straightforward. Some of the key changes and challenges that result from such simple economic theories are as follows.

Utilities reduced efforts to stimulate demand for power

The large integrated utilities had an interest in selling more power under their traditional structure. Thus, utilities have long been partners in economic development efforts because they know that an increase in the economic prosperity of their region will lead to stronger sales. Even under regulation, growth is over the long run a favored outcome for utilities, and they see it in their best interest to assist local officials seeking to attract, retain, or assist with expansion or creation of firms in their area. Most of the leadership in economic development at the local level is done through economic development corporations which are usually nonprofit organizations with extensive community representation on their board.

Alternatively (or in addition), cities or counties will have economic development departments or agencies that provide very similar services that are part of the government, and they provide linkages between policy makers and the business community. In some communities business interests are represented through chambers of commerce which conduct economic development efforts within their community on behalf of their business members.

These economic development organizations or corporations work closely with and are funded in part by the business community, local governments, state programs, federal block grants, and other sources. Their activities include marketing the community, providing assistance to businesses wanting to expand, raising money, planning, recruiting, and hosting firms looking to site plants or offices in an area, and holding informational conferences and meetings (Blakely and Bradshaw, 2002).

An increasing emphasis of the programs is on what is called "third wave" activities, supplementing business attraction and assistance with programs that help create the local business climate in which firms can be competitive and grow. The number and scale of economic development organizations is huge, with at least 300 in California alone. Cities feel that they need these organizations to compete, and utilities are strong supporters.

Utilities across the country have been enthusiastic participants in local economic development efforts. For example, both Pacific Gas & Electric (PG&E) and Southern California Edison (SCE) in California have members on the boards of the state economic development organization, the California Association for Local Economic Development (CALED), and they contribute strongly to many local organizations. However, SCE is the only utility in the State approved by the CPUC for economic development activities. This is due in large part to SCE understanding the need to assist their customers (businesses of all sizes) and retain them within their jurisdiction. This is not true for other utilities in California. In other states such as Missouri, Georgia, among others, local utilities have very large and active economic development programs. They will market and advertise on behalf of the jurisdictions in their service area in order to promote energy conservation and efficiency.

Utilities also are called on to offer price incentives to key firms with the assumption that strategically awarded discounts would be made up by general growth in the region. Thus, utilities may give a large-price discount to a new factory seeking a location with the assumption that its increased sales to residential and commercial customers will make it worthwhile. In addition, the factory may stimulate the attraction or expansion of other firms. Utilities have also been active in promoting civic events, donating considerable money to community activities to show good will.

These roles in economic development are weakening as the utility structure is dismantled under deregulation. For example, as utilities end their vertically integrated role and purchase more power that they do not generate, they have fewer earnings with which to engage in civic activities. In addition, many utilities shifted some of their investment to separate power generation companies that sell on the open market, independent of any community to whom civic investment would be noticed.

Certainly multistate power generators and merchants have little local commitment outside of the community in which their head-quarters are located. Enron might have been a good citizen in Houston, but there was little reason for it to invest in the Fresno Economic Development Corporation. Sadly, within the State, firms like PG&E stopped playing a role in their local economy as the amount of power sold within the region no longer made any difference—just how much of that was sold by them.

Electricity problems have made the State the target for business attraction by out-of-state economic development offices

As soon as the blackouts occurred in California, Michigan and other states started advertising that they had lower electricity rates and more reliable service. Since the east coast grid collapsed in August 2003, which plunged many states and over 50 million people into several days of blackouts, the California crisis does not appear as bad. More significantly, the California multilevel state and regional response to its energy crisis now appears to be a "road map" for the entire eastern USA and perhaps the nation as well as Europe and other parts of the world.

Yet in 2001, according to an article in the Los Angeles Times (Dickerson, 2001), some of the economic development schemes were highly creative to lure companies out of California. For example, economic development officials in Tennessee sent 3000 flashlights to targeted California businesses, claiming that the lights were always on in Tennessee. In addition, the out-of-state business hunters met with local companies, offering executive trips to Tennessee and a lavish cocktail reception. The same article reported that a UC Irvine story found that 44% of Orange county executives had received an out-of-state energy-related solicitation.

It is not clear how effective these business recruitment efforts are, but it is clear that energy has become a key factor. However, in September 2003, the LA Business Journal, contrary to popular belief and "urban myth" reported that "the numbers refute the popular notion that companies are leaving California, and LA in particular." Almost 500 companies worth a combined $38.6 billion have been brought in and moved tens of thousands or workers in the Southern California region alone (Kate Berry, 2003: 1). California businesses have been targets for many years which is in large part because the economy is so huge with many active, innovative, and growing firms. What seems to be increasingly clear, however, is that the energy crisis has complicated the State's efforts to sustain its image. Nonetheless, and despite the demise of the "dot.com" economic bubble in Northern California, the State continues to attract businesses and employees. However, in mid-2003, the State legislature eliminated the entire Technology, Trade, and Commerce.

Utilities are no longer interested in participating in the energy services market, including conservation assistance

One of the significant trends in utility management has been the on–off emphasis on utilities providing a bundle of power services, not just bulk electricity. The earliest electric companies did not try to sell electricity, instead they sold lighting in the tradition of Thomas Edison. Customers paid by the light bulb, not a measured amount of power. Today, progressive companies have taken an interest in providing a range of services such as conservation, demand side management, and investment in clean and dispersed technologies. To the extent that these programs can reduce total power costs for consumers, they are a benefit to local economic development.

However, with competition and deregulation, these economic incentives were lost. The goal of utilities is to compete to provide the most power to customers, not to help the customer buy less power. Customers want these conservation and environmental benefits spread over all rate payers, not concentrated in one company with higher rates. While conservation programs and other public goods or energy-efficiency programs are good for economic competitiveness of firms, in the emerging utility structure the old utilities no longer provide these services.

The municipalization debate is engaged by many communities

Public anger over deregulation brought up issues of municipalization across the State (Bradshaw *et al.*, 2003). While most countries are embroiled in battles to privatize or liberalize public utilities, the opposite battle is significant in the United States. Deregulation has given added incentives to the debate in California. The rising prices of power and public outrage over the energy crisis has led many communities to look into the prospect of buying their power system from the private utility and running it on their own. Historically in California these efforts have been going on for many years, pitting community power advocates against well-financed private utilities that do not want to lose their business.   •

Public power advocates have a number of financial incentives that make their proposals more attractive. First, public utilities pay no taxes on their earnings and no property tax on their holdings. As a unit of local government the public utility operates as a nonprofit corporation and is exempted from most tax obligations. In fact, however, public utilities usually contribute funds to the community and schools in lieu of taxes at about the rate of local property tax.

Second, public utilities can use public bond authority to borrow money from lenders who do not have to pay state (and usually federal) income tax on the interest they receive. This means that lenders are willing to lend at a lower rate since earnings are tax free, and public utilities can borrow money at a few percentage points lower than private utilities. Third, public utilities do not pay dividends to stock holders. Private utilities pay dividends instead of interest to investors, and utility stocks have been attractive investments because regulators can assure a constant return on investment when setting rates. On the other hand, dividends are paid instead of interest, so the difference is smaller than some public power advocates wish the public to believe.

Finally, public power companies have access to cheap federal hydro-electric power that does not go to private companies. The cheap hydro power available to municipal utilities has given them an historic price advantage, although the hydro power constitutes only a small proportion of total power sold by the State's municipal utilities (Bradshaw *et al.*, 2003). A current trend in California, based in part upon the opportunities brought about due to the energy crisis, such as regional and local utilities needing to meet the State's Renewable Portfolio Standard, is a replacement of fossil energy with renewables such as wind and solar. Increasing amounts of power generation are moving into the portofolios of these companies. For some, in fact, renewables are needed to oft-set increasingly the decreasing amount of energy supplied by hydroelectric power plants due to global warming and lower rain fall and hence snow levels.

On the other hand, public power advocates often cannot turn these financial advantages into enough of an advantage to enable them to acquire the assets of private power companies currently serving their community. For one thing, the private power company is usually an unwilling seller and the municipality has to use eminent domain to force the sale. These proceedings can be held up in expensive court battles for years and the utility usually can outspend municipalization advocates and hold up the process through litigation and delay tactics. In addition, the price of acquiring the distribution system and other assets is expensive, and its payback over years can actually cost community residents more than when it was privately owned. Then, the problem of access to cheap sources of power emerges.

Several California municipalities are seeking to municipalize because they obtained a share of a municipal power plant in Glendale that was being refurbished and would produce additional power. However, most municipalities have to compete for power in the same market that private companies do, or to install generators that cost about the same as they do for private companies. Finally, one of the incentives for municipalization is that communities want to avoid the costs of repaying bonds from the deregulation debacle and the cost of high-price long-term contracts, but State law will impose an exit fee on these customers to assure that all pay their fair share. When all is added up, the costs of establishing a new municipal power company do not offer many incentives. This is why most of these proposals have failed over the last 50 years—only two new municipal utilities have been established in the last 50 years, and both had special access to low-priced power (see Bradshaw *et al.*, 2003).

From an economic development point of view, municipalization promises local businesses local control over their electricity system, but in fact it is hard to leverage municipal advantages into a viable new utility. What is happening and making sense, however, are partial municipal involvement in power production. As we will see in Chapter 12, San Francisco has initiated a program to install solar panels to meet the needs initially of municipal buildings, schools, and other public facilities. They are also assisting businesses to become independent power producers. The municipal advantage in doing these projects is not only an advantage for the power grid, but it stimulates local development.

Job and business creation for advanced power production
provides a stimulus to the economy for transition to the
new agile energy system
Changing new advanced technologies have historically created significant alternations in the economics of communities and the availability of jobs. The increasing scale and sophistication of large centralized power plants has generally been associated with increased worker productivity and fewer overall jobs relative to the power produced. However, the changes that occurred after the California energy crisis

with the legislative requirements for increasing use of renewable power lowered greenhouse gases and statewide planning, altered the employment patterns by stimulating new jobs, careers, and business opportunities.

Employment in the electric and gas industry is significant in the national economy with over 600,000 workers in 1998. Coal mining, engine and turbine manufacturing, and distribution equipment added another 250,000 workers. Today, the American power industry is worth over $300 billion annually in revenues with at least $30 billion invested annually in improvements, upgrades, and new capital costs (Economist, August 23, 2003: 16–18).

The extent to which renewable and distributed energy generation creates jobs is provided by a paper produced by the Renewable Energy Policy Project (Beck *et al.*, 2002). They compare different jobs that are involved in three types of renewable power with coal plants. The first is employment in photovoltaic applications which in 2000 required a total of 35.5 person-years of labor to manufacture, install, and service 1 MW of capacity. Interestingly almost half of this was professional or clerical personnel.

Solar/PV systems require over 60% of installed costs to be in labor alone. The high costs for labor are due to the lack of a trained workforce, an issue that the State of California is aggressively addressing. Solar/PV industries are also intent on solving the problem with their own "certification" programs and in-house system installation training. Furthermore and perhaps, even more significant are the labor unions where programs and curricula for solar/PV seminars are being implemented throughout the USA. California is one of the key target markets for the labor organizations as it is in their best interests to focus on this growing industrial sector.

The second renewable technology was wind, with much lower labor demands and more initial capital expenditures for the machine. Wind requires 4.8 person-years of labor to install 1 MW of capacity. A third option was to fire coal plants with some proportion renewable wood with hugely different employment options based on the type of bio-fuel used and the labor requirements to grow, harvest, transport, and feed it into the coal plant. Over 10 years (same comparison as the previous options) mill residues would take 3–7 person-years, while growing tress or grass range from 9 to 21 person-years. Urban waste is estimated to require 3–13 person-years. Coal for comparison ranges from 4 to 8 person-years depending on coal supply. These data are shown in Table 7.1.

Clearly, photovoltaic applications are much more labor intensive than coal, but there is not as much difference between coal and wind.

Table 7.1.   Jobs per MW capacity by technology

Technology	Jobs per MW
Photovoltaic	35.5
Wind	4.8
Biomass co-fire	3–21
Coal (low)	4
Coal (high)	8

Source: Singh (2001).

In the California context, without coal plants in state, the comparison should be made with natural gas plants which probably have much lower labor demands than coal. This makes both photovoltaic installations and wind a considerable jobs improvement.

More recent data, however, tells a more compelling story for both advanced technologies and renewable energy systems providing employment and business growth in California. Cal PRIG (July 2003) reports that the renewable energy industry has more than doubled in California (in terms of jobs) since 2000. More significantly is the report from the solar/PV industry, only one subset area, whereby over 4000 new jobs have been created in California since January 2002 (Cal SEA, draft "Job Creation Report," July 2003). Given the even more dramatic growth in the wind and geothermal industrial sectors in California, creation there will be even greater.

In addition, the Public Interest Energy Research Division within the California Energy Commission has documented even more evidence. As the CEC reported on a review of PIER contracts completed through 2002,

> it revealed a total of 20 commercialized products with projected benefits of $221 to $576 million. Based on the estimated disbursements through 2002, the benefit-to-cost ratio is between 2 and 5 to one. For tangible products (hardware, software), "commercialized" means that the product is commercially available, economically viable without subsidies, and has been sold in its intended market. (CEC, Review Report on "Commercial Successes," August 2003)

In sum, deregulation has altered the linkage of utilities and electricity with economic development. The future will not be shaped in the same way as the past where the utilities had incentives to be a participant in the economic development of a region, but it will be shaped by the power of new forms of power development which will be a major stimulus to the overall economy. Southern California Edison (SCE, 2003) has a strong economic development program which is actively working in this area. However, two key elements are missing: one is finance and the other is a customer. Both elements are actively being developed by 2004 (more details appear later) in the former area lead by California State Treasurer Phil Angilides (2003a,b), who as head of the California $300 billion California Retirement System, has initiated public policies that commit over $20 billion to environmental companies and sustainable development.

The second element is the customer. While the State rebate and buy-down programs through both the CPUC and CEC were successful in stimulating the solar/PV sales, installation, and entrepreneurial companies, there needs to be sustainable business development in the State that is not dependent on government incentives. One such large real-estate developer in Southern California (Arden Realty with over 220 million square feet of commercial space) did just that.

Arden invested over $18 million in energy-efficiency and conservation programs within their own holdings and earned over a 30% profit from energy savings in less than half the time to recover the investment (Ziman, 2003). The internal program was so successful that the company formed a subsidiary (NextEdge) that specializes in this area and contracts out to non-Arden building owners and developers. Clearly more customers need to follow Arden's lead.

7.3. The Energy Crisis Derailed the California State Economy

The combination of the energy crisis in California and the 9-11 terrorist attack on New York and Washington DC on September 11, 2001 dealt a devastating blow to a relatively normally functioning state economy. While it is impossible to separate out the independent consequences of the two events, there is no doubt that the energy crisis has had a serious impact in reversing economic growth and creating challenges for firms and employees. While the "dot.com" collapse of thousands of technology industries in 2001–2002 is not due to the energy crisis, the combination of energy and technology industry decline has led to serious increases in unemployment and declining earnings by taxpayers, leading to a state revenue crisis of unprecedented proportions.

What did the energy crisis cost California? It is hard to arrive at a firm number and there are few overall studies or analyses that come close to providing comprehensive and inclusive data. Our best estimate is at least $40 billion.

The PG&E bankruptcy amounted to about 13.5 billion, while SC Edison lost between $3 and $4 billion. The State assumed about $10 billion in costs that were not covered by revenues and required a long-term bond to be repaid by electricity consumers, and then the DWR negotiated about $40 billion in contracts, estimated to be about $10 billion too high. There are surely other costs, and estimates are notoriously hard to verify. Weare (2002: 4) published an estimate of the impact between $40 and $45 billion, noting that this is about 3.5% of the total state annual economy. Before the California energy crisis, he noted that the largest energy shock to the economy was the default of Washington Public Power Supply System which overbuilt power plants (read nuclear) and lost about $800 million. This was a much smaller part of the Washington economy. We feel that these estimates are conservative because they are direct losses and do not include the economic losses during the blackouts or the costs to companies to protect against them. Nor does it account for the economic multiplier which estimates the ripple of the losses through the economy.

This is a huge cost, at the level of more than the expected 2003–2004 personal income tax revenues for the entire state (33.6 billion), or well over half of the entire state revenues of $69 billion. The usual revenue for the electricity industry in California only totals $20 billion per year. During the energy crisis customers continued to pay utilities their $20 billion, but because of the extra costs of power during this period the State and utilities accumulated another $30 billion in expenses which were not passed on to consumers but came out as debt which will eventually have to be repaid. This will be more difficult because of the high price negotiated for the long-term contracts.

James Walsh (2002) wrote a book titled *The $10 Billion Jolt: California's energy crisis: Cowardice, Greed, Stupidity, and the Death of Deregulation* that tells the story of the problem. However, we believe that he got the numbers very wrong. Clearly his subtitle is correct.

Where did all this money go? Governor Davis and others blamed the leakage to greedy out-of-state merchant companies, and to a large extent that is right. Now, few of these companies are in a position to repay the illegal profits and money because they are bankrupt and gone like Enron. Most of the others are in relatively weak financial positions, having lost their ill-begotten windfalls to other schemes. For example, Mirant Corporation of Atlanta, one of the large players in purchasing California generation capacity and providing power during the crisis, is now in Chapter 11 bankruptcy, having a total debt of $11.4 billion dollars. The company owns several prominent plants in Northern California including the San Francisco Portraro Hill plant and several plants in Antioch and Pittsburgh which it purchased for $801 million (Tansey, 2003). Mirant continues to seek favored and subsidized funds from the State and Federal government as it attempts to emerge from bankruptcy. The California ISO and PG&E along with local community groups and the State Attorney General's Office are looking into the continued contractual relationship between the State and such companies.

Some of the money lost in the power crisis went back to the utilities who operated more than one firm—their independent generating units were able to charge the distribution utility, but it is not clear how much this was. Before and during the crisis, many utility executives took large pay raises and retention bonuses, though the direct impact of these costs are probably small compared to the public relations losses of the company due to their publicity, and compared to other losses from high prices charged the utilities.

California has argued that it deserves refunds from the utilities who overcharged the State through market manipulation. Some of the utilities have negotiated settlements with the State. For example, Reliant reached agreement with FERC in January 2003 to repay the State $13.8 million for schemes that drove up prices. Most critics think that the settlement was far too light and that much more should be refunded to the State. However, FERC continues to be gentle on the firms involved at the time in California. The real problem, however, is that most of the firms that exploited the State no longer have the financial capacity to refund their ill-begotten gains.

7.3.1. *Financial drama and looming public and private bankruptcy(s)*

One of the most challenging stories unfolding from the energy crisis is the fate of the large utilities that could not afford to continue buying power at higher prices than they could charge their customers. As a consequence of rapidly rising prices at the wholesale level that could not be passed on to customers because of the rate freeze, all three major investor-owned utilities faced financial disaster. SC Edison had debts of $3–4 billion and they negotiated with the CPUC rates that would recover these funds. This has been largely completed now. By August 2003, the CPUC approved a small rate reduction for SC Edison signaling the end of the energy crisis and the new solvency of the utility itself.

Another utility and one of the first to be hit by the energy crisis in the spring of 2000, San Diego Gas and Electric was able to ride through the energy crisis by passing increased costs on to their customers because they became free from the retail price cap once they paid off all their stranded assets. San Diego was the first utility to become free from the cap and their customers experienced the price cuts early in the form of huge price increases in 2000.

Agile Energy Systems

However, the largest utility in the State, PG&E in Northern California, was not able to negotiate a solution with the CPUC or the legislature to resolve its financial problems. By the time the State started buying power for the utilities in the winter of 2001, PG&E accumulated a debt of over $13.5 billion, leading to the declaration of Chapter 11 bankruptcy on April 6, 2001. The key issue is that creditors, under guidance from the courts, must find a way to either assure that PG&E is restored to financial health, or to oversee the dissolution of the firm without repayment of the creditors. From the start of the bankruptcy hearings, the assumption has been to restore the firm rather than to dissolve it, which means finding a way to repay the $13.5 billion debt.

In a somewhat unusual procedure, PG&E and the California PUC both filed Plans of Reorganization for the company to emerge from bankruptcy. While both plans promise to pay all creditors in full and to restore PG&E to full financial health, there are significant differences in the two plans, which have costs and benefits to various, but different interests. These plans were revised and put to the vote of the creditors several times, with the results being advisory to the Oversight Judge. The vote reflected the creditors' interest in the firm coming to health, but reflected the difficulties in both options. The Official Committee of Unsecured Creditors recommended in early 2003 that the interests of creditors would be best served by favorable votes of creditors on both plans, acknowledging that the plans compete and that the Judge might strive for a compromise.

At the present time the PUC and PG&E have reached a tentative agreement to resolve their differences, but the PUC is sharply divided in whether or not they would approve it—reflecting unresolved tensions that have been evident since the start. In this proposed settlement, the utility will remain whole and under control of the PUC who will guarantee rates to cover debt, while the PUC will not insist on the dilution of PG&E stock to help repay outstanding debt. Californians will be paying for the energy crisis incurred debt for about 10 years. Stockholders share some of the costs by foregoing dividends for a while, but the bulk of the payment will be added to customer bills which will drop a little initially, but not to precrisis levels. As we write public hearings are being scheduled.

With regard to the resolution of the bankruptcy, it should be noted that key players hold starkly contrasting views of both how the utility became financially insolvent and who is to blame. The utility perspective is that it was placed by state and federal legislation under impossible business conditions by not being able to raise retail rates to pass on escalating wholesale prices in spite of appeals to the CPUC and state government. In contrast, the CPUC assumes no responsibility for events which were largely outside its control and proposes shared responsibility with stockholders absorbing some of the loss and customers the rest. The CPUC seeks to return to more-or-less previous regulation of the private utilities. Other advocacy groups believe that the deregulation policy was crafted by the utilities for their own interest, and they should alone be responsible for the consequences of its demise.

These competing perspectives are not resolved and continue to drive the debate over reorganization. A large group of consumers still want the shareholders in the company to shoulder a major share of the responsibility, while the company and some analysts feel that the company has paid a very high price already and that the state interests are best served by whatever it takes to restore the firm to financial health, meaning that rates should remain high enough to allow the recovery of funds in deficit. No one has convincingly argued that the State (which passed the legislation deregulating utilities) should pay for it through general funds, but instead the agreement has always been that the deficits should be paid by ratepayers in their individual utility, through a continuation of the rate increase that was imposed early in the power crisis.

The other major state utility, SC Edison, did not declare bankruptcy and worked out a similar agreement with the PUC to shift costs to consumers. Since their deficit was smaller, they will impose additional fees on electricity rates for a shorter period of time than their Northern Californian counterpart. San Diego Gas and Electric, the first state to experience deficits, was in a stronger position to accumulate revenues and their debt will be repaid before the other major utilities.

7.3.2. *Reliability, costs, and the environment*

The economic development issues of the California power crisis revolve around four key factors: reliability, costs to customers, environment, and long-term confidence.

Reliability

Reliability in power supply is essential to a well-functioning advanced economy. Blackouts and the threat of service interruptions cost the economy billions of dollars in 2000–2001, and the extent of the disruption led to a loss of confidence in the California economy that at times gave the impression of being like a third world economy, at least from an infrastructure point of view. Examples of huge economic losses resulting from blackouts include Silicon chip manufacturing plants that lost production and had to recalibrate instruments, food processing that spoiled, oil refineries that had to shut down, and data processing facilities that had to reconstruct massive data files. People died in traffic accidents and others with medical problems were stranded because power stopped. These problems illustrate the critical need for reliable power supplies.

The energy crisis showed how important reliability is for the economy to function properly. The vertically integrated system had relatively few firms in control of all aspects of the provision of electricity, and while that system did not guarantee reliability, the regulatory commissions could determine who was lax when reliability problems occurred and required that these problems be fixed. For example, winter storms often topple trees and power lines, and the PUC has fined the utilities for not doing proper tree trimming. Even in its bankruptcy, PG&E was allowed to spend money to keep trees trimmed. But with deregulation, the overall reliability of the system fell to the Independent System Operator, who lacked long-term perspective of working with the parties since this was a new organization, and it lacked authority to mandate spending on many reliability issues.

In this reliability vacuum, the Electric Power Research Institute (EPRI) has undertaken a number of studies and programs to increase reliability. One report evaluated 117 documents that reported on the costs of unreliable service, and concluded that the methodologies of these studies did not lead to a definitive answer (Eto *et al.*, 2001). For example, commercial and industrial economic loss for a one-hour outage ranges from a few cents to over $50 per kW unserved demand. The middle range of estimates are between $1 and $5 per kW for outages during peak time of operation and without advance notice. This means that a one-hour blackout outage of 1000 MW would be a million kW, or between $1 and $5 million loss. LA Times report that each undelivered MW of electricity causes $16,000 in lost economic output, or $16 million per 1000 MW (see Dennis Silverman energy data) www.physics.uci.edu/silverma/crisis/html. These estimates are very imprecise, but seem low.

Fundamentally, utilities need to provide reliable generation, transmission, and distribution services to their customers. The restructuring of the utilities and bankruptcy resolution need to assure that firms have the capacity to provide reliable service. However, if financial or legal issues block the company achieving investment grade credit status, the ability of the company to continue offering reliable service is questionable.

One of the points being made in early consideration of the East coast blackout in August 2003 is the fact that the utilities under deregulation have had no mandate or funds with which to invest in grid reliability. Reliability could also be seriously undermined as utilities become financially unable to invest in electricity infrastructure. New transmission lines, monitoring and protecting distribution networks, maintenance of power stations, and all the preventative maintenance and safety steps that are taken to run a modern utility are always a necessity. Moreover, if the utility has financial difficulties or if its stock has low value, its potential for growth and service to customers could be badly hurt. In the post-September 11 era security expenditures will continue to be necessary and costly.

Costs to consumers

The large consumers were upset about energy costs which led to the effort to try deregulation. Overall, California as a State has few heavy energy using industries, such as aluminum mills, and heavy industry. In the heavy industry categories, the State has more specialized segments of industry which tend not to take as much power because the cost and availability of power is limited. Since demand is less, the cost implications are a smaller part of the overall costs of doing business. In these cases, other location factors have to make it worthwhile for a business to stay in California.

The energy crisis has resulted in rates that are much higher than had been predicted before deregulation, and there is little likelihood that they will fall in the postcrisis period. This will surely have strong economic development implications for California.

The utilities have little room to manage lower rates for their customers. Given that they now own only a small proportion of the plants and are dependent on other suppliers for all their power means that the State's long-term contracts and other operational strategies will have a higher impact on prices than local decisions. From an economic development point of view, the State has accepted the fact that rates are going to be higher, but the consumer has little certainty on what the prices will be. From an economic development point of view the cost impact of the energy crisis turns on several concerns:

- How much of a difference will higher prices make on the average bill?
- Will certain user classes be affected more than others?

- How long will high prices be felt (12 years?)
- Would it be better to have higher prices for a short period and then reductions?
- How will technological innovations and policy initiatives that could lead to lower power prices be passed on to consumers, and will they see and appreciate this?

From an economic point of view, lower rates are very important to all consumers especially businesses. Industry has absorbed more of the recent rate increases than have residential customers, but one can assume industry will try to find ways to reduce rates soon. The reason remains that businesses are in competition with firms in other states with lower electricity costs, as well as costs of labor, land, pollution abatement, and many other factors of production.

In the future, the economics of the electricity industry will lead to increased pressure on utilities to reduce rates. After all, need for lower rates was a key driver underlying deregulation in the first place. California was acknowledged as one of the higher cost power states in the nation, with rates some 30% above the national average. These rates were not too serious a problem for economic growth because energy efficiency in California was so impressive that per-capita use of electricity was one of the lowest in the nation. However, the belief that competition would lower rates was one of the key promises of deregulation.

The unreliability of electricity supply during crisis in spring 2001 with spiking prices and blackouts was so severe that most consumers (residential and business) tolerated increased rates to restore stability to the power system, but this willingness to pay is temporary. The pressure for lower rates is beginning to be heard, and it will become louder.

Finally, many regulatory and market factors outside the control of either the bankruptcy proceedings or the cost of power will affect market prices and their perceived fairness. One of the most significant of these factors is the resolution of the legal battles with producers and marketers who have signed long-term contracts with the State. The evidence of market manipulation by electricity wholesalers is increasing daily with disclosure of the gaming that led to market manipulation, and as the evidence mounts concerning illegal or inappropriate activities, some become optimistic that contracts will be renegotiated and refunds obtained. While the outrage over these activities remains high, it is not clear what the legal results will be and what financial implications if any will benefit customers in the form of lower rates.

Environment

To the extent that the restructured utility can offer reliable and inexpensive power, attention needs to turn to environmental issues. The concern is with the negative impact that the energy crisis has had on environmental protection issues, though the new power plants are cleaner than the older ones. In this period of crisis, utilities have little capacity or incentive to work for environmental goals, and with divesture of their power plants the local utility is less likely to be the one to whom claims for environmental protection will be heard. In addition, a financially starved utility will have little ability or interest in advancing environmental goals.

There is some evidence that a growing proportion of the residential base is interested in obtaining renewable or "green" power. During the short period where customers had choice under deregulation, one of the most successful competitors to the regulated utilities was alternative or green suppliers, who accounted for one or two percent of the market. While small, this is actually significant because these customers had to pay more for their power. The environmental values issue may be an opportunity and historically the CPUC has been more innovative than FERC in promoting diversified and distributed power.

If environmental innovation becomes possible for utilities, California utilities have had a long history of success being diversified and environmentally innovative. Many conservation and demand side management efforts were also implemented by PG&E where its leadership role has been well-recognized. These programs have a significant economic impact on customers and the State because in a growing number of cases conservation remains cheaper than provision of additional power and renewable sources such as wind are now competitive with other sources of new power. We think that there is economic benefit to flexibility to innovate in these areas regardless of the bankruptcy restructuring plan or the solution by the State to reregulation of the utilities.

Long-term confidence

The final economic metric for examining the consequences of the energy crisis on economic development is that business needs confidence in the gas and electric utility system in order to stimulate long-term investment necessary for global competitiveness. However, the accounting scandals that have been uncovered at Enron and more recently the misreporting of expenses to inflate profits at WorldCom have seriously eroded corporate confidence to an all time low.

One of the major concerns affecting the State in the post-deregulation period is the confidence in the regulatory bodies to provide a stable framework for investment in business infrastructure in the State. Utilities that are diversified and have a place in the global market have resources to contribute to local economies. This should assist firms either in California or looking to do business in the State to have confidence in their utility. Firms are unlikely to be reassured that either the CPUC or FERC have the capacity to handle complex problems. It is not clear how the relations between the State and federal regulatory agencies will be responsive to the economic needs of the State or the utilities. In sum, it is increasingly clear that neither agency has adequate legitimacy.

7.4. Conclusion: Economic Development in an Agile Energy System

One of the most significant studies of the impacts of moving to an agile energy system that rests on efficiency, conservation, and renewable power assumptions and standards is a series of simulations reported by Geller (2003). Comparing a business as usual model with a "clean energy scenario," Geller shows that a series of 10 clean energy strategies would in combination produce a decline in total energy consumption in the US starting in 2010. Further data from Wiser and Bollinger (2003) document the same results.

In addition such renewable energy assumptions would reduce the national energy intensity from 7.4 kBtu per dollar (1999 value) based on business as usual to 5.5 kBtu per dollar with these and other clean energy strategies implemented. These policies would cost by 2020 $674 billion in the US, while saving a total of $1229 billion over the same period. Hence, a net gain of $554 billion would be achieved in addition to reducing American dependency on international oil and gas supplies. In other words, the investment would not only pay for itself, but would produce a gain of 82%. These savings would keep on growing into the future.

Such savings would reduce per-household costs for energy from all sources (household, industrial, transportation, etc.), from about $5500 in 2000 to $3800 in 2020 under the clean energy scenario, compared to an increase per-household to about $6250 in annual energy costs with the business as usual scenario. In short, the average household would reduce their energy bill by $2400, or 40%.

Jobs under the clean energy scenario would increase rather than decrease, multiplying the economic value of the strategies. While not a part of the Geller study, one estimate is that the clean-energy strategy would create 870,000 jobs. This is a clear example of the puzzling technology implementation question—if people could gain so much and it would not cost them anything, why are we not doing all these good projects that would also clean the environment and create jobs?

We have argued here that public policy directed toward advanced, renewable technologies with agile energy systems, which are dispersed and distributed energy generation on the regional and local level, mean the creation of local businesses and jobs. The evidence is mounting in California that such is the case with the enactment of measures to stem the California energy crisis, legislation to set new standards, codes, and protocols. Above all, government programs are needed to stimulate initially the clean energy sector while other programs are needed to limit the growth of fossil energy power generation.

What California has learned and its citizens embraced is the basic concept of "social capitalism": clean environment and renewable energy can be profitable. The citizens of the State do *not* want to see more oil wells off their coast or in their parks, nor do they want to import fossil energy fuels from other states who must violate their environments as well. Instead, the citizens of California have embraced what the Europeans call "social constructions" whereby they believe that both can happen—a clean environment and profitable businesses.

The pathway has been set with government and the public sector taking the lead in "greening public buildings" as well as procurement of "environmentally sound technologies." The private sector has rapidly taken the lead and appears poised to implement "civic capitalism." A win–win scenario is not far behind for all Californians.

PART II
Progress Toward an
Agile Energy System

Part II
Agile Energy Systems: Solutions for California and the World

We introduce the term *agile* to refer to an energy system that is flexible but more importantly, a system within any energy, environmental, waste or water infrastructure able to change quickly.[1] An agile system is adept at change, where innovation is welcomed rather than opposed. Agile energy systems are resourceful and find ways to avoid conflict, while deconstructing social–economic barriers that slow down effective solutions to problems. Agile systems are dynamic and progressive. Agile systems are not limited either from political pressures or constraints from lobbyists and special interests. Instead, they foster and promote diversity and dynamic growth and change using knowledge, intellectual capital and advanced technologies.

Even more fundamental is that agile energy systems anticipate new laws, regulations, and emergency measures so that adaptation and change can occur effectively and efficiently. In this way an agile energy system is proactive and takes a leadership role in order to balance the need for growing amounts of electric power with civic, economic, and environmental benefits. In short, agile energy systems grow out of civic markets where societal benefits are merged with private sector needs often creating what some call "triple bottom line" benefits.

Agile energy systems are a market-oriented paradigm, built upon experimentation and policy developed today while remaining open

---

[1]Dictionary definitions of "agile" emphasize things that are readily able to move quickly and easily. Other adjectives are nimble, mentally quick and resourceful, brisk, and spry. Agile implies dexterity and ease in movement. In contrast, the word flexible applies to things that are capable of bending, responding, or conforming to new situations. Flexible may or may not be resilient or elastic, but simply the ability to be bent or folded without breaking. In our use of agile we emphasize quickness, dexterity, and include flexibility as well.

and flexible for the future. Agile systems are neither a particular technology nor a finite market mechanism. Instead, an agile energy system is a set of technologies, policies, and programs creatively linked to be superior to any one of them alone. Above all, agile systems respond to immediate as well as long-term needs. Compared to the restructured but business as usual option which emphases shareholder profits over public goods and service, agile energy systems find solutions to the deregulation, privatization, and liberalization mess. The characteristics of such a system include:

- *Diversification.* By relying on diversified and renewable sources through the transition period, the type of agile energy systems we have described will be more reliable and less vulnerable to disruption. These systems will also be more environmentally friendly. The restructured centralized utility system without additional incentives will be large and centralized with several competing units providing power through traditional technologies. These power providers run the risk of dependence on fuel shortages and price increases as with oil and increasingly with natural gas. The ultimate objective of diversified renewable sources reduces dependence on distant suppliers.
- *Balance.* Agile energy emphasizes the beneficial use of power, not simply the amount of power. An agile system will balance supply with conservation to achieve an optimum output for the need which is being met. The traditional business as usual competitive system has every interest in selling power and lots of it, and has no financial incentive to promote conservation or reduce consumption, or even to shift to less demanding periods or fuel types. An agile system tries to meet consumer objectives at the lowest price which often means selling less power. Restructuring has systematically undercut demand management, but we argue that it has to take precedence over supply. The problem of balance in the restructuring system is that deregulated markets fail to adequately value reserve or peaking demand, for example. Both are essential for proper system reliability, but in a short-term competitive market there is no way to value the capacity to meet demand that may be at peak only a few hours a year.
- *Interdependence and interconnection.* The key to an effective energy system is to integrate the producers and consumers through well-designed transmission systems. Electrical transmission in most ways is a monopoly because there are few justifications for establishing redundant transmission systems that cover the same routes. That said, any piece of the transmission system is

inseparable from the rest with electrons from a generator at one point following multiple routes to end use according to laws of physics, threatening to overload parts of the system. This requires central dispatch over generators to balance the transmission system. Agile systems find ways to avoid bottlenecks in delivery of power.

At a deeper level, the strength of agile energy is that it looks at energy system needs as an interconnected and interchangeable whole, so that fuels, electricity, and waste are all in dynamic balance. In the traditional energy system the provision of electricity is separated from heat systems, but it should not be so. We need more cogeneration, but we also can save huge amounts by looking at the pairing of technologies so that they increase efficiencies for each other. For example, wind systems that produce storable electricity in the form of hydrogen that can be later used in a fuel cell, or photovoltaic systems that pump water into reservoirs at a higher elevation, achieve system efficiencies well above that of any single technology. In the traditional deregulated system these linkages are often made difficult by short-term competitive market pressures.

- *Spatially appropriate.* Agile energy systems are dispersed and non-critical. The appropriate scale for an energy system is not a region or nation, but a neighborhood. Self-reliant neighborhood-based systems not only recognize their environmental costs, they also rely on the grid for reliability and peaking. Whereas the old technology was more cost effective as scale increased, leading to power plants and clusters of power plants that produced several thousand MW in remote locations, today's technology is more cost effective when it is smaller, located closer to where it is needed, and closely coupled with available solar and other renewable resources.

- *Regional.* The locally appropriate power nexus links the community to the economic development objectives of the community and regional, national, or even global issues. An agile energy system easily bridges community interests in economic development and community well-being with the benefits of reliability from trading and being interconnected to a regional network. The agile system can quickly and easily move between these levels, achieving objectives that benefit all.

- *Public good.* Agile systems benefit many goals, but the general public good is primary. Rather than large corporations or elegant engineering models, the real "stakeholders" in any energy system are the public good. In a similar way, agile energy systems may be the appropriate paradigm for other infrastructure sectors confronted with deregulation and privatization such as waste, water, atmosphere/climate and even transportation, telecommunications, and education.

In the post-restructuring world, agile energy systems are a public good to which private competitive firms play a part. Agile energy meets the goals of restructuring in that it gives each person, group, community, state, and nation the power to chart their own course and achieve maximum benefit at the lowest costs. It is highly competitive in that there is no one way to obtain economic power, but it relies on public oversight, active participation, and decision making to define public goals.

In this second section, the emphasis is on solutions for the emerging era of the energy industry. From the traditional vertically integrated utility that ended around 1972, we are now in a transition era that is giving rise to the agile energy system that will follow. The chapters that follow cover the same five core themes that were discussed in Chapters 3–7, but these themes are used to explore the potential changes that will overcome the limitations of the current energy system.

Chapter 8
Advanced Technologies for an Agile Energy System

8.1. Introduction

Technological change is one of the primary drivers in the solutions for problems in the energy sector. Furthermore, advanced technologies provide the energy sector with more modern and efficient tools to deliver services. Historically, the research and development (R&D) of these new advanced technologies in the USA has been through the public utilities. More recently, since the late 1970s, the USA federal government with the formation of the US Department of Energy has been the focal point and often the initiator of new basic energy, and environmental-related technologies. Since deregulation in California and elsewhere in the USA, however, little basic research and limited development has occurred from the power utilities.

In the same way that the old vertically integrated monopoly based power utility systems were forced to change by the availability and pricing of different power-generation options, the future configuration of the power system is driven by technological innovation. The drivers for this innovation include the historical tenants by which technologies are commercialized, as well as the need for technologies that adhere to environmental and climate change protocols, laws, and regulations.

During the 1990s, while deregulation legislation began to sweep across the USA, President Clinton's administration made a series of attempts to develop emerging energy and environmental technologies through the leveraging of defense funds (what was known when Clinton took office as the "cold war dividend" of $1.2 billion) with national laboratories and the private sector (Clark, 1997). Using the Bayh-Doyle Act of the mid-1980s, which opened the door for private companies to commercialize federally funded R&D, the

Clinton administration aggressively sought mechanisms to "transfer technologies."

One significant mechanism was the Cooperative Research and Development Act (CRADA) which required public–private partnerships in transferring technologies to the private sector. As a means to promote and advance such transfers, the Clinton administration created a number of public–private partnerships. One, the Partnership for New Generation Vehicles (PNGV), focused upon commercializing basic research into private sector companies. There were many problems with the program, the least of which were that the private sector companies were only American ones and these firms tended to want to protect their current technologies, rather than to either seek or accept new advanced technologies (Clark and Paolucci, 1997, 2001).

This chapter outlines the theoretical and conceptual framework for making agile energy systems operational, demonstrating both the benefits of technological options that have been installed and their potential in the future. Agile energy systems provide a far more flexible approach (Clark and Lund, 2001) to demonstrating and commercializing new emerging technologies since the regional ability to innovate tends to be more progressive. Additionally, agile systems mean just that—the local energy supplier need not be one or two companies but many. In fact, the idea is to have a diverse energy supply so that power can come from local grids, buildings, and complexes as well as individual homes and businesses.

We pay special attention to how the individual advanced technologies can work together as in a systematic manner in which benefits multiply as technologies form advantageous "hybrid systems" (Grandy et al., 2002). When renewable energy generation, such as wind or solar, are combined with energy storage devices, the result is not only a far more inexpensive system but also one that qualifies as being base load (Lagier, 2003). The chapter proposes criteria for such agile energy systems and suggests what needs to be done to convert opportunities into a sustainable energy/environmental plans. Furthermore, the costs and benefits are explored briefly but presented more in-depth in Chapter 10.

8.1.1. Background and context for energy systems

The traditional energy system, established worldwide primarily as a public monopoly over a century ago, had become lethargic and unresponsive to the changing potentials of advanced technologies and the new needs of a complex society. Deregulation was to change all that, but it did not. Instead, new and emerging technologies were left in California, and similarly elsewhere, to the California Energy Commission, Public Interest Energy Research (PIER) program which has $62 million annually (four years with renewed legislation) from rate payers to spend on R&D.

The problem with state-substituted R&D programs for regional or local ones is basic: not enough R&D money; and with those funds available, any applications of the R&D were not only prohibited, but too far removed from commercialization. Another issue emerged, contrary to the deregulation assumptions about the market, the private sector companies simply did not invest in R&D. It was a negative investment on their bottom line. Market forces were only concerned with maximizing shareholder value and executive incentives and benefits, rather than protecting or enhancing the public good.

The future, however, suggests that civic benefits will be greatest if policy makers consider power systems as "agile"—that is energy systems must be quick and responsive, adaptive, flexible, and robust. An "agile energy system" not only fits with the needs of "the next economy" (Hinton, 1997), but also is interdependent with residential and business needs as well as setting public goals which include environmental and atmospheric protection. In short, as the social and economic structure of modern society gets more complex, the energy system that ties it together needs to be responsive to the complexity of the social system it serves.

Emerging technologies are being commercialized at the local level more and more in California. This phenomenon was unpredictable but a practical solution to the lack of State funds and a strong need and desire at the local community level to finance advanced and especially renewable technologies for energy generation. Numerous examples will be given later, but the most dramatic one was the public approval of a $100 million bond measure in San Francisco for Solar Systems that was vigorously opposed by the public utility (PG&E). Other examples abound in California. The creation of an agile energy system is possible to create and implement as a viable energy future from the current traditional central grid systems through three major technological principles:

- First, an agile system is characterized by increasing use of *distributed technologies* that are efficient on a smaller localized scale rather than being grid-centered. Centralized systems with a relatively few large and often distant power generators connected by major transmission lines favor large generation plants and utilities that can finance and run them. Increasingly electrical system benefits from smaller generators that are closer to users, connected by a grid for backup, distribution, and efficiency, rather than generation plants tied to transmission lines. The new agile (read: local) grid accommodates electricity flows in all directions, more like the "internet" than a municipal water, waste, or other infrastructure.

- Second, an agile system includes a greater diversity of power generation resources that can take advantage of available and free primary energy (renewable energy for example) from the sun, taking advantage of attractive economics of solar power with fewer negative environmental consequences. This means that the agile power system will favor *renewable and sustainable* energy generation options. The technological transition to a portfolio of diversified renewable fuels and power sources is not just an ideological response to environmental public policy. Renewable energy systems are cheaper, cost competitive, more reliable, and offer consumers life-long benefits (documented in Chapter 10) of a healthier and more productive physical environment along with better sustainable communities.

- Third, an agile system is not a single technology or several separate technologies operating in parallel. Agile systems are interconnected as *hybrid energy systems* in which advanced technologies and traditional resources are integrated into a whole new network of collaborating producers and users. The strength of a hybrid system is that the strengths of one part balance the weaknesses of others, creating a more robust technological system. When solar PV systems are operating on business complexes along with energy storage devices, for example, they provide both backup and off-peak power supplies when the sun does not shine or during the night.

Technological advances support agility in the energy system. Local or regional energy systems are not dependent upon a single technology or package, but are a strategy for creatively linking new technologies, policies, and programs in a way that is far superior and efficient to any separate part operating by itself. An agile system responds fast to opportunities and demands, is not captured by segments that can restrict either supply or manipulate demand to the advantage of any one part of the system. Furthermore, agile systems require public–private partnerships that seek to promote civic markets, rather than short-term profits and market force gain.

8.2. Technological Development and Agile Energy Systems

The technological basis for the proposed agile system paradigm must achieve the goals of lower cost and better environmental performance for local and regional energy systems. California is the appropriate place to pursue this new agile energy model because of the need to find low-price solutions in the postderegulation era and because the state has long been a leader developing innovative solutions to environmental crises. Indeed, it appears that California may be the first nation-state to define and implement "sustainable development." Its citizens are ready and apparently the new bipartisan leadership is following. As the Economist (2001) has noted, "the world is watching for California to take the lead again." We believe that the agile energy model is what should be exported to other states and countries, rather than the failed deregulation and privatization debacle.

The events after "9-11," global military tensions, international terrorism, and war all give more urgency to solving the basic issues of the fuel supplies for any energy system. Without doubt, recent history has shown that energy is directly related to issues of the economy, environment, community, and social well-being. The heightened awareness of the vulnerability in power system means that future technologies must be more robust, flexible, and reliable. Yet at the same time, they must be less costly.

> From a technological and regulatory perspective, innovative ideas need to be introduced while protecting against both misguided business interests and dangerous terrorists. Agile power systems provide a strategy for "security" through diverse energy generation and supplies rather than centralized grids, plants, and transmission. (Clark et al., 2003)

The best solution for a secure, reliable, and sustainable future is to work toward an "agile energy system" based on innovative and advanced technologies, renewable generation, distributed systems, conservation, and hybrid systems. This type of system is neither hypothetical nor inevitable. In fact the future is available now. However, its implementation requires more public commitment at all levels, not less. Reducing the public role, such as was tried with deregulation which failed in California and elsewhere, is not the answer. Just the opposite is required. The agile energy system's model increases independence from fossil fuel energy suppliers, because it substitutes conservation, local renewable energy generation whenever possible through new advanced and hybrid technologies.

8.2.1. Visions of the future

The technological vision for the future of state and regional power systems are ambiguous. The Worldwatch Institute's Christopher Flavin and Nicholas Lenssen argue that the status quo options is the least likely scenario for the future. Instead, they argue that energy efficiency, renewable resources, electric-hybrid vehicles, dispersed production plants, and ultimately hydrogen will lead to a revolutionary energy transition that "will have profound effects on the way all of us work and live, and on the health of the global environment on which we depend" (1994: 18–28). In a similar vein, Lester Brown (2002), the founder of Worldwatch and now President of Earth Policy Institute, offers an integrated vision as the "eco-economy."

In an interesting book Michael Brewer argues that "it is not only desirable but practical to make the transition from fossil fuels to 'cool' renewable energy. By doing so we will help preserve the environment and sustain our economy at the same time" (1994: 1). He shows that remarkable progress has been made in the technological development of the wide range of renewable technologies and that they are reaching the point where they are competitive in terms of cost and integration into the power grid. However, Brewer issues a cautionary note that is more true now than when he wrote it. The industry, he says is "in the doldrums" (1994: 173) and that in spite of broad political support, research financing is dwindling, financial support continues to flow to the fossil fuel industry, regulatory strategies are not supportive of diversification, and opportunities are being lost.

Amory Lovins, among others, sees a combination of energy-efficiency mechanisms with the commercialization of renewable sources to provide a low-cost energy that was also environmentally sensitive (see Hawkin and Lovins, 1999; Weizsacker *et al.*, 1999). Lovins and his colleagues at the Rocky Mountain Institute showed how simple technologies and renewable resources provided a higher quality of life with more sensible energy use. Lovins sees the energy system in an integrated way in which common sense solutions simplify the technological basis of energy provision and use, reducing costs as a byproduct. This concern focuses on the health of society rather than on meeting market or private sector interests. He consistently outlines a vision of a society in which the private sector was a partner with government.

David Morris (2002) took the basic issue of social responsibility further, based on his work in the mid-1980s. He saw the problem as who owns the electrical system itself as the critical issue. That entity or group who control energy systems, translates into their motivation or lack of it, for providing clean and reliable energy. Morris advocates factors, therefore, such as local ownership to capture the benefits of conservation and decentralized production while basically "democratizing" the energy sector. Agile energy systems benefit from these factors.

More recently, a number of visionary scholars and thinkers have focused upon hydrogen as a set of technologies that will avoid some of the problems of the old fossil energy-dependent world order. For example, Jeremy Rifkin sees the future in terms of the "worldwide hydrogen energy web (HEW)" that "could decentralize and democratize energy and recast commercial and social institutions along radically new lines" (Rifkin, 2003: 9).

Rifkin has a broad vision, tying the fall of Rome and the success of the Allies in World Wars I and II to energy policy. He argues that the ability to pursue a diversified strategy to manage energy is essential to survival of civilizations, and that the US and other developed countries are in a hopeless situation now because of their dependence on hydrocarbons. Not only is the supply of oil more vulnerable than most think, so is the long- and short-term availability of natural gas. The crisis is that shortages now will become critical within 10–20 years, multiplied by the increasing reliance on supplies from foreign countries that are likely to be inclined to use oil availability as a weapon.

Rifkin looks, furthermore, to technological advances as supporting his argument due to falling prices of photovoltaic and fuel cells and other technologies. He notes how the rapid decrease and now competitive costs for wind energy as well as other renewable sources generate ample electricity that can be used to produce hydrogen from water. The key in Rifkin's model is that the hydrogen can be stored and used either as a fuel for transportation and combustion, or in fuel cells to generate electricity. This vision is neither abstract or off into the distant future.

Many major companies including Daimler-Chrysler and ChevronTexaco have proposed similar approaches to bring hydrogen into the economy sooner rather than later (Clark, 2003–2004). Moreover, the influential and reputable South Coast Air Quality Management District in Dimond Bar, California has promoted a similar program through funding and requests for proposals of "energy stations" throughout the greater Los Angeles region (SCAQMD, 2003–2004).

Rifkin, himself, is not far from the current application of the hydrogen economy as he is the Advisor to the European Union President, R. Prodi, on the subject. The hydrogen economy, Rifkin argues, can be commercialized at the local levels where individuals can produce and add to an interconnected network as well as take from it. This increases reliability and reduces the potential for international energy terrorism. But most importantly, the hydrogen web economy for Rifkin redistributes power to the individual and avoids the pending environmental destruction of global warming associated with hydrocarbon economies.

These visionary plans differ greatly from the plan advocated by the Bush/Cheney scheme that was put forward by the White House in May 2001 and the proposed Energy Bill of 2003. In that plan, the American President and his administration reiterated their ties to the oil and gas industries from which they made their fortunes and received political contributions. The Bush/Cheney Energy Plan retains emphasis and dependence upon fossil fuels, including more coal and oil from the Artic. Indeed in the chaos of planning for war in Iraq, seeing early evidence of the turmoil caused by global warming, and uncertainty in supplies of oil and gas, many industry leaders are advocating old solutions such as a new generation of nuclear power plants, further deregulation of oil (Ballonoff, 1997), or an expanded grid by which to import more power from Mexico or the other side of the continent.

While visions of the future remain uncertain, they ultimately remain visions rather that reality. Power systems throughout the world are changing rapidly without adequate road maps and strategies for the future. EPRI (Gehl, 2004) drafted in 2003 and issued in 2004, its five-year road map which begins to address distributed generation and regional energy systems. Agile systems are, however, a new realistic and obtainable model that are comprehensive, affordable, and viable, by providing both a technological and social-eco systems approach that drives the economics. In short, agile energy systems are rapidly becoming a reality today.

8.2.2. Implementing advanced and emerging technologies

Below is a more detailed account of what new, advanced, and emerging technologies are. Consider now that a set of advanced technologies is both feasible and cost effective. However, this does not mean that they will be easily introduced, especially when there is a complex embedded system and bureaucracies into which they must fit. For this reason, the introduction of technologies must work in tandem with public policy and institutional changes that facilitate their adoption. Thus, each new technological strategy requires a commercial and civic partnership (later discussed in Chapters 9 and

10 as "civic markets") to overcome the barriers to effective implementation.

Technological implementation is more than ever dependent on civic or public action. California, due to the energy crisis in 2001, created a number of innovative strategies for environmentally sound energy generation. The State held forums focused on renewable energy that gathered firms together with government officials to discuss barriers, problems, and strategies for clean energy in the State. These Forums brought about a number of creative changes including the publication of a revised Standard Practices Manual for project finance of state facilities (Schultz *et al.*, 2001). The Manual, originally issued in 1987 from the California Public Utilities and the Energy Commission, includes "life-cycle analysis" and economic externalities such as health, social, and environmental factors in cost–benefit analysis.

Public–private partnerships for the promotion of new technologies are essential (Clark and Lund, 2002). One of the most ambitious efforts took place in California during 2001. A California Stationary Fuel Cell Collaborative (CSFCC) was formed from the California Air Resources Board, University of California, Irvine, National Fuel Cell Center, and the Governor's Office. This group (not motivated by government regulations, but by the need for new clean energy technologies) structured a public–private partnership that prepared government agencies, departments, and commissions to issue proposals for purchasing, installing, and maintaining fuel cells. Through the newly created California Power Authority (CPA) and local bonding authorities, funds were available for commercialization of fuel cells.

The CSFCC aims to reduce the costs for the fuel cells through the use of master purchase agreements and power purchase contracts. It will also help to standardize technology by having a process for assessing "superiority" of a technology and showing how the technology has a positive impact on the economy and on the environment. This process is considered to be of more general value, and addresses new models of technological innovation in a world where the development of more complex technologies is usually subject to patterns that slow it down and decrease social returns of R&D expenditures.

In the high-technology industry, several public–private technology initiatives were undertaken with federal and state governments in the early 1990s. These two examples also exemplify the regional basis for innovation, since one was located in Texas and the other in California. In both cases, significant "bidding" occurred between the two states to get the associations to locate there, and both states were correct as each association yielded uncalculated economic benefits to their respective regions (Clark, 1994).

One was the Semiconductor Equipment and Materials Institute (SEMI), located in Austin, Texas. While the semiconductor industry in America in the 1990s was centered in Silicon Valley, Texas was able to both out maneuver local California communities and the State of California to get SEMI in the late 1980s. However, the other association, created to advance emerging technologies, was the Flat Panel Display Consortium (FPDC). FPDC was a different story. It began in the early 1990s. This time, California was not to be left behind. By the early 1990s with the decline of the American economy and a recession in California, the region south of San Francisco formed Joint Venture Silicon Valley which was a large public partnership to advance and protect the high-tech industry in the region. Along with a bipartisan State government, the FPDC was able to win the bid for federal funds to support its creation in Sunnyvale, California.

Technological innovation often is described in terms of the dual economic forces of the market "pull" or whereby innovation is demanded from consumers. The opposite perspective is technology "push," whereby innovation is created by industry or academic R&D programs and then new markets are created through advertising or promotion to purchase the technologies (Cooper and Clark, 1998). The opening of a new feature film is a good example of creating market demand for a product where none existed heretofore.

The role of universities in creating technologies and the difficulty of getting them implemented suggests that implementing innovations is a very challenging task where there is no single strategy. Instead, commercialization of advanced technologies is often an interactive process of both the pull and push economic models (Clark and Fast, 2004). Hollander and Schneider (1995) review how energy technologies are impacted from these conflicting perspectives.

The "technology push" model argues that R&D centers have developed technologies that industry needs and will therefore make them available. The most common manifestation of this approach is the widespread use of "technology transfer" programs within national laboratories and universities (as well as increasing numbers within industry). The basic assumption is that research organizations have to spend large sums of money on research and the outcomes must be a technology that can then be licensed to industry or entrepreneurs.

The "polarization" between the push and pull economic models "persists to this very day and remains a major factor determining the character of the energy-efficiency debate" (Hollander and Schneider, 1995: 5). Ten years later this same technology model is still in place and now more bureaucratized in both the public and private sectors (Clark *et al.*, 2003). In the real world of business and government, the process is far more interactive and nonlinear (Clark and Paolucci, 2001).

On the one hand, government regulation and funding of research programs must take into account these technology models when considering efficient allocation of financial resources and social benefits. The final objective is to reconcile societal demands for innovation, reducing pollution, and industrial requirements. Funding must support technology-based consortia, to facilitate spillovers and diffusion of knowledge in as many industries as possible; it must also provide incentives to universities and research laboratories to play an active role in moving innovation into products, and to help select "targets markets," and introduction patterns. In this model, the role of regulation is to reduce market uncertainty and stimulate utilization of new technologies.

On the other hand, a company's strategy must reflect these issues. While the technology (or market) pull model has some merit for certain activities, it is usually counterproductive for American corporations who are too often short-term and shareholder oriented. Market pull works in other industrialized countries, however, more effectively, since it fosters close industrial and governmental relationships in order to seek long-term research and development objectives. It is this issue (government role in commercialization of R&D) that is one of the key conflicts between the USA and Asia as well as within the EU.

Short- and long-term markets and technologies must be balanced repeatedly. Often there is a need for quick short-term research solutions to immediate problems as well as longer term enabling technologies for competitive posturing. A new technology commercialization model appears to be the best solution to provide that delicate balance or interaction between that push and pull models of technology commercialization. Companies and firms have to consider product architecture as a function of technology, depending on inter-firm relationships; vertical and horizontal integration are both technology and market driven.

8.3. Power Generation Technologies for an Agile System

The technologies to create an agile power system are largely available at the demonstration level, though most have not been commercialized to the point where they are competitive without subsidy. The most important breakthrough is in cutting-edge photovoltaic systems.

As this book is published, a major Japanese company, has claimed that it can provide and guarantee solar/PV power systems for $0.035 per kWh by 2004 into the California market (Kenidi, 2003). This price is competitive with natural gas and other renewable energy costs which are about half the cost of the long-term contracts signed by the Davis administration.

In addition, wind energy costs have fallen below fossil fuel alternatives. Utilities are purchasing wind energy wherever there are wind resources based on economic criteria alone. Renewables, with wind and geothermal energy production, are helping the State to meet its Renewable Portfolio Standards. Geothermal power generation plants, such as at the Geysers in Northern California and Imperial County, have been economical for over 30 years. Biomass plants are still in need of tax and government incentives. The new CEC Renewable Energy Generation Plan (December 2003a) sets more stringent economic demands upon industry to reduce costs for government support.

Consider hybrid technologies (Grandy *et al.*, 2002). With hybrid technologies, combining technologies can reduce the costs of renewable energy, be competitive with fossil fuels, expand the industry and hence economic and sustainable development. For example, in geothermal energy generation, the hot-steam resources are particularly attractive in terms of producing other mineral-based products. A geothermal plant in the Imperial County (Salton Sea) region of California is a good example of this. The production of geothermal power also yields zinc from the plant that is used as a raw material in other products.

Iceland has also become an excellent example of the use of geothermal power production along with these same reliable energy resources for hydrogen production. In Kalenborg, Denmark in the mid-1970s, a concept was developed whereby the waste from one industry became the raw material for another. The process, known as 'industrial symbiosis," involved five local industries including the "ash" from the local power plant being turned into "gypsum" for use in building materials. Some large corporations have even developed complex computer matrices to identify waste from companies in order to colocate other companies in need of the waste for raw materials in their production processes.

The key point about energy generation with advanced technologies for an agile energy system is that they are not new or exotic technologies. Instead, they all have been in use before the California energy crisis occurred. Some emerging technologies are rooted in renewable technologies and others utilize existing fuels at least as a transition to a more fully renewable system. What is interesting and new, however, is that they provide a comprehensive alternative to large centralized power plants. Renewable technologies will account for almost all of the energy-generation capacity growth in California.

Renewable energy generation and associated advanced technologies are the logical and economic choice for replacement of power plants. Renewable energy technologies can supply power in place of outdated and environmentally hazardous power generation plants, modernization or upgrades of those plants, installation of new fossil fuel-based plants, and the expansion of natural gas production or storage especially. Such concerns are particularly significant when considering the California emphasis on the need for more natural gas, including liquefied natural gas with all its attendant problems in production, distribution, and transmission (CEC, 2003b). Some advantages of the renewable mix of emerging technologies are:

- Small scale
- Diversified in their fuel and not dependent on single sources
- Relatively near to final demand, and in some cases colocated with demand
- Quick construction timelines
- Environmentally benign or with minor impact
- Increasingly cost effective as scale increases

According to an EPRI study (2001: 1–3), California has about 5536 MW of renewable energy capacity, out of a peak capacity of about 52,000 MW. These figures include small hydro (< 30 MW), excluding large dams and their hydro capacity. Thus the State now generates about 10% of its power from assorted renewable sources, the highest in the nation. Most of these renewable power facilities were built prior to 1995 and thus current technologies and their attractive economics are not taken into account. In addition, California companies have plans to add another 1150 MW but these plans are hampered by a number of uncertainties, including

- Market mechanisms and favorable regulations assuring confidence for intermittent sources such as wind,
- Improving transmission from wind and geothermal sites,
- Solving technological problems for low-head hydro, solar thermal, and other technologies,
- Demonstrating effective biopower technologies such as ethanol production from biomass coupled with cogeneration.

An added benefit of expanded renewable power in California according to the EPRI study is that it could "contribute up to 20% of the State's electrical energy demand, create over 18,000 jobs, and produce over $4.8 billion in state revenues within 11 years" (EPRI, 2001: 1–6). As will be discussed later in Chapter 10, the economic benefits from building a renewable industry in California are unknown. Even more significant is the fact that renewable industries become the basis for sustainable development companies which contribute to job creation, societal needs, and economic expansion.

The cost of alternative power is a critical issue, and one that is not yet resolved. The spot-market price of 2–3 cents before (and now after) deregulation seems to be setting the price expectation. However, the retail cost expected to be paid by consumers for generation forecast alone is between 6 and 8 cents per kWh. This is the range for most of the long-term contracts of the State as well, though these are overpriced, based on prices since the energy crisis in 2001–2002.

Future prices will likely increase as natural gas shortages work their way into the system. The price assumed to be reasonable for additional supply in California is critical and it depends on regulatory policies, government incentives, as well as markets. If one assumes that new sources of power are competitive at 6.9 cents per kWh, as does the 2001 EPRI study, then at least an additional 4400 MW of grid-based renewable power ("reserved capacity" needs according to the CPA) is cost competitive now, largely from geothermal and wind. However, at a higher price of 9.1 cents nearly double that amount could be available.

As we will see, these attractive sources of power are limited by rules but also by the return of a surplus of traditionally generated power. In spite of the past shortages and projected long-term shortages, today there is little spare room in the California electrical system for a lot of new capacity that will demand relatively high prices under the type of contract that a supplier can get financed through commercial lenders. State programs can assist in funding, but the real issue is to assure that producers of alternative power have a central place in the power system on a long-term basis, rather than a temporary role subsidized by state programs.

8.3.1. Wind

California was a global leader in wind energy under PURPA during the 1970s, along with Denmark. However, the State fell behind especially in manufacturing of wind turbines. California wind developers under PURPA developed large wind farms with small machines, an innovation that has been retained even as the machine size has grown. California has already about 1700 MW of utility scale wind installed, and another 650 MW are planned (EPRI, 2001: 2-1). Today, larger and more economical (per kWh generated) wind turbines have been developed. The cost of producing wind power has fallen by more than 80% since the first wind farms were installed in California during the late 1970s, and now at 3–5 cents wind is competitive with many fossil fuel options (Markels, 2002: 40). In addition, wind is expanding in response to several state renewable development mandates, notably Texas, New Jersey, Pennsylvania, Wisconsin, and Arizona. Similar laws are motivating investments in wind in several European countries.

Rinie van Est (1999) completed a recent book comparing California and Denmark wind innovation and deployment of wind power. He traced the interplay of policy and innovation in the two countries and concludes that the lack of clear focus of policy in California toward wind development led to weak and ultimately ineffective efforts to develop an effective export industry and continuing development of technology and installations. In contrast, Danish policy was not so ambivalent, but also was more "flexible" (Clark and Lund, 2002). This led to strong collaborative arrangements between government research which supported commercial development as in other Danish industries (Clark and Jensen, 2001). By early 2004, the two largest Danish wind turbine producers merged into one company primarily due to external threats of acquisition and the need for larger capital investment.

Wind is widely claimed to be the technology of choice for low-cost power. Even without considering environmental benefits such as zero pollution, the new machines are cost effective, and provide power at a lower cost than gas-fired plants, the other option. For example, new utility scale projects are costing what works out to be about 3.5–4 cents per kWh (Brown, 2001: 115). This means that wind is not only competitive with most other sources of power, with the prices falling it will clearly be the most attractive source of power regardless of the current reliance on tax credits. California has around 7000 MW potentially developable wind resources in areas that have high enough wind speed for enough hours per day/year to be commercially viable. EPRI (2001: 8-3) estimates that under their high-growth scenario an additional 5100 MW could be installed, bringing total wind output to 6700 MW producing about 6% of the State's electrical requirements. Wind in California is generally strongest during summer peak demand periods, minimizing the disadvantages of its intermittency.

Major innovations have improved the cost effectiveness of wind power. The most obvious has been the growing size of wind machines, increasing in size from 50 kW or smaller during the 1980s to several MW now. The larger size is coupled with more complex electrical generation systems that allow operation at slower wind speeds and greater control in high-speed wind situations. However, the United States and California now lag behind Europe in wind innovation and implementation.

For example, General Electric Wind Energy purchased the remnants of the Enron Wind Company when Enron went into bankruptcy. Enron had purchased the only American wind manufacturer of wind turbines, Zond, located in Tehachapi, California. With the growing interest in wind and the financial scale of a company like General Electric, wind has seen considerable recent technological innovation. In early 2000 the largest machines were the Zond 750 kW turbine, but under General Electric turbines are now being built at over 3.5 MW.

The most common wind turbine now is in the 1.5 MW range. In February 2003, the Los Angeles Department of Water and Power contracted to purchase eighty 1.5 MW GE turbines to be located in the Pine Tree project, 12 miles north of Mojave, California. General Electric announced that it now has produced over 1000 of the 1.5 MW turbines. At the largest scale, GE has produced a new prototype turbine to be installed in Spain rated at 3.6 MW which indicates the continuing increases in size, efficiency, and cost effectiveness of wind for the growing international market (GE Wind, 2004).

In addition, reliability increases from improved blade materials and design to reduce maintenance costs and downtimes for repairs. Wind installations used to cost over $3000 per installed kW while the new turbines cost around $1200 per kW (California Renewable Energy Plan, 2002). These prices are expected to continue to fall.

In spite of lower price, wind has not been accepted as widely as one might expect. The most significant reason is that the wind power is not dispatchable, which means that it is available when the wind blows but that cannot be controlled. While the wind typically blows hardest over passes surrounding the central valley near the peak demand during hot summer afternoons and evenings, operators have a hard time predicting the amount of power that will be available. Moreover, storage of electrical power from wind has not been possible and many wind resource areas are distant from transmission lines, requiring expensive new lines and switching stations.

In some ways the good news in wind is that the policy and interface problems are being solved so that wind energy can be more effective. For example, Governor Davis' Office of Research and Planning brought wind producers, utilities, and the transmission dispatchers together to resolve dispatch problems, and agreement was reached to accommodate the unpredictability of wind resource, as long as best available estimates are provided (Clark and Morris, 2002). Once wind producers became free from penalty fees for not delivering power, their ability to finance expansions increased (CAISO, 2002). This is an example of how technology and policy work together in an agile way (FERC, 2002). In addition, a number of innovative programs to link wind to pumped storage have allowed backup power to meet demand when wind resources are weak.

8.3.2. Geothermal

Geothermal is the largest current renewable source of power in California, not counting large hydroelectric power. Today the State has about 1750 MW of geothermal power plants, mostly in the Geysers area of Sonoma and Lake counties, and in Imperial county in the southern corner of the State. These plants use either direct steam from the ground or draw power from hot water that goes through a binary cycle. Geothermal power is a well-established technology, though many complex problems need resolution concerning chemical discharges and replenishing the water to hot underground chambers at the Geysers.

Geothermal systems are somewhat more expensive than wind, and today some areas have excessive generating capacity for their declining steam resource. Nonetheless, about 300 MW in new geothermal capacity are under development and 150–200 MW more are under consideration in Imperial county. The State estimates that the Imperial County (Salton Sea) area could develop at least 1000 MW of new capacity and that the State has a mid-term development capacity of 3000–4000 MW. This is the largest, most cost effective, and most easily developed new renewable source in California, but it is relatively remote and requires considerable initial investment (Grandy, 2002; CEC, 2003a).

Other end-user resources could be developed, including geothermal for use as direct heat in green houses or other uses rather than generation of electricity. A number of innovative geothermal projects have been built including a district heating project in San Bernardino, and various projects in Lassen county. However, these projects will have little net impact on the electricity system in the State.

8.3.3. Biomass

The biomass fueled power generation system in California also has extensive capacity, though it has suffered in recent years when many producers were not paid during the price spikes, bankruptcies, and blackouts. These could be restored to operation and the biomass-electricity industry could expand significantly. Today, agricultural and wood-waste burning systems are about three quarters of the 1000 MW operational biomass capacity, landfill gas collection and utilization contributes most of the remaining capacity (EPRI, 2001: 4-1). The bulk of the biomass in California comes from sawmill residues, forest-wood residues, and other agricultural and domestic waste products. At its peak in the early 1990s the California biomass industry had a capacity of 660 MW, consumed 10 million tons of waste a year, and generated 4.5 billion kWh of electricity. More recently biomass has produced about 3.2 billion kWh per year, consuming about 6 million tons of waste. With the decline of the California timber industry, the cheapest source of fuel is less available. However, at the same time clearing the forests of excessive flammable material is an increasingly significant goal since the huge fires that burned in Los Angeles and San Diego counties in October 2003. Landfill gas systems are important because they capture methane that would otherwise create air pollution, and so they are doubly attractive.

One of the least fortunate results of the deregulation debacle is that biomass plants got left out of the mix. While biomass in California is large and diverse, the future can be much more attractive if attention is given to the dual problems of technological innovation and expanding markets. However, careful projections show that the maximum potential for the biomass industry is about double the current 660 MW capacity, or about 1300 MW. This goal could be reached by forest cleaning and thinning for fire protection and greater use of urban residue. (Interagency Green Accounting Workgroup: 18–24).

8.3.4. Solar thermal

California has several solar thermal plants that were built in the 1980s and they continue to produce inexpensive power. However, the cost of new plants is high. The extensive solar sites in the Mojave Desert are available with few environmental consequences. Two technologies have been deployed to date—parabolic troughs and central towers with mirrors that reflect sunlight to a tower receptor. A demonstration solar tower project was built in Daggett and is rated at 10 MW. Heat is turned into power using traditional techniques. Experts consider that solar thermal plants have potential if the price can be reduced (EPRI, 2001: Chapter 5).

However, the corporate and private sector investment needed to commercialize these technologies seems to be lacking. While costs have traditionally been cited, new technological advances, primarily from Israeli companies such as Solel Corporation, appear to have dramatically cut costs and made the systems far smaller and hence more conducive to local and regional power generation. One hybrid application, for example, is the use of solar thermal energy for desalinization plants (one of the key barriers for desalinization has been the high costs for energy). This hybrid application fits both public policy and societal needs in California for both energy and water.

8.3.5. Photovoltaic systems

The long process of development of photovoltaic (PV) cells is paying off. Data on photovoltaic system implementation are hard to obtain since many systems are placed on individual businesses and residences. However, incentives to install PV systems continue to attract users and the price is falling. As noted above the costs for solar/PV systems will be cost competitive to other traditional energy sources, according to one large Japanese manufacturer in 2004 (Kenidi, 2003). Nonetheless, some manufacturers and contractors continue to rely upon government programs for tax relief, subsidies, and purchase contracts. These may be needed for a few years in order to make the industry more sustainable.

The potential for PV systems is great for California. If only 1% of the State surface area were covered with PV panels, it would generate on average about 100 GW, about twice the current power demand. Much of the PV coverage could be on top of existing buildings. Schultz *et al.* (2001) and Grandy *et al.* (2002) looked carefully at projections for on-site energy generation, primarily in the PV area. The results were striking in that they indicated both cost competitiveness with energy conservation and efficiency as well as exceeding the targets for State renewable energy standards by the year 2017.

One of the major incentives for PV installation is net metering. What this means is that a PV system owner can generate power for his own use while still hooked up to the grid. If the owner needs power when the PV is not generating because of night or poor weather, the power is supplied by the utility in the normal way. However, if the owner does not use all the generated PV power it will flow back into the grid. With net metering the amount provided back to the grid is deducted from the power that is used and the owner pays only for the balance, net over a period of a year according to new rules. If the owner supplies more power to the grid than is used, the utility according to new rules will pay the owner for it. This makes it very attractive for small installations since they use the entire grid as a battery. Moreover, the PV displaces power at full retail value rather than a wholesale price. Net metering is also good for the utilities because the PV supply will reduce demand and in many cases will supplement supply on hot sunny days when power is in shortest supply.

The growing PV market is subsidized in California. The State has agreed to a rebate of up to half the price of PV systems, to maximum of $4.50 per watt (CEC Emerging renewables resource account, 2001). One of the limitations of current policy is that the cap on rebates has frozen prices at that level, with little downward price pressure. Many industry observers feel that the price would fall if the rebate program were restructured. On the other hand, the support at this level following the rise in energy prices led to requests for rebates of over 1500 kW per month in September 2001, and a total of 14 MW had been approved (Garbesi and Ramo, 2002). The real price of PV systems is debated and hard to determine. However, Garbesi and Ramo offer the following calculation: PV systems are being installed commercially for about $8 per watt, and adding 20% for maintenance over a 25-year life span, PV energy costs about 17 cents per kWh. However, with rebates the cost falls to only 8.5 cents per kWh compared to around 12 cents per kWh for retail utility energy delivered to a residence. In other words, PV with net metering is well below retail and could easily pay for itself if it receives rebates.

However, the level of support for the PV industry is less in the US than in other countries. For example, in Japan a well-funded and coordinated program has enabled PV growth at the rate of 50% per year, making Japan the largest PV market in the world, consuming about 40% of world production. Germany increased its PV market five-fold in two years (Interagency Green, 2002: 28). These programs are challenging the US lead in the PV field, but planning is underway to respond. Today industry leaders are expecting PV end-user costs to fall to about $3 per watt by 2010, a price that is competitive with retail prices without subsidy. This assumes financing (interest and principle of 12% per year or $0.36 per year per watt), which could be recovered if the PV cell averaged 10 h a day for 360 days, totaling 3.6 kWh per year. At 10 cents per kWh the watt-sized PV would generate just enough to repay the loan, and then all the power is free or can be sold. A 500 W system would cost $1500 and could pay for itself and earn its owner $35 a year based on these estimates. However, since the PV will be producing power on peak, if real-time metering is added the value of the power generated will go up even further.

8.3.6. Cogeneration or CPH (combined heat power)

The potential for additional cogeneration installation in California is not known now. The State built many specialized power plants when it could have given contracts for independent producers through cogeneration which would have added little to the demand for natural gas in the State. In addition, many hospitals, computer centers, colleges and universities, and other users are looking for increased reliability and installing large backup generation capacity in case power goes out. The same firms adding this backup capability could easily become more regular cogenerators and contribute power to the grid as needed.

There are some regulatory problems with expanding cogeneration into self-generation or more permanent grid producers. For one thing, many of these generation facilities will be in urban areas where strict air quality rules prevent consuming any more fuel and making air quality any dirtier. Further, the "do not build here" syndrome often occurs. Renewable fueled systems are far more preferable and likely to be advanced in California with special incentives and programs.

The experience in California with cogeneration is varied, but extensive. Some of the cogeneration in the State is simple combined heat power engines (typically fossil-fueled turbines) that supply both electricity and heat to building occupants. The recent placement of a natural gas-fired turbine in the parking garage of the California Public Utilities Commission in San Francisco is an example. It quietly sits outside the building, supplying heat for water and interior heating, along with electricity for lights and other office uses. This cogeneration unit is supplied by a private company. While most of the natural gas would be used anyway for heat, it is much more environmentally responsible than not cogenerating.

Other cogeneration processes have been tapped and provide a model for the future wherever fuel is burned for heat. For example, to increase recovery of oil, hot steam is injected into oil wells throughout the central valley. Some burn oil and others natural gas, often from the well itself. In these cases the fuel making the steam first powers a cogeneration electricity unit, and the remaining steam is injected.

This model is another example of how the system can be virtually free to run and generate electricity from existing sources.

In the concern over the worldwide energy crisis cogeneration has largely been forgotten as a potential source of additional and reserve power. It is highly dispersed or distributed, and it makes double use of short natural gas supplies. Moreover, cogeneration systems are very quick to design and install, as most are off the shelf applications. Such systems and applications have been extremely successful in Scandinavia (Lund, 1998, 2003), for example, with entire communities receiving power from such power supplies.

Most European countries, in fact, refer to cogeneration or CPH as distributed generation (DG). Later distributed generation will be discussed at length as part of an agile energy system model. In such agile power systems, cogeneration (along with conservation) or DG is in the front lines of any response to shortages and high prices.

Indeed the PURPA experience showed that tens of thousands MW of power can be obtained very quickly when cogenerators are offered attractive rates (Summerton and Bradshaw, 1991), though the PURPA formula was clearly not the right rate. Nonetheless as nation-states consider what their policies and programs must be to address energy shortages and crises, such systems must be central part of planning and their strategic use of resources.

8.3.7. The hydrogen option

In order to have long-term viability of renewable power, storage is critical for the economical generation intermittent power (e.g., solar, PV, run-of-the-river, and wind) into hydrogen, which is nonpolluting. A key in the hydrogen economy is that using electricity to generate hydrogen is very efficient, operating at an efficiency of 75%. This is comparable or superior to other forms of storage including batteries and pumped hydro (Isherwood *et al.*, 2000). In addition, it is also the fact that hydrogen is no more dangerous to store and work with than any other fuel such as natural gas, and in fact it is safer than gasoline because its vapors do not concentrate on the ground. In addition, fuel cell efficiencies are increasing and costs are falling, spurred on by automakers.

Hydrogen has long been of interest to the academic research community. Unfortunately, the public image of hydrogen is as a volatile fuel with the Hindenberg tragedy in the 1930s before news cameras from around the world. Until recently the explanation of the airship explosion was viewed as the hydrogen fuel itself (Kamin and

Lipman, 2003). Now advanced data analyses conclusively point to the paint used for the outer shell of the Hindenberg as the cause.

Additionally, advances in understanding both the production and safety needs of hydrogen (Norsk Hydro, 2003; Stuart Energy: 203) have been internationally proposed in new codes and standards. The need today is to educate and implement fire and safety codes at the local level (CFCP, 2003; CSFCC, 2003). More is discussed on this topic in Chapter 13. Extensive data is available from a series of over 23 presentations made before State government officials in August 2003 (Clark, 2004).

With the end of World War II and the advent of the Cold War, hydrogen was used in the making of the H-bomb led by Nobel Laureate Edward Teller. Research conducted under the American Atomic Energy Commission, and later through the US Department of Energy (USDOE) in the mid-1970s at the Lawrence Livermore National Laboratory (LLNL), established the USA as one of the world's leading centers for hydrogen research. More recent research from the USA national labs now focuses on economic issues (Berry, 1996; Berry *et al.*, 1998; Isherwood *et al.*, 2000).

The USDOE through LLNL and other laboratories and facilities (Rambach, 1999) continued its efforts primarily deriving hydrogen from fossil fuels such as oil, gas, and nuclear processes. More recently, a number of R&D projects with "clean coal" production into hydrogen have gained some currency. USDOE convened a Hydrogen Technology Advisory Panel in the 1990s that reviewed policies and plans for hydrogen. By the end of November 2002, USDOE released its "Hydrogen Strategic Plan" including suggestions for national standards and codes.

8.3.8. Fuel cells

The California Fuel Cell Partnership (CFCP) was formed in 1999. As will be discussed later, the Partnership was designed to resolve the needs of government and industry to create solutions to the California zero emission vehicle (ZEV) regulations of the early 1990s. The Partnership, located in West Sacramento, near the State Capital, has a center with all the major car makers renting office space, supplying funds and vehicles, and providing technical and administrative support services. Until July 2003, General Motors did not have a presence with the CFCP, since its policy was instead to fight the ZEV rules in California. A change in GM strategy has led to a resolution between the State and GM. Now GM is not only collaborating closely with CFCP but also establishing a major business presence in

Southern California (Clark, 2004). The CFCP estimates commercial fuel cell-powered cars to be in the market place (California first) by 2005. The California Stationary Fuel Cell Collaborative (SFCC) was formed in August 2001 by leaders of CARB, the National Fuel Cell Center (UCI) at University of California, Irvine, and Governor's Office of Planning and Research (OPR), respectively. The mission of the Collaborative is to promote stationary fuel cell commercialization as a means toward (SFCC, 2002):

- reducing or eliminating air pollutants and greenhouse gas emissions,
- increasing energy efficiency,
- promoting energy reliability and security,
- promoting energy diversity,
- promoting energy independence, and
- realizing a sustainable energy future.

From the CFCC (2004), it:

- envisions fuel cell installations pursued by state, local, and public organizations as well as private entities. In aggregate, the Collaborative has established a minimum goal of 50–250 MW of installed capacity by the year 2006 in California. We believe that California represents a critical market for the fuel cell industry. Therefore, it is anticipated that California will capture 5–25% of the global sales volume over the next several years;
- takes specific actions to promote a wide variety of fuel cell technologies, sizes, and applications for installation in California. These actions will include facilitating the installation of fuel cells in a variety of applications including: industrial, commercial, residential, premium, remote, backup, and base-load power applications—as the market dictates;
- provides unparalleled leadership in facilitating the installation of fuel cells in State buildings as well as support the installation of fuel cells in other markets.

The technological principles underlying fuel cells[1] are older than internal combustion engines (ICE), since it goes back to 1839; until now they have been expensive and used only in space rockets and some military applications. As in any technological development

---

[1]A fuel cell is an electrochemical engine that produces energy; it combines fuel and air to produce electricity with no moving parts.

linked with defense or military application, the costs are far too high for commercialization. Below we outline the role of regulation and technological innovation in changing the shape of technological trajectories toward the commercialization of environmentally sound technologies in the energy sector. In Clark (2001), the point was made that the energy crisis in California is really an opportunity for the creation of business cases for new advanced technologies like fuel cells.

The fuel cell is inherently twice as efficient as ICE, but costs are still high since military applications had to be made by manufacturers with secret and precise specifications for only a limited number of products. Today with the fuel cell more commercially viable the spillovers between transportation and energy seem to be likely.

A new hydrogen company in Los Angeles has made the public announcement that it will begin converting ICE vehicles into hydrogen fuel cars by 2006. Governor Schwarzenegger made the same announcement in his September–October 2003 campaign for Governor. Commercialization of fuel cells to transportation needs has been inhibited over the decades by two significant factors: one is economic or cost for research as well as development into prototypes and commercialization; and the other is market demand.

The key issue is bringing the costs for fuel cells into the range of conventional batteries. Now with better electrochemical technologies and improved materials, fuel cell costs can be made competitive with batteries as well as being environmentally more benign. In late 2002, the University of California, Davis Institute for Transportation received two Toyota fuel cell-powered cars; so did the University of California, Irvine. The City of Los Angeles took delivery of four Honda fuel cell-powered cars. The list increases in 2003–2004.

The hydrogen future is here today. Iceland has proved it already. Several large and small companies have developed and begun to commercialize the needed technologies. Shell, BP, and Chevron-Texaco are world leaders in this area as they foresee both a diminishing oil fuel supply and an increased world demand for renewable energy for hydrogen systems. Every major carmaker is heavily involved with fuel cell cars, some transitioning to renewable energy fuel for hydrogen production faster than others (Clark, 2004).

8.3.9. Transmission and distribution innovations—energy webs

The potential of an improved technological base for an agile power system is vastly increased if the inputs of power are connected to each other. The grid used to be the backbone connecting the various parts of the system but it was prototypically lethargic. Power flowed one way from producers to consumers, and there was no other information carried along the route except to assure that supplies balanced demand so that voltage could be adjusted by more supply as needed. Demand was not controlled but could be roughly predicted based on statistical models that averaged individual decisions into relatively stable aggregated demands.

The lethargic grid and distribution network of the past will be transformed as part of the emerging agile power system. The key to this new network linking producers and consumers is a change in the way the system is understood. Producers of power will be distributed, small scale, and responsive to quick changes in demand, just as consumers will increasingly be able to be informed about changes in price and availability of power. In some instances consumer demand will be controlled by smart devices (run by locally based chips that monitor prices and availability of power, and then respond with decisions about whether or not to buy power at the available moment). In other cases consumers will be able to turn control of their power usage over to a central source that can balance grid demand by simple commands that, for example, raise air-conditioner thermostats two degrees—not noticeable by the occupants of a room but able to save considerable power.

One of the keys to improvements in grid management and design is control over the flow of electricity along different paths. Innovations in switching and power controls are allowing more active management, necessary if the grid is going to become the two-way carrier of excess power from distributed generation to consumers whose systems are not producing enough power. It can also be a carrier to hydrolysis stations where excess electrical power is turned into hydrogen so that it can be used later in fuel cells or burned in regular turbines.

8.4. Conservation and Load Management

Conservation remains the least expensive way to expand the power system. The fact that California avoided blackouts during the summer of 2001 is in large part the result of conservation programs that combined with some increased capacity and legal actions that reduced the market power exerted by Enron and other brokers. While new power plants helped prevent further blackouts, conservation was the clear winner in the California strategy and it was at a much lower cost with long-term benefits.

Conservation and load management go hand in hand on the demand side of providing power to California. The advantage of conservation is that it is the front line of attack on excessive power consumption, and savings tend to have long-term effects. For example, improved energy efficiency in industrial, commercial, and residential applications has saved thousands of MW at relatively low cost. Compact fluorescent lights use only 20% of the power as equally sized incandescent bulbs, and now have very comparable performance qualities. Even larger gains are available in industrial settings. These new lighting technologies pay for themselves in a matter of months and save both the utility and the customer without additional cost for the lifetime of the use. In general, conservation programs have been successful at costs of 1–3 cents per kWh saved, well below replacement costs. Some of the easiest conservation efforts have already been pursued, but many more exist. Most are in the 2–3 cent range. Industrial efficiency programs could save 3.5 GWh or 544 MW peak at a cost below 6 cents according to the California Power Authority Clean Growth report (2002: 15).

While conservation has been a feature of advanced energy systems through the recent decades of energy crises, the agile system takes conservation another step to implement what Lovins calls cutting through the cost barrier. This allows, in his language, many instances of "doing twice as much with half the resources," or improving efficiency by a "factor of four." Much of the progress to be made is more efficient design, and paying attention to resource use. Other progress involves . understanding the overall cost benefits by simplification of some existing systems to the point where large parts of the original design can be omitted (Hawkins *et al.*, 2002; Weizsacker *et al.*, 2002).

Conservation has been proven in the old system to be possible without behavior change and to lead to increased quality of life rather than reductions in lifestyle. The US Department of Energy (USDOE) program, Energy Star, has proven to be extremely useful in this regard with labels for products that demonstrate certain conservation goals. USDOE also funds research programs and national laboratories for data and demonstration of new conservation energy-efficient technologies.

Huge increases in refrigerator efficiency are illustrations of both the research and applied programs from USDOE. In each case incentives and mandates to manufacturers has led to increases in efficiency which allowed people to save considerable power without any sacrifice in convenience. From 1972 average electricity use in new refrigerators declined from 1725 kWh per year to about 500 kWh per year in 2001, even though the size and number of features increased during this period. Also efficiency of central air conditioners increased about 54% over this time frame (Geller and Goldstein, 1998; Geller, 2003: 98).

In addition, the new refrigerator efficiency provides even more benefit because as they operate they loose less heat into the house during the summer which then needs to be taken away a second time by air conditioning. In the agile system this premise is continued, while at the same time solutions are found that cost nothing initially while saving resources over a lifetime. The best example of this is the cutting edge in housing design where energy efficiency is so high that the house can be built with minimal heating or cooling system, saving more by the elimination of these systems than is spent on the energy-efficiency measures themselves (Bradshaw, 1996).

Demand side load management programs have also been very successful. In general, they work by offering large energy users options where they pay a lower price overall for power with the agreement that when supplies are low the user will curtail a certain amount of use for a certain period of time. Governor Davis during the energy crisis issued an Executive Order requiring public buildings to not only lower energy costs, but also purchase energy-saving devices.

The "Flex your Power" program was started to educate and inform the public about energy conservation and efficiency programs. Both the CEC and the CPUC expanded their conservation incentives and began to widely promote conservation goals. The results over the summer of 2001 were dramatic with a 12% saving in public building energy usage. What this means is that industrial processes that can hold for a few hours will do so when needed, while other users may choose to allow air conditioning to be turned off for a period of time or even that a business will close for the duration of the energy demand period. In other cases the user will shift to a backup generator and not rely on the grid. While these demand reductions do not work for all users, and they are most efficient when targeted to the largest users, they have a concrete and very low cost of managing peak demand.

The State estimates that a potential of 3750 peak MW are available via load reduction (see CEC 2002–2012 Electricity Outlook Report, P700-01-001). This is much more power than could easily be built in a short period of time, but on the downside, each saved kWh means that users have had to change their preferences for when and how they use energy, an argument to turn these interruptible savings into permanent conservation gains.

In the agile economy a variety of demand side programs will be essential, but ideally users will be less dependent on grid-supplied power and have more self-supplied power and the ability to not just curtail use but increase the supply of excess power fed back into the grid from dispersed locations.

In addition, the model of improving conservation by increasing the efficiency of refrigerators and home air conditioning means that previously one might decide to cycle a refrigerator or air conditioner off for a short time as part of a demand reduction. With efficiency increases, such as zero peak demand houses or efficient refrigerators, the decision to turn the unit off during peak is not an issue because it already uses little power.

8.5. Renewable Portfolios

8.5.1. The California State Renewable Investment Plan

The benefits of the investment agenda in renewable sources of power set out in the five-year State Renewable Investment Plan (Schultz *et al.*, 2002) are substantial. First, state and local governments can regain control of their energy bills through restoring stability to on-going budgeting needs and focusing on improving the public services that they are expected to provide to their "clients"—the citizens of California. By creating local and regional power generation, public and private customers can free themselves from the vulnerabilities of the central electric grid and hence be more "secure" in terms of power supply and from attack or unwanted emergencies. Hence, government services will become more reliable.

Second, by installing environmentally sound local generation products in government buildings, state and local agencies can contribute to the amount of renewable electricity in California. As documented in the Plan, for example, accomplishing the self-sufficiency goal will contribute approximately 3000 MW of renewable power. This amount plus other renewable generation projects is almost equal to the amount of additions expected by 2005 from central-grid renewable resources such as wind, geothermal, and biomass. The Plan in other words helps meet or even exceed a Renewables Portfolio Standard (RPS) such as proposed by the California Energy Commission Investment Plan with a goal of 17% renewables in 2006.

Third, the systematic build out of energy generation systems, for example, in public buildings that can be distributed throughout the State, will accelerate the public's awareness of these products for consideration in buildings owned and operated in the private sector. State and local agencies and their buildings throughout California will become "show places" for these alternative energy technologies and demonstrations of how these on-site generation systems work. Moreover, the costs for such products to the general public will be reduced due to increased manufacturing and supply.

Fourth, implementation of the Investment Plan by state and local agencies will signal manufacturers and vendors of these products that California represents a growing and secure market. With additional economic incentives and development plans these firms will become a core part of business expansion plans for many years to come, thereby contributing to the growth of additional high-technology industries locating in California and bringing an expansion of job opportunities, training, and educational opportunities.

Fifth, by meeting the self-sufficiency challenge, government agencies can directly contribute to reducing the amount of electricity imported from out of state, hence contributing to a longer-term opportunity for the State as a whole to become self-sufficient. Renewable and clean energy contributes to efficiency as well as local or on-site generation.

Sixth, by meeting the self-sufficiency challenge, state and local agencies can contribute to other state and local goals such as air quality improvements without causing land use problems that will necessarily accompany most new central power plant additions to the central electric grid without adding to California's dependence on natural gas.

Finally, given the events of September 11, 2001, California, like the entire country, must address the issue of secure infrastructures. Energy is one of the key sectors. The Governor implemented such an emergency plan in January 2001 where none existed before as part of his plan to provide sustainable energy to the State. Now the implementation of a secure energy infrastructure is imperative on the regional and local levels in order to provide dispersed energy supply, local power needs, and independence from central grids.

The conclusion of the State Renewable Investment Plan is that there are sufficient financial resources available to get started on a five-year plan which will also be part of the Economic Stimulus Package. The focus of the Plan is to install on all state and local government buildings on-site PV, fuel cell, and microturbine products, which provides the basis for helping to define the "new energy market" in California.

The new energy market in California is in "transition" but will not be like the regulated market and certainly not close to the chaos that defined the deregulated market. Most likely the future energy market will be a combination that provides for clean, renewable local-distributed energy systems, on-site and cogeneration, and regional generation. This new energy market will redefine how integrated resource management is implemented in a public market where private companies can compete in a socially responsible manner.

8.5.2. *Renewable energy and state policy*

The California Consumer and Power Authority's (CPA) Investment Plan and the Renewable Energy Plan for the Governor both rely on data that have been gathered from a number of sources including the CPA Request for Bids on Fuel Cells completed in February 2002 by the Interagency Green Accounting Working Group (IGAWG) (Schultz *et al.*, 2002). Essentially, the costs for renewable energy technologies such as wind but also solar and fuel cells is cost competitive when seen in the aggregate, compared to fossil fuels, and purchased in large quantities. Similarly, Bolinger *et al.* (2001) analyzed the bids received by the CPA for wind and geothermal power facilities to find that both technologies were competitive with traditional power resources.

Additionally, the IGAWG published a revision of the Standard Practices Manual (Schultz *et al.*, 2001) that took into consideration for project financing life-cycle analysis of new technologies as well as externalities such as health, climate, and environmental impact. What has yet to be considered are the fuel source costs for development. For example, what does it cost to drill for oil or mine for coal as compared to the use of the Sun or wind (Weil, 1991).

Many other dramatic innovations took place including the change of the Independent System Operators' "Imbalance Penalty Rules" against wind and solar power (CAISO, 2002). These industries until the fall 2001 were penalized for not delivering power based on day-ahead forecasts. Hence the industry was not able to get financing for their renewable energy projects. The rule change relaxed the imbalance penalties and thus new projects were started.

When these economic factors are included, the costs for renewable energy will be considerably less. As James and James (2001) review about the European Union's research in a study of "the true costs of electricity":

> *The results of a major EU-funded study undertaken over the last 10 years and released in Brussels in July show that the cost of producing electricity from coal or oil would double and the cost of electricity production from gas would increase by 30% if external costs, such as damage to the environment and health, were taken into account. These costs amount to up to 2% of the EU's gross*

domestic product, not including any costs associated with global warming, and
are absorbed by society at large rather than through the cost of consuming energy.
The study was conducted by researchers in all EU member states, and in the US.
It is the first study to attempt to quantify the damage resulting from all different
forms of electricity production across the EU. (James and James, 2001)

What is clear from the 2000 to 2001 energy crisis in California is the need for new affordable and environmentally sound technologies that can be commercialized. Throughout 2001, a number of plans were proposed to stimulate investment in these technologies, including plans by the California Energy Commission in June 2001. Various organizations such as the California Bay Area (San Francisco) Economic Council hired consultants to make plans. The Union of Concerned Scientists, Center for Energy Renewable Energy, and the Energy Foundation, all have advocated solutions.

All the plans made one basic assumption: the deregulated market would exist and be modified or adjusted to allow market rules to govern new energy generation. While regulation will not be reinstituted in California, it is significant to note neither will further deregulation as advocated by many economists (Borenstein *et al.*, 2001 among many others), power companies, and nonprofits (see California Commission on the 21st Century Report, 2002; Clark, 2001; Clark and Lund, 2002). What is good for the market is not necessarily good for the general public.

Morris and Clark (2002) documented in early 2002 that California has ample supplies of a variety of renewable energy resources, each of which offers the State the benefits of clean, renewable energy, and energy diversity. In order to realize its full renewable energy potential, California needs a comprehensive, coordinated set of policies to encourage renewable energy development and production. The goals should be both to encourage instate renewable energy production, and to attract instate manufacturing of renewable energy goods and services. Five policy areas must be advanced.

1. First, an overall policy should be developed and implemented that supports renewable energy production in general in the State. Gradually increasing goals need to be mandated that combine both central grid and distributed systems as well as on-site energy generation which fall under the overall renewable energy Statewide Objectives.
2. Second, recognizing that a "one-size-fits-all" policy is not sufficient, targeted policies should be employed that recognize and address the specific needs of various strategically valuable renewables.

Without doubt, the major immediate-term need for central-station renewable power generators in California is the development of a stable and predictable market for sales of their power. This should be followed up by the development of specific targets for increasing the amount of renewable content in the State's energy supply over the coming 10–20 years.

3. Third, new advanced renewable technologies must be "linked" or developed as integrated (e.g., pumped storage and wind or solar and fuel cells) in order to be cost competitive with more conventional energy systems including single renewable and efficient energy areas.

4. Fourth, economic consideration must be given (incentives, credits, tax breaks, finance, and public investment) to renewable energy companies that locate in California.

5. Finally, related to economic development policy decision making is the need for training and education of a workforce who can install, maintain, and operate renewable and clean energy facilities. Such an educated workforce of today can be seen as the innovators and entrepreneurs of tomorrow.

8.5.3. California power authority

In the spring of 2001, the California Legislature formed the California Consumer Power and Conservation Financing Authority (CPA). It began its operations in August 2001 with a difficult mandate: create reserve energy capacity for the State. Later this was defined as primarily in renewable energy. After months of determining its role in the energy mix within California, the CPA focused on finance and investment issues surrounding energy in California. With legislation authorizing it to raise $5 billion in the bond market, the CPA developed and released several studies, including one on "Clean Growth" (CPA, February 15, 2002).

The Power Authority programs have a huge potential impact. For example, the CPA Portfolio reduces out-of-state natural gas purchases by $10–15 billion.[2] Indeed a study by the Electric Power Research Institute (EPRI) projected that by the end of the decade an additional 4400 MW of grid renewable power could be economically available in California at a price of $.069/kWh or an additional 8200 MW could be

---

[2]The $15 billion assumes natural gas prices of $2.50/mmBTU over the next 20 years. Some scenarios project costs 60% or higher than this.

available at a price of \$.091/kWh under normal market forces[3] (CPA, 2002: 17). This system should become a model for other jurisdictions, promoting renewable energy development nationwide. However, now after one year, the CPA has not had its \$5 billion bonds authorized and hence has had to focus on long-term low-cost energy loans (CPA, June 2002) for public and private sector partnerships. The future of the agency is uncertain.

8.6. Distributed Energy Production

The notion of distributed production or dispersed production (Summerton and Bradshaw, 1991) is really at the core of what makes the new technological fix different from the old traditional model that needs replacing. Deregulation had an immensely negative impact on the markets and control of electricity, leading to escalating prices, whereas an agile system needs to radically deconstruct the centralized large-scale power plant (of which there are perhaps 100 major ones in California). Following PURPA, California had thousands of distributed producers who accounted for up to a quarter of the State's power needs. We argue that renewable technologies and other strategies can expand that to tens of thousands of producers generating most of the State's power. Fortunately, renewable power especially photovoltaics and hydrogen are ideally suited to distributed systems.

A distributed system has many producers typically located near to demand, whereas a dispersed system simply has many producers. The distributed system allows for self-generation and varied technologies, many of which are intermittent and not dispatchable. Distributed systems at a large scale may need new strategies for grid management, but as a supplement to the existing system the availability of distributed resources may enhance grid performance. Isherwood defines "distributed generation" as

> *Distributed power systems generate electricity in close proximity to the end users, and can thereby avoid dependence on a network of long-distance transmission lines and provide opportunities for efficient use of renewable resources. Distributed energy systems may or may not be connected to a regional power grid. Where they are grid connected, distributed generating capability must compete with large-scale power generating systems, which use*

---

[3]Electric Power Research Institute, "California Renewable Technology Market and Benefits Assessment, Final Report to the California Energy Commission," November 2001.

technologies that benefit from the economies of scale. Advantages from being grid-connected include the ready availability of backup power and the possibility of selling excess locally-generated power back through the grid. (Isherwood, 1998)

There are a number of agility advantages of distributed power systems. First, distributed systems reduce reliance on long-distance transmission by supplying more power closer to end use. This reduces transmission loss (up to 10% in many cases). Second, distributed systems increase reliability because there are more independent suppliers who have a smaller share of responsibility for reliability. The greater numbers of generating units reduce the impact that the loss of any one section of the system would have on the whole. Rifkin (2002) notes that this feature greatly decreases vulnerability of the power system to terrorism or catastrophic failure. Third, the large number of units increases the chances that new, more environmentally beneficial, and economically attractive systems can participate.

On the other hand, distributed production has a number of challenges that need to be overcome. For example, each of the small producers needs to have contracts to sell power (all or surplus self-generation) in order to obtain financing for their project. Second, there is little control over the system in case too much distributed power enters the grid or if too little is available at any one time. Planning needs to be done using statistical projections for supply in the same way that energy planners estimate demand. While this is not too serious, it may cause problems in grid systems that have limited capacity in critical places.

In mid-summer of 2002, the California Energy Commission (CEC) issued its DG plan after spending six months in hearings and debates. The plan noted that California has made progress with distributed generation. About 2000 MW distributed generation is now connected to the grid, while another 3000 MW is used as backup. Both PG&E and Southern California Edison have over 500 distributed generation plants and San Diego has half that many.

However, this plan lacked a comprehensive vision which would link expanded renewable production into the markets in an attractive way to investors. The State needed to fit distributed production into a Comprehensive Renewable Energy Finance Plan for the State (Matteson, 2002b). Along the way a State Renewable Energy Workshop (August 2002) helped refine the State-distributed generation plan (Matteson *et al.*, 2002).

Distributed generation is most useful to the agile power system when it is decentralized or on-site electric generation connected at the distribution level to the transmission and distribution grid. Such a broad definition supports financial investment planning for renewable energy. It is critical that the distributed generation issues be solved for a viable renewable energy effort to succeed. As the Governor of California's Commission for the 21st Century put it in its Infrastructure Report, "To achieve sustainability, Californians must think differently about energy infrastructure," and to capture the "great potential for distributed energy generation systems, especially renewable or clean energy systems." (California Commission, Infrastructure Report, 2002).

Distributed generation is linked to renewable electricity generation (Clark, 2003). Both should be contained in the State of California's Energy Plan, especially seen as a flexible power system. Any nation-state plan must define, in quantifiable terms (financial amounts, timelines, and carbon amounts), the following elements: (1) amount of generation, including targets for renewable energy; (2) customer's options on purchase of electrical energy (wholesale and retail); (3) energy-efficiency targets for every household and business; and (4) permitted levels of impacts on the environment (Matteson *et al.*, 2002).

8.7. Hybrid Energy Technologies in Agile Systems

Hybrid technologies or hybrid systems (Weare, 2003) are a combination of two or more technologies (that is, wind with pumped storage or solar with fuel cells—here both renewables are linked with storage devices). Hybrid technologies can be seen as the future for solving the issue of intermittent resources both as firm energy source and qualifying the energy produced as "base load" (NPS, 2002). Northern Power Systems has implemented such systems with good numbers in terms of costs and results. A number of companies are beginning to explore the possible implementation of hybrid technology systems for their operations.

Hybrid technologies offer substantial benefits for both "green grid power" and renewable-only systems, which are often not the most reliable or economic approaches. Some benefits of hybrid technologies from Northern Power System (2002) may include:

8.7.1. Cost savings

- Reduced fuel costs, including storage, handling, and maintenance
- Reduced utility power consumption, especially during expensive peak hours

- Buy-downs, tax credits, other incentives reduce installation cost and shorten payback period
- Reduced impact of utility rate hikes

8.7.2. Environmental benefits

- Reduced greenhouse gas emissions
- Improved efficiency
- Reduced fuel consumption
- Less potential for leakage and spills

8.7.3. High reliability

- Uninterrupted power supply
- Reduced risk of financial losses due to power outages
- Reduced downtime

8.7.4. Energy independence

- Lower vulnerability to power outages
- Own your own power supply
- Incorporate multiple energy sources

Some examples of hybrid technologies on a regional level are:

- Oak Creek Energy Systems plans to combine wind turbines with storage systems such as pumped storage or electronic storage to create a wind-driven system that can provide firm energy with some dispatchability.
- Sharp Solar Systems Division of Sharp Electronics is researching the combination of photovoltaics with electrolyzers and fuel cells and developing a control system to optimize its operation.
- SunLine Transit Agency in Thousand Palms, California has a number of experimental fuel cell buses, and they are making hydrogen fuel for the buses in electrolyzers powered by photovoltaic arrays.

What is obvious is that the energy cost numbers begin to "add" correctly and the power supplied is cost competitive. Some of these hybrid technologies were under development in Japan with strong government support for many years (Clark and Chung, 2000). Today they show that with technologies integrated into agile energy systems over 1–3 MW, the costs are extremely competitive (Wiser *et al.*, 2001).

Intermittent generating resources (such as wind and solar) are fundamentally different than conventional resources with regards to how they affect the operation of the electricity grid. The difference results from the fact that unlike conventional generators, whose output is controlled by the operator, intermittent generators produce electricity in amounts that are dependent on factors beyond the operator's control, such as wind speed or cloudiness. This intermittent source of power creates two problems.

The first is a problem of management of the resource in relation to the grid, which has traditionally been by operator control and now has to be seen as a statistical problem much like demand that cannot be controlled. The second problem is a utilization problem which has to be solved by integrating the intermittent sources into a whole utilization pattern including storage.

The integration of renewable intermittent sources has progressed considerably. Wind was discovered in California to be an attractive addition to the power mix because of the location of high-wind areas on low passes in the ring of hills surrounding the great Central Valley. As summer temperatures increase in the Valley the hot air would rise, sucking cool coastal air into the valley. Thus, the wind over the passes was greatest at just those times when power was most needed for air conditioning, a factor which allowed early wind-farm operators to benefit from peak-power prices. While these special circumstances were known within the management of integrated utilities, there was no way to value them after deregulation. This led to a series of efforts to find a policy solution, a process that is interesting because of its reliance on a public–private partnership to find a solution.

The process went beyond an initial proposal that simplified the needs of the grid operators by simply allowing wind producers to sell on the spot market, which would usually be too low an average price to justify the capital expense of building the wind resource. Similarly, wind operators could not afford to pay penalties if their day-ahead forecasts were wrong, though all parties admitted that the forecasts were relatively good. What was resolved was a strategy that allowed intermittent producers to sell power based on best available forecast without penalty, within some broad long-term performance objectives. This worked to everyone's satisfaction. Proper implementation of these new scheduling rules will open the California market to new intermittent renewable generation. The benefits of low environmental impact, rural economic development, and source diversity for the State greatly outweigh the small cost of accommodating intermittent generators into the electricity grid.

However, the breakthrough for the system requires agile linking of renewable power sources to improve reliability and management. For example, California's many hydro resources on mountain reservoirs are already being used to stabilize the grid and provide peaking power because they are readily dispatchable, they may be reserved until most needed with virtually no loss in value, and they are relatively ample. Some amount of hydro resource needs to be used on a regular basis to keep rivers flowing to protect fish species and to provide water for farming irrigation, the flexibility in the hydro resource coupled with wind allows expanded renewable capacity.

The next step was to provide incentives to expand pumped storage coupled with nearby wind energy resources, so that the hydro increases reliability of wind when the wind resource is weak. This allows wind to remain as a more valuable peaking power resource. Pumped hydro storage is about 70–75% energy efficient, which means that there is a loss but easily valued considering the premium of peak power.

Another approach to increasing reliability with hybrid systems is to link wind and more conventionally fired fossil fuel generators— either diesel or natural gas. Another strategy is to link fuel cells with hydrogen production through more than one system. In Sweden a cogeneration fuel cell system will be built with solar and biogas sources of hydrogen. Along with the solar-powered hydrogen generation, municipal waste biogas will be processed to make hydrogen. The electrical system will be connected to the grid with net metering.

Hybrid systems may also benefit from some new storage systems including flywheels and electronics. However, these are relatively experimental technologies. Public interest and investment will be needed to support further commercialization efforts.

8.8. Conclusion

The technological basis for an agile system is not particularly new nor hypothetical. The technologies are known for the most part and some are even well-established. Others are in the later stages of development and with some commercialization will become cost effective. What is new is seeing this as a long-term strategy that goes beyond simply trying to figure out how to bandage the broken California system and repair the damage of deregulation without creating a new set of crises. We argue that this is a new vision. It is a vision where agility is obtained by focusing on many renewable technologies that avoid the greenhouse gas problem of the hydrocarbon-based system, and that moves directly to hydrogen as a storage for electricity generated during peak times.

The key to the agile future is that it does not require dismantling or replacing the existing system in the short run but supplementing it. It is built on four key foundation blocks. (1) The agile energy system utilizes conservation as the first building block because saving power in the first place is by far the least-expensive alternative to make sure that it is available for those who need it. (2) The expansion of cogeneration especially through self-generation and expanding dispersed production is the second line because it helps establish more redundancy and the two-way network of producers and consumers linked in a less-hierarchical system. This is the least-expensive transitional alternative to building new large centralized power plants and it has additional system benefits. (3) The third building block of the new approach is renewable sources that displace reliance on traditional fuels and that protect the environment. The key here is that renewable technologies are already cost effective in some situations, and with continuing research and deployment the cost will continue to fall. This is especially true for photovoltaics and wind, which are both very close to being the technologies of choice to displace centralized power plants using carbon-loaded fuels. (4) The final building block is to develop system approaches that store the energy generated from renewable sources as hydrogen to allow its flexible use in transportation and fuel cells, ultimately linking vehicle cells with buildings so that every place of work or residence becomes not just a consumer of power but a generator in a democratic web.

The benefits of an agile power system are based on renewable and distributed technologies. Future energy systems must encourage the coupling of several alternative technologies into mutually beneficial hybrid power systems. Such agile energy systems reduce reliance on long-distance transmission plans. Agile energy systems localize both the demand and supply of energy. Moreover, such systems stand in contrast to a free market solution which aims only to change behavior through real-time metering under the theory that if consumers know and understand their energy needs, costs, and usage then they will cut back or alter their time of use.

Agile energy systems can (and have) created other market mechanisms at the local or regional levels which are flexible systems rather than the traditionally central gird-oriented monopolies or new market forces who would monopolize power generation. Agile systems, since they are local, allow for more democratic public participation in setting public policy and hence provide strong public oversight.

The benefits of an agile system go well beyond simply fixing the mess that deregulation has caused. Agile systems benefit early and quick adaptation of new technological breakthroughs. Agile systems favor reduced environmental destruction as they promote the health and social benefit of local communities. Finally, such agile systems are cost-effective solutions to a system that is now overpriced.

Chapter 9
Civic Markets: Public Oversight of an Agile Energy System

9.1. Introduction

A number of good progressive public polices and programs emerged in California from the administration of Governor Davis in the months and years following the chaos caused by deregulation. Aside from the basic recognition that energy is a vital ingredient to any industrial nation-state, Governor Davis, and the new Governor Schwarzenegger, made strong new commitments to renewable energy generation standards; acknowledged the need for conservation and demand management programs; advocated and supported environmental and climate protection; and reinforced the California tradition for government acting in the best interests of all energy consumers within the State, but also in neighboring states and countries.

No one can see the future clearly, but there will be a new type of state energy system in California in the New Century. Governor Schwarzenegger has indicated the same and appears ready to "modify" deregulation. His plan is not to restore it nor revert back to energy regulation. Instead, California is seeking to solve the problems of the traditional rigid vertically integrated gird-centric system while taking advantage of technological "clean" energy breakthroughs that promise to make energy reliable and renewable for future generations.

In order to implement such advantageous energy infrastructures, the institutional regulatory system must change. State political leaders and regulators are continuing to explore options that will facilitate the transition from the current "deregulated" system toward a future clean energy system. The future is *not* a return to the regulated past. Nor is it a furtherance of theoretical economic models. Instead, California is leading the world in becoming a "sustainable economy"; it is "growing up" through its transition. The future is moving more in the direction of defining, outlining, and implementing an "agile energy system" in both providing reliable power supply (especially renewables) and orienting far more to the public good, rather than corporate greed and market forces.

As we write, one significant result of the crisis in California that is often overlooked is the redefinition (reorganization, restructuring, downsizing, or whatever business terms fits) of private-regulated utilities. As a group, they experienced near catastrophic financial losses from deregulation and the subsequent energy crisis. Each was forced to sell most of their generation capacity, leaving them financially weaker (in terms of tangible assets, cash flow, and market capacity) than they were before deregulation.

The short-term cash gains from the overpriced sales of these assets was just as short lived. In addition, with the end of any immediate plans for renewing retail competition or direct access, the traditional utilities retain their position as "distributors" of power to the local consumer (the last few miles or less). Hence, the utilities have little or no control over prices, let alone costs for conducting daily business.

The pooled power purchasing organization, the Power Exchange (PX), has gone bankrupt and closed. Yet the new California Independent System Operator (CAISO) has taken increased responsibility for managing the grid, securing supply, and managing demand. Because of the 2001 energy blackouts, various California state agencies had to take over many of the functions that were previously in the domain of the public utilities, such as assuring supply through long-term contracts (DW in RA),[1] conservation and efficiency (CSA, CEC, and CPUC) in securing peaking power (CASIO), and running the transmission system at constant cycle and voltage (CAISO), setting codes and standards (CPUC and CEC); providing funds (CPA and State Treasurer). The list goes on.

If one of the theoretical economic goals of deregulation was to reduce government involvement or control over prices and supply of power, exactly the opposite happened. Instead of less government involvement, there is more. Furthermore, the number of different agencies, departments, and commissions involved with energy policy making has not only grown but also is often in conflict with one another.

---

[1]Names of abbreviated organizations are: DW in RA, Department of Water in Resources Agency; CSA, California Consumer Agency; CEC, California Energy Commission; CPUC, California Public Utility Commission; CASIO, California Independent System Operator; CPA, California Consumer and Power Authority; State Treasurer, California State Treasurer, an elected official.

However, neither the regulators nor legislature of the State have figured out how to restructure the system in a permanent way now that the immediate energy crisis has subsided. Settling on permanent energy infrastructure mechanisms are critical both to the public and private sectors. Each must know that there is stability as well as certainty. On one hand, some legislators and interest groups want to pursue a strategy of "reregulation" which would set prices based on return-on-investment criteria and would allow public oversight of all programs and expenditures.

On the other hand, some legislators, free market economic theorists, and interest groups (especially out-of-state generators and large users) want a "more deregulation" strategy. They believed that the deregulation scheme was basically solid, but went wrong when the State did not go far with open retail competition and imposed price caps. In addition deregulation advocates argue that rules could be enforced to protect consumers from market manipulation. These interests would allow full retail competition with real time pricing and more effective policies to prevent market manipulation.

However, neither of these extreme options are viable. Instead, as shown elsewhere, the competitive model for electricity is blatantly unfeasible, misguided, and only theoretical. Further deregulation is not an option under any circumstance. Moreover, there is no viable way to restore the old system under the regulatory scheme that served the State well for nearly 100 years. Even if the utilities could repurchase their generators and be restored to financial health, the system change that led to deregulation in the first place would make the old system obsolete in the first instance.

What is needed is a vision for an entirely new framework that is a deliberate mix of the old, new, and transitional structures that are characterized not by one fixed centralized solution, but by an agile process aimed to merge technology and economics in a civic market for the public good.

9.2. The Role of Government: Reregulate or Deregulate

The option to "reregulate" the energy infrastructure is not feasible for two reasons. First, the replacement of the regulatory system would be different because now the utilities no longer own most of the energy generation. Thus, the utilities have little control over their largest cost factor, which is obtaining their primary source of power. Similarly, the long-term energy generation contracts entered into by the State have fixed the prices of power at a relatively high level that leaves little room for regulatory flexibility to achieve public goals.

Secondly, the drive to reregulate the power system neglects the fact that political conflicts, tensions, and vested economic interests in the regulated system caused the pressures for infrastructure deregulation in the first place. What this means is that the same pressures and stakeholders who demanded change during the mid-1990s and resulted in the energy crisis remain powerful forces today. These same market forces (for-profit and not-for-profit) would lobby against and certainly destabilize a return to an integrated and regulated system.

In addition, many energy consumers will want to opt out of the regulated system entirely. Often, consumer needs are better met by self-generation or contracting with private generators without any utility hookups except as stand by power. In addition, the municipal utilities or power suppliers still can undercut regulated utility prices because they can avoid some high costs of a regulated utility system such as operations, maintenance, and transmission lines. The regulated utilities remain unable to capture the increasing efficiency of small scale operations and distributed power generation systems. Further, they are limited because they need to reduce prices in order to retain large power users. In short, reregulation will return the State to the same tensions that it stared with 10 years earlier.

The "proper deregulation" model is no more feasible than re-regulation. Energy infrastructures are not suitable to the competition market forces, though some parts could be competitive, especially at the local and regional levels. Such a negative view of the deregulation option is based on two considerations.

First, the failed deregulation system was fundamentally flawed in ways that more deregulation would not fix. Consider the lessons worldwide where power systems universally tend toward monopoly. Even if more retail competition were present, little market force would counter the possibilities of major anti-competitive consolidation taking place. In fact, one business school "exit strategy" that is universally taught is to start, grow, and then sell or merge the company.

Additionally, full deregulation is both problematic and theoretical because market systems have little incentive to pursue policies for the civic good. The corporate goals are to get a good return on the investments. Yet, the most problematic parts of any energy system is assuring adequate peak power and pursuing demand reduction (conservation and load shifting) strategies. The public good is not a market force concern or consideration.

When power generation plants are used but a few hours on only the highest peak demand days, there is little incentive for any firm to pay the high costs involved with having this capacity available. Peak power is already high priced, but looking after proper capacity reserves for use only on the hottest summer afternoons is not attractive to purely market forces—reliable peak power has been one of the most remarkable successes of the regulated system.

Similarly, the public interest is well served by conservation and demand reduction programs. However, market forces reward competitive firms for selling the maximum amount of power, not for selling less. This has been a persistent problem that California addressed with a large publicly run conservation program paid for by a charge to ratepayers on all power sold. Such programs however leave little room for efficient pursuit of these goals by private firms looking to maximize local opportunities.

The second reason "more deregulation" is not feasible is that we have no models of deregulated private competitive markets that have really succeeded anywhere in the world. While some would argue that United Kingdom is a success, recent critiques and events there suggest otherwise. Growing evidence has shown that the British attempt to deregulate or "privatize" or "liberalize" their energy infrastructure (and perhaps other public sectors) is a failed tragedy. Earlier, the issues surrounding the nuclear power plant bankruptcy in the United Kingdom were discussed. While the UK has had some positive side effects in the energy sector, such as experimentation with renewable energy generation systems such as wind and advanced technologies like fuel cells, even these innovations were well under way before "privatization" took place.

The questions surrounding the British energy sector are far deeper and more profound. In 2003, other European countries (especially Norway, France, and Italy) began to experience energy problems. Norway had a rainfall shortage in the winter of 2003 which left its hydroelectric system at its lowest levels in decades. The result has been for the Norwegian government to accelerate its pursuit of new energy generation. The economic issue for Norway is the fact that they are one of the world's largest exporters of oil and gas.

Hence, much of their energy generation could be supplied by increased generation from these fuel sources. However, the country has a limited supply of these fossil fuels (most estimates are at 20–25 years maximum) and the resulting emission pollution problems violate both European and Kyoto Accord Standards to which the Norwegians are historically stanch supporters. Accelerated efforts to become an "hydrogen economy" with more and more emphasis on renewable energy generation began in late 2003.

On the other hand, Italy suffered some of the worse energy blackouts in the summer of 2003. France recorded over 12,000 deaths associated with the heat wave during the summer of 2003, a crisis that was aggravated by power shortages. Italy, however, had realized that dependence on 25% of its energy coming from nuclear powered plants in France is both risky and not a good public policy. The country had long ago (late 1980s) engaged in changing from a government-regulated monopoly energy infrastructure into something else. Like California, Italy is in transition with many market changes. What appears to be a parallel set of public policies to California is the move toward agile energy markets with the core being to start building a hydrogen economy. The regions of both Lombardi and Piedmont have been leading the Italian transformation into the civic market structures.

Nonetheless, it has been the British government, for example, that has placed strong pressure on other European Union member states and new applicant nations to be "competitive" in energy and other sectors. Yet at home, the privatized energy markets have failed. Moreover, within the EU a growing skepticism has arisen while nations watch California experience their own energy problems and monitor the entry of a dozen new members to the EU in 2004. What is clear for the practice of deregulation and privatization, and not the theory, is that market forces should not replace publicly regulated energy suppliers and services. The civic market must be established and must provide the framework for regional energy public policy and practical market mechanisms.

In addition, the EU countries are developing some interesting energy models of "privatization" that might be far more useful and practical. In several areas civic markets operating as public–private partnerships have been successfully documented and evaluated for years (Clark, 1997; Clark and Jensen, 1994, 2000, 2001). For example, some European countries prefer to maintain partial government ownership in the energy companies, including shares, board membership, and regulatory oversight. This model appears to be working well in the Nordic countries as well as in Germany and France. Italy is experimenting with it now.

9.3. Civic Markets: Partnerships in "Agile Energy Systems"

The transition from the traditional vertically integrated utility to the emerging "agile power system" is a struggle between two different perspectives on how to increase the public good—on the one hand "privatization" and on the other hand "civic markets".[2] Deregulation was proposed under the premise of privatization, which is the neo-classical economist view that competitive markets reduce prices and allow maximum choice, while providing optimum conditions for technological innovation. The belief has been a cornerstone of Prime Minister Margaret Thatcher public sector reforms during the 1980s as well as the philosophy behind relaxing regulations in many other industries from banking to airlines. In all these cases proponents look at the declining prices and innovation, but also have to acknowledge gaps in service and occasional scandals such as the collapse of the American Savings and Loan institutions. The failure of the California deregulation can be added to the list of failures.

The philosophical premise that the public good rests at the core is the theoretical basis for any analysis of market options and is key in any discussion of the energy sector. The public good is a concept linked to community wide, shared benefits by people that transcends special individual or group interests, and hence benefits everyone collectively. Put another way, public good is a shared benefit that in aggregate exceed those that might otherwise be retained as exploitive benefits for only a few individuals.

We think that the model for resolving the tension between those who want to see the energy sector reregulated and those who wish for more deregulation lies in the pursuit of civic markets that encourage programs for the public good. The public good in the energy infrastructure sector and for power systems is represented by the benefits of electricity that are:

- cheap,
- reliable,
- predictable in terms of future availability and costs,
- safe with few negative social costs (externalities) or health impacts on local communities,
- environmentally friendly in protecting air quality and natural resources, and
- oriented to the future needs of society as a whole such as convenient transportation, pure water, waste removal, and renewable energy generation.

These characteristics are the cornerstone of most of the restructuring proposals that have recently been published such as the Bay Area

---

[2]This point was made by Clark and Lund (2001) with regard to the Danish restructuring, using the concept of privatization and democratization.

Forum and the California Policy Institute (Weare, 2003). These characteristics are generally well represented through consumer pressure and public advocacy for government oversight of the energy sector. Regulatory systems generally have had an easy time assuring these goals because the goals are largely identical to the marketing goals of the utilities, which are being regulated. The key issue for regulators is to keep the price reasonable, while preventing the utility from making excessive profits.

On the other hand, some aspects of the public good are not so easily represented in the market. Individual consumer interests, for example, do not tend to be closely aligned with utility interests. To be specific, the public good is enhanced by environmental and equity issues that do not have traditional cost–benefit market values for utilities. Environmental issues are important because of the scale of the electric power industry and the fact that power generation creates a number of types of pollution, including smog, particulates, and other air-born wastes that contribute to global warming, ash which needs disposal, nuclear waste which needs long-term isolation, heat pollution, and visual pollution from plants and power lines.

These same environmental problems impact the public good in another way: health. A growing amount of literature in "environmental justice" (Salazar-Thompson *et al.*, 2003) documents the health costs for communities surrounding power plants. San Francisco has been active in meeting the concern through its Bay View Hunters' Point community action group which seeks to close two local power plants and replace them with renewable energy generation. The concern then for public good translates into high medical costs for society. Community-based action groups (Citizens for better communities, among others; see Greenpeace, Casper and Ross, 2003) have provided technological expertise and contact networks to provide solutions to local community clean energy needs.

Some of these energy-environmental problems can be addressed by regulatory prohibitions that reduce or eliminate some of the offending behaviors. However, the record both of utility regulations and environmental laws shows that much progress can be made by also being proactive and requiring that technologies be developed and installed that reduce pollution, even if the market would not voluntarily select them.

In addition, a range of environmental problems need to be addressed by experimental technologies and considerable investment in alternatives that may cost more at the early stages, until the economies of scale make them more price competitive. The requirement for including advanced technologies that are not immediately competitive in the energy sector mix, until they reach enough volume that they become cost effective, is one of the key objectives of progressive regulatory agendas. Clark and Chung (2000) prove this argument with an international study of environmentally sound technologies. Moreover, California has pursued this strategy during the energy crisis through several civic market partnerships, collaboratives, and agency and commission programs (CSFCC, 2002) discussed earlier in Chapter 8 on advanced technologies.

Other technological issues also benefit the public good in ways that need public encouragement and regulation to assure that the technological advances are provided. The three most important of these are renewable energy generation (grid, distributed generation and on-site), peaking power, and conservation. The public sector through government programs such as regulation, standards, and codes as well as public procurement policies can assure that these benefits are met.

The equity issue also remains one for nonmarket regulation. The problem in power is that it needs to be available to a range of people who can not afford it but who need it for their safety. Similarly some groups of people have very strong needs but the cost of service is greater than they can afford at least initially. For example, rural populations were last to get power because of the high cost of providing lines and distribution networks for power over much longer distances on average than in urban areas, and rural populations tended to be poor. This led to public rural electrification programs in most countries. Both of these issues contribute to public well being, safety, and security.

9.3.1. Markets in other contexts

Kuttner (2002) noted that deregulation was a faulted concept before the energy crisis hit California. He specifically mentioned the American savings and loan industry in the mid-1980s whereby the federal government in the end had to bail out saving industry customers for $100 billion. Kuttner and others have pointed out that the American transportation industry might suffer the same fate today, and that the airline industry was deregulated and more oriented toward cost savings rather than security and safety of passengers.

Other examples can be given, but perhaps the other most current issue of market failure is workers compensation in California. Here, like energy, the pattern is similar. In the late 1980s and early 1990s, the ideology that government is bad and should not be regulating this

Agile Energy Systems

industry lead to deregulation in 1993. After a few years of market forces competing with prices stable, only a few companies survived. By the late 1990s, two companies controlled the entire California market. The results are the same as the energy sector—public control and monopolies were given away to private sector.

In contrast, civic markets are a form of regulatory oversight, whereby the emphasis is on giving consumers real choices rather than a "free" market which ultimately manipulates only a few choices. The private sector is, in fact, a partner in the creation of regulations; operation of companies; and potentially an equity partner. The goal of creating civic markets is consistent with helping reduce prices and lead innovation into the market, while maintaining a watchdog that protects the public interest. Civic markets provide choices that are practical and flexible.

Consumers, in civic markets, can purchase alternative solutions to their personal and public needs, recognizing that there are many ways to provide services. In a civic market, the abuses of monopolies are controlled under the premise that the public interest should be represented in making key market forming decisions. Instead of open competition, the civic market model increases choices through regulated licensing combined with public participation as it is needed.

Of course, no market system is purely one form or another. Especially during the current transition phase in energy where there are few choices, any market mechanisms aimed at improving free enterprise conditions will adopt a mixture of competition and nurtured creative options. All must be under the scrutiny of public sector oversight mechanisms. The future of the energy market, perhaps many other infrastructures, will be much more like the scrutinized choices of a civic market than the brutish competition of the unfettered "free" market. Indeed, one can argue that in the cases where deregulation of the power system has succeeded, it succeeded because choices were introduced slowly and carefully, assuring the public good, and revising the rules as disparities are discovered.

A parallel to the internet can be made. The internet, as Clark (2002) and Rifkin (2003) both note, was developed by the federal government specifically for dispersed communication. Not one central computer was envisioned, but an "ethernet cloud" in which electrons flowed freely. The concept, originally seen as a defense network to thwart any direct attack from destroying all communications, was to have small and dispersed computer centers so that if one failed the others would operate.

The role of government in the internet is a relevant example. It has oversight capability from First Amendment Rights to technological bandwidth but plays only a supportive role by providing research and development financing along with increased technical advancements. The internet was invented by researchers and academics through initial public investment. The main public role was to set standards and assure open access. No provider was able to monopolize any part of the system, its standards and structure were transparent, and it was flexible enough to grow over time while accommodating previous users. Moreover, users were seamlessly networked together with huge local autonomy. This allowed public interest to take priority over all aspects of the web. In power too, the competition will be enhanced by more public involvement rather than less. The private sector simply uses the system. Other sectors are similar including transportation (highways and airways) as well as water and atmosphere. Each successful model has similar qualities: government's role is the creator, monitor, and overseer for the public good.

Perhaps one of the best examples coming in the near future is atmosphere. Aside from the Kyoto Accords in which most nations have signed, except the USA (California and New York State have signed similar legislation to the Kyoto Accords putting them squarely in opposition to the American federal government), the world community sees atmosphere and climate as a global concern. Hence nations, must now create mechanisms to account for climate change—such as greenhouse gases, carbon, and other particulates. United Nations Environmental Protection had put forth the Clean Development Mechanism in a series of reports and studies. The basic approach was to create a trading market for green credits.

In 2000, before the energy crisis, California created a Climate Registrary and later convened within the Resources Agency a Joint Agency Climate Team (JACT). The Registrary is a voluntary organization but with a growing list of companies which has been heralded as an international model in this area. JACT has provided both frameworks and scientific policies for California in climate change.

Both of these have monitored climate issues in California and the west coast leading to a three-state Pacific Coast Summit in late 2003, whereby Governor Schwarzenegger endorsed Governor Davis' initiatives in this area. Nonetheless, theoretical economists have appeared again. This time to argue that "green tags" or "credits" need to be created in order to make clean energy and environmental technologies cost competitive.

One company (Energy Info Source, 2003) issued a 70-page Report advocating green tags which are a variety of different market mechanisms for companies to get financial credits in the form of 'tags" or units or credits so that they can trade them. Usually energy generation companies that pollute or discharge waste will get certain credits as financial benefits for clean up, newer technology upgrades, or closing the plants such that:

> *a comprehensive look at what green tags are, how they work, the role they can play in spurring renewable energy development, the different models for implementing green tags, government programs in support of green tags, current offerings of green tag suppliers, and customer purchases of green tags. (Energy Info Source 2003)*

The United Nations Environmental Program in Paris has been tracking these market mechanisms for the last decade. Some entrepreneurs have started exchanges in various cities, one of the most active of which is in Chicago, Illinois. California government is monitoring these international developments through a Joint Agency Climate Team in Sacramento and its Climate Registry in Los Angeles.

9.4. Partnerships to Create Civic Markets in Energy

The problem however, as noted by Clark and Chung (2000) among others, is that the private sector has taken over these "mechanisms" and will try to control and manipulate it as is its typical approach to the market. A number of private "exchanges" have been created and more are being formed. The government must oversee and regulate these exchanges, especially as they begin to conduct business.

However, an even more compelling and significant infrastructure development is on the near-term horizon in infrastructure development: hydrogen. But as Stipp (2001: 1) notes in Fortune magazine:

> *The greatest hurdle is cost: Fuel cells are too pricey for all but niche applications, and they're likely to remain so until economies of scale kick in. Likewise, fully installing the infrastructure needed to produce and deliver hydrogen on a massive scale—think of the refineries, pipelines, and gas stations that have been built to support the oil economy—will take decades and require tens of billions of dollars.*

Surprisingly, the problems confronting all new massive innovations (like the internet) are not insurmountable. Hydrogen and fuel cells are well into the marketplace. Government is leading the charge. In California by late 2002, three major efforts were underway: one with the South Coast Air Quality District in the Los Angeles' region;

another inland in the Palm Springs area with Sunline Transit; and the last in Northern California with Alameda-Contra Costa Transit District (east of San Francisco).

The transit systems have led the building of a hydrogen infrastructure as the government can exercise both planning and procurement (noted below). Civic markets are just that role whereby the government and industry collaborate together for mutually common and supportive ends. See various plans by these public organizations as well as private sector companies supplying hydrogen systems and major automobile companies providing vehicles (CFCP, 2001) and stationary fuel cells (CSFCC, 2002). The future is now.

In terms of how agile energy systems work and are organized, for example, the plans of regional transit systems are one of the driving forces. The California Fuel Cell Partnership (CFCP) is an excellent example of how agile systems work in an area related to energy: transportation and air pollution. The State has a long history of air quality problems and there is no need to review them here (Clark and Paolucci, 2000). But it is important to note how public–private partnerships have helped to resolve the problems. The background of air quality problems in California rests in the regions but became institutionalized into the California Air Resources Board (CARB) in the early 1990s. The CARB set up zero emission vehicle regulations (ZEV)—hence requiring automobile manufacturers to "sell" ZEV cars into California under an annual formula.

The ZEV regulations basically saw electric vehicles as the future form of transportation for the State. The key to the success of the program was to have the public sector oversee the regulations for vehicles sold in California by working with the carmakers to produce such vehicles. By the late 1990s, it was clear that electric battery vehicles were not the "only" solution to the problem. One clean alternative would be "fuel cell" vehicles (Cooper *et al.*, 1995; Cooper and Clark, 1996; Clark, Paulocci and Cooper, 2002) and especially those that ran on hydrogen (Rifkin, 2003). Resistance from the carmakers, especially the American companies, was overwhelming as they attempted to stop the California deadlines.

However, the carmakers had made great technological advances and with the collaborative efforts of the CFCP were able to not only find compromise technological solutions but also regulatory avenues to get the ZEV into California. While the time lines have been pushed back slightly, the public–private effort has worked successfully. The same is now true for the SFCC where companies and public sector leadership appears to be moving clean fuel cells into the marketplace.

Much of the progress in both mobile and stationary fuel cells is on the local and regional levels.

Government and the private sector can collaborate rather than be adversaries. This civic market approach has been very significant with the Fuel Cell Partnership and other collaborative efforts in the State to derive practical approaches to implement public policy: in this case with ZEVs and in other cases with energy and environmental policies. Porter (1995), not normally recognized for the positive role that government can play in stimulating new technologies, let alone good public policy, also makes the point that the Dutch government passed some rigid standards for tulips in their country that not only protected their domestic market but stimulated international market growth.

The same principle, government setting of codes and standards, is responsible for California being the market leader in new advanced technologies for emission free and hybrid vehicles (Reinhart, 2003) leading to a hydrogen economy (Clark, 2004) and environmentally sound technologies (Kenidi, 2003). Market leaders in environmentally friendly vehicles note that if it was not for the ZEV and clean air emission regulations in California, "there would be no industry in California or worldwide" (Reinhart, 2003). The same is true in renewable energy technologies and the industries that follow. According to one industry leader, "California set the standards and then established the markets for everyone to participate. Either we do that or we lose." (Kenidi, 2003).

The practical issue of how civic markets are discussed throughout the book is in terms of partnerships, collaboratives, and networks such as interagency working groups, task forces, and forums. At this point, it is noteworthy to mention that civic markets set the framework for which public and private sectors can work together rather than at odds and in conflict. Such cooperative meetings bring about the solution to issues (Clark and Morris, 2002) in a variety of areas and technologies, especially when there is a crisis.

9.5. The Public Role in Creating a Civic Market for Agile Energy Systems—Five Principles

The goal for modern and future energy systems around the world is now well established through "social constructionism" (an European concept meaning the development of a societal or national social consciousness around a particular topic, Poole, 1997): to introduce renewable, clean, and hybrid technologies in rapid succession to diversify the energy sources so that price and reliability is not based on any one dominant set of fuels, as well as to promote the use of renewable power in order to protect and enhance the environment. But from a policy point of view, this goal is hard to enact let alone accomplish.

From the California energy crisis, came a challenge and an opportunity to do what no other society had done heretofore. Garnered from the California experiences are what we propose as five fundamental principles for creating a "civic market" structure that best meets the electricity needs of modern societies. These five principles constitute a framework from which specific policies can be designed and replicated throughout the world. It is the subsequent policies that can respond to the political, social, economic, and cultural conditions of the place, region, community, or nation-state where they will be applied.

Furthermore, these principles are not beholden to neoclassical economic principles, but instead provide the basic fundaments for creating market rules which are clear, concise, and consistent. Industry and government both need clear and concise rules so that they can move ahead to accomplish mutually agreed upon goals for society— the civic market as defined in any community.

In large part the failure, even today, of California, other states, and Federal agencies to establish and agree upon any standard market mechanism is due to lack of clarity and the inability to start with any set of principles. Herein we set out the framework of basic principles to follow in order to derive market rules, standards, codes, and operating protocols.

9.5.1. First principle: sustain government oversight of existing utilities to make energy systems agile

The first principle for an agile energy future is to address the existing utilities and their historic regulatory framework. We argue that government has a continuing role in the power system relative to the private utilities, and it is to retain oversight. The regulatory framework for private utilities actually worked well enough for most purposes, though there are problems with the classic regulatory framework that need to be addressed. Given the California experience no citizen or its representatives can not accept the premise that the utilities if unregulated in the future would pursue the public good. The role of public utility commissions remains to continue their historical oversight, rule-making role and to adjudicate and provide leadership to monitor the private utilities and to protect consumers from the worst abuses by private companies seeking profit.

On the other hand, utilities and their regulators have been less than visionary about promoting technological change and staying ahead of the mounting complexity of modern power systems. The classic regulatory framework which is to monitor all aspects of the utility and to judge all expenses and prices charged consumers may be too much micro-management. We use the word *oversight* instead of regulation to denote the responsibility of regulatory bodies to look out for the public interest while setting practices and policies which will allow private power markets to serve the public interest. This does not mean that oversight would retain the old utility structure in its classic form—new alternatives to utility power could provide a competitive framework that would assure that private utilities provide the best possible service at affordable rates.

The agility of the existing utilities is a key part of assuring that the whole electrical system is agile. Today, the existing utilities have virtually all the capacity needed in the short term, and they have a public mandate to supply power. The key issue is not to replace the existing utilities but to help them operate better. What this means is that the existing utilities need to explore ways to assure that their power supply is more robust and efficient over the long run. The objectives of this system include the following:

- Diversification of generation technologies and fuels, with increasing reliance on renewable resources that promise to be more cost effective.
- Selection of system options to assure protection of the environment, reduction of greenhouse gases, and promoting other public goods.
- Provision of adequate transmission links to permit flexible and robust interconnection and substitution among suppliers, minimizing the possibility of bottlenecks and preventing suppliers exercising market power to raise rates.
- Increasing the distributed character of the power system so that more power is supplied to customers without dependence on long-distance transmission and where local innovation and investment help to solve regional as well as national or global issues.
- Protection of public good values such as conservation that can not be valued in a fully competitive market system for the well-being of communities and the environment.

The specific type of regulatory structure that is used to achieve these goals depends on the political and economic heritage of the State or country implementing it. Our goal here is not to suggest one model or an ideal structure, but to outline the broad objectives that can be reached by a number of different regulatory or oversight structures.

However, the fundamental reality is that the existing centralized utilities are the only organization that has the vertical integration and the financial capacity to achieve the system objectives listed above. A deregulated and fragmented system would pit generators using the cheapest and dirtiest technologies for the short term against responsible integrated firms looking toward the long-term benefit of the public. In contrast, well-managed existing utilities could adequately invest in networks and flexibility, and promote distributed service and conservation as part of a balanced and interdependent multifaceted system.

How the existing utilities can achieve these goals is the key question. The core oversight issue is to find the right combination of incentive and mandate to enable the existing utilities to reach the objectives of becoming an agile power supplier. Utilities have one huge advantage to partner with providers of renewable and distributed power and that is they have the ability to make long-term contracts and they can blend resources into their overall pool, providing backup and reliability for individual resources that may be intermittent. Utilities have also had considerable experience since PURPA with making these contracts, though most have fought it. On the other hand, some of the municipal utilities such as Sacramento Municipal Utility District (Smeloff and Asmus, 1997) have worked on stimulating other sources and have done it successfully.

The first strategy is to assure leadership from PUC and State to establish favorable contracts for renewable power and distributed power. The provision of flexible but standardized contracts is essential. As shown in previous chapters, independent producers need to have stable long-term contracts in order to obtain financing, and these contracts must be fair but have a long enough time frame that lenders can verify an income stream to enable the firm to repay the loan. The utilities and their needs can be balanced by the lenders and their financial requirement, but the key point is that a real working partnership be established to negotiate contracts that meet the needs of all parties without anyone loosing money. These contracts should be standardized for similar firms providing similar types of power, but they can reflect variable costs and flexibility into the future.

The second way in which the utilities can assist with the provision of renewable and distributed power is to enable producers to use the grid and other suppliers for backup and to cover intermittent production. Some distributed and intermittent producers have complained that they are given very punitive contracts for backup connections or for intermittent power even though the demand caused by the power is minimal and easily managed. Public and private sectors need to work collaboratively in order to solve problems. Rather than be opponents, the two sides must seek the greater good to benefit society.

Example: Intermittent power agreements. The wind industry was able to sit down with the utilities, for example, and negotiate reasonable contracts for intermittent wind that enabled firms to invest. This did not really cost the utilities more than they might otherwise pay for power and it solved a big problem for wind generation. This came because of the need in early 2001 to find a way for the California Independent System Operator (CAISO) to account for intermittent resources (e.g., wind and solar in particular, but could be renewables in general) into the state power grid. Heretofore, the CAISO would penalize intermittent power generators if they failed to supply the power when contracted to deliver it. These "imbalance rules" put a damper on the renewable generators to even contract with the CAISO. A solution had to be found (Clark and Morris, 2002).

Upon approval of the CAISO Board, a large group of renewable power suppliers (over 30 companies) got together as an "Intermittent Team" under the leadership of the Governor's Office and CAISO to meet weekly for almost 10 months in order to formulate new rules. The results were new rules and tariffs that were submitted to the Federal Energy Regulatory Commission (FERC) in early 2002. The FERC approved the rules and hence they applied for the entire USA (CAISO, 2002). This is an example of agile energy systems.

Consider also cogeneration which remains one of the large untapped resources for power in the United States, and to some degree in other countries. With the need to be more agile this source of power should be encouraged for many reasons. For example, by generating electricity at the same time a firm uses heat for processing or other manufacturing tasks, less energy is wasted. This contributes to cleaner air and lower costs, but it also provides distributed power that can be used closer to the source. However, the cogenerator needs to have backup power from the grid when the cogeneration plant is not operating and when demand exceeds available capacity.

The utilities have often used their contractual power to discourage cogeneration because it will mean that they loose a customer. They can charge a very high connection fees regardless of the amount of power used, and they can refuse to purchase excess power from the cogenerator. At the residential level this problem got solved when the State established a net metering program for photovoltaic installations. At a larger scale, policy needs to do the same for a wider range of applications.

Agile systems need to create institutional mechanisms as well. Even now that the FERC rules are in place, few CASIO intermittent contracts have been signed. The problems have shifted to costs to the CAISO and financing for the power generators. The basic need for long-term contracts drives the process for the private sector to invest in renewable energy while the public sector (or market mechanism) must have cost-competitive power supplies. It is at this point that other agile system components come into play: competitive aggregated procurement, hybrid technologies, and power purchase contracts.

9.5.2. Second principle: develop societal strategies for transitional costs

The process of transition from a regulated vertically integrated system to an agile complex civic market for power was done in the worst possible way in California, leading to crisis. Now as the State tries to restore confidence in the power system and create a viable future, the challenge is greater than ever to find tools by which an effective power system can operate.

In California, as elsewhere, the transition from the current situation to a more responsive civic market is a process that opens up the technological system to policy influences that are unknown and have high possibilities of creating negative unintended consequences. However, in California some of the negative conditions of the current situation can be turned into assets for change.

It is important first to assure that the costs of transition are identified and borne equitably. For example, the deregulation debacle cost the State at least $40 billion and this has to be paid for somehow. While legal efforts continue, to recover some of the losses and to renegotiate long-term contracts, the possibility of recovering much of the loss seems increasingly slim.

FERC has consistently been reluctant to either demand refunds or to mandate renegotiation of contracts, and in their most recent ruling, as we write, they restated this premise again saying that the contracts must stand. Moreover, even if recovery of some excess profits were permitted, most of the companies involved have found themselves in severe financial difficulties, or are bankrupt such as Enron. Recovery of funds from these firms is not possible, and for others the windfall has largely been lost so that recovery would have to be delayed and possibly based on future revenues from the company, which would then come from consumers.

The equity principle means that the losses from deregulation need to be shared by all private power users at the time of deregulation. The State of California has in principle accepted that there will be an exit fee for any consumer of power who was served by IOUs to cover the cost of state power debt and overpriced contracts. The amount of this fee and its coverage are still being worked out, but it seems to be a fair process. What this means is that communities or firms can not bypass the existing utilities to avoid the costs of deregulation by becoming a municipal utility, joining a municipal utility, finding another utility (perhaps out of state) to supply power, or entering into a direct supply contract. It is not clear how the State intends to apply this rule to self-generation, with the exception that individuals installing renewable power such as photovoltaic panels would be able to avoid the fees.

Second, the utilities are being required to assume the long-term contracts of the State. The cost of these contracts will be passed on to the consumers, but the amount of power involved in the contracts is large enough that there is little flexibility for utilities to develop alternative sources of power. In some cases the utilities are in an excess supply mode based on the contracts and will have to resell that power on the spot market for a loss. Finally, the volume of power involved in the long-term contracts means that there will be less demand for power on the spot market and as a consequence, prices will be very low. This will present serious political pressure on regulators and system operators because consumers will seek to buy this cheap spot-market power and, as occurred in the State earlier, it will be considered a reasonable avoided or marginal price, when in fact it is not.

Because of the rigidity of these market conditions, the power system in California faces huge difficulties in being agile. The cost and large amount of contracted power is like a freeway gridlock and solutions that promise long run flexibility can not get started. We have demonstrated that wind and within a short period photovoltaic power will be available at lower price than some of the contract power. The public good, however, will be best served by not letting these overpriced contracts block innovation.

Creative programs to deal with this surplus are needed. At the core is the realization that maintaining flexibility in the system is essential and it may add to the costs of the deregulation debacle. For example, one solution to assure that the surplus power retains flexibility would be utilizing the excess power in electrolysis to generate hydrogen and in so doing jump start the hydrogen economy. Even though the hydrogen would be expensive because it is made with expensive electricity, the system benefits would be so great that the civic value would be worth it.

Similarly, in an agile system renewable off-grid application should be seen as a system asset rather than a liability. These should continue to be encouraged. With some reservations, the same should be designed for cogeneration which is a highly effective distributed technology. While cogenerators using natural gas applications should not be exempted from all exit fees, perhaps a flexible scale could be used to encourage cogeneration especially on peak.

The agile system needs to find ways to encourage conservation and load management during the transition period because civic markets would value conservation greatly, though it is not reflected in utility interests. One incentive in the current structure in California might be to allow utilities to invest in conservation in order to displace high-priced long-term contracts which would then be assumed by the State. Southern California Edison is trying to do some of this through its economic development programs whereby the company receives some financial support from the CPUC to market and reach out to consumers in order to inform and educate them about conservation, energy efficiency, and demand reduction measures to be taken.

The same is true for the CPUC regional programs where it allocates funds to regions of California to do similar tasks through energy-related organizations or nonprofits serving local communities. The CEC has implemented similar educational outreach programs (CEC, 1999, 2002). The CAISO has seen the importance of such consumer educational programs and supported staff efforts for participation in conferences and meetings throughout the State (CAISO, 2002).

9.5.3. Third principle: promote joint public–private investments that leverage private funds with public dollars

While public ownership of utilities is often promoted as a solution to problems such as experienced in the State, the opposite trend is being pursued around the world. We think that joint ownership is often the best solution. For example, public retirement funds could invest in private utilities and obtain a large enough block of stock to have a strong influence on the operation of the utility. While the pension fund will want to maintain utility profitability, the fact that they have some investment is central.

As noted in the chapters on economics, State Treasurer Angiledes has argued for double bottom line in setting priorities and strategies for state pension funds as "pension funds must take the lead in encouraging corporations to provide meaningful, consistent, and robust reporting of their environmental practices, risks, and potential liabilities. We must also push companies—through dialogue, share-holder resolutions, and other actions—to improve their environmental operations." (Anglides, November 2003: 3). In short, the State is following the civic market framework in its investment strategies and programs.

Further, the State created the California Consumer Power and Conservation Financing Authority (CPA), with $5 billion bond financing capacity in order to expand the State's grid-based renewable capacity. These low interest funds to government and private sector partnerships (CPA, Pulse Program, 2002) will be able to stimulate investment of over $17 billion and achieve a total contribution of 8000 MW to the State. Two major barriers were noted by the CPA however in its "Clean Growth Report" (2002: 17): the lack of a wholesale market either with long-term contracts or short-term bidding opportunities. The second is the high cost of capital for financing projects compared to conventional power plants.

The type of commitment to support green solutions to the power crisis are illustrated by several additional efforts by the CPA. They have a program called "Greening the Peak" which aims to find renewable solutions to peak needs. Both an advanced load shedding program made possible by automatic meters, and the use of renewable sources to supply peak power has been proposed. For example, some biogas operations with limited production are economical if they operate only at peak times.

The CPA, CEC along the CPUC have been focused on clean distributed generation. Renewable energy is financeable. As Stipps (2001) put it:

> Renewable energy, excluding hydropower, which currently dwarfs other renewables, provides only 2% of U.S. electricity today. But its potential is huge. The harnessable wind power in Midwestern and Western states alone could supply as much electricity during a 15-year period as all of Saudi Arabia's vast oil reserves if they were burned in power plants, according to a federal study. Such factoids are no longer merely the stuff of environmental confabs and engineering conventions—they are guiding boardroom decisions.

The state government and public sector must take the lead in the implementation of renewable and clean energy generation. The California Consumer Affairs Agency, for example, has produced a Sustainable Public Building Road Map (CAA, 2001), the California Interagency "Green" Accounting Working Group (IGAWG, 2001; Clark and Sowell, 2002), and the university system with support from a variety of organizations, including Greenpeace (Casper and Ross, 2003) provide ample evidence that buildings can have their own "green power" generation at competitive costs.

The financing of renewable energy has shifted from the State level (due in part to the budget crisis in 2003 of a $35 billion deficit) to the local and regional levels. Distributed energy generation can lead the efforts for renewable energy generation. While this is not in conflict or competition with the central grid approach to energy generation, it does signal a reconfiguration of how renewable energy can be more efficiently implemented and be more cost effective.

When public institutions like Community Colleges along with other university campuses, State Public Buildings, and local government buildings target new or retrofitted sustainable buildings the costs for the renewable energy products will decrease as well as the costs for operating the buildings themselves, thus saving funds for future operations and maintenance. In November 2002, Californians approved over $20 billion in other bond measures for affordable housing, public school construction and infrastructures (e.g. water and waste). Many of building codes, standards, and protocols for these facilities will include sustainable measures such as LEED and state sustainability requirements (Sowell *et al.*, 2002–03).

With decreasing costs due to large public sector market demand, sustainable buildings are more readily achievable. The further reduction of costs can be accomplished on the local level from combinations or "hybrid technologies" whereby solar PV, for example, is combined with fuel cells so that the customer has continuous reliable energy. Some local communities are installing wind turbines with biomass facilities for continuous energy generation. This approach to distributed generation has been successful in Europe for over a decade (Münster, 2001) through cogeneration or combined heat and power (Atwood *et al.*, 2001).

In southern Sweden, for example, BoO1 (2001) is a city within a city where renewable energy has been successfully used for on-site building power generation as well as energy for the community from wind and larger renewable power systems in the region (Vernamo, 2001). The Ecological City of Tomorrow in the western harbor district, City of Malmö (southwestern Sweden near København,

Denmark). The new district runs exclusively on renewable sources of energy. A large portion of the heating needs are extracted from sea and ground water and is supported by solar collectors. Electricity is generated entirely by wind and solar cells. Biogas is produced from the area's waste and used to heat homes and power vehicles.

An effective energy usage is essential in order to reach the target of entirely locally produced renewable energy. The buildings in the district are designed to minimize energy demands for heating and electrical equipment that installed is highly energy efficient (according to Swedish Energy Standards). Malmö's existing sewage system has been fitted with improved equipment to extract nutrients (for reuse in agriculture) and heavy metals. Most of the organic waste is transformed into biogas and biogas digesters.

Energy is linked to other infrastructures. Hence transportation and traffic are designed to promote "foot" and cycle usage. A bus system using electric vehicles is in operation with cars using environmentally friendly fuels are planned (fuel cell in particular when available). Furthermore, information technology is used as an active tool to help residents to monitor use of water and energy, with increased broadband network to enable residents and business to use the Internet and related IT services.

The district is a good example of civic markets and agile energy systems at work since its residential population of 3000 with over 1000 homes, offices, shops, nurseries, cafes, restaurants, schools, libraries, and more includes public and private partners such as the City of Malmö; Sydkraft Power Company (largest in Western Sweden); BoO1 City of Tomorrow (European Housing); Lund University and Swedish National Energy Administration. The BoO1 exemplifies how hybrid technologies operate at a cost-effective level.

9.5.4. Fourth principle: facilitate innovative renewable technological systems

Above and in other chapters, the importance of governmental code and standard setting has been highlighted. Other technological fields than energy and environment have also been noted within civic markets, whereby public and private sectors have sat down and worked out differences that allow new regulations and technologies to become real and practical market drivers.

At this juncture it is important to note how codes, standards, and protocols can set benchmarks for industry from which all can agree. Nonetheless there are significant differences between regions in how these standards are measured, evaluated, and enforced. At the end of

2002, for example, testimony before the State Senate Energy Committee exemplified the significance of civic markets and regionalism. The legislature was considering a bill on standards for washing machines. The Senators were challenged by a large manufacturer and the National Association as to both California's far more rigid standards and to the current national committee considering standards now. The Chair of the Committee, supported by almost everyone in the hearing including industry representatives, retorted, "California has different needs and thus higher standards (just like in air and environment) for water. And since top loaded washers use 50% more water than side loaded ones, we need to pass this bill." The Committee passed the bill and it became law.

The same issue was apparent during a national meeting on hydrogen lead by the US Department of Energy and the University of California, Davis in the summer of 2003. When the US Department of Energy (USDOE) keynote presentation was completed after which there were comments, the speaker was reminded that he neglected to include geothermal in the renewable energy generation area for producing hydrogen. "California has a large supply of geothermal and needs to develop this renewable source of energy." USDOE corrected its mistake in the presentation and in its Hydrogen Standards. Civic markets encourage the participation and interaction among different groups of people in order to solve problems and set high codes, standards, and protocols.

As a result of the civic market approach to solve public and private sector issues, the US Department of Energy has broadened its definition of hydrogen fuels to include geothermal. However, more significantly, the USDOE appears likely to both set policies and award funds to regions of the USA based on the strengths of their renewable energy fuel sources. California, therefore, would be one of the prime areas for hydrogen from geothermal generation, as well as solar, wind, and water.

Codes, standards, and protocols
An increasingly significant concern for any energy systems and civic markets are regulations. Without debating for or against "regulations," the argument has been made that "civic markets" are a viable and workable combination of both. Weare (2003) picks up this same theme when he notes the need for hybrid systems which combine both approaches to the energy sector. However, his and other concerns with basic conventional economic mechanisms (Weare, 2003, Appendix A) trap the argument into the ideology of neoclassic economics: markets

must be open and free to conduct business unfettered by the government.

Given the assumption that government must have a significant role as oversight and often arbitrator in the energy sector (as others) then what are the mechanisms for an agile energy market? As noted above, sustainable buildings can be achieved today at cost competitive levels. When economic externalities such as fuel source, health, and linked infrastructures are factored in, there is no competition. Nonetheless, a key to bring renewable energy into the marketplace are the codes, standards, and protocols. Looking at these issues is different and part of the civic market approach to implementation of an agile energy system.

Since reregulation will not occur in the energy (and other) sectors, the new civic markets will be public–private partnerships focused on implementation of legislation. A good successful example of civic markets that provided a legal framework and tariffs for agile energy systems is the FERC Intermittent Resources Protocol (FERC, 2002; Clark and Morris, 2002; Hawkins, 2003). When confronted how to account for intermittent energy like wind, the results under a civic market where a protocol, not regulation, that provided for industry financial needs to eliminate uncertainty, CAISO power reliability, and government concerns for the public good.

Such protocols with related codes and standards are the new market mechanisms that result from the civic market. As the market mechanisms are developed and implemented, agile energy systems can function, be overseen by the public sector, and open up new and existing market opportunities. The same public–private process is currently underway in California to meet the Greenhouse Gas Bill signed by Governor Davis in July 2002 (OPR, 2002; CARB, FCP, 2002) and the Environmental Goals Policy Report (EGPR, 2003) due to the Governor and Legislature annually.

The EGPR is an excellent example of how civic markets work in the environmental field. The goals included in the EGPR (GPR, 2003) must be consistent with the three state planning priorities established under AB 857 (Wiggins) passed in 2002. EGPR is intended to promote equity, strengthen the economy, protect the environment, and promote public health and safety in the State, including in urban, suburban, and rural communities. These priorities are to:

• Promote infill development and equity.
• Protect environmental and agricultural resources.
• Encourage efficient development patterns.

The EGPR further implements the civic market by modification of its own strategies and plans (EGPR, 2003):

- Having a broad focus, addressing issues related to the environment, the economy, and equity.
- Serving as a basis for decisions about the design, location, and priority of major public programs, capital projects and other actions, including the allocation of state resources.
- Guiding the development of state functional plans.
- Addressing the policies, programs, and expenditures of state government only.
- Striving to bring consistency to state policies, programs, and expenditures.
- Building on existing research, reports, and recommendations including the work of the Commission on building for the 21st century, the Speaker's Commission on Regionalism, the California Environmental Protection Agency's Environmental Protection Indicators for California (EPIC) project, the Resource Agency's Legacy Project, and the California Economic Strategy Panel.
- Developing through an inclusive and collaborative process, utilizing advisory and working groups consisting of state agency staff, a broad range of private stakeholders, and the general public.

State and public buildings lead the way to develop markets

The goal of energy independence is being pursued by aggressive programs that require energy investment in state buildings. This program is aimed at creating a market for renewable technologies. The State invests over 2.5 billion dollars annually on state facilities, and they are a major energy consumers. In total state buildings cost over 600 million dollars in energy, water, and waste disposal. While not all this can be eliminated, the investment potential to save and to lead by example is substantial. A number of specific projects are important (Sustainable Building Task Force, 2001).

- Sustainable building design program which will encourage state design teams to increase energy and materials efficiencies.
- A new state office building, the Capital East End project is being designed using state-of-the-art technologies, with an expected savings of $400,000 annually.

- The Leadership in Energy and Environmental Design program developed by the US Green Building Council rates buildings, and the State has a supplement to that rating.
- The Fuel Cell Collaborative is working on fuel cell technologies which can be used both in cars and then hooked to buildings to provide distributed power in a community.
- The greening the Capital project seeks to define sustainable energy, water, and waste projects that can be championed by state agencies.
- The University, State University, and Community colleges have over 200 campuses which are major power users, and each is targeted to adopt energy-efficient technologies. The university systems comprise nearly half of all state buildings, and they will become leaders in energy efficiency.

These various programs for the building program have been linked into a state infrastructure investment plan that sees state spending as a resource for sustainability and economic development.

These state building programs have a dual objective. They need to set standards that demonstrate that energy efficiency is viable and cost effective. Second, they will create a market for photo-voltaic cells, better lighting, and efficient heating and cooling equipments. The greater market will entice manufacturers to drop prices and will encourage private sector buildings to adopt similar standards.

9.5.5. Fifth principle: systematic and regional implications to the power system

There are two basic ways to structure agile energy systems: one is for on-site power generation (CPUC, 2002; CEC, 2002); and the other is for regional systems (CPUC, 1999; CEC, 2002; Bollman, 2002) that are fundamentally more like the internet (Rifkin, 2002) than the present central grid configuration. By the late fall of 2002 and looking toward the future, California has begun to rebuild its infrastructures. Governor Davis (2003) has called for a "Building California" program that focuses on its infrastructures as well as developing its workforce and advanced technologies. With a large budget deficit in large part created by the energy deregulation, the State now needs to look to its historical creative and entrepreneurial spirit for rebuilding.

The tools, including financial resources and workforce development are local–regional. The voters have passed over $40 billion in bond measures while the university system continues to lead the world in research and development. Jobs are created and business developed from a variety of emerging technologies, including the energy and environmental sectors.

For example, there is now a shift in the roles in the California Public Utilities Commission (CPUC) and the California Energy Commission (CEC) as seen in recent governmental appointees to these Commissions. Now there will not only be an oversight function for the Commissions, but a specific economic development role. In other words, California has provided large contracts and projects for energy programs in the State. Now it wants the companies to be both located and grown in the State. In other words, California may be the first nation to define and practice "sustainable development"—in both the scientific and economic context. There are enormous amounts of money at stake.

The second area is on-site power generation. Here typical accounting "cost–benefit analysis" strategies are the norm but fail to focus on real costs of energy (e.g. fuel source, historical technological development, health costs, and future needs of society). Thus while it may be cheaper and "cleaner" (than coal or oil) to have natural gas as a fuel source, the financial analyses fail to consider the original costs for exploration, discovery, and distilling the fuel as well as the particulates' health impact.

What is particularly interesting are the lack of data on historical costs for any fuel infrastructure, such as natural gas. Aside from its dramatically increased use in electricity generation, natural gas is being increasing used for vehicles and fleets. However, what were the original research and development costs for natural gas—and more importantly who paid for them? Much of the research and development was subsidized in the USA by the federal government; and in other countries by various government entities.

Critical to the costs of natural gas or other energy supplies are the transmission or pipe lines. Again, consider the costs for these systems when they were originally proposed? And what might be the costs today for new systems that use renewable energy? The comparison is even more compelling when the costs for transmission are seen as being underwritten or financially supported by national governments.

The future of agile energy systems might be advanced far more aggressively, if, as with historical energy power systems (generation and transmission) government support and financing play a key role. When governments on the local and regional levels are involved, as is increasingly occurring today in California, the solutions to bring online more clean intermittent energy is more than just probable. It becomes, with strong state support, financeable and eminent. That is why California can see a Hydrogen Economy future—sooner than later (Rambach, 1999).

Related to both gird and on-site energy generation is distributed energy generation (DG) or as they refer to it in Europe, combined heat and power generation (Münster, 2001) or CHP. The concern for distributed energy systems is not new. In Europe and especially the northernmost countries, DG or CHP has been fundamental to basic energy needs for decades. Most of the systems, however, are very dependent upon fossil energy of some sort. Natural gas within the last decade has been the most pronounced (Lund, 2001) due to its availability, reliability, and low costs. However, wind and biomass are both strong competitors and increasing in use (Lund, 2001; Bolinger and Wiser, 2002a, b).

In the USA a growing concern for DG can be seen to follow the European pathway with natural gas dominated systems leading the way. Public entities in California (CPUC, 1999; CPA, 2002; CEC, 2002) all argue for the need for DG but few integrate intermittent resources, as they are considered too costly and unreliable. New analyses and programs (Morris, 2003) are needed to direct this important concern for regional energy systems that incorporate renewable energy technologies (Clark, 2003) and focus on the future energy infra-structure needs such as hydrogen (Rifkin, 2002).

What do the worldwide changes in the energy sector all add up to? The goal of deregulation or privatization was to create competition, whereas the goal of flexible power is to create a civic market in which private companies operate with the government as their partners. These new entities might be formed under "joint public–private agreements" (as in California) or through third party vendors (companies that create new clean energy for an industry or region) distributed in terms of location and function. In any case, these entities are a direct consequence of regulatory and policy intervention on behalf of the government for the public interest.

An agile power system is a new regulatory and policy orientation in California which is not a restoration of the old regulatory scheme. It is a proactive set of policies on behalf of the civic culture in which the power system serves the goal of sustainability and environmental responsibility. California in this way is forging a new model of restructuring based on choices that support sustainable development. Civic markets structure a role in the following manner:

Power supply. The State is moving boldly to assure that consumers have more clean and renewable options in terms of power generation. The emphasis on 20% renewable power sources by 2010 assures that the monopoly of natural gas-fired central power plants will be weakened, and eventually reduced further. California clearly recognizes that without strong public leadership, financing, and regulation a single focus gas powered power supply system will result, emphasizing short-term financial objectives while leaving the State vulnerable to long-term crises. The State role is clearly to support a more diversified fuel supply system.

Self-generation. California is encouraging through regulation and incentives greater use of dispersed production that allows customers to supply greater proportions of their own power either through clean on-site energy such as photovoltaic installations at their property or through cogeneration (heat-power) systems. Since self-supply requires some backup and grid connections, these contractual barriers are being broken down so that generators can contribute to the grid when they have excess power and draw from it when they do not. This is especially important with intermittent power sources such as wind and solar.

Conservation and load management. The State is also expanding the public incentive programs in conservation through a variety of programs including the California Power Authority and fees charged to consumers. For the most part these programs provide incentives to increase important conservation activities that lower overall demand, especially at peak times. In addition, it is likely that consumers will have more choices of rate schedules based on time of day pricing. The extent to which time of day will include "real-time" costs based on the actual blend of contractual and spot-market costs is not clear, though the largest purchasers are already operating with similar contracts.

Retail level. The State is continuing to see the value in offering a greater range of choices among retail providers, but it is not clear how fast this will expand. On the one hand, large industrial customers are already able to select from alternatives to the local utility, and this may expand. On the other hand, there is no immediate plan to open the system to presumed widespread retail competition. The State appears to be working with the nearly bankrupt utilities to assure that they recover and for the most part it is likely that they will continue as major retail providers. What will probably happen is that the previous utilities will retain their role as a regulated monopoly or near monopoly for the distribution of power to the local customer, but they will not have a monopoly over supply of power. New suppliers will probably be added incrementally under the principles of aggregation where members of communities and industry associations or other bargaining groups will secure supplies to be transmitted and distributed by existing regulated utilities to final demand.

However, a very important caveat on retail choices is that all consumers, with the possible exception of municipal utilities (and their prederegulation customer base) that were not part of the original deregulation, will have to share in the costs of the crisis purchases of power and the uncompetitive costs of the long-term contracts that were negotiated by the State. The total costs of these statewide expenses will be a non-bypassable assessment on future energy sales. How these costs will be computed and allocated are being discussed now (spring 2002), and any estimate of the costs will depend on the outcome of the current legal uncertainty over the contracts given the increasing evidence that Enron and other firms manipulated the market.

9.6. Placing Principles into Action: Civic Markets that form Agile Energy Systems

California has been one of the world's leaders in promoting and installing alternative and renewable technologies in the early 1980s following the first energy crisis. Under PURPA contracts were signed for over 15,000 MW of small scale, qualifying facility power generated largely by independent power producers. This equivalent of 15 nuclear power plants was designed and brought to contract within a period of just two years, overwhelming the utilities and causing an oversupply problem (Summerton and Bradshaw, 1994). However, under the pending deregulation, virtually all new construction came to a halt in the early 1990s. The major reason for this was that there was adequate power and with the changing regulatory scheme, no utility or other generation provider wanted to lock in any new production capacity, especially under the conditions of uncertainty surrounding the changing policy environment.

For California the creation of a civic market that supports an agile energy system must start with the current situation which is that deregulation has been halted and rolled back, but the old system can not be restored (see Fig. 9.1). This is the most important structure of the California electricity system following the electricity crisis, with the CPUC regulating the three major utilities and their remaining generation, transmission, and distribution systems. For the most part the rates have been set by negotiation as a resolution to the financial crisis and bankruptcy, and the regulators and utilities have no long-term strategy to balance private business and public regulation once the crisis-related debt is paid off. Presumably the remaining parts of the utility will return to return on investment regulation, which is a stable but not very agile structure.

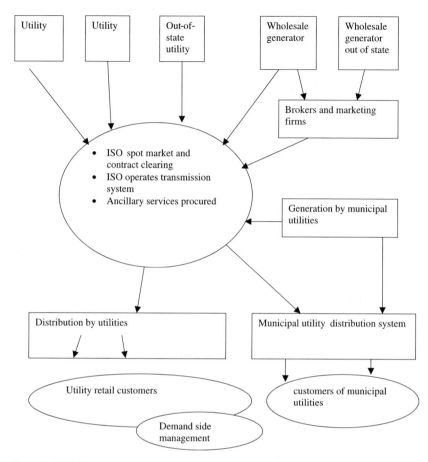

Fig. 9.1. 2003 Competitive generation and retail market coordinated through the ISO after energy crisis.

The five principles outlined above help to create the conditions for agility in the energy system by increasing generation options, retail options, and innovative use of the transmission system. Regardless of the existing structure of the energy system in other states or countries, agility is increased to the extent that the system encourages new options for advantageous new technologies and markets that work in the public interest.

These options can be encouraged by regulators, government agencies, coalitions, partnerships, nonprofit organizations, and communities. Instead of relying on private competitive markets, the agile energy system is built on the premise that expanded alternatives provide the best competition, and that it is the public role to propose, support, encourage, finance, and protect options that may have long-term civic benefit. In this way the public sector is what Henton *et al.* (1999) and others call "civic entrepreneurs". In the electrical power system, civic entrepreneurship is clearly more advantageous to the public good than private competition.

The agile energy system model

Figure 9.2 shows what some of the civic options might be for the California electricity system. Included in this model of an agile power system are options that either are proposed or currently being implemented, or are viable options that could be added within a year at the most. These options are not esoteric or unreasonable, as they are all projects or programs developed in this book. The creation of an agile electricity system requires that public interests create the partnerships and conditions under which these programs can function as core parts of the electricity system.

Moreover, the goal of the agile energy system is that the publicly initiated and overseen parts of the system grow in keeping with the five principles. In Fig. 9.2 the publicly involved parts are shaded and the goal of a civic market is to increase the shaded components until they so dominate the system that public good exceeds private greed as a motive driving the electrical system. There is no magic pill that will reduce rates by competition, but the goal of an agile system is to assure that technologies and markets in the public interest can compete fully and fairly. The agile system introduces new ideas into a broken system rather than completely destroying the old system and hoping for some future good—e.g., it is David versus Goliath rather than World War III. Agile systems are not created by getting a few big players to compete, but in this model the civic interest is best served by a strategy of helping innovative firms or programs develop technology in a protected environment.

Agile electricity generation. As of the present time the State will not and cannot change the fact that a majority of its power is supplied by a combination of old utilities and out-of-state firms that bought the old generation plants. Much of the output of these plants is now under long-term contracts that seem to be legally binding and expensive (but if fuel prices increase they may not be such a bad deal). The remainder of the power to be used on a daily basis is bought and sold under a bid process through the ISO, which also procures ancillary services such as spinning reserve and power to stabilize the voltage and frequency on the transmission and distribution systems.

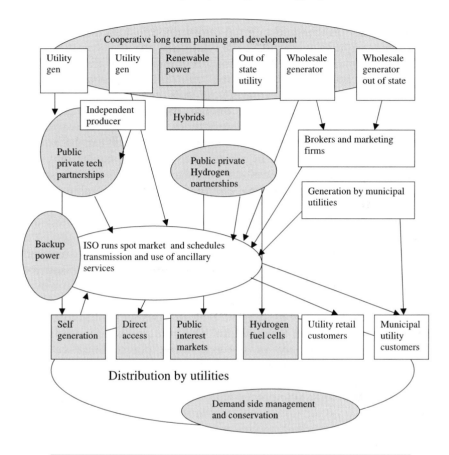

Fig. 9.2. An agile energy system and the civic market.
Source: Authors.

Cooperative planning. The first civic market component in the agile energy system is cooperative planning and system design. This is shown underlying the various generating options at the top of Fig. 9.2. In the traditional regulatory system, the vertically integrated utility accomplished system integration and forward planning since all the generators were under control of a single firm. While sometimes misguided, the utilities had internal information that allowed effective planning and they typically had relatively effective strategies to integrate their resources. In contrast, the integration and planning function becomes more important, not less important, in the transitional or deregulated market. This is critical since there are many more generators operating outside the internal control of the single firm, and for the civic interest these need to be coordinated. The planning function is the first point where agility can be added to the system. For example, in a competitive market short-range cost competition creates the conditions for reliance on too much natural gas generation capacity, making the State overly vulnerable to gas shortages. The goal of long-range planning is to identify this problem and cooperatively find solutions that diversify supply and assure adequate backup in case of shortage.

Renewable generation. The second public function is to nurture and expand generation from renewable sources. Some renewable sources may be more expensive in the short run, but they have environmental and public interest benefits that exceed their short-term costs. When this is the case we suggest that the public should plan for renewable sources, fund technological research, and offer subsidies as needed. The center piece of the renewable power initiative is a collaborative effort involving renewable portfolio standards for the utility suppliers who must either develop their renewable technologies or purchase the renewable power which may require a higher price or subsidy.

The portfolio standard model is very attractive because it puts the burden on all participants in the electricity system to develop renewable sources, without specifying exactly which sources are to be developed except through cooperative planning. Furthermore, we have discussed at some length how many of the renewable technologies are now cost effective or nearly cost effective on the open market without subsidy. These technologies will become even more cost effective as the scale of their use increases and their cost falls with larger scale production. This has already happened in wind and most geothermal applications, and photovoltaics are nearly cost effective.

Hybrid generation systems. The capacity of renewable technologies to supply reliable power is increased to the extent that viable pairings of technology permit storage or backup of intermittent systems. To the extent that wind or photovoltaic systems are coupled with either pumped hydro or other, their reliability and value goes up.

Another hybrid coupling of photovoltaic power is when it is used for cooling. When power is available it can cool water, perhaps making ice, that can be used to supplement cooling systems that are not large enough for the hottest days, and to cool buildings after dark or on days when there is limited sunlight. Chilled water storage systems have been used for years and are relatively inexpensive given the otherwise high price of peak power.

Also wind can be coupled with regular hydro. When there is ample wind the hydro plants do not have to run especially in hot summer afternoons. Then when the wind is still there is more adequate supplies of hydro to meet needs. Financial calculations show that these technologies together can be cost effective (Lamont *et al.*, 1999). Projects in developing countries as well as in northern parts of Europe demonstrate the feasibility of these systems. At least two wind developers in California have projects combining wind and pumped hydro now under development (Clark, 2002). The key will be to have the energy supplied as base load and dispatchable during peak demand periods of time where the price for energy are highest.

Hydrogen partnerships. Another linkage with renewable technologies include development of appropriate hydrogen facilities that can store energy for fuel cells or other uses. For example, the public–private fuel cell collaborative and the initial experimentation with fuel cell buses and cars has led to the development of fueling stations and vehicles to use the hydrogen. The critical issue in hydrogen is that it is closely connected to the development of renewable sources of power where it serves as a storage medium, thus increasing the value of the renewable source (Rifkin, 2002; Rambach 1999; Clark, 2004).

Public–private technology partnerships. With all the attention given to hydrogen, it is hard to remember that there are many technologies that are and could be developed by public–private partnerships. For example, cogeneration could save California and all other US states considerable amounts of money, and the technology has largely been developed. A public–private effort has been formed to expand the use of cogeneration. Their effort requires working with manufacturers and others who use lots of fuel, and developing the newest models of the technology that will meet the users needs. The parallel effort is to find and assure that the utilities or other power suppliers and users will buy the power generated.

Thus from the generation side there are already many opportunities that will utilize the five principles. Regions such as Los Angeles, Sacramento, San Diego, and San Francisco among others have been seeking means to implement the State's renewable energy standard portfolio. The problem for some is simply the financial resources. Yet for others it is that the regions already have sufficient energy to meet their needs. Shifting to renewables will mean either eliminating, downsizing, or increasing the energy supply reserve margins. All of these strategies can work.

However the civic market approach is the only way to achieve them; get public and private interest groups in the same room and discuss how to find the mutually beneficial solutions. The other gold mine of opportunity for increasing the agility of the power system is to create new, open, and fair markets for renewable and clean energy generation within the region or customer sites.

Self-generation. The expansion of self-generation is probably the most significant and immediately beneficial step a State can take to increase agility. The widespread use of self-generation, to the extent it is fuel and cost effective, can achieve distributed goals readily. To some extent the key to solar is self-generation. However, the technological barriers to widespread self-generation are nowhere as great at the market barriers. For decades the utilities had tried to stop self-generation, including the reduction in rates for industrial customers who threatened to pull off the grid. The utilities also retaliated with exorbitant rates for backup and connection. The goal for an agile system is that self-generation would be embraced with enthusiasm. There are several roles that the public regulatory boards can play in encouraging self-generation.

First the whole grid can be a backup for self-generators whose own capacity can go out unexpectedly. While the new load caused by an intermittent and unexpected interruption by a self-generator could be a problem for utility or CAISO dispatchers, to the extent the self-generator has excess capacity, the system also gains a resource they can draw upon when they have other problems with the grid and suppliers.

The most beneficial aspect of self-generation is that it is distributed and the power is used where it is generated without relying on the transmission system. So, for the most part expanding the distributed part of the overall energy system by encouraging self-generation increases agility in the system. However, it is in the public interest to see more self-generation and requires public participation to overcome the barriers of securing reliable backup from the grid and calculating the costs and fees of such interconnection. Historically, these fees have been what most consider to be unreasonably high because they undermined the interests of the monopoly utility which would loose customers. But to increase agility, the public and private interests need to find ways to increase self-generation.

Direct access. Like self-generation, direct access allows some generators and customers to contract for power directly without going through the utility. Direct access has been proposed in a number of different configurations, and its implementation raises policy questions that are beyond the scope of this book. On the other hand, the logic of direct assess is that some customers by themselves or in aggregated market clusters are linked to generators bypassing the utility. The direct access customer and their supplier arrange for generation, transmission, backup, and all other services, often contracting for capacity as needed. For the most part the local utility delivers the power through the local distribution system for a fee, just like other power is delivered.

Direct access helps by providing options that increase agility in the system. The major abuse is if some customers, either large ones or groups of clever customers, pick off the cheapest sources of power, leaving the old public utility or supplier of last resort with the most expensive power with which to serve the segment of the market least capable of paying for it.

However, "competitive aggregation" can be another government-initiated tool for the purchase of goods and services. The California Power Authority along with the California Stationary Fuel Cell Collaborative did just that for fuel cell in the fall of 2001 (CFCC, 2002) and also for solar PV systems. While the Request for Bids list still exists, the actual funds for purchasing were not available. The competitive bid list may become a significant item with the newly passed $40+ billion bond funds passed in 2002.

A good example exists now for on-site generation with the Los Angeles Community College District. In 2001, the community passed a bond measure for $1.3 billion to renovate and rebuild the 30+ year old campus. Half of the funds were to be used for renewable technologies. In the spring of 2002, the Board of Directors approved the contractors and building for "Silver Level LEEDS" standards at some for the campus buildings. Voters in the fall of 2002 then approved another $2+ billion in bonds for the entire "greening" of the 9-campuses within the System. Similar measures passed 17 or the 19 Community College Districts in 2002, leaving the System with the potential to competitively aggregate goods and services bidders.

Public power advocates are very interested in direct access. They perceive the option of building a municipal generation facility or many distributed facilities and supplying the community through the existing distribution system (Bradshaw *et al.*, 2003). Some of the options for direct access in support of publicly owned power are the purchase of new generation capacity owned by other municipal utilities, as is being done by Cerritos San Marcos who have bought a share of the increased capacity of the Burbank power plant that was being upgraded and expanded.

Direct access generally was used by large purchasers to secure a more favorable bulk power contract than they were getting from the utility. Since their retail rates were not frozen, when prices escalated during 2000–2001, many of these customers temporarily returned to their old utility; when prices stabilized a bit in the fall of 2001 most returned to direct access contracts. However, the State had spent public funds of over $8 billion for power for the financially strapped utilities, and projected the need to spend another $10 billion by the end of 2001. These funds were to be repaid by customers of the utilities for whom the power was purchased. Consequently, the State was worried that too many customers would leave their utility for direct access, hoping to avoid the repayment costs. To correct this possibility, the State eliminated all new direct access on September 20, 2001.

Today, direct access is still frozen, though there has been legislation proposed that would allow communities to aggregate their local citizens into a direct access municipal utility to obtain advantageous power prices. The original legislation allowed community aggregation, but only to the extent that customers signed up for the service. The new proposed legislation allowed communities to enroll everyone, giving anyone the option to opt out if they wished. The municipal utility interests were very optimistic that this would lead to many new municipal utilities in the State. However, the legislation still would require that the new municipal utility pass on an "exit fee" to cover their share of costs born by the rest of the State. At the present time this option remains undecided.

It is not clear yet how or when customers will have limited access to alternative suppliers, or how the State will get out of the power purchasing role. It is ironic that the premise of deregulation was to have more open and competitive markets, but the result has been the opposite—much greater state roles in the provision of power. On the other hand, the consistent emphasis by the Governor and the State has been to first stabilize the system which was in chaos, and then to find ways to increase flexibility.

Public interest markets. The key to many green and renewable programs is that the State can become the public interest market, that is a market that is specifically invests in and uses the energy from advanced sources. The State has already taken the lead with green buildings and has frequently been a leader in innovations such as fuel cell cars and buses. The great state and municipal purchasing power is one of the keys to transition to a renewable future, and this increases the agile quality of the system. The public can innovate in many ways including putting fuel cells in government facilities to provide a test for new technologies.

Procurement is critical especially for state and public buildings. As the California Consumer Affairs Agency noted in its "Blue Print for Sustainable State Buildings," (CAA, 2001) the driving force for clean energy and lower costs should be the state buildings. Along with cost accounting based on life cycle analyses (IGAWG, 2002), the competitive costs for renewable on-site energy technologies can be competitive.

San Francisco has taken an aggressive approach by installing PV and other renewable sources for its city buildings and schools, and intends gradually to make the locally generated power available to users who are not in city owned buildings. Several cities are also interested in installing wind power for some of their uses. The logic of using a municipal market helps to provide an alternative market for innovation in the electrical generation sector, as the public benefits from the diversification and it is a reasonable approach to use public funds to help create new markets for innovation when the other utilities are less willing to take the risk.

Demand side management and conservation. The fact that with deregulation the investment in conservation and demand side management slowed dramatically helped create part of the shortage that was exploited by the electricity brokers leading to the California crisis. This shows the great importance in the continuing public oversight role in the power sector. Fortunately, California's experiment in deregulation included some provisions for continuing conservation programs, and many of these in California are among the most aggressive and successful in any state. The municipal utilities such as Sacramento Municipal Utility District have been very successful in promoting conservation because they have less to gain from increased quantity of power sales.

9.7. Conclusions: An Agile Energy Future

Governor Davis set a primary goal for the state of "energy independence" in 2001 which means decreasing reliance on out-of-state generators and out-of-state natural gas for power production. Governor Schwarzenegger appears to be headed in the same direction. While full independence is only a very long-term goal, many steps are being taken toward the goal. Since the State is in the position of purchasing substantial portions of all the power distributed in the State since the collapse of the regulated utilities, this gives the State considerable leverage.

Clearly the deregulation or privatization of energy sectors has led to new market forces who provide generation, transmission, and distribution services. While central gird energy generation still dominates the utility sector, an increasing number of new private sector, local, on-site, and regional companies, are providing energy to public and private buildings. Civic markets capture the systemic and overall approach to infrastructure with less regulatory and governmental control.

First, the State now holds long-term contracts for about a third of the power that will enter the grid. While these contracts are high (and given the Enron "smoking guns" appear to be contrived as well by other energy trading firms), the contracts are being renegotiated and reduced.

Currently the State purchases power into a common pool from which distribution utilities draw. The Independent System Operator (CAISO) needs to control supply to balance the system demand so that the transmission lines do not get overloaded. How choice will be increased while the State controls so much power that will need to be shared by all consumers is still not resolved. Any option selected by state policy makers will require approval by FERC with whom California has had a strong ideological difference on the marketplace.

Similarly, the current system still has not figured out how to assure that the capacity is built and maintained ready to meet the very top of the peak demand.[3] Peak demand means that capacity has to be available to serve demand for only a few hours on that hottest summer afternoon. This is very expensive, indeed, and no clear plan exists for meeting the demand under current models.

In sum, the evolution of the California deregulation debacle has moved in the direction of embracing many options that will lead the State toward an agile energy infrastructure system. The goals are to

---

[3]Some peak demand is shaved by conservation or load shedding, while other demand is met by hydro plants and old of less efficient plants which are reserved just for peak periods. Utilities also meet peak demand through long-distance transfers from other states where night has already fallen, or where weather differences result in less demand. However, it remains uneconomic to build or maintain peaking plants for the very highest loads.

achieve independence through expanding the civic market, rather than deregulation, which is about laissez fair "free market" competition. The California experience has shown that deregulated competition leads to instability and fewer choices, whereas the current response is to carefully use regulation in the public interest to increase choices.

Chapter 10
Civic Capitalism — A New Approach for Public and Private Collaboration

10.1. Introduction

The energy crisis in California was a challenge for all its citizens. The "design flaws" or "restructuring" as some economists now label it, were not the only problems. As new energy systems are envisioned and constructed to respond to the crisis, policy makers must reformulate the basic premises that led to the crisis in the first instance. This means reevaluating the political–economic foundations that led to deregulation. These assumptions must be recast to provide a new direction that will provide electricity that is cheap, reliable, and environmentally friendly without relying on price competition as the main economic tool.

The extent to which the old basic premises need to be replaced is clear not only from the failure in California, but also from the more widespread problems with deregulation or privatization in other states and nations. Growing evidence appears to indicate serious problems with energy sectors worldwide where unrestrained competition has been tried (Kapner, 2002), and this is not just a minor adjustment but a huge mistake. The energy crises during the summer of 2003 in Northern USA and Southern Canada along with those in Europe point dramatically to something being wrong with the deregulation and privatization of economic models.

The current energy crisis created a challenge which provides the opportunity to look at energy economics in a new and different manner. While neoclassical or conventional economic theory looks at energy from the perspective of the market, energy economics needs to be examined from the perspective of the society in general. The object of an energy system or sector should not be to maximize corporate profits, but to assure that civic interests are protected for all citizens and best developed for future generations.

In the current predominant deregulation model, the pursuit of profit is assumed to lead to public good. As evidence mounts, the pursuit of the public good when it leads to profit only, is a disaster for not only the company, but also the general public. This "public good" argument is parallel to Hawkin and Lovin's (1999) concept of "natural capitalism" rather than neoclassical economic theory. It is consistent with the findings that socially and environmentally responsible firms are profitable, sometimes more profitable than average (Angelides, 2003a).

However, this alternative economic framework is only beginning to be articulated. While it is not possible to present a complete new theory of civic capitalism here (Clark and Lund, 2001), this chapter will outline the basic economic elements of a new approach to electricity structure that supports the development of an "agile energy system." "Civic markets" define the role of government and regulatory oversight which is embedded in public–private partnerships. This is not a socialist or communist model (Clark and Li, 2003). The public good is not maximized by central planning and control or by the elimination of private ownership, but from the integration of public and private goals and objectives.

Cooperation between the public–private sectors in the form of partnerships, collaborations, rule making, setting codes and standards, and implementing programs is the new civic market model. This approach to economics and politics is an alternative to the theory that competitive market forces would increase the public good of any nation-state. By letting private monopolies control the supply (or demand) of any infrastructure sector like energy, government opens the door for mistakes like what happened in the California energy crisis between 2000 and 2002.

The worldwide energy crisis has reinforced the basic tenant that all governments must adhere to higher standards for the public good. Leaving energy, water, environment, or waste, among other infrastructure sectors, to the "market" or "competitive forces" of supply and demand was wrong in the first instance. The predictable results were that private monopolies gained legal control of energy supply and generation. These market forces only replaced the publicly regulated monopolies that had supplied California with power for a century of economic growth.

The task in this chapter is to argue for a new set of tools by which the economics of the power sector can be reformulated to create new solutions and opportunities for the future of all citizens. The old neoclassical competitive model, which gave deregulation to California, most of America, and now the world, needs to be replaced with a new energy/environmental economic model that builds on networks, flexibility, and innovation. Such a new economic model is well-rooted in civic markets.

10.2. A New Framework for Understanding Energy and Economics within the Context of Civic Society

The concept of "civic markets" is put forth in this chapter in order to highlight the differences that need to be addressed in managing a complex industry such as electricity. However, civic markets also apply to other infrastructure sectors like water, waste, transportation, and education where reliance on the market forces can be either technically relied upon or financially trusted to be honest. In addition, civic markets are likely to be in the new economy and concentrated in industries that are expanding rather than contracting.

This is most clearly seen not only in monopolist industries such as energy, but also in industries involving other public infrastructure such as airlines and airports, information and telecommunications, industries with high environmental impacts such as the natural resource industries, and service industries such as health and welfare. Even industries dependent on a steady stream of innovation from university and government research labs such as pharmaceuticals, life sciences, and biotechnology are moving rapidly toward civic markets or partnerships between public and private sectors. The framework for the new economics is rapidly evolving and is reflected in a growing body of thought in politics as well as business and economics (Clark and Lund, 2001).

According to conventional neoclassical economics, companies should operate with little or no government interference. Ideally companies have no regulations and taxes etc., but contribute to societal needs on their own. Adam Smith's (rev. 1934) concept of the "invisible hand," and more recently the Bush Administration's (2001) application of it in outlining its "energy plan," are good examples of the neoclassical economic perspective gone wrong with odd contradictions. Government should not be involved in energy business activities, especially setting regulations, yet government can and should support big corporations through incentives and tax breaks by which only they can benefit.

In any industry, as in any country, the conventional economic argument is made that there is a "balance" between supply and demand which keeps prices low due to competition among the companies for customers. It is the supply–demand balance that is the basis for all energy economics and the rational for deregulation in

California (Marshall, 1998), as well as similar conventional economic justifications elsewhere in the USA and worldwide.

The energy system points out the limitations to the conventional economic models and gives priority to new concepts. Many of the contrasts between the neoclassical and civic market models are matters of degree and centrality; the civic issues are "externalities" in the current models used by modern economists rather than being at the core. Civic market functions must take prominence in framing competition and market economics. The main differences are:

- Neoclassical economic models are based on concepts of independent firms competing to gain advantage over other firms because of efficiencies, product, technology, and price, and thus meeting the public interest because they better produce what the public wants at the lowest cost. In contrast today, we better understand that the firms are in networks where innovation, efficiencies, and price are the result of the inter-firm sharing and cooperation rather than simply competition.

- Neoclassical models assume private sector involvement whereas the new system is based on an increasing number of public–private partnerships and shared responsibility between the public and private sectors. Shared ownership and management control are at the root of programs that blend the public good with private initiative.

- Neoclassical models are based on premises that markets, and technological systems are largely self-regulating and that government's role is limited to protecting against market power and unfair competition by enforcing laws preventing price gouging, protecting patents, enforcing contracts, and prohibiting malicious misrepresentations or corruption, etc. In contrast, we now see an expanded role for government that goes well beyond rules creating the context for public good in expanding markets, promoting employment, and protecting the environment.

- Neoclassical models left innovation and technological change to the marketplace, whereas the new model relies on government leadership to introduce and stabilize markets for innovations that serve the public good but which may not be in the short-term private interest of market leaders.

- Neoclassical models make minimal distinction between industries where it is easy for companies to enter or leave, compared to companies in grid or network industries where control of the grid constitutes a public obligation to serve and a natural monopoly. In fact, barriers to entry in a number of industries is growing because of increased interdependency and specialized materials, information, and markets that limit participation in the industry to those already involved.

The transformation away from the neoclassical and now conventional economic model that was the basic philosophical and theoretical basis, along with a bi-partisan political agenda, and hence responsible for the deregulation framework which led to the California energy crisis and to changes in the electricity system structures in other nations, must be discussed in some detail. It is important to understand that not all existing economic philosophy and theory is dismissed. Nor are the accomplishments of neoclassical economics in solving other industrial and business problems. Nonetheless, a full discussion must be made (see Appendix A for some details from Clark and Fast, 2004).

Neoclassical economics and its conventional contemporary proponents derived from a particular economic philosophy are not appropriate for the energy and many other infrastructure sectors. Furthermore, there are other economic philosophical paradigms that lead to very different economic principles and rules (Clark and Fast, 2004). In short, the explanation of economic issues surrounding the electricity industry require new tools, framework models based upon a different social science philosophical paradigm. It is this paradigm, called "interactionism," elsewhere by Clark and Fast (2004), which is framed by the civic market theory.

Interactionism is, in short, the theory that because people (actors) interact in specific situations (everyday behavior such as business), companies and their behaviors are better understood. The decisions of business actors is not dependent upon numbers, figures, and statistics alone. Instead, business people form strategies and plans, such as deregulation public policy, knowing that they can maneuver the newly formed markets. A key component in understanding business in the interactionism paradigm is to also know, influence, or control the role of government. Much has been written on this subject, but the "invisible hand" of government needs to be influenced to do as business wants it to do.

Economists want to be scientific and therefore, ignore this influence over government. Instead, they tend to think that the use of statistics and numbers place them above the interaction between people. Economists see themselves akin to the hard and natural sciences. There is almost a sense in economics that if the field is not scientific (e.g., statistical or numbers-oriented) then the field is not professional. For most economists, however, the perspective and view or definition of what science is and does bears little proof in reality (Blumer, 1969).

Science is not a simple matter of statistics or numbers (Perkins, 1997). While some field or qualitative studies have been conducted, especially on productivity (see Blinder, 1998), economists remain steadfast in their belief that fieldwork is the main research area for sociologists and journalists. Yet, the need to explore the "productivity paradox" as Nobel Laureate, Robert Solow, called it in 1987, promoted statistical research in the 1990s only to crash land with the explosive truths behind the "productivity miracle" of that decade by the turn of the next century.

Clearly statistics did not tell the "truth" about productivity in the 1990s. The popular journal, *The Economist* (see *Economist* issues 1998–2002), often tries to "sugar coat" or marginalize the accounting scandals of CEOs, major American corporations, corporate governance and bankruptcies in 2002, as simply downward revisions of company financials, when in fact these crises represent only the beginning of corporate illegal misbehavior (Demirag *et al.*, 2001). The issue of validation and verification of economic data is simply neither statistics and numbers (quantitative) versus fieldwork and observation (qualitative) data to prove points or hypothesis, but a combination of both (Casson, 1996).

Implementation of energy economics today has been traditionally done (prior to deregulation, privatization, or liberalization) through a variety of "mechanisms" by energy experts. HarvardWatch (2002) looked behind the scenes of public policy and discovered, however, questionable direct links between the objective experts at some universities and the energy private sector. The "links" between scholars and experts and the companies violates the credibility of economics as being either objective or scientific. Far more important are the "networks" of people who develop and implement government policies that impact the public through the private sector. As will be described below, government policies do not just mean regulations, tax, and incentive programs. They should also include, as California has championed, economic accounting for projects/ programs (Schultz, 2001) and the creation of market demand (CCAA, 2001; CAFCC, 2002 among others).

At this point, it is important to make note of how California government found itself in the middle of redefining energy economics. The energy crisis can never be fully explained (CEC, 2002), but one basic economic issue is clear: the state government had to take an active role in solving the crisis. For California, this meant a number of measures and legal steps had to be taken from long-term energy supply contracts, to emergency funds for conservation and efficiency programs, to incentives such as buy down and rebate programs, to expedited siting of new power plants.

As discussed earlier in some detail, other economists such as Borenstein *et al.* (2001), Woo (2001), and Nobel Laureates (2001) all agreed that the energy crisis could be averted and changed if the government simply took off all the price caps on energy. What is ignored traditionally by economists is a focus on the firm itself (Teece, 1996). Energy economics, however, only discusses the companies as end-users of energy such that the energy flow, hence costs, should be controlled by the consumer's awareness of "real-time prices" (Borenstein *et al.*, 2001).

Elsewhere Clark (2004) argues that "qualitative economics" is a new area of economics, within the interactionism economic paradigm. The purpose of qualitative economics is to understand how companies work. Much of field is concerned with case studies, corporate descriptions of operations, and people. But the most significant concern of qualitative economics is to gather data in order to understand what the meaning of numbers is. For companies when they add, as Enron allegedly did, 2 plus 2 and got 5, the meaning of those numbers is critical. The issue is that economics must understand how businesses work, and can only do that with deeper definitions, meanings, and backgrounds of organizations, people, and their interactions.

The goal of economics must be to take quantitative and qualitative data and derive rules. Economics needs to expose universal rules based and tested in reality upon a combination of statistics and interactions. From rules, laws can be articulated (Perkins, 1997). Scientists in fields, such as linguistics (Chomsky, 1968, 1988) and developmental cognition (Cicourel, 1974), have long investigated science in terms of developing universal rules and laws. Just like the natural sciences, social sciences use observation, description, and hypothesis testing (Chomsky, 1980). The science argument is spelled out in other works (Clark and Fast, 2004) and some aspects of the qualitative economic theories are presented below. Appendix A provides more details.

10.2.1. The advantages of cooperation over competition

The first economic principle supporting an agile energy system is that cooperation among companies and among consumers helps to increase civic good and societal purpose. Clearly an important side benefit, however, is sustainable development; or to put it another way, the growth of environmental and clean energy friendly businesses is needed as an overall public policy. As California State Treasurer put it in a speech delivered to the UN in November 2003, California must "mobilize financial capital in new and innovative ways, consistent with the highest fiduciary standards, to meet our 'triple bottom line' goals of achieving positive financial returns and fostering sustainable growth and sound environmental practices" (Angelides, 2003: 1)

One of the lessons of the personal computer technological revolution is that by having an open architecture and allowing other firms to follow standards and achieve standardization, the IBM model succeeded over other firms that were trying to go alone. Indeed, the notion of firm cooperation is not new or unique to alternative economics, but it is clear that it plays a central role in thinking about how to introduce a new technology and energy system.

Competition will not, and should not, go away in California. Governor Schwarzenegger appears to be headed into a middle pathway as well, following much of the "civic market" approach to economics. Today, California has a electrical generation system, and a minimally competitive retail market. Owing to both legal and practical reasons, there is little reason to consider reverting to the market structures of the vertically integrated energy system dominated by three monopolies that the State had before deregulation. The companies that purchased the bulk of the State's generation capacity after deregulation now, since the energy crisis, have medium-term contracts of up to 10 years to sell power to the State's utilities at fixed rates. This is a significant shift from the spot-market mechanisms.

The California Power Exchange, which is now bankrupt, was created by deregulation in 1996. It still holds (2004) over $2 billion in assets as the courts try to decide on how to disperse the funds. Nonetheless, the dozen or so Exchange staff remain on payroll. After some significant conflicts, due to the California energy crisis, the Federal Energy Regulatory Commission (FERC) and the California Independent System Operator (CAISO) are now cooperating.

Although the mid-term contracts were negotiated while the State was in its energy crisis, and by all estimates are overpriced, significant reductions were later negotiated. In addition, most of the new power plants that are being proposed or built are seeking and usually obtaining long-term contracts on more reasonable terms. The large number of fixed contracts has reduced price competition among electricity generators on the day ahead and spot market to a very small proportion of power that is needed. Looking ahead, the State now has a modified market structure for buying and selling power which the FERC is expected to approve in 2004. That market structure will continue to operate. As the existing long-term contracts end, this market may become more robust for supplying the core demand of the utilities. But given the past performance of the market mechanisms, there will be a need for alternative plans.

On the retail side, some limited competition may emerge over the next few years. Now, the existing utilities serve virtually all customers in their geographical areas, with the exception of a few large consumers who had direct access contracts before the energy crisis. However, pressure remains on the CPUC to allow other large users similar contracts. Modified direct access and limited exit fees have allowed the continued development for on-site generation, especially with new solar/PV, microturbine, and fuel cell technologies.

In addition, some interest groups and municipalities are intensely interested in aggregation of customers to obtain power from their own contracts (Bradshaw et al., 2003). The California Stationary Fuel Cell Collaborative and the California Power Authority developed such aggregated master purchase contacts for new advanced on-site technologies. The premise of the CPUC and most legislators is that those customers who want to bypass their utilities and the existing system must continue to pay their share of the energy debt and overpriced contracts that are a residual of the energy crisis. If these "exit fees" are added, the advantages of leaving the traditional utility become limited except in some exceptional cases. So compromises have been worked out to mitigate the negative impact on business development for retail customers. A significant side benefit is the economic development of new technologies and companies providing the technologies, services, and operations.

The issue, then, is not whether price competition will be eliminated in California—some competition is here to stay and may beneficially increase. The issue, instead, is to identify what will replace competition as the organizing premise for the evolving energy system in California. What should be the organizing premise for other states and countries looking to restructure their power system, given the California experiences? From an economic perspective, the strategic driving force of civic capitalism is to increase cooperation not competition.

The premise is that since full and legitimate price competition in electricity is not possible, and indeed its pursuit is catastrophic, the alternative is to structure multiple options for cooperative solutions to the energy problem of how to deliver the best electrical services to the population with the lowest possible cost. In a particularly interesting article, Henrik Lund (2000) contrasted the conflict model of energy policy to a "democratic" model that involved broad public participation in decisions to reduce fossil fuel dependence and innovate with renewable and conservation alternatives in Denmark. That country is the world leader in innovative solutions to the energy crisis without focusing solely on getting firms to compete on short-term prices.

The vitality of cooperation and collaboration among firms is highly valued in studies of economic success. For example, Saxenian's (1994) study of the conditions leading to the ascendance of Silicon Valley over Boston Route 128 in microelectronic technology. She showed that the networking and interaction among competitors in Silicon Valley gave these high-technology companies a competitive edge. One high-tech entrepreneur from Silicon Valley, for example, made a fortune in the dot.com/IT industry, but then turned his attention to sustainable environmental companies. He has formed networks and raised capital for such firms.

In addition, firms in many industries have collaborated to find solutions to major technical problems that affect the whole industry. In electricity, the Electricity Producers Research Institute (EPRI) model is an example of how the utilities have contributed the funds necessary to do fundamental research on power plant design, maintenance, operations, modeling, and many other factors. Deregulation and competition have led to serious cuts (over 33% since the mid-90s) in funding and programs at EPRI because the new market players have no incentive to look to long-term collaborations and financial participation in programs to research, develop, and deploy new advanced technologies.

Finally, the potential of cooperation is seen in building regional networks of firms that can take advantage of specialized infrastructure and supplier industries, becoming a type of regional node. This type of industrial concentration that gives individual firms competitive advantage has been called an industrial cluster by Bradshaw *et al.* (1999). The cluster concept has been used in other less-specific ways by Porter (1998, 2000) and others, but what is important is that research is showing that industries concentrate in certain areas and that gives them an advantage. This economic advantage is one that increases the economic value of each of the firms in the region.

The California State Assembly took the lead in understanding and seeing the need for regional public policy. Under Speaker Robert Hertzberg (2002) and then continued under Herb Wesson (2003), the State issued a report recognizing the realities of the State's diversity in both cultural and physical makeup. Guided by a series of regionally convened forums throughout 2002, the Public Policy

Institute gathered opinions and perspectives from citizens and leaders throughout the Golden State. A constant theme was the value and concern for protecting the environment. Because of that, the State legislature took the initiative in passing laws to protect the environment as well as plan for the future growth of California.

A good example of the regional approach undertaken by the Legislature is the California Environmental Goals Policy Report (EGPR) passed as the Wiggins Bill (AB #857) in September 2002 that requires the Governor to form a statewide environmental plan which must go to the Legislature for approval. This statewide plan is the first such plan in over 25 years, but does not dictate to the local communities and cities as to what to do. It basically establishes public policy and provides some direction as to the State's plans for growth. The first report was issued at the end of Governor Davis' term in office before the Recall took effect (EGPR, 2003).

10.2.2. The economic advantages of public–private partnerships

The second theme that underlies civic capitalism is the importance of public–private partnerships. Building on the first theme of cooperation, the public is a favored cooperator with private firms. From an economic perspective, the public role increases in complex industries and economies because of the special role of public participants to facilitate business activities that are beneficial to business and that pursue the public good. The partnerships in energy have become more complex over time and the beneficial partnerships are markedly different from the early regulatory relationship. Whereas regulators primarily tried to keep the monopoly utilities from raising rates too high, the new partnerships try to use public resources to help better meet civic interests. In the past the public role with utilities was the power to say "no," however, the emerging role is for the public to say "yes."

What is the role of government in business? Much of the economic literature has been focused on the dichotomy between free markets and tight regulation as in the historical electrical industry. The emerging era of public–private partnerships is neither. The justification for public involvement in the power industry is two fold. First, the transmission and distribution monopoly and technological nature of electricity networks mean that the public has an interest in overseeing the private suppliers of such an essential part of modern life. This point has been mentioned consistently in previous chapters. Second, the public has many social and environmental interests that intersect with the provision of electricity, such as environmental protection, public safety, equity, economic development, and long-term reliability. Simply put, given the extensive public agenda, it is more effective to try to reach these goals through partnerships than rule making. This is not unique to the electricity industry, though it stands out in a very clear relief.

In Denmark, for example, the free market has historically involved a partnership between government and business (Sorensen, 1994). If shared societal goals (free universal education, national health care, jobs, strong social services, and high standard of living) are to be achieved, then business and government must work together toward common economic goals. The "partnership" between government is not always smooth or cooperative, but it remains dedicated to the shared values for the common good (Sorensen, 1993).

Government is deeply involved in many industries in more than a regulatory role. For example, government provides over $16 billion annually to the US Department of Energy and its over dozen "national" laboratories. Two of these scientific laboratories receive over $1 billion annually in research funds: Los Alamos National Laboratory in New Mexico and Lawrence Livermore National Laboratory in California. Both of these labs, as well as Lawrence Berkeley National Laboratory, are operated by the University of California System which receives over $25 million annually as a management fee. The amount of research funds flowing through these and other labs clearly influences both public policy and business strategies in the USA and worldwide.

The recently passed national energy bill included assistance for coal and nuclear power as well as expanded incentives for oil and gas, and most parts of the electricity industry. The electronics industry credits high-price defense contracts with giving them the capacity to develop and market early transistors and integrated circuits when there would have been no private markets for these products given their costs. In addition, the US agricultural incentives have become hotly contested by Europe and Asian countries claiming unfair competition in trade. Also, the Bush administration's favoring of government support for industry is seen in the prescription drug bill recently passed. In short, the myth of industry operating without government support and control is hopelessly inadequate.

The local and regional level is also a critical resource for public–private partnerships. The role of local governments is often forgotten, but together they have extensive planning and program activities because their residents and constituencies need and want it. Thus, local level governmental entities, such as government and counties, are one focal point for renewable energy generation and hence noncentral grid energy systems. In 2000, the voters of California passed Initiative #38 which allowed local governments or districts to use finance measures such as bond measures.

One of the most successful has been the Community College Districts, the largest college system in the world with 1.3 million students on 108 campuses. By the spring of 2002, six districts followed the lead of the Los Angeles Community College District (LACCD) and its Board of Directors who passed a bond for $1.3 billion. At least half of the bond measure funds are being used for "sustainable" (green) buildings in LACCD under international green building standards. In other words, the public colleges are leading the way to renewable energy in their facilities.

Part of the evidence of the political and economic success rests in the fact that the Board of Directors for the California Community College District appointed the Chancellor for the LACCD to head the entire State System in 2004. The success of the LACCD meant that the Board saw the need throughout the entire system. The advancement of "green" college buildings throughout the State will certainly be far more rapid and cost effective. The political and economic repercussions to this are significant. Local communities are the market drivers for renewable and clean energy systems.

In California, the mass purchasing of sustainable systems has reduced the price and expedited the implementation of these systems. The State and the agencies and programs it funds are a huge market and the mobilization of this market is large enough to change the economics for the production of many items. The State mandated some level of internal consumption of recycled paper, green building, and renewable energy, for example, which creates enough of a market to help establish these industries at a level where they have economies of scale and become cost competitive in open and unsubsidized markets. Many examples exist of this financing practice such as the State purchase of police and other vehicles which are zero emission; incentives are offered through the Energy Star program for energy saving appliances, efficient equipment, and conservation. The Department of General Services has led the State in this effort and included new technologies, such as fuel cells and solar devices (CSFCC, 2002).

Government partnerships rather than regulatory power help create more successful programs to meet civic goals. Using moral persuasion and the legitimacy of the State, governments can lead by demonstrating their willingness to invest in what they are telling private companies to do. California has the public policies and mechanisms in place for local and regional clean-distributed energy systems.

The State Government Code already provides for Community Energy Authorities (No. 5200) for local and regional energy systems (not municipal utilities).

With local governments, the private sector, educational and research institutions, as well as nonprofits, all working together as partners, clean energy is viable along a business model for recovering costs and providing for innovation and change (Clark and Jensen, 2000). A number of these strategies include promotion of dispute resolution and conflict mediation as a way to resolve differences between private firms and state agencies or programs. The competitive model is based on a win–loose model whereas economic growth and public interests are increased with win–win responses to differences of opinion on what direction the power system should take.

The public role in partnerships is often and most importantly the collection of information and data on power demand, technological change, environmental resources and pollution, and national and global trends. As discussed in the earlier chapters, one of the major contributions of the California Energy Commission when it was formed was to help the utilities come up with a standard methodology forecast of power demand which led to the reduction in expected number of nuclear power plants needed. The fact these plants were not built protected the State from even worse disasters of stranded assets and high costs.

Resource mapping and technological feasibility studies are also an essential function that government can provide. Again, the Energy Commission had as one of its initial mandates the collection and dissemination of information on the location and extent of renewable resources such as geothermal hot spots, wind resources, untapped hydro capacity, solar capacity, etc.; these resource inventories became essential for firms looking to invest in these technologies in the State. These studies were done in partnership with the industry, pooling their private information and setting up methodologies for collecting additional data. Because the data came from a partnership involving the firms intending to use the data, it had a higher level of credibility than if it had been developed in order to force business partners to do something.

Provision of additional resources and technical assistance to implement best practices, including green building and site design, product development, and installation of energy-efficiency systems (CAA, 2001). The public role in partnerships can also include developing and providing training, conferences, best practice reports, and consultations with staff experts that will eventually lead to more successful private developments meeting state standards and agendas.

Finally, the partnership can encourage California-based philanthropies and the commercial media to work with the public sector on public education and participation, and inform readers and viewers on energy issues. The partnerships in the State that encouraged conservation that eventually broke the price spiral of the energy crisis show that broad partnerships can work very effectively.

The implementation of new policies and programs cannot be done until basic public finance issues are addressed and resolved (Clark and Sowell, 2002). The state investment in conservation, new environmentally advantageous technologies, and public energy infrastructure is not an expenditure but a down payment that will generate considerable return. State Treasurer Phil Angelides has implemented two major policies that leverage the vast $300 billion State CALPERS retirement fund. Two policies were launched since 1999: (1) sustainable development as "Smart Investment" with a $12 billion investment; and (2) The Triple Bottom Line which is investing in "California's Emerging Markets" at $8 billion and another $1 billion to developing countries.

In addition, the public sector has many financial tools and mechanisms to stimulate development while providing environmental protection and safeguards. For example, the California Infrastructure and Economic Development Bank makes funds available at lower rates and to projects that do not necessarily qualify for bank financing. The Energy Commission has identified a number of financing tools available to assist private firms to obtain the loans necessary to start their businesses. In particular, a number of new tools (e.g., CEC, 2001) are available for regional- and community-distributed generation capacity, purchase of energy savings equipment, retrofits, etc.

For the consumer market in partnership with utilities and homebuilders, the FHA has established a new Energy-Efficient Mortgage that has been rolled out by the California Housing Finance Agency. Publicity about it and its benefits to the State can increase its use and the energy savings associated with housing that goes well beyond minimum standards.

Finally, it is important to note that the public role is not likely to include much in the way of funding in the future. The state budget is over $35 billion short, and the new Governor Schwarzenegger is making deep cuts in virtually all existing programs, and has had to borrow large amounts of money from bond markets. This means that even state-supported bonds which have lower interest rates will not be available for other uses because there are limits to the amount of money the state can raise without becoming fiscally unstable. That point may be near.

10.2.3. The civic markets at work

The third issue involved in the new economics of energy concerns the interface between electricity firms and the State. Under regulation and deregulation the issue was to control the market power of the large utilities to assure that they did not overcharge; the new energy economics aims to assure that the market is broadened to include the broader concept of the public good including environmental protection, economic growth, and long-term stability. Especially after the energy crisis, the commodity markets for power are narrowly based on short-term prices for power. The new economics recognizes that the important market for the public good is broad and long term. This difference between narrow and short-term versus broad and long-term markets is not easily managed by making adjustments to how electricity is sold. It is not something easily woven into a PX of power pool. The new comprehensive market reflects the diversity of markets that constitute an agile power system.

With globalization and increasing scale of corporate structures, the conditions for and effect of competition needs reassessment. Today more multinational companies have significant shares of the global and local markets and they shape demand rather than responding to it. While large parts of the economy are strongly competitive, many trends of consolidation of firms, interlocking ownership, and corporate–government linkages contrast with innovative and price competition characteristic of small business markets.

The new civic economic model must take into account the growing power of large firms and the inability of competitive markets to work effectively without oversight. It is the role of oversight that restrains these large firms from being uncompetitive and to exercise market power. In James Scott's (1998: 8) words, "Today, global capitalism is perhaps the most powerful force for homogenization, whereas the State may in some instances be the defender of local difference and variety." Thus, the civic market is not built on the premise that a competitive market must be created and maintained; instead, it is built on the premise that such a competitive market is impossible to guarantee and that the public good must be served and assured by active public partnerships between empowered state agencies and innovative and socially responsible companies.

A number of economists have argued (see various issues in the Economist in February–March, 2002) that the collapse of Enron proves how neoclassic economics works. As the argument continues, if a company cannot perform in the market, then it fails. Other companies come in and take its place. The free market economy moves on.

The problem with that argument is that it ignores what allegedly Enron did in the first place—set-up and influence the deregulation of the energy market, then manipulate it, and finally use or profit from investors so that in the end, the collapse of the company was based on inflated shareholder value and unsecured creditors who lost their funds. Employees lost their retirement and with the collapse in the value of the stock, thousands of stockholders outside the company as well as mutual funds and retirement portfolios suffered. Thus, the consequence was not just a failed company; it was a cascade of pain for people all across the nation, and it was a leading contributor to the $40 billion electricity charge to the citizens of California.

The most common supply side economic mechanism is "integrated resource management" in which the supply of energy into a system is based on what are known as "base load" or firm supply of power (Patel, 2001). Base load is usually dependable fossil fuel sources such as coal, oil, natural gas, and hydroelectric or nuclear. However, in the past few decades, geothermal has been considered base load. Renewable energy such as wind, solar, and even biomass are considered nonbase load or intermittent (Bolinger and Wise, 2002). Hence the challenge is to have renewable energy calculated and treated as base load power supply (Lund and Clark, 2002).

The issue of energy management is critical for understanding how the economics of energy works. In short, the integrated resource management approach places the burden on the power system for delivering energy. Hence a "firm" or base load must be established which has reliable power from traditional fossil energy such as coal, oil, or natural gas. Nuclear and hydroelectric power are also considered firm load as the fuel can be constant and uninterrupted. The problem is that each of these fuel sources (hydroelectric usually has social and environmental side effects) pollute the atmosphere and have waste disposal problems. Thus the use of current "technologies" for firm load are unacceptable, given the increase in greenhouse gases and atmospheric particulates.

The problem in the energy sector, therefore, is the definition and operation of the market itself. When government does not regulate and directly oversee the energy sector, then the private sector can manipulate and game the system as it is constructed (Clark and Demirag, 2002). What is also not often stated or acknowledged is that the private sector, unlike the public sector, need *not* invest or even explore renewable technologies since they cannot foresee immediate profits (Clark and Demirag, 2001). As Schumpeter (1934) noted many decades ago, innovation for companies will only occur when they see it in their own best interests.

*10.2.4. Stimulating innovation for sustainable environment
and energy systems*

The fourth change from the neoclassical model is the observation that in marginally competitive situations (mature or established industries) innovation is limited because it would render otherwise profitable investments obsolete. Lovins (1997), among others, has demonstrated the "factor of four" whereby new technologies get twice the productivity from half the input of resources. These technologies are sensible and environmentally friendly innovations that not only are cheaper to use, but often cheaper to install in the first place. One can ask the same question about most conservation strategies and many cogeneration (combined heat power) projects, as well as other renewable projects.

Why is this type of sensible innovation so difficult to introduce to mass markets? Simply, according to the logic of the alternative strategies, it is because existing industry does not look for opportunities to cut costs and increase output, and when it sees opportunities it perceives the change too difficult. Costs and profits do not drive this behavior and aversion to change does.

However, there is a growing environmental economics tradition in which strategies for valuing the economy are made. For example, in business, making a profit may not be the only motive for the firm itself, individuals working within it and shareholders themselves. Ritzau (1992) indicates in his study of Danish researchers that success is not defined totally by monetary reward. The survey results from 63% of about 350 researchers indicate that there are other rewards (what we call deep structures) for inventing and patenting new ideas and innovations.

As Ritzau puts it "for the majority of the scientist economic benefits are not the primary motivating factor for them to patent their research. Much more so is it the prospect of being able to contribute to the development of society and at the same time secure their own research projects. An economic benefit is considered nice and indeed motivating, but seems not to be the primary incentive of patenting" (Ritzau, 1992: 19).

Kuada (1994 and 2002) indicates much the same in his work with African entrepreneurs and companies. Ritzau appears to summarize the universal concept even more precisely with a focus upon "Scientists who have filed patent applications" (Rizau, op cit., 19) notes that these successful scientists, by any quantitative measure or scale, "emphasize even less the chances of any personal economic benefit. They focus on personal satisfaction of realizing their own ideas and ensuring funds for their own research" (Rizau, op cit.: 19).

For example, the US automakers failed to invest in change until faced with catastrophic drops in sales as foreign cars flooded the market with fuel efficient, safe, and attractive vehicles. American energy companies still have exploited only a tiny fraction of potential cogeneration which could be its cheapest generation source as shown in California under PURPA. Conservation programs which saved billions of dollars for utilities were proposed and mandated by regulators, not the industries that benefited from them (along with huge consumer benefits). In short, the classic economic model is not adequate to establish advanced programs that develop and implement cost-effective and profitable innovations in dominant industrial systems.

10.2.5. Networks and social relations as opposed to only numbers

Entry to the grid or the network's for large consumers, like industries, shopping plazas, and commercial users, is critical. Most companies want to have reliable and inexpensive power. Technically, having dispersed or distributed generation (DG) is not much more difficult to manage than dispersed consumption, but for a long time the grid has been managed in the simplest way possible by a centralized utility able to control a small number of generation plants. Generation can be tailored to meet demand on a moment notice, and generation levels can be shifted to assure transmission capacities do not get exceeded. Dispersed production poses new challenges since a single utility does not own all the power generation plants making input to the system and there are many more of them.

The key issue is that local, distributed power generation is potentially far more cost effective and reliable than the central grid supplied energy. The importance of local energy generation means that control and oversight can be far more effective and "democratic" in that citizens have control in their communities including on-site generation and local power systems. Networks are critical in this DG process. Grabher (1993) correctly argues that networks, and not just social ones, have become of increasing interest to researchers. Hakansson and Johanson (1993, 35) point out that "there is an important difference between these social networks and the industrial networks of interest... Social networks are dominated by actors and their social exchange relations."

Hakansson and Johanson (1993, 35) argue that "activities and resources in interaction are the more significant factors" in networks. Network theories can fit into the basic social constructionist framework and work within a subjectivist perspective for an understanding of everyday business life. Nevertheless, many scholars in the field find themselves rapidly moving into the objectivist paradigm because it offers structures that provide predefined and convenient explanations of the business activities. Thus in 1994, Hakansson and Snehota argue that:

> *We are convinced that adopting the relationship perspective and the network approach has rather far-reaching theoretical as well as managerial implications. It seems to open up a quite new and different theoretical world compared to the traditional way of conceptualizing companies within markets. It offers new perspectives on some broad traditional problems of business management and yields some novel and perhaps unexpected normative implications for business management. (Hakansson and Snehota, 1994: p. 1: 4)*

Therefore, "Relationships between companies are a complex knitting of episodes and interactions. The various episodes and processes that form business relationships are often initiated and triggered by circumstances beyond the control of people in companies. They are however never completely random, they form patterns." (Hakansson and Snehota, 1994: Ch. 1: 15). In order for the authors to understand a network, they revert to "structural characteristics, such as "continuity," "complexity," "symmetry," and "informality" (Hakansson and Snehota, 1994: Ch. 1).

Enron appears to prove to be a good negative example of networks or the building of business relationships (also known as cronyism and the "old boy" network) in order to influence and control markets. In the American energy sector, Enron indeed used "some novel" management skills and tools which have shown how it manipulated energy markets (Bryce, 2002; Cruver, 2002; Fusaro and Miller, 2002; Harvard Watch, 2002; Smith and Emshwiller, 2003).

Various court cases are proving how Enron executives misled regulators, cheated their customers and clients, pocketed unreasonable personal gains, and influenced public energy policy through social and business networks. Much of that influence was paid for by Enron corporation and its executives in donations and grants to scholars and politicians who deregulated without anticipating the negative consequences.

While all the evidence is not in as of late 2002, it is clear that these networks which Enron built were to influence political decision makers. This use of networks and personal relationships was supported by money that influences entire sectors of the economy and therefore markets. The behavior of Enron and other firms is not unusual, but in this case, the end result was not an open or free market but initially their control and domination of an entire sector. The plan almost worked.

The key to networks is "trust." This can only be achieved after people work together on a common problem and find that others are able to keep secrets, share valuable information, and exchange new ideas. The interactionist economic theory (Clark and Fast, 2004 and overview in Appendix B) best describes, understands, and explains how networks are created and operated. In themselves, networks are neither theory nor scientific. Instead, the understanding of networks allows both the scholar and the business person to pursue shared goals. If networks are institutionalized as formal permanent structures, they will implode from their own administrative weight. The very notion or idea of a network is something that exists at a moment or situation in time to accomplish some task(s). People know one another and form the network to solve the problem at hand.

The basic issue for most people in firms is how to make the company survive and grow during any particular point in time. They must be free to move in the marketplace, but also be secretive enough to protect its privacy. More importantly, firms must have concern for others and their environment. The public good must be protected because it is in the best interests of the firm to maximize its profits for shareholders and executives alike. The protection of the public good is essential in various infrastructures and sectors (Clark and Lund, 2001). In recent months, the protection of the transportation sector must be embedded in the government. The energy crisis in California has clearly shown that the energy sector is a public trust. The same could be argued for environment, water, as well as telecommunications.

In a highly dispersed system grid managers do not control much of the system and must have control over ancillary service capacity to respond to changes in generation quantity and location as they occur rather than by control over all the generators. With new computer and monitoring technology, this is more feasible and technologically efficient, though given the crisis that the utilities have been reluctant to engage in any experimentation or investment in system change. The goal for the new civic markets is to help bypass the control roadblocks of the old system and to facilitate the transition to an agile system in the interest of the public good, even if the changes are not necessarily beneficial to existing institutions in the short run.

A significant component at the microeconomic level is the use of "Networks" or relationship between people and organizations. These personal connections, partnerships, and relationships between technical staff and separately between business executives are collaborations in which often intense exchanges of information are common in place. Some networks (Hakansson, 1994; Hakansson and Snehota, 1995) form in many different ways, but primarily link businesses with compatible strengths (and in some cases weaknesses) to achieve common goals. Other networks form between government and private industry (Sorensen, 1993; Sorensen and Nedergaard, 1994). Networks can form on horizontal and vertical plains, depending on the nature of the interactions between the actors, organizations, and situations involved (Clark, 1995, 1996).

10.3. Economic Collaborations and Partnerships in Action

The California Stationary Fuel Cell Collaborative (CSFCC) is an example of civic markets at work. In this case the participants include all the major Japanese and American car manufacturers, as well as firms interested in hydrogen economy. The collaborative works on a variety of technical and marketing issues needed to get the technology introduced. One of the most significant trends in many industries is the collaborative programs undertaken by industry associations.

For example, the National Association of Home Builders, in the fiercely competitive homebuilding industry, sponsors many programs to increase research on new materials, techniques, and markets for members. The Biotechnology industry also has collaborative industry programs. In sum, even in the sectors of industry which are most heralded as being models of the free market, most have deep cooperative and sharing strategies for building capacity.

The most interesting new addition to the economics of power is the growth of networks of firms and consumers that strive together for advantage. The pervasive networks of firms are not only the generators who are connected to the grid, but many firms in diverse industries that are networked in buyer–supplier networks. For example, equipment manufacturers work with installers, parts manufacturers, computer venders, software designers, and hundreds of other related companies, and all benefit when a new generator is ordered. Understanding the existence and nature of networks in the new economy is one of the most pressing challenges for civic economics. In many countries the energy system includes equipment manufacturers as well as suppliers of transmission towers and transformers.

Cooperation between suppliers and the manufacturers of generators will also pay off. While this form of cooperation has long been active and beneficial, supplying equipment for changing and expanding markets is very competitive. For example, in the case of pollution control equipment: multi-fuel plants that can use renewable resources is another example of how different parts of the industry can cooperate with utilities and grid suppliers.

One of the mistaken assumptions about the regulated California electricity system is that it was not competitive. However, in the US the technology and equipment side of generation is not regulated. In several countries the utilities own the equipment manufacturers and this has led to serious problems. In the current situation the manufacturers and the utilities can collaborate to produce more efficient and less polluting generating plants.

Renewable energy generator companies can also cooperate. For example, wind generators have in the past worked together to build and secure the transmission capacity to bring their power to market. More importantly, they cooperated with each other and the utilities to resolve problems around intermittent production. Mention has been made already of the Los Angeles Community College District (LACCD) with not only its funding for green buildings but also meeting the Silver LEEDS standards. More bond financing for other college districts appear to be spreading the LACCD initiative not only statewide but also nationally.

In July 2003, for example, the University of California System Board of Regents passed its own green building initiative for all 10 campuses. A similar resolution will be considered by the California State University System with its 26 campuses. The cost savings and benefits from the installation of solar/PV and other "green" technologies are substantial, based on the actual experiences from the LACCD. All public buildings are also now benefiting from these programs and creative financing mechanisms.

Governor Schwarzenegger appears to stand by the greening of the State buildings as well. During the last six months of the Governor Davis administration in 2003, a number of "green building" initiatives were under way based on both Governor Davis' Executive Order on Public Buildings in 2001 and the Consumer Agency Road Map Report (2001) reflecting the need to have renewable technologies for on-site generation in public buildings. From these governmental perspectives grew a number of private sector investments and programs (Kenidi, 2003; Ziman, 2003).

Most significantly, the public sector has been on the State's Green Driving Working Group Team under the Consumer Agency whose goal has been to develop demand and specifications for new "green" vehicles in the State Fleet. This team continues to meet and move aggressively in this sector. Moreover, the Team has explored and put into place a "sustainable historical building" initiative that provides over $128 million in associated bond funds along with state speci- fications and coordination with the State Architect's Office as well as the professional architect associations.

Similarly, the Governor Davis Administration's Office of Planning and Research led an effort to quantify the costs for installing and maintaining renewable and "green" technologies for on-site power generation. The result of an Interagency Working Group (over 50 active participants) was the revision of the 1987 California Standard Practices Manual (SMP) to a version in 2001 that uses life-cycle analysis and externalities to get the correct costs for renewable energy in buildings (Schultz *et al.*, 2001). The SPM is becoming widely used by state and local governments in costing out their installation of energy-saving technologies (Clark and Sowell, 2002). Governor Schwarzenegger is expected to continue these programs and efforts.

Nonetheless, two critical issues remain and appear to be solvable. First is the need to aggregate the demand for green building technologies and services. The State Community College District did just that under its Foundation which has a program to provide a competitive central purchasing contract using LEEDS standards, criteria, and codes. This initiative implements the attempts of the CPA and CSFCC to do the same on a voluntary basis. With a "competitively aggregated contracting" mechanism substantial amounts of funds can be saved and controlled.

The second, and perhaps even more significant issue, is the standards, codes, and rules themselves. The California Fuel Cell Partnership took the lead in implementing a civic market mechanism in 1999. In answer to the need to get industry and government to identify and solve mutual issues surrounding the California clean air acts, especially the zero emission laws enacted in the early 1990s, the Partnership holds semiannual meetings in Sacramento, requires paid memberships not only among the auto industry but also with fuel suppliers (oil and gas), research labs, universities, and technology companies.

Another civic market mechanism formed in the Spring of 2001, in part to meet the energy crisis, was the California Stationary Fuel Cell Collaborative (CSFCC) whose role was to get all the fuel cell companies to identify their problems and find solutions either from government or the private sector. A number of actions have resulted including the setting of codes and specifications for competitive aggregated contract bids for fuel cells in State public buildings.

Finally, one of the most successful collaborative efforts was advanced by the Governor Davis administration and appears to be duplicated and expanded under Governor Schwarzenegger: setting renewable energy goals. Davis set in 2002 a Renewable Energy Portfolio Standard of 20% by 2017. Governor Schwarzenegger announced in 2003 a shortened time period for 20% renewables by

2010. Moreover, Schwarzenegger is far more aggressive in pushing for a "hydrogen economy" in the State sooner than later. All indicators are that the civic market will be ready to make such goals a reality.

For example, in the summer of 2003, Governor Davis' Office of Planning and Research held an industry–government (civic market) one-day Forum on "The Hydrogen Economy in California" (see Chapter 13 for more details). The Forum was held in Los Angeles, which is the focal point for hydrogen transportation applications in California due to the air quality need, high-volume of traffic, and a series of regional initiatives. One result was the strong recommendation from the over 60 active participants for a Governor Executive Order to pronounce California as embarking on "The Hydrogen Economy" with a hydrogen freeway and economic development. Yet a number of outcomes came from the meeting, but the Davis administration failed to announce a "Hydrogen Economy" and did not implement any policies including issuing the "Hydrogen meeting minutes" and a comprehensive collection of the presentations and data from the meeting on a CD.

None of these actions ever occurred under the Governor Davis administration. Yet three weeks later, the soon to be elected Governor Schwarzenegger issued these ideas and related items on his Election Web Site. During his administration, Governor Schwarzenegger is expected to implement most if not all the August 03 Hydrogen Forum recommendations. Since the Recall Election and the installation of Governor Schwarzenegger, the Forum Meeting Minutes, Hydrogen presentations, and data CD were released (Clark, 2004).

10.4. Conclusion: Maximizing the Public Good in Energy Economics

Civic markets have many attributes that are different from neoclassical theories, though none are topics unfamiliar to those working in energy economics. What is different is the emphasis that is given to besides the fact that it is an emerging focus. At the root is the fact that the objective is not to maximize sales and profits but to maximize the public good.

The public good is not assumed from economic theory to follow from firms competing to lower prices through higher productivity, but lower prices and a higher value are assumed to follow from maximizing the public good. While evidence on this topic is increasing, we acknowledge that it is not definitively proven. However, we simply know that the old economics did not work.

California is the global laboratory for the agile energy system and
the first "sustainable nation-state" that is building its energy system
on a new set of economic assumptions after being blacked out by
deregulation built on the old assumptions. To fully develop the agile
energy system, Californians must continue to put civic concerns over
private profits, and build an energy infrastructure based on what is
good for the public. As a "bellwether" nation-state, California has the
opportunity to lead the world in the new energy system.

Appendix A: Linguistic Paradigm and Energy Economics

Source: Clark and Fast (2004)

The acts or exchange of goods and services between human beings is
the central theme in most economic theories and traditions. However,
a different approach to the notion of exchange is needed. The basic
assumption for interactionism economics, unlike Smith and almost
all economists since, is that first there is a need to define the topic:
exchange is interaction between two or more human beings. But,
following Herbert Blumer and Alfred Schutz among others, exchange
is much more.

As Clark and Fast (2004) draw particularly from Blumer, along
with George Mead, Alfred Schultz, and other philosophical traditions,
interactions or exchanges (not just as the good and services, but also
social, verbal, nonverbal, and group interactions) among the people or
actors within any setting or situation, has meaning to those actors
and others within and outside people of any firm. Attached to these
exchanges are values which are used, in the case of an economic or
business situation, to buy and sell goods, services, information, and
contacts. What needs to be considered far more carefully is what, for
example, is the meaning of an "electron"? It is simply not the price
or whether an individual can afford electricity. Indeed, electron, like
water and clean air have a far higher value based on social meaning ñ,
one that is immeasurable.

When we discuss exchange, we are talking about a subset of
interaction. Exchange, as in the buying and selling of goods and
services, is the foundation of modern neoclassical economics. Yet
exchange is a part of interaction. When a person interacts with
another for any reason, that person is part of an act to exchange
something. Linguists have long seen this with their analyses of
discourse and verbal communications. Again, such studies are
components and parts of interaction. Interaction is core or basis than

to any exchange in business activities. Interaction, as we have seen, is far more complex in that it presumes the ability of the actors to think and reflect upon their actions.

In Mead's and Blumer's perspective, interaction involves the actors literally talking to themselves. This use of the "generalized other" provides the act of exchange, for example, with a far more comprehensive and significant definition. Exchange from the interaction perspective is an "engagement" between actors. Two or more people have established a relationship. They have engaged each other for some purpose.

It is this notion of engagement that underlies all business activities when understood as exchanges within our interaction perspective. It is also the understanding of these engagements through symbolic and nonsymbolic activities that we are able to understand everyday business life. While some scholars might describe these interactions through the use of dialogue or language analysis, we are more concerned with the subtle and observable situations that surrounds these actions and the meanings and interpretations involved. Therefore, we are more inclined to use varied methodologies including quantitative ones when appropriate to describe the phenomenon.

Elsewhere, Clark and Fast (2003) provide the basic arguments for the subjectivistic perspective in philosophy or as seen in economics as civic capitalism. Here, however, a theoretical refinement of the interactionist perspective drawn from transformational linguistics (Chomsky, 1975, 1988, 1989) takes the philosophy of science arguments into more practical applications with our case study and other empirical examples. At this point consider only the basic arguments for our merging or integrating the subjectivist perspective with interactionism and linguistics.

With the interactionism view, the understanding of networks, as interpersonal and linkages between the interactions of people that networks, takes on a new meaning and dimension. In short, networks cut across and even violate company or firm organizational structures. While government and business networks are familiar in other industrialized countries, they are new concept for American industry and government.

Economic actors neither behave as atomized individuals outside a social context nor adhere slavishly to unchangeable habits or norms. Consequently, opportunism, bounded rationality, and uncertainty—basic elements in Williamson's (1993 and 1996) approach—are not treated simply as exogenous determinants of economic behavior. Rather, they are seen as emerging in the course of exchange processes (Williamson, 1993: 5). Lundvall (1992) notes the limitations of the transaction–cost model in business economics as lacking "interactive learning (which) involves both the learning of substance (technical learning), learning of communication (communicative learning), and learning of proper behavior (social learning). Organized markets present themselves as sets of stable and selective social and economic user–producer relations that adapt only slowly to new technical opportunities" (Lundvall, 1992: 62). However, he does not provide direction for how to understand everyday life in business interaction.

Linguistic (transformational grammar) theory is modeled on science, and has been generally accepted by academics as a science since Chomsky's seminal work in 1957 and other publications (especially 1966, 1968, and 1980) since then as well as transforming linguistics into a science with theory, rules, laws, and predictable results. Consider now how we can apply linguistic theory to help describe and explain the economic relationships for firms. Once the basic concepts are understood of actors, their action and interactions as part of relationships in forming networks, then we must develop a theoretical paradigm. Transformational linguistics appears to offer the best theoretical model (Clark and Sorensen, 2001).

Consider now Chomsky's transformational linguistic paradigm (1957 and 1975; see Chart 10.1) in more detail as it could apply to business economics and specifically firms. If the linguists' sentence-dependence principle is correct, "then the rules of grammar apply to strings of words formed into abstract phrases" that is in the technical

```
                      Universal Grammar
T------Surface Structures-------------------------------------------------^
R       (Syntax -- the formal structure of language)                      |
A                                                                         |
N                                                                         |
S                              R                                          |
F                              U                                          |
O                            RULES                                        |
R-------Deep Structures----------------------------------------------------^
M       (Semantics -- meaning to words/sentences)                         |
A                              E                                          |
T                              S                                          |
I                                                                         |
O                                                                         |
N                                                                         |
S-------------------------------------------------------------------------v
```

Chart 10.1. Representation of linguistic theory.
Source: Clark and Sorensen, 2001.
Note: Within linguistics there is considerable debate about the basic theory and especially at deriving the "meaning" in language expressions (Lakoff, 1970a,b). We will not go into the debate and refinements of the basic theoretical construct here.

literature to structures that are called "phrase markers" (Chomsky, 1980: 79). In a business concept, a basic universal grammar of economics exists which can generate rules which apply deep structure meanings to surface structure interactions. The action of actors can thus be explanatory and predicable.

Linguists call these rules as transformations (shows the occurrence of a word corresponding to a yes–no question) which "map phrase markers into (other) phrase markers." The transformational component of language is "One component of the syntax of a language consists of such transformations with whatever structure (say, ordering) is imposed on this set." For the transformation component to function in generating sentence structures, there must first exist some class of "initial phrase markers" (Chomsky, 1980: 80). The present state of the field of economics provides such descriptive classes. Since the economic corpus of terms and concepts (especially since the end of the Cold War) are international, they constitute a "universal grammar" to which "transformational rules" can apply.

Syntax contains a "base component" that generates a class of "initial phrase markers." The initial phrase marker class must be finite, thus "assigning to the base component the recursive property" which is central of any grammar. In order for rules to be useful, they must reoccur and be applicable to numerous situations. The base component itself consists of two subcomponents: "a categorical component" and a lexicon. The categorical component presents the basic abstract structures by means of "rewriting rules" that state how a syntactical category can be analyzed into a sequence of such categories" (Chomsky, 1980: 80).

In summary, having outlined the theory of transformational linguistics, the next step is to apply the theory in order to develop a new way of looking at business operations. While the application of these theories is to energy economics, there are compelling considerations to apply the new theory to other economic and business concepts.

Surface structures

Surface structures are simply those activities and words that people hear and read from the firm. Aside from the annual report and tax statements, firms are quoted in the stock market, give briefings to analysts, and lobby with particular perspectives to politicians. What is never known in the public are behind the scene realities of the business and its operations.

The surface structure is clearly seen in the activities of Enron, now that activities behind the scenes have themselves become public since its bankruptcy in December 2001. Below we identify these activities as "deep structures" as they not only explain the firm's behavior but provide predictions for its future activities. At this point, what firms want to do is satisfy their shareholders, investors, and bankers. Demirag (1999) labeled this corporate behavior as "short-termism," since it was only focused on quarterly earning statements. The motivation for corporate leadership and behavior, therefore, was the "bottom line." Bonuses and rewards are given to company executives if they can influence and enhance the bottom line each quarter.

The revelations of many corporations came about as a result of "accounting" irregularities. Nonetheless, as more and more evidence is amassed, it is clear that the corporate executives of firms either directed or agreed with the accounting schemes since the very positive economic reports personally enhanced their own incomes and bonuses.

Deep structures

What is a firm, company, or business? Most companies start with the entrepeneur. Ask most families, spouses, and colleagues of any new business venture, for example, and the answer would be that the entrepreneur is a "bit crazy." Schumpeter characterizes the entrepreneurial experience as that of a sort of "heroic figure." The "cowboy" image has now achieved the folk lore status of almost cult figure today, as with a Bill Gates. However, the entrepreneurial experience is not that of an individual. Many entrepreneurial ventures are the results of partners, usually forming a balanced relationship. Network theory underscores that point whereby social networks either form new ventures or support them (Sorensen, 1996). Many new companies are the result of family or extended family relations. Yet within the new venture, one person tends to exhibit the basic characteristic definitions of an entrepreneur.

If following our use of transformation theory, the basic characteristic definitions of a firm can be described in a common lexicon, then a universal grammar exists for how companies actually work. With the use of theoretical considerations from linguistics, transformational rules allow explanations and predications to be made of key people as they interact with variety of actors and in numerous situations.

The energy crisis in California has been a reaction at the surface structure level, but also a far more comprehensive understanding of how firms act. Through various public legal proceedings and hearings, deeper understandings of a firm's actions are now known. This is true in the context of bankruptcy, declared by Pacific Gas & Electric (PG&E) in the late spring of 2001 whereby testimony had to be given before the California Public Utility Commission. Such evidence indicated behavior by PG&E heretofore unknown.

Court testimony and legal depositions are a mechanism for getting at the deep structures of a firm. Some public interest groups have also used the "American Freedom of Information Act " to gather information and data often withheld by the companies. This is the case now with bankruptcy of Enron and with a number of other American companies in not only the energy sector but also in telecom companies. What will most likely occur is that a number of the corporate leaders (actors) will be found responsible for suspicious if not illegal actions taken by their companies to enhance and falsify their corporate financial performance (surface structure).

However, what does this mean for the need to research firms before tragedy (either in terms of an energy crisis or a firm bankruptcy) occurs? The issue for economics is how to get at the deep structure of a firm? In order to describe, understand, explain, and perhaps predict its actions? This deep structure information about any firm is critical for any scientific consideration of economics. The aggregation or identification of principles and then rules from the actions of a firm allow economics to then be scientific.

A number of papers and disciplines in the social sciences have argued for "qualitative" research methods to be used to gather this corporate level data. Interviews, participant observation, and surveys are among the methods suggested (Clark and Fast, 2003). In the context of the energy sector, economists need to know what makes the firm "tick"—operate or work? Not in theory but in practice, the economics of energy depends on the firm and its actions. To get at this issue and be able to develop a theory of the firm, a number of quantitative and qualitative methods need to be used to get at the deep structure meaning of the firm.

Without reviewing all the statistical or quantitative methods, a few comments on getting at the deep structure might be useful. Assuming that the key is for the economist to ask questions in order to get definitions and meanings of the actors and their activities, then there is what some scholars refer to as asking the "2nd Question" (Clark and Sorensen, 2001). Basically, the idea is to assume that the actors in any firm will give an answer to a question that is superficial or surface structure. What is important is to ask the next or second question that gets at a deeper understanding of the individual or activities of the firm.

The use of these methodologies and techniques are useful in constructing the principles and rules by which the firm operates. Once the surface and deep structure rules are understood, they can then be used to construct relationships between the structures—known as transformational rules. With these rules constructed and abstracted, a different approach to economic theory will result.

Transformational rules

Consider the overall use of transformation rules in theoretically connecting and explaining business interactions. Business leaders are many actors in a situation. The economic must observe/inquire/reflect on the firm interactions and determine if they are "appropriate." In transformational linguistics, this would involve answering the question: does the language act conform to common sense and everyday usage? If appropriateness is observed and recorded, then the question is to identify the specific phrase markers attributable to the defining characteristics of the firm.

Finally, the generative grammar theory allows the researcher to make the connections around situations in terms of the actors, interactions, and symbols thereto described. When transformational rules are applied, the explanations for business actions become apparent and predictable.

With these theoretical concepts in place, the actual transformation rule making process can be seen. That is, a firm becomes successful or unsuccessful because s/he draws upon the defining characteristics in the deep structures (universals or common properties across cultures) of the new business creation interactive process (surface structure) and applies the proper rules. For example, when a firm appears to have been very successful (e.g., material wealth, power, or head of large company), there were many transformational rules that got the firm to that place (surface structure or where society sees and categorizes the firm).

The transformational rule-making process is often intuitive and based upon common sense. That is one reason why "teaching" and "learning" about firms is so difficult. All too often, the firm's experience is forced into the context of traditional business practices. The use of "Business Plans" is seen, for example, as the process that all companies must go through in order to create, manage, and succeed in their business ventures. The problem is that business plans violate the transformational rules for firms.

Consider the right side of the transformational process. In the deep structure across all cultures are relationships and interactions based upon family, relatives, and other interpersonal interactions. These universals build or transform as "trust rules" whereby people interact and demonstrate their ability to perform. Teams or networks are then formed. Once these transforms build and grow, then surface structure successes can be seen and acknowledged.

Given the defining characteristics of the firm as the lexicon for the deep structure for a new business, the actual surface structure can be seen as the set of interactions observed between actors such as the firm and others necessary in conducting the new business.

Clearly, success for a firm can be many things: money, status, ego gratification, family values, nonmonetary rewards, etc. While businesses may want success in terms of profit or wealth, that is not the only criteria. Application of other transformational rules may define success in a variety of other ways. When those transformations are "mapped" over other transformations then a much clearer picture emerges as to the explanations for the surface structure results of interactions within firms.

Success, defined in any number of ways, is itself the result of a series of transformational rules that result from interactions between actors. When these actors are seen as firms operating in a context, a variety of constantly changing situations emerge. As the firm conducts everyday business (solves problems), new rules must be applied. The firm, therefore, draws upon the deep structures formed from past experiences. Creating new and different ways to solve problems is the direct application of these rules in everyday life.

Economics and Linguistics: The Sciences of Discovery, Description, Meaning, and Understanding of Rules in Everyday Life

Structures in language theory are not rigid, as in the conventional functionalist paradigm in social science, but fluid and flexible. They are not stagnant in either time or space as with the determinist paradigm, but dynamic. In language structures simply provide a set of universal rules (grammar) and data base (lexicon) upon which to draw. Language skills and their application to everyday life must be dynamic and fluid by definition.

For the linguistic, a surface structure allows the action researcher to describe and understand organizations and the actors within them. This is done through investigation and continuing analysis of groups within larger organizations. The surface structures are often seen in terms of their events and situations that occur within the group. It is this dynamic through constant interaction among the actors that defines surface structures.

Deep structures are the basic building blocks of surface actions and interactions because they define and refine concepts, ideas, and objects in terms of their meaning. In other words, deep structures are the "meaning" attached to actions. Deep structures cannot be seen, as surface structures, because they are the mental representations that people bring to situations. It is the deep structural level in which people communicate (or do not communicate). Here people interact because they define and thus understand one another. While particularistic legal constraints and covenants are defined as rules and apply to both organizations (due to government, foreign ownership, and nature of business), they will not be considered here (see Clark, 1996).

The interactionism perspective provides a perspective in which actors within groups and organizations can be described and understood in situations (e.g., meetings, discussions, or work sessions), activities (e.g., daily work as with computers, conference calls, telephone usage, and research), and events (e.g., conferences, travel, and larger level or management meetings). Each representation is an example of the discussion from Blumer and Mead, whereby A → B → A (A interacts with B and then interacts back again to A after some thought and planning).

Beneath the surface structures with its set of rules are the deep structures with its own set of rules. Think of the deep structure as the level of interaction that defines business actions within situations. In short, deep structures provide the meaning behind the observable behavior seen of actors and organizations at the surface structure. The transformational linguistic concept of generative grammatical is equivalent to the dictionary or lexicon of a grammar for providing definition of ideas and concepts in the deep structures.

Conclusion: Understanding Everyday Business Life is the Science of Economics

The interactionism perspective is particularly significant since there is an extreme need to define these ideas and concepts in the international business arena, even when business is conducted in the same language. The outcome of defined concepts and even the meaning of specific English words (as in "commercially viable" has different meanings between the Americans and Australians leading to misunderstandings) are the representations in the deep structure. Owing to the interaction within the deep structure and the interactive transformations with the surface structure, terms, concepts, and hence common goals become clearer. With common "lexical" definitions, the actors and their organizations can move forward into business activities.

Chapter 11
Complex Infrastructures: The Role of the State in Planning for Agile Energy Systems

We need "a little more 'reverence for life', a little less straitjacketing of the future, a little more allowance for the unexpected, and a little less wishful thinking." (Albert Hirschman in Scott 1997: 345)

11.1. Introduction

In the first section of the book, Chapter 6, the complexity of the California electricity system was discussed in some detail. Complexity, and its similar and parallel systems such as data, archives, information processing, and networks, was not the only problem that led to a number of operating and policy decisions. Nonetheless, it contributed to both the forces urging the State to deregulate and to the catastrophic failure of the resultant deregulated system.

In this chapter, these same forces of complexity are analyzed and shown how to fashion them into an agile energy system. In short, there is an increased public role in organizing any power system that has never been developed before using technologies yet to be commercialized. Energy systems are complex ones. Energy companies must meet public goals and needs, rather than just their corporate objectives. They must pay off their debts, provide reliable service, and recover from the tragedy of deregulation while helping to create alternatives for the California public.

In hindsight, it is also known that small mistakes can lead to catastrophic grid failures because all power system components are so tightly coupled through the transmission system. It would be naive to assume simple solutions about the scale, economies, technologies, and difficulty of the challenge this poses to public or private companies when society is dependent upon the constant flow of electrons. On the other hand, not addressing the challenge is even more risky and dangerous. By proceeding with business as usual or continuing to find ways to further deregulate and privatize power systems, policy makers will perpetrate even more catastrophic crises, including those initiated by terrorists. A new mindset must be established and implemented.

The private firms that now own the generating capacity in California are still looking for additional opportunities to earn profits in California. Even though Enron is bankrupt (it still exists as a company), corporate power needs to be "governed" (Demirag, 1998). Moreover, following the "Recall" of Governor Davis, the State administration includes some former proponents of deregulation. While it is not known how Governor Schwarzenegger will pursue energy and environmental policies, campaign policies and top political appointments favor renewable energy and a hydrogen future. One can hope that the State will not revisit failed agendas of the past. What appears to be occurring for the new Governor is a balance between the regulated and deregulated energy sector.

The agile energy infrastructure system appears to fit this approach. Planning that looks after the public good is essential to the implementation of the agile energy system. By far, the greatest value for these agile systems is in the long-term planning that will enable easy transitions from the current nonsystem to one that is based on renewables, distributed, flexible, and hybrid systems.

The extent to which this new approach to energy infrastructure systems is true and viable is indicated by changing perspectives at the World Bank. There, while applied to developing nations but reflecting the concerns of the developed world, new power sector reform guidelines are arguing that effective governmental capacity and a stable investment climate are necessary before power systems can be privatized and opened to competition. Mitigating uncertainty and financial risk are critical factors for both the World Bank and nation-state. Just look at what happened to California, now with a USD$35 billion debt, in part driven by the needs of the energy crisis.

Setting these economic, political, and social preconditions are much more difficult than anticipated, as institutions and governments now look at 10-year efforts, instead of one or two years. However, as one deals with complex power systems, planning requires an understanding of much that is uncertain and perhaps unknowable, requiring that new strategies be adopted for the planning of uncertainty. The goal of planning in complex system, therefore, is to strive for system simplicity, rather than assuming system ability to withstand unknown forces.

11.2. Planning for Uncertainty and Risk Aversion

Planning theory offers some perspectives on planning for conditions of great complexity and uncertainty. The core idea of the agile energy system is that it is flexible (Clark and Lund, 2001) and not dependent on any single event, structure, calculation, or transmission that can dominate and control the whole energy system. The agile system is inherently self-correcting, yet it is not brittle or fragile. The system is one that is continually changing and evolving, responding to system changes in a way that a simple competitive market mechanism could never do.

Electricity markets have an inherent propensity when uncontrolled to become rigid. Agile ones do not perform that way. The question for this chapter is to demonstrate that it is possible to plan and establish a continuing advanced electricity system that is agile enough to prevent debacles like the deregulation crisis in the world's fifth largest economy.

Contingency planning and planning for uncertainty and risk administration are well-established areas of research and writing within management and policy fields, but they have only been occasionally used in the field of energy studies. As more flexibility appears in agile energy systems, they become more technologically feasible. However, the strategies for implementing agile systems require a new approach to shape policy.

The key characteristics of such a strategy is to recognize the level of uncertainty that is inherent in such an undertaking and to utilize strategies that build on that uncertainty rather than deny that it exists. For example, international security after the 9–11 attacks on New York city and Washington, DC have led to very different concepts of vulnerability of key infrastructures. The basic assumption of global security and availability of oil and natural gas supplies now remains uncertain.

The starting point is uncertainty. Risk and its variations of aversion, mitigation, and management are closely linked as companies must ascertain these issues for making corporate decisions, plans, and investments. In his book Hugh Courtney (2001) suggests that there are four levels of uncertainty.

1. The first level is near term unexpected changes in a relatively predictable future. The uncertainty about the summer temperature

on any given day will be within relatively predictable ranges and this first level change is really within reasonable limits. Similarly, the risk that an employee will be sick follows statistical averages that tend to average out. This level of uncertainty operates as "noise" in an otherwise predictable way of operating.

2. The second level has a deeper level of uncertainty, where there are several identifiable options that constitute a closed set of outcomes. For example, the voters will pass a bond measure for energy investments or they will reject it.

3. In the third level, uncertainty becomes more complex in that the options constitute a range with unknown boundaries or statistical limits. In this case the outcomes do not include discrete options but by a continuum (prices will rise but we can not say how much).

4. Finally, level 4 uncertainty is virtually impossible to describe and define. We did not have any idea of the electrical system crisis that would follow deregulation.

From a policy and public perception, the fourth level is the hardest to work with because the variables that define it and the odds for anything happening are by definition impossible to detail. The fear of an asteroid hitting the earth is not anything that can be planned for at the present time based on current knowledge. However, policy makers looking to the energy future often have to work at the third and fourth levels, though they may not recognize that their uncertainty is too high.

Not only are there many options for the energy future, but all of them are imprecisely defined and the scale of their impact is a continuity rather than a discrete option. Moreover, the interaction between many options create uncertainty best described in complexity and chaos theory as described in Chapter 6. While this book argues that the alternative to reregulation and more deregulation is the pursuit of an agile energy system, planning for such a system is highly uncertain.

The scientific world is not helping. As more is known about the different options, scientists find more that is not known. In an interesting article on environmental planning in face of uncertainty, Johnson and Scicchitano (2000) argue that uncertainty in the scientific world manifests itself to the public as conflicting messages about what to do, and public uncertainty "creates paralysis in policymaking" (Johnson and Scicchitano, 2000: 634).

On the other hand, when the public is convinced that there is only one solution, support tends to overwhelm uncertainty. Many policy mistakes, such as deregulation in the first place, can be traced to a misplaced confidence that there is likely to be one outcome with only minimal uncertainty.

Organizations, both policy setting bodies such as legislatures and agencies that implement policies, generate trust among the population. When uncertainty is high (such as after 911) the policy makers' solutions generate broad support. Whereas when the public trust in the organization is low, public oversight on actions often leads to a lack of willingness to take action. In the energy sector, the failure by government, agencies, utilities, and markets to perform as expected has led to a serious erosion of confidence that tends to magnify both the tendency to paralysis and the skepticism of the public to plan ahead with any confidence.

Johnson and Scicchitano (2000) also suggest that uncertainty increases the amount of risk that actors in the system perceive and must deal with. Some things are very uncertain but the risk is low (who wins a lottery), whereas some uncertainties are high and they carry a very high risk (nuclear waste contamination). The response to the high-risk situation is often unclear because not enough is known about potential solutions to be able to effectively select a response. In highly uncertain and high-risk situations, such as shaping a future energy system for developed countries, it is unlikely that the public, and usually experts, will ever understand enough of the technologies, social systems, options, economics, and environmental consequences to be sure that the policy options are sensible.

John Holdren (1992) suggests two alternative policy strategies. One is to pursue options that have the lowest risk of negative outcomes. The other is to pursue policies that provide insurance against worst case options. These alternatives help to set a floor for avoiding paralysis, and offer for a skeptical public some assurance that their actions can be beneficial even recognizing the huge level of uncertainty and the high risk of catastrophe in the future.

Planning for the energy infrastructure in the future requires a very different approach than that taken to deregulate. The parallel to the restructuring of formerly communist and socialist economies is illustrative. With the collapse of the former Soviet Union, economies were quickly restructured and the old economic systems were quickly dissolved under the world belief that they needed to be quickly replaced with more efficient market driven economic institutions and firms. However, these new structures did not emerge quickly, total economic activity fell by about 40% of their pre-1989 level, and small changes rippled into catastrophic market failures.

In China, on the other hand, the economy is making a gradual transition with many parts gradually opening to market opportunities

(Clark and Li, 2001) in a semi-unplanned way. Rosser (2002) describes the difference between these cases as a "shock therapy" model and a "gradualism model." The economist, Heilbroner (1993) called "beyond capitalism." In the gradualism case the boundary between new and old, between structured and unstructured, between planned and unplanned is at the edge of chaos. In this transitional zone, institutions emerge, successful firms grow, unsuccessful experiments vanish, and the old is gradually adapted, consumed, or eliminated.

The world's energy system is facing somewhat the same opposite conditions. The California model for deregulation was a "shock therapy" model. It attempted one of the most rapid "deregulation agendas" of any nation-state aimed at power sector reform. The result was that the institutions capable of handling uncertainty were not established. Moreover, these public and private institutions had no body of trust and capacity to handle unknown situations. The small impact of the market manipulation by Enron and other generators created geometric impacts throughout the system, eventually costing the State $40 billion dollars in both long-term contracts and debt. Energy system planning for the future must learn from this mistake.

The best thinking in the planning field recognizes the limits to planning under conditions of uncertainty. Planning needs to be open rather than limiting in opportunities. It needs to set fair rules, standards, and protocols so that experiments can be evaluated to succeed or fail on their own merits. Furthermore planning needs to anticipate some of the most interesting innovations that may take many years or decades to fully emerge. Meanwhile, society needs protection during the transition. The chaos of a system full of experimentation should be seen as an asset, rather than a problem. Redundancy (Landau, 1969) should be embraced rather than discouraged.

At a practical level, planning in any complex society, where uncertainty exceeds certainty, may appear not to be planning at all. The following key components, therefore, must be considered. Planning needs to:

* Creatively find and explore alternatives. If a system has so much uncertainty that the full range of options are not known, and we have made the case that this is characteristic of California, then the planners need to create an environment where all parties start thinking creatively to generate the widest range of options. The reports done by the California Governor's Office of Planning and Research documented below show this creativity. When the

planners are creative, the system they are planning with becomes creative too.

- Find the barriers to successful implementation of good ideas. The goal of planning under conditions of uncertainty is not to make something happen, but to make sure that when something positive is being proposed that it can happen without unreasonable barriers. Sometimes this means that old systems should not continue doing what they have been doing, like building more gas-fired power plants.
- Understand the infrastructure and support systems that are needed for the widest range of options. Funding for infrastructure is often expensive, and planning tries to identify ways to meet infrastructure needs for an evolving system without limiting options. This is sometimes impossible, but a flexible infrastructure for multiple directions is highly beneficial.
- Identify resources to support long-term thinking. The market system always wants to maximize for the short term, while long-term goals get pushed aside. The goal of good planning is to assure that longer time frames can be pursued, even if it means short-term support of projects that will ultimately not be viable.
- Support networking and partnerships rather than creating isolated islands. In the energy system we have demonstrated the value of promoting hybrid technologies, of forming partnerships between public and private companies, of finding ways producers and consumers can work together, to find value in the economic opportunities from sustainable options.

Consider now, some of the ways planning can help to create the conditions for an agile energy infrastructure system, using examples from California and elsewhere.

11.3. Meeting the Energy Infrastructure Challenge

A reliable supply of cleaner energy is clearly essential to California's continued economic progress and quality of life (Governor Davis, 2002, 2003; Governor Schwarzenegger, 2003, 2004). It is a foundational component of the State's energy infrastructure (CCSA, Commission, 2002). The demand for energy is pushed upward both by structural changes in the economy and lifestyle decisions. Over the next 20 years, California must solve the problem of matching cleaner supply with increasing demand.

11.3.1. Role of government in planning

In the fall of 2002, the Governor signed legislation that put the State directly in the role of overall planner. While not dictating planning to regions or communities, Assembly Bill (AB) #857 established the Environmental Goal Policy Report (EGPR) and set the Governor's Office of Planning and Research (OPR) in the role of coordinator and facilitator for all state planning. The California Energy Commission (CEC) was given a similar role but only focused on energy for an Integrated Energy Resources Plan Report (CEC, 2003).

The CEC planning was the first one required by the State legislature since 1996, when they did away with any statewide energy planning. The role of OPR had evolved under Governor Davis into being more of a planning organization than it was under other Governorships where it only reacted to legislative actions. The CEC has developed in that regard. However, OPR during the energy crisis took it on the role of thinking progressively ahead (Schultz *et al.*, 2001; Grandy *et al.*, 2003; Clark, 2004). EGPR was another example in that "energy" and "hydrogen" were not apart of the original legislative mandate but included later.

Each of the key State infrastructures had been carefully considered and reported from the Governor Davis' Commission for the Building of the 21st century (Infrastructure) which was completed in September 2001 but due to the terrorist attack on the USA in that month, released in February 2002 (Commission, 2002). Some of the conclusions in the Commission Report are noted below. The significance of the Report is that through EGPR effective environmental and energy planning were implemented directly through OPR.

Finally, California State Planning has taken the additional role of setting goals for renewable energy through Senator Byron Sher's Bill Senate Bill (SB) #1038 which established a Renewable Portfolio Standard (RPS). The law requires the State to double its current level of 10% renewable energy (e.g., biomass, geothermal, wind, solar, and "run of the river" but not nuclear or large hydroelectric) to 20% by the year 2017. This is one of the most aggressive State planning policy goals in the USA. Several European countries have enacted more aggressive laws, which are now under "political" attack and perhaps threatened by privatization. Data from Gellen show how much ahead this standard is.

The basic issue will be how to finance the more inherently "expensive" renewable energy sources. The State of California has convened an Interagency Renewable Energy Investment Plan task force that issued an internal government report on that issue in the fall of 2002 (Grandy *et al.*, 2003). While refinements are being made on the financial impact and leveraged incremental costs for renewable energy, it is clearly doable even with California's current debt of $35 billion for 2002. The issues will be redirecting and leveraging state and local level financing mechanisms. A final finance report on renewable energy will be made public in early 2003.

Table 11.1.   Renewable portfolio standard policies in the United States as of 2001.

State	Renewables requirement	Eligible technologies
Arizona	0.2% by 2001; 1.1% by 2007	Solar photovoltaic and thermal electric must supply at least half the total
Connecticut	6% in 2001; 13% in 2009	Existing technology (hydro and municipal waste) limited to 7% in 2009; new technologies (wind, new biomass, solar, landfill gas, and fuel cells) must provide 6% by 2009
Hawaii	7% by 2003; 9% by 2010	Wind, solar, biomass, hydro, geothermal, landfill gas, waste, fuel cells, and ocean energy
Lowa	2% by 1999	Wind, biomass, solar, hydro, and waste
Maine	30% by 2000	Biomass, wind, solar, hydro, fuel cells, geothermal, landfill gas, and cogeneration and municipal waste projects under 100 MW
Massachusetts	11% by 2009	Biomass, hydro, municipal waste, wind, solar; existing hydro and municipal waste limited to 7% of total
Minnesota	1% by 2005; 10% by 2015	Wind, biomass, hydro, and solar
Nevada	5% by 2003; 15% by 2013	Solar, wind, biomass, and geothermal
New Jersey	5.5% by 2006; 10.5% by 2012	New solar, wind, geothermal, landfill gas, biomass, and fuel cell facilities must provide at least 4% of the total by 2012
Pennsylvania	2%	Wind, solar, biomass, geothermal, and municipal waste
Texas	Approx. 3% by 2009	2000 MW of solar, wind, biomass, hydro, geothermal, and landfill gas
Wisconsin	2.2% by 2011	Solar, wind, geothermal, biomass, fuel cells, and small-scale hydro

Notes: MW, megawatts.
Sources: Grandy *et al.*, 2003.

Several specific cases and programmatic ideas are given as examples as how to meet the challenge. Much of the content of the discussion provides the basis for a formal presentation and inclusion into the Commission's final report itself, due in the summer of 2001. Hence the long-term (10 years) goals for the California energy challenge are:

- Ensure that all Californians have reliable, affordable, and clean energy.
- Achieve a diversified energy base, by increasing the share of renewable sources of power to one-quarter (25%) of the total.

The more immediate or short-term challenges are:

- Meet the short-term energy needs of all Californians through conservation, efficiency, and emergency measures that lead to a long-term integrated system.
- Develop a plan for increasing the diversity of future power generation sources and transmission methods.
- Create a cabinet level entity to consolidate energy-related functions, and coordinate interagency resources for greater efficiencies.

The energy crisis in California continues to be a challenge for all its citizens. This crisis has deep historical roots. As discussed earlier in the book, various experts have shown that the problems associated with the current situation are the result of a complex web of events many of which predate the State's actual electrical restructuring, and many that were not even part of the restructuring.

Californians rallied successfully to the challenge in the 1970s and 1980s with innovation, public–private sector partnerships, new bipartisan public policy, public investments, and supported by public education. It became a leader in the energy efficiency field and is now fast becoming the world leader in addressing the overall energy issues.

11.3.2. Short-term energy trends and issues

Projected state requirements for year 2020 energy needs are: 40% more electrical capacity, 40% more gasoline, and close to 20% more natural gas (California Energy Commission, 2001). Additional large gas-fired energy plants need land, water, and fuel; they produce air emissions and other impacts requiring mitigation. The CEC Integrated Energy

Resource Plan (CEC, 2003) concludes that more natural gas is needed in the State to satisfy the demand. Hence, the CEC recommends in its Executive Summary the approval of liquefied natural gas facilities (2003: 1–4).

There is a need for additional oil refinery capacity with no plans for new capacity of 6 billion gallons of natural gas would need to be imported. However, gasoline when combined with increasing transportation demand and traffic congestion, a significant increase in air emissions will occur. Furthermore, the need for additional natural gas pipelines into and within California will most certainly create stranded costs. And as Meyer (2000) notes, before the end of this century, the worldwide gas supply will be exhausted.

Whilst the energy crisis in 2000–2002 has the attention of the public now, over the long-term, demand reduction strategies are a more expedient approach that can become a "way of life" for California businesses and residents. California ranks as the tenth largest user of energy in the USA and is the top among the three states in conservation, efficiency, and demand reduction. Over the long run it is not feasible to build enough capacity to meet demand that is not mitigated by strategies to reduce the amount of power needed, especially at peak times. While the State seems to have enough power now, pending natural gas shortages and price increases pose a greater challenge than can be met easily. Some of the conservation and load shifting behavior that got the State through the blackouts must continue.

By the summer of 2001, following the worst of the crisis, over 10 new power plants were in operation and another 17 were under construction. Most of these plants were power peakers designed to address the immediate need for more capacity in the near-term summer and fall of 2001. This additional power supply primarily required the use of natural gas, most of which must be brought into the State. Many are forecasting a shortage of natural gas that will drive prices to crisis levels, though the price estimates are a high level of uncertainty (third or fourth uncertainty level, following Courtney, 2001).

Planning for a highly uncertain and politically volatile future requires strategic steps to reduce uncertainty or to minimize and contain the uncertainty that will remain. One of the immediate strategies, however, must include a long-term fuel source diversification strategy so as to limit future dependency on any one type of fuel. As Chart 11.1 indicates, the State by the spring of 2001 derived already 52% of its fuel supply from natural gas.

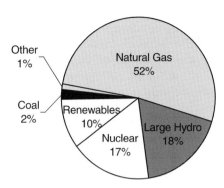

Chart 11.1. Share of current in-share power generation fuel mix.
Source: California Energy Commission, 2001.

All but one of the new power peakers and plants approved and funded are natural gas-fired facilities. By mid-summer of 2001, 9000 MW of new power plants were natural gas fired. However, also by mid-summer, over 4000 MW of renewable energy facilities were under active negotiations to round out the California Power Portfolio. This diversification can reduce the impact of uncertainty in any one fuel source or generation technology.

11.3.3. Long-term plans: renewable portfolio standards

In developing its long-term strategy for energy, California needs to address energy issues such as supply and transmission. Part of the tactical definition of sustainability includes the control over or at least the setting of rules for commerce and business. Governor Davis in the spring of 2000 convened a Commission for the 21st century whose task was to examine the infrastructure in the State and make recommendations. Energy was a key component to the Commission's considerations and the Report was approved in late May 2001. In that Report, the Commission adopted a 25% renewable energy goal for the State by 2020.

Shortly thereafter, the State legislature approved a similar goal of 20% renewable energy by the year 2010, while the Energy Commission weighed in with a 17% renewable recommendation by 2006. These renewable portfolio standards are among the strongest in industrial states or nations. While they were determined by a collaborative process, it remains unclear if the current Governor will continue to work toward these goals.

The impetus of Governor Davis' Infrastructure Commission for the State to set a renewable energy goal was echoed by other major elements of the government. To help achieve this longer-term goal, the State and its local government, business and civic partners are implementing specific policies such as:

- Promote pricing structures that change behaviors through energy conservation and efficiency programs.
- Create the public acceptance of new price structures (including higher but capped prices) through public education and other means will help to achieve the goal.
- Develop financial mechanisms including incentives and investment strategies (such as use of incentives for energy-efficient programs for rebates, tax credits, etc. to consumers and industry which could be linked to economic development programs for manufacturers and suppliers to locate in California) to assure that long-term demand reduction is built into return on investment calculations.
- Provide venture and risk capital for the basic research and technology transfer required to generate large-scale and effective technological innovation and adoption.

The California experiment in increasing renewable electrical generation rests on political and economic strategies. The benefits will be substantial but will require planning and policy initiatives that recognize the difficulty of the task and the interests that can profit if it is not implemented. One of the most important objectives is to increase control over energy sources through a combination of public and private sector policies, consortia and contracts to assure self-sufficiency over the long term.

The Energy Commission has long been interested in future planning and has engaged in a number of long-term strategic planning efforts. One of the scoping efforts came up with the following trends, but given the energy crisis soon thereafter was shown to be off the mark as Chart 11.2 shows the figures, but when compared to the estimates of the CEC in its Integrated Plan (2003) three years later, the problems of just numbers can be seen as woefully inadequate:

The statistics in either Report (2000 or 2003) fail to show the whole picture. For example, as shown in Chapter 13, hydrogen has become an important topic and energy consideration for California. It will represent the future. But the transition to a hydrogen economy will be through the reforming of "natural gas" (SCAQMD, 2003). As more and more demand for hydrogen grows, if the State only looks at natural gas as its immediate future energy supplier, then it will

- Projected requirements for year 2020 energy needs: 40% more electrical capacity, 40% more gasoline, and close to 20% more natural gas.
- Additional large gas-fired energy plants need land, water, and fuel; they produce air emissions and other impacts requiring mitigation
- Need for additional oil refinery capacity—no plans for new capacity—6 billion gallons of gas would need to be imported
- Additional gasoline, combined with increasing traffic congestion, will increase air emissions
- Need for additional natural gas pipelines into and within California
- Additional stranded costs

Chart 11.2. The California Energy Commission outlines trends for the future.
Source: California Energy Commission, 2000.

soon run out of that supply source. What needs to be done today is diversify the fuel supplies now in order to meet the State's increasing and future needs.

11.3.4. Framework for energy infrastructure planning

Given these issues, trends, and strategies to meet the California energy goals, as well as new positive opportunities on the horizon, what are the new ideas that can guide California's plan to meet its future energy needs. Clearly, there are a number of perimeters that frame a plan for the future by turning a crisis to a challenge and thus into an economic opportunity. California will be the leader in sustainability—with energy and environment synonymous with economic growth and business development. The basic areas to consider are:

- Learn from the past. The past 30 years of energy trial-and-error is a vital source of lessons, both positive and negative, about how to manage our energy future. We must be candid about what has worked and what has not.
- Make decisions in the near term that aligns with long-term goals and strategies. The current crisis which no doubt will be resolved in the near term—provides our challenge and hence an opportunity for all sectors to provide future Californians with reliable,

affordable, and clean energy for the long term. Our decisions today clearly frame our choices for tomorrow.
- Operate through collaboration and partnership whenever possible. With the necessary changes in policy, resource commitments, behavior and increased capacity, all partners from the household, community, and regional levels in the business and civic sectors together must help to solve this problem.
- Enhance California's energy self-sufficiency. California must accurately project, measure, and monitor its actual energy needs, and develop a sufficient supply to meet those needs, using a mix of conventional and alternative energy suppliers, coupled with increased efficiencies and demand management strategies. Future fuel supplies should be based on a diversity of sources, to avoid market distortions from overreliance on one or a few sources. Waste, through biomass and other environmental methods potentially can generate large amounts of power.
- Use new "return-on-investment" models for public sector investment. Create an investment finance model, as used in other states and industrialized countries with considerable success, which allows equity investment, particularly venture and risk capital for energy and environmental research, early product development etc. Typically managed through a public–private partnership, a high priority is a return on the investment for all investors. Government needs to be able to have an "equity stake" in its investments through grants, finance mechanisms, and incentives.
- Create new public sector accounting methods such as those used now in the private sector, known as "green accounting." Traditional accounting cost–benefit models that only promote governmental incentives, including tax breaks, rebates, or loan guarantees, with varying degrees of success are not adequate.
- Integrate energy efficiency and self-sufficiency into all infrastructure systems. All California infrastructure investment, whether land use, housing, school facilities, or water delivery, should be held to the highest standard of energy efficiency.

Efforts should be made to ensure efficient technology transfer across infrastructure systems, for example, fuel cells can serve two infrastructures at the same time such as energy and transportation (Clark and Paolucci, 1997). The fuel cell can be used in a vehicle for daily usage, and also be used to power one's residence.

That is the challenge from the energy crisis. Building on the investments that the State has made already in the diverse tools and technologies for renewable and alternative energy sources, we can develop our future energy capacity consistent with the State's commitment to clean sources of energy. We can work with leadership companies to foster and disseminate information on best practices for use by other public, civic, and private sector partners.

11.4. Case Study: Distributed Renewable Energy Systems

Distributed energy systems or local and region control over energy within the overall State framework for sustainability and form the basis for a new energy infrastructure. There is great potential for distributed energy generation systems, especially renewable or clean energy systems (Clark, 2004). Developed primarily in Europe, many communities in the United States, where they are called distributed energy or distributed generation (DG) systems, are now developing similar programs, focused in many cases on cogeneration or combined cycle (the combined production of heat and electricity) using renewable energy.

Energy can be a "dispersed" energy system (Summerton and Bradshaw, 1991) or distributed energy systems on the local level (Lund, 2000). Energy will not be subject to a central grid and control by only a few companies. Isherwood *et al.* (2000) outline in an optimization model on how such distributed energy systems would work in remote communities. Examples of renewable distributed systems were done in Alaska and Maine. Chart 11.3 is an illustration

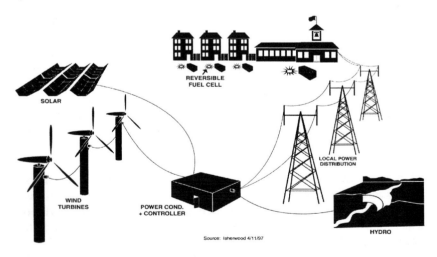

Chart 11.3. Using renewables to sustain disturbing power and heating needs.
Source: Isherwood *et al.*, 2000 and reprinted in California Commission for the 21st Century Report, 2002.

of how a local distributed energy system could work in a "model remote community."

11.5. Return on Investment Public Finance Model: The Potential for Renewables

Public incentives to support the wind industry in the late 1970s and early 1980s led to many investments for tax breaks instead of business development. When the subsidies ended, most companies went out of business. However, one wind energy firm emerged from bankruptcy under a new management team with only one of the original investors. Others replaced the team but more importantly, the company management refocused from a tax credit-driven company to a profit-making firm. This also required some new investors and a large Danish wind turbine company (NIG MICON, now merged with another Danish wind turbine manufacturer, Vestas) to invest as well as provide turbines. Today the company is growing and profitable (Ramonowitz, 2003).

Distributed generation operates at a good profit and provides excess power for the grid in its region (Clark, 2004). The business model works for over 400 investors (shareholders) who believe in the value of renewable energy. Other wind developers and manufacturers (including PV, biomass, and geothermal energy) see opportunities to mix clean energy with business prowess. A key element for renewable power generation is energy storage.

A number of "best practices" exist that demonstrate in a practical manner that new forms of energy infrastructures can be implemented across industrial and public sectors. For example, over 25 years, the city of Kalenborg in Denmark has had an industrial development project involving at least three sectors: energy, environment, and waste.

The city created a program called "industrial symbiosis" where the waste of one company became the raw material for another. This local business-energy model is a public–private sector partnership involving companies in the three sectors, with a very positive economic benefit. Another advantage is the location and control of the energy infrastructures at the local level.

The industrial symbiosis model has gained international attention and major industrial corporations replicate the process in other communities. Energy infrastructure firms have developed tools and computer programs for use by communities and regions for replicating the model. Chart 11.4 illustrates how this integrated system works.

382   *Agile Energy Systems*

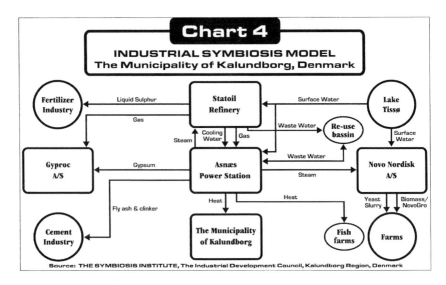

Chart 11.4. Best practice: Industrial symbiosis—Integrated Systems.
Source: Reprinted in California Commission for the 21st Century Report, 2002.

11.5.1. Proposed strategies for state government

"Energy efficiency gains come without adding to air pollution, ecological disruptions or global warming. And energy efficiency improvements cut the risk of power shortages." (Geller, March 2001). California has the potential to become a "sustainable nation-state" relative to energy. To achieve sustainability, Californians must continue to think differently in the future about our "energy infrastructure." The California energy policy and plan will need to focus on increased efficiencies and development of a diverse mix of energy supply, both generated in or imported to the State. It will need new ways to distribute these power sources.

Governor Davis signed into law what is refered to as the Pavley Bill (Greenhouse Gas), after Southern California Assembly woman, Fran Pavley. While the law is not perfect, it is the first in the USA which calls for vehicle emission reductions and establishes both guidelines and responsibility to the California Air Resources Board to implement within five years (2007). The day (July 22, 2002) Governor Davis signed the Bill, the Governor of New York State called him to get advise and the next day, himself, signed a similar Executive Order.

More importantly, the law put California in line and close association with the Kyoto Accords and the UN meetings in South Africa that met to implement the Accords. The US Federal government refused to comply with the UN majority (actually the US was the only nation to resist the Accords). California, seeing itself as a "nation-state" and the fifth largest economy in the world, however, felt that it had a responsibility to be part of the worldwide effort to reduce greenhouse gases. So the State did just that. Now the law is being challenged in the courts by some industries and the federal government.

Nonetheless, California as a "bellwether," nation-state, led the US in the effort to reduce its impact on the climate. California continues to lead the world in energy efficiency and self-sufficiency. Now with the Renewable Portfolio Standard and its goal for energy independence the State Plans are being implemented. Governor Schwarzenegger is following this same pathway but accelerating the pace.

11.5.2. Technology transfer and commercialization

Technology transfer is key to the development of an agile energy future. The "polarization" between the push and pull models "persists to this very day and remains a major factor determining the character of the energy-efficiency debate" (Hollander and Schneider, 1995: 5). However, in the real world of business and government, the process is far more interactive and nonlinear. The Stationary Fuel Cell Collaborative and Vehicle Fuel Cell Partnership in California exemplify such a dynamic process. The role of government is to work with both the "market" to "pull" innovation and with research and with development programs to "push" new technologies into wide spread use (see Hollander and Schneider, 1995). However, the thesis of this book is that these processes do not happen by themselves but need a strong civic partnership to make them happen. The civic role is to provide structure and incentives in the market so that innovators can sell their product and gain market share, but in addition to provide incentives to the technological side so that viable products are developed (Clark, 1996).

Thus, government regulation and funding of research programs must take into account these facts when considering efficient allocation of financial resources and social welfare. The final objective is to reconcile societal demands for innovation reducing pollution and industrial requirements. Funding must support technology-based consortia that facilitate spillovers and diffusion of knowledge in as many industries as possible. Funding also must enable universities and research laboratories to play an active role in moving innovation into products, selecting "targets markets," and introduction patterns. Regulation must reduce market uncertainty and stimulate utilization of new technologies.

On the other hand, firms must be receptive to technological changes. Indeed, the technology (or market) pull model relies on firms seeking technologies that will fill their marketing agendas. However, the technology transfer process is widely acknowledged as a long-term strategy that is not the objective of many American corporations who are short-term and shareholder oriented. Market pull works in other industrialized countries, however, since it fosters close industrial and governmental relationships in order to seek long-term research and development objectives. Short- and long-term markets and technologies must be balanced repeatedly and often: there is a need for quick short-term research solutions to immediate problems as well as longer term enabling technologies for competitive posturing. A new technology commercialization model appears to be the best solution to provide that delicate balance or interaction between the push and pull of technologies. Firms have to consider product architecture as a function of technology, depending on interfirm relationships; vertical and horizontal integration is both technology and market driven.

11.5.3. Planning and implementation

California does have an energy plan. The USA in general does not have an Energy Plan as of early 2004. The one put forth by the Bush Administration continues to rely heavily upon fossil fuels and foreign oil. Numerous published reports call the Bush Energy Plan a "little bit for everyone" but in the end it is assuming a fossil and nuclear energy future for America.

The misdirected notion that energy could be planned by the private sector guided a number of decisions in the 1980–90s actually disbanded the planning unit of the California Energy Commission for most of the 1990s. With the basis for a State Environmental (Energy) plan, such as the EGPR, but also based on goals as outlined herein, the following are some specific strategy recommendations:

- Create a new cabinet level entity (e.g., California Energy Agency) to develop a State energy infrastructure vision and plan, building on the Governor's already announced concepts and strategies.
- Ensure that energy planning and infrastructure developments are linked to the capital budget planning process and other investment programs.
- Continue to implement strategies regarding under-utilized state-owned land and facilities, military bases, and other state-owned facilities for possible siting of generation and transmission.

- Provide incentives for regional planning and monitoring for long-term energy supply and demand.
- Monitor mismatches in regional energy supply and demand; address by providing resources to targeted local governments to prepare an energy element as part of their comprehensive and integrated General Plan.
- Work with regional entities to ensure that energy planning is linked with land use, housing, water, transportation, and other infrastructure planning, incorporating conservation and efficiency strategies.
- Continuously retrofit state-owned facilities for energy conservation and resource efficiencies; use as demonstration models.
- Develop enhanced model building ordinances, building standards, subdivision design standards, and other planning tools for energy efficiencies, including different land use models to reduce dependency on automobiles.

11.6. Conclusion

The challenge of planning for a complex task, like restructuring a failed deregulation program, is daunting and beyond the expectations of a single book. However, the objective of this chapter is to recognize the complexity of modern systems and to construct the framework for a more complex set of policies for the future. The evaluation of this can be done by reference to Scott's (1997: 345) four rules of thumb for making development planning less prone to disaster. Scott argues that successful projects typically involve taking small steps, favoring reversibility, planning on surprises, and counting on human inventiveness to improve on initial design.

The lesson learnt in California include a clear conclusion that in very complex situations that making incremental changes through small steps is superior to a fast and early broad-based change. The California crisis was so severe in part because it did not make some adjustments and see how they were working, and then go on to the next set of changes. The ambition to do it all at once reflected the arrogance of the planners of deregulation and their assumption that they could design a whole system reform at once and implement it quickly.

Scott's second criteria is to favor reversibility. While some decisions are technologically or socially irreversible, when it appears that some programs are not working out it would be advantageous for a state or country to have a plan that would allow a low-cost return to the previous status. This notion of reversibility would have saved

California from bad planning in the PURPA era when the plan generated too many contracts, and the contracts should have been halted.

The third criteria is to plan on surprises. In systems characterized by uncertainty, surprises are to be expected by definition. In the emerging energy system planners do not know the future and new technologies and applications not currently envisioned will create options that may be better than those currently being explored. On the other hand some surprises will be so catastrophic that they will require major adjustments.

Finally, Scott urges planners to be bold in their visioning of the future while counting on human inventiveness to keep improving initial designs. Conservative design strategies that include small steps, reversibility, and openness to surprises will necessarily not have a well-scripted long-term agenda. Such systems will necessarily be agile, while systems that are overly scripted are brittle.

Chapter 12
Economic Benefits of
Agile Energy Systems

12.1. Introduction

The premise of this chapter is that agile energy systems are good for economic development at local, regional, and nation-state levels of society. The process of encouraging the expansion of renewable, dispersed, and locally appropriate energy resources is both a source of jobs and business opportunities at the local level.

Furthermore, agile energy systems fit well into the distributed energy generation (DG) approach to energy which is becoming increasingly touted by energy experts as a viable and important approach to energy transformation and markets. The civic market process whereby State officials convene, cochair and facilitate problem solving at the local level for various conflicting stakeholders yields important energy savings and generation possibilities, as well as combining significant synergies that create jobs and economic well-being.

Local economies are vulnerable to crises and benefit from opportunities originating outside their jurisdictions. However, not all communities are equally vulnerable. Communities can control the extent to which external events alter local preferences by building a diversified economic base and being attentive to flexible responses to changes as they occur. Communities across the State have historically benefited from rapidly growing technology commercialization into entrepreneurial businesses that offered new jobs, career ladders, and tax revenue.

More recently, California has had its share of crises. The energy crisis deeply threatened confidence in the State. The "dot com" crash further eroded that self-confidence. New technologies were particularly hard hit, and the State lost thousands of companies and tens of thousands of jobs. The falling stock market during the 2002 recession and following the 9–11 attack on the World Trade Center in New York led to declining public tax revenues. The California state government was faced with huge unreimbursed electricity costs and spending that greatly exceeded revenues, leading to an unprecedented fiscal crisis with a $35+ billion budget deficit. These problems continued to spiral the economy into a weaker position as private business earnings fell, investment slowed, and jobs continued to be lost.

The energy crisis contributed greatly to the State's economic woes. The national and global economic slow down in the first years following 2000 was compounded by the economic dislocation associated with unreliable electricity and skyrocketing prices. In addition, repayment of the debt associated with keeping the lights on most of the time added to both State and utility costs, and these were added to utility rates, but they also loaded the State with so much debt that the State's credit rating started falling. What was once an energy problem became a more general social and economic problem which, in the end (fall 2003) helped to bring on the Recall of Governor Davis.

Nonetheless, local communities should look to the energy infrastructure systems as an opportunity for broader local economic revitalization beyond just getting enough power so that blackouts are avoided. Distributed generation, especially with renewable and hybrid technologies, along with extensive conservation create local economic benefits regardless of whether they are done by investor-owned utilities or some other mix of public and private entities.

An added benefit is that local communities can address long-standing problems of environmental justice associated with old and existing power production. Issues of environmental justice have been concentrated in finding legal solutions for the poor and ethnic minority communities. And in the decision below, it was under the overall need to help mitigate environmental justice issues that prompted the State government to act and intercede in supporting local needs for energy reform.

The purpose of this chapter is to show how agile energy systems promoted by national and state governments can use changes in their energy system as a tool for economic revitalization of communities. The State can only identify and inform entrepreneurs about the technological possibilities, create the civic markets, and promote the public–private partnerships that will solve energy problems.

Along the way local communities need to work with their local businesses, economic development organizations, educational and job training institutions, and civic leaders to promote new renewable agile energy systems that will provide local power and economic wellbeing. It is not possible to know how many jobs can be created and how much local business can increase because it depends on the programs selected to meet community goals. However, the only way to reverse the economic downturns as well as provide solutions for the energy crisis is to be active at the local level to implement agile systems where the benefits are most important.

12.2. Third Wave Local Economic Development

The context for understanding economic development in the energy industry is what has been called "third wave" economic development strategies (Bradshaw and Blakely, 1999). The theoretical foundation for local economic development is based on increasing evidence that local communities can play a role in creating jobs and expanding wealth in their community, but that the strategies for doing this have changed and become more sophisticated.

Local economic development includes the tools and strategies that can be used at neighborhood, community, and regional levels, but it does not include national economic policies such as trade policy, monetary stability, interest rate adjustments, labor law, or most tax policies. Local development works with many national and federal economic development programs such as infrastructure investments, education and research, programs such as enterprise zones or federal incentives for local development, and social service programs (Blakely and Bradshaw, 2002).

Analysts of local economic development including Ross and Friedman (1990), Herbers (1990), and Fosler (1991) have identified three waves or broad sets of strategies that describe a cumulative expansion of approaches to economic development intervention. The first wave identified was simple business attraction strategies where communities offered incentives to businesses to locate in their community. The assumption is that the businesses would generate jobs and pay taxes, allowing the community to recoup their incentive expenditures, and along the way the community would benefit.

This business attraction strategy was initially introduced in Mississippi in the 1950s, but it was quickly adopted around the country. The first wave development strategies worked well for many communities and it still constitutes a large share of all economic development activities. Incentives offered by communities to attract businesses include property tax breaks, subsidized interest rates, donation of land, low-cost utilities, cost sharing for buildings and moving costs, and worker training, as well as other incentives as appropriate.

However, some limitations to first wave strategies have became apparent to local officials and observers, leading many to name the technique "smokestack chasing" with a negative connotation. For example, the firms attracted by incentives were often in declining industries under intense competitive pressure on product price such that they had to search for lower costs, which favored places with nonunion labor, nonmetropolitan and southern states where they could obtain cheap land and utilities, and low taxes. As a consequence, many jobs were for lower-skilled labor earning marginal wages with few benefits or opportunities for advancement, and the industrial processes often were environmentally damaging. Tax breaks given the firms meant that the community had less revenue to pay for schools, parks, and other amenities.

Also, some of the communities found that the "footloose" firms they attracted would quickly leave after getting a better offer from another place (often in developing countries) in competition for the same type of firm, creating more instability in the community and not repaying the initial incentives. Most critically, communities got into bidding wars with other communities, with the result that packages offered exceeded local benefits. The most expensive package offered went to a Mercedes Benz plant in South Carolina that cost over $300,000 per job, an amount that got the National Governors Association involved in trying to reduce the size of incentives.

Against this overlay of competitive incentive based attraction, economic developers pursued a second wave of development strategies, targeting business expansion without focusing on attracting outside businesses but offering improvements to new and old businesses alike (Bradshaw and Blakely, 1999). The core idea in the second wave is that new businesses offered many incentives gain an unfair advantage over the businesses currently in a community, and that the best strategy is to assist all businesses.

An advantage of this approach is that it helps retain existing firms so they are not recruited by outside communities. Second wave strategies include programs for business such as offering training programs that assist all firms, improving transportation linkages, assisting small businesses through small business centers, and offering loan programs allow stronger business growth without favoring outside recruits. Utilities were often involved in these second wave strategies of providing services to local businesses. Industrial parks, redevelopment, and community infrastructure investments are widely used second wave programs.

Following these changes in economic development, emerging third wave economic development strategies take a logical next step and look beyond the needs of firms for reduced costs and build a framework of collaboration among firms and with the community. The third wave is built on growing number of ideas about how firms form "clusters" in a region where agglomeration of firms benefits all because they support a more sophisticated infrastructure and gain marketing advantages (Bradshaw and Wahlstrom, 2000).

In addition, the third wave realizes that the most attractive firms are those that create permanent jobs, contribute to community wellbeing, and stimulate the conditions for new growth. These firms typically are interested in other factors than simply lower cost. For example, they want highly trained and skilled workers and superior quality of life for executives and workers (Henton and Walesh, 1998). Clark *et al.* (2003) documented this need in California as a direct result of energy and environmental public policies, including new technology areas such as in the life sciences with "stem cell" research (Clark and Feinberg, 2003) and in energy/environment/climate change with the "hydrogen economy" (Clark, 2004).

As Governors Davis and Schwarzenegger (2004) both advocated, there must also be concern for "sustainable companies" which are concerned about the environment, health, and community. The Davis administration called for the "Next Economy" (Henton, 1999) in California which embraced these concerns (Clark and Feinberg, 2003). State Treasurer Angildes (2003) argued for the same third wave concern in what he and others label the "triple bottom line."

Thus if the first wave was about attracting "footloose" or marginal entrepreneurial firms, and the second was about reducing costs or managing business, the third wave is about creating a favorable context for sectors of the economy. Such a political and regional context can grow most rapidly in a local community, creating business environments where innovation and success flourish (Saxenian, 1994; Bollman, 2002). Some would argue that the best approach for implementing the third wave of the next economy is from a "clusters" approach (Porter, 1990, 1998). However, others would point out (Castells and Hall, 1994; Clark, 1993, 1997; Henton and Walesh, 1998) that regionalism does not mean industry clusters must be geographically bound.

The tools of third wave economic development differ dramatically from the tools that are used in the first and second wave. The processes are cumulative, however. All economic developers will mobilize incentives for firms looking to come to their community, and they will try to offer second wave community improvements to businesses when they can. What third wave economic developers add is that they see networks of firms, not just individual firms. They seek to find the intersections between firms and to build regional collaboration that will lead to clusters that are more competitive than if the firms operated alone.

Whereas first wave developers viewed themselves in competition with other communities, the third wave developer looks for potential cooperative arrangements where all firms win. Leadership and the ability to broker deals where firms cooperate are the hallmarks of the third wave; conflict resolution is often necessary to form the trust that allows cooperation. Interestingly, third wave development strategies are more complex and skilled than the efforts associated with the earlier strategies, but they are generally inexpensive. Building partnerships is complex, but the purpose is create value in partnerships rather than to spend a lot of money.

For communities looking at the changing energy situation and trying to figure out the economic development implications for themselves, this constitutes a new opportunity. New energy investment brings value and jobs to the local economy, though most communities have not wanted large centralized power plants because of their negative environmental impacts. Moreover, large power plants employ relatively few people to build and operate, with fuels coming from outside the local region. Renewable and distributed plants on the other hand are sometimes more labor intensive and do not send lots of local money outside the local economy. Today, communities are in a competition to become the next "silicon valley" of wind, fuel cells, or the hydrogen economy. Saxenian (1994) makes the significant point in comparing silicon valley to Route #128 surrounding Boston that the two regions are very dissimilar in so many ways that neither can be replicated. Hence in subsequent works, Saxenian (1999, 2000) expounds upon those differences which are really competitive advantages in the Porter (1980) context. The "valley," as the locals call it, "is unique" and can not be replicated nor should it be (Clark, 1993).

The new energy system is good for local economies because of jobs and cash flow. The strategy by which local communities benefit requires intervention, however, from an economic development perspective to broker the relationships and build the partnerships that allow new agile power systems to be established in a community and to contribute jobs and wealth. Economic development and sustainable energy development based on renewable sources and conservation are not in opposition, but in fact are symbiotic (Bradshaw and Winn, 1999). The case study of a San Francisco neighborhood that discovered this helps to prove the point.

12.3. Energy Infrastructure and Technological Innovation

The key to a third wave response to the energy crisis is local innovation. While there is little potential for quick fixes, new thinking about technological innovation places emphasis on the type of public–private partnerships that have been advocated already in terms of solutions to the energy problem. The technological solutions that enable an agile energy system do not come directly from university research labs, but from a complex model of technological transfer that builds on collaboration between research, business, and economic development efforts as outlined by Bradshaw and Westwind (2004). Examples exist in other high-technology industries.

See, for example, insulin (Stern, 1995), the biotech industry (Zucker *et al.*, 1994), the computer mainframe industry (Iansiti, 1993), and the pharmaceutical industry (Arora and Gambardella, 1994), where there are some important aspects in technology development and commercial transfer, concerning division and coordination of innovative labor among firms. The basis for California's next economy is precisely a combination of many factors, but foremost is the basic research milieu, including the intellectual capital, facilities, and finance surrounded by a variety of innovative geographical areas, support services, and public polices.

The main point is that communities must consider innovations requiring that firms "assemble" information and knowledge coming from different scientific fields with different and sometimes conflicting methodologies, theories, test procedures, and the like, that are part of technical knowledge-base. Furthermore, the innovation process is creative by definition, requiring constant change by its very nature. Often, sources of knowledge are located inside different organizations, which constitute a "locus of innovation" where significant and high-priority information can be stored and processed (Clark, 1996; Clark and Paulocci, 1997, 2000).

More often than not, innovation and creativity reside in the head of the team and individuals of researchers. This "knowledge capital" is key to the success of any research as Narin (1997a, b) demonstrates in his research on intellectual property. Nevertheless, as Clark showed in the study of energy and environmentally sound technologies in the USA, private sector research funds often were not available (Clark, 2000a). The primary source for research funding for these two areas was the American government, especially the US Departments of Energy and Defense in recent history with the US Environmental Protection Agency. Support also came from the National Science

Foundation and the National Health Centers, but proportionally less than other high-technology fields (UN, 97).

According to this perspective, it is impossible to treat innovation as made up of homogeneous parts, with well-defined borders, where economic and technological aspects can be separated. The key element is the mutual interaction among these parts that change patterns of technological evolution: depending on how interfirm interactions are made, starting and ending points and of a technological trajectory may remain unchanged, but there will be different ways in reaching the "full" development of an innovation.

At the same time the legal aspects, concerning patenting and property rights attribution, cannot be considered as sufficient for completely determining the movement of an innovation as it enters into the market. Elsewhere, these facts are analyzed by explicitly considering the role played by organizations involved in "zinc air fuel cell" (ZAFC) development and commercialization (Cooper and Clark, 1997; Clark and Paolucci, 1998). However, this role changes with different stages of innovation. This model is nonlinear rather than chain-link linear one, because it explicitly considers all sources of knowledge and of scientific research at the same time.

Another aspect concerns the structure of the innovation's life cycle. Existing models consider a life cycle where incremental and/or radical innovation improve product performances (or trade-offs among variables defining a technological trajectory). In the case of most advanced new technologies, the main issues are: (1) the market structure before and after "discontinuities," (2) shakeouts caused by introduction of innovations, (3) emerging of a dominant design, (4) period of new entrants success, and/or (5) incumbent displacement.

Conversely, it is far better to concentrate attention on technology development and refinement, at least in early development stages, and not on product definition. In order to introduce technologies that are "pulled" by environmental regulations, innovation life cycles must be considered as made of different steps, each focused on different products and market segments. New markets, where technology is introduced, can be different from the traditional ones for which the technology was designed (Clark, 2001). The introduction to "target markets" may take place in later stages, when there is larger diffusion of the new technology. Hence "learning by using" in new industries and application fields can be created and well-established.

In sum, the economic development potential of new technologies in the energy system can be enhanced by effective technology transfer programs (Bradshaw and Monroe, 2000; Clark and Paolucci, 1997, 2000). The most effective technology development involves active consideration of the economic development potential of the innovation process as well as focus on certain problems and the solutions, such as the energy crisis. Consider now the City and County of San Francisco, California, as a very concrete example of one situation where the third wave theoretical perspective focused on the regional impact of the energy crisis as it began to be implemented using civic markets to create agile energy infrastructure systems.

One of the authors (Clark) was directly involved in this case study, but the entire process lasted almost two years and involved dozens if not hundreds of people. Moreover, the case constructed below is based on many resources, including community activists, government officials at the local and state levels, community college staff, and the private sector companies. Key players were essential in all of these areas. While the basic case study is directly derived from an official report by the San Francisco Public Utility Commission (2002), everyone contributed. What follows is an attempt to pull all the data together, but the authors apologize in advance for not identifying and naming everyone involved; and take responsibility for the content, focus, and conclusions of this material.

12.4. Case Study: Bay View–Hunters Point in San Francisco

In mid-2001 but starting many years before that, community activists in the Bay View/Hunters Point (BV/HP) southeastern part the City and County of San Francisco (SF) approached the California State Government for assistance on closing two power plants in their poor working class, mostly ethnic minority, neighborhood. They claimed these 30+ year old plants, operated by Mirant Corporation, were polluting the air and causing severe illness to children and older adults. Evidence abounded on the high-health risks from living in the area. The City and County had already agreed to "phase out" the power plants, but the community wanted more. In short, BV/HP was a classic environmental justice (EJ) issue.

The coalition of the community presented a strong case for reliable clean energy replacements, which would serve the City and County, but also the local community saw the need for local sustainable development in terms of job creation, training, and business development as well as a far more viable and livable community. Numerous local and state agencies have jurisdiction over the power plants and their replacement. The California Independent System Operator (CAISO) played a critical role as it oversaw and controlled the electricity market. Nonetheless, the SFPUC had already begun to examine the issues and make alternative plans for phasing out the power plants.

The issue was contentious on many levels. Moreover, the California energy crisis starting the year before (2000) added to the drama in San Francisco. However, when the issue of clean power for SF was elevated to one of "environmental justice," the State had the mandate to take action—not punitive or controlling action (as some of the activists demanded) but a leadership role that centered on "civic markets." In other words, State Government under the Governor's Office or a similar state level "ombudsperson" role implement the civic market approach to problem solving.

Such proactive strategies would support the public good proponents (activist, community leaders, SF officials, and State/Local governmental agencies) together with the private sector market forces. The CAISO, created under deregulation who buys/sells power, is responsible for reliability. The Pacific Gas and Electric Company (PG&E) oversees the northern California transmission grid as well as contracting for electricity from power companies. The local community college and local business owners all saw a strong role in the BV/HP energy changes (third wave).

The Governor's Office of Planning and Research (OPR), whose Director at the time had served on the Board of the CAISO where he first encounter the EJ problems in BV/HP was asked to bring all the parties together (civic markets) in order to resolve the energy and environmental issues. EJ became the basis for assembling state and local leaders along with private sector interests including members of the CAISO Board and its senior staff in one large meeting (about 50 people attended) held in BH/HP community center. At that meeting the OPR Director publicly assigned his EJ Director and Energy/Environment Policy Advisor to assist the BV/HP efforts through convening a series of meetings over many months to identify the specific problems and come up with creative solutions. Among the many consideration would be upgrading the plants, introducing new technologies in order to provide clean fuels for the community and financing for the plants and related education, training and business development. The third wave was launched.

In this chapter, a detailed discussion of what occurred in San Francisco between spring 2002 and winter 2003 illustrates what civic markets can do to accomplish mutually shared goals for the public and private sectors: clean reliable energy that provides jobs and businesses for the local community. This approach illustrates how agile power systems can provide clean/renewable distributed energy generation for a major city. It also defines what sustainable development is in economic terms for the local community. Finally, the example shows the role that financial programs play in encouraging civic markets that create agile power systems to meet the future demands of the region.

12.4.1. Municipal involvement by the City and County of San Francisco

As the San Francisco Public Utilities Commission (SFPUC) Energy Plan outlines (November 2002), the City and County of San Francisco is at crossroads on energy policy as it faces the harsh realities on how and whom electricity will be produced, delivered, and used today and over the next 20–30 years. Concern for environmental justice at the local level has focused concern on the City's economic and environmental health.

Environmental justice is driving this effort as much as the drive for more local control and lower costs. An important initiative in that direction is the "Human Health and Environmental Protections for New Electric Generation" ordinance passed unanimously in May, 2001 by the SF Board of Supervisors. The ordinance directed the San Francisco Public Utilities Commission (PUC) and the Department of the Environment (SFE) to develop plans to implement all practical transmission, conservation, efficiency, and renewable alternatives to fossil fuel generation in the City.

The ordinance was created in response to community concerns over the construction of a large (540 megawatt) new power plant at the Mirant facility in the southeast sector of the City. The communities in these neighborhoods have already been suffering an unfair burden of the price of modern-day society's dependence on electricity. Mirant's facility already has one 207-megawatt plant (Unit 3) and three 52-megawatt "peakers" for use during times of peak demand. The only other power plant in San Francisco is nearby at Hunters Point, where PG&E operates one 163-megawatt plant (Unit 4) and one peaker. These plants are old, inefficient, prone to failure, and extremely polluting. People living in these neighborhoods experience an exceptionally high incidence of respiratory ailments, especially among children and the elderly. (SFPUC, 2002)

Central to the debate over the proposed plant, aside from its size, is if the City will close the Hunters Point power plant. In 1998, Mayor Brown and PG&E had already agreed that the plant would be shut down as soon as replacement power became available. Since deregulation took place in 1996, the California's Independent Systems Operator imposed this restriction due to its responsibility for assuring the state of reliable energy. However, the final decision on the plant has yet to be made due to precise data from the Pacific Gas and Electric company. By the spring of 2003, the reworking and refinement of the data for analysis was continuing. And at the same time, the SFPUC is building new renewable capacity to replace the older power plants. In short the shut down might shortly become more a political statement rather than an energy issue. There is a clear consensus within San Francisco (as opposed to the PG&E utility position) that the plants need to be shut down and replaced with renewable energy power generation.

Because the City is located at the end of the San Francisco peninsula, importing electricity to San Francisco is highly constricted. Only about 60% of the power needed for SF can be provided during periods of peak demand over existing transmission lines, and the Hunters Point and Potrero Hill power plants meet the balance of need. San Francisco uses about 5000 gigawatt-hours (GWh) (or 5 billion kilowatt-hours) of electricity per year and reaches a peak demand of about 900 megawatts (MW) in a given year. Thus, San Francisco is dependent on power plants located within the City limits (see Fig. 12.1).

Fig. 12.1. San Francisco power infrastructure.

The neighborhoods of Southeast San Francisco have historically been the recipient of a disproportionate burden of environmental, health, social, and economic impacts. Southeast SF is predominantly the home of low-income, nonwhite residents shattered among public housing and industrial warehouses. Many of the local residents have developed ailments related to these environmental impacts. Causes of the health problems come from a number of places including the air emissions from the Hunters Point and Potrero Hill power plants. "Children in Southeast San Francisco have higher rates of asthma than in other parts of the City. While these communities bear the negative environmental and health costs of these plants, they do not have access to the financial benefits that accrue to the owners of the plants nor to the businesses outside their neighborhoods whose success is so reliant on electricity." (SFPUC, 2002).

Growing scientific and anecdotal evidence points to severe and costly health problems in the community associated with the power plants. Both Potrero Unit 3 and Hunters Point Unit 4 are subject to more stringent NOx emission limitations beginning January 1, 2005. However in order to meet this requirement and continue operating, both plants may have to shut down in 2004 and be retrofitted.

The plants may be able to continue operation for a time using emission reduction credits if the plant owners acquired and "banked" such credits. Without the retrofit, the Potrero plant could be derated from 207 MW to 47 MW in 2005 to come into compliance. As the SFPUC Energy Plan (2002) indicates, the possible shutdown of Potrero in 2004 presents two problems for San Francisco.

First, during the period of time that the plant is out of operation, electric reliability in San Francisco will be highly dependent on the operation of the Hunters Point Power plant. Given its age this plant has a higher rate of forced outages than do newer power plants. If the Potrero Plant is not available because of its retrofit schedule and the Hunters Point Power plant experiences a forced outage during a period of peak demand, then it is likely that blackouts would be experienced throughout San Francisco.

Secondly, the retrofit of the Potrero Unit 3 would be costly. Mirant would only make an investment in such a retrofit if it were guaranteed by the CAISO that it could recover those costs through an RMR contract or similar mechanism. This investment would be amortized over time and could result in the operation of Potrero Unit 3 instead of the development of more efficient and reliable sources of generation.

PG&E, as the owner of the Hunters Point Unit 4, has indicated a strong desire to avoid having to invest in emission reduction retrofits at this 44-year-old plant. PG&E may be able to operate Hunters Point using emission reduction credits into 2005 and 2006. The number of hours they can operate will be determined by the Bay Area Air Quality Management District.

As voiced at public hearings, and by using the civic markets process, the most pressing issue is the closure of old polluting power plants and the prevention of the construction of any new polluting sources of electricity generation in Southeast San Francisco. More renewable sources and the expansion of energy-efficiency programs were proposed as alternatives. This approach and strategy within the goals of the community leads to economic development as the most productive, vital, and long-term solution to the issue of environmental justice.

In addition, diesel-fueled generators are used to meet peak demand and to provide emergency backup power for critical facilities. There are four 52 MW diesel-fueled combustion turbines, or "peakers," located in Potrero Hills and Hunters Point area. These power plants are limited in their operation to 10% of the hours in a year by the Bay Area Air Quality Management District. Diesel fuel produces many times more pollutants than natural gas. Thus significant air quality improvements could be achieved if these units were not used to meet peak demand, but reserved for emergencies only.

The consultation and negotiation process took over 10 months and has yet to be finalized with all the stakeholders which includes regulatory agencies, commissions, and local government among others. However, the final results as reported in this chapter look promising. Moreover, what started as an environmental justice issue soon encompassed and helped to shape an agenda for sustainable economic development—that is, helping expand local businesses and training workers for jobs of the future. While economic development and job training can become apart of any community plan, the SF community focus upon clean energy and environment gave them a particular focus and direction.

The results of the local community energy plan will be shutting down polluting power plants as well as putting online clean energy generating facilities. More importantly, the local community will be able to train workers, employ them at this and related facilities, as well as create and grow new businesses in the energy and environmental sectors. The community is calling this their "94124 Plan" after their local postal zip code. And is strongly supported by the local SF community college staff and students. With some leveraged support from the State, local government and the private sector, the Plan appears to on its way to success for a "sustainable community."

12.4.2. Local control over energy resources for the future

San Francisco has continued to lead the way to clean energy with several voter initiatives passed in 2002. Among the most significant was the Vote Solar which yielded the City $100 million for solar systems for its buildings. A number of programs support the effort with major new construction ramping up daily. The City has had plans to create its own energy power company which would be the holding company for local energy generation from communities, public and commercial buildings.

Where local control can be most effective is in the promotion and development of small or on-site energy generators. Permitting of power plants under 50 MW in size is subject to local review under the California Environmental Quality Act (CEQA) administered under OPR. Plants over 50 MW are required in California to be permitted by the California Energy Commission in Sacramento.

The siting of these smaller power plants requires that a local agency assume the lead in determining what the environmental impacts of a proposed power plant are and providing for their mitigation. Hence it is possible for the City to either own smaller power plants through the Hetch Hetchy Dam (near Yosemite Park, about 70 miles east of the SF Bay area) Water and Power System or enter into contracts for the power. Very small generators, particularly renewable energy generators, are completely within the domain of oversight for the City.

12.4.3. Promote opportunities for economic development

The choices San Francisco makes about its energy future will have a bearing on the local economy. Not only it is important that homes and businesses have reliable and affordable energy, but also that some of these businesses become part of the local energy supply infrastructure. This goal would consider to what extent different energy technologies are able to keep dollars in the local economy by supporting local community or City manufacturing, production, distribution, and installation services. Local employers would need local workers trained at the Community Colleges and available for work and advanced education.

Some advanced technologies are available outside the local economy such as combustion and combined-cycle turbines, micro-turbines, fuel cells, and large wind turbines. However, with the exception of wind turbines since they can be installed, operated, and maintained, the fuel needed to run these other technology systems involve revenues leaving the City. Solar technologies, peak load management systems, and energy-efficient products are all available locally in the SF Bay area and can reduce spending on fuel.

Communities within SF saw new opportunities for the local economic development and growth in an increased demand for solar products and energy efficiency, especially with the passage of local City wide energy Propositions. An expanded and growing market in San Francisco would support new business enterprises, encourage training and education programs, and create jobs while reducing air pollution.

The basic strategy for the civic markets process in SF was to create and implement a local "agile energy system" that consisted of clean energy generation, lower energy demand through conservation and efficiency, and providing a new economic basis for a sustainable community with job training, advanced education, and business creation.

12.5. Economic Development Strategies for an Agile System

Programs and the people who run them can make an agile power system work in ways that contribute to the economy rather than draw from it. Theoretically, Coase laid the ground for how "firms" are developed in 1937 (Coase, 1937, 1993) when identified the importance of many contributing factors for companies to be established in areas and subsequently develop and grow. Related work from Schumpeter (1934 and especially 1942) formed the basis for much of the current entrepreneurship literature (Vesper, 1990). Most of the literature and graduate business school programs focus on forming companies themselves and ignore the local economic development in communities. However, Bradshaw and Blakely (1999) argue that three key components are essential to enabling communities to obtain economic development benefits from new or old business development such as energy projects.

The first is leadership which in this application refers to the ability of individuals and organizations in public–private partnerships to set priorities, establish a vision, communicate an agenda, and mobilize resources to make it happen. The notion of leadership is not one of position, but one of ability to establish and implement a vision. Leadership expands the network of people involved in a project and helps to set priorities.

The second component of an effective economic development strategy for the future is information. In the classical economy, people are assumed to have an adequate or perfect information in order to act rationally, but we all know that most decisions are made with inadequate information, some of the actors involved in a decision are easily exploited because they lack key pieces of information such as the regulators who were manipulated by private companies during the blackouts.

In addition, information is often better collected by the community and made available to the widest number of possible firms and investors. For example, knowledge of available wind sites had not been mapped in California prior to the early efforts of the CEC and their charting of wind areas became available to private and public entities who could develop the State's wind fields. The public role in making this information available was essential.

The third key component is brokering. In complex society someone with a leadership vision and adequate information is needed to put critical interdependent parts together. The broker role is essential because it recognizes that connections between necessary parts are not formed in the most efficient way by accident, but they need to be facilitated. Brokers are essential to create the networked industrial fabric of the new economy. Their role is to solve problems, form coalitions, identify markets, expand the network of people in an industry to gain strategic advantages.

The three components of an effective third wave economic development program link directly to the creation of a civic market. This is a partnership in this case with the public and private firms that can jointly solve economic development objectives while creating the framework for a successful energy system (Fig. 12.2).

The Hunters Point San Francisco example clearly illustrates these interconnected factors in crating a civic market for renewable

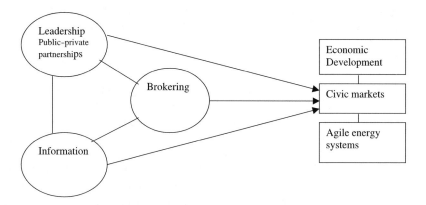

Fig. 12.2. Economic development for agile energy systems.

energy systems that will also create jobs and employment in the local community. The leadership came from community members, nonprofit organizations, colleges, and government in identifying environmental justice issues and striving to find a collaborative way to resolve problems and gain benefits for a wide variety of organizations and firms.

The information role was played by the state agencies who shared understandings and facts. The broker role was played by senior members of Governor Davis' administration and their associates who kept the process of target, identified state resources that were available, and helped the group to see the value in what they were doing.

This process at the neighborhood level can be extended to the state or regional level where the legislature and governor set goals and strategies such as for the renewable portfolio standard, based on widely shared information, and the key players are brought together to make it happen. One should note that the documents of this process are often not made public at the early stages of the process of forming leadership, collecting and disseminating information, and brokering. The process of partnership building is iterative and good leadership assures that many pieces are working together.

12.5.1. Leadership for economic development

The leadership that led to the local program in Hunters Point and the overall strategy in the city of San Francisco is the critical reason these programs went ahead when many other areas with environmental justice and energy supply problems stagnate. Leadership is the elusive quality that takes ordinary conditions and infuses them with vision and positive steps to create change. The critical part of the leadership role is the legitimacy that comes from local and ground up involvement. This is not to say that all leadership for economic development and building new civic infrastructure is local without state or regional assistance; in fact it is the opposite. But the experience in San Francisco and other places suggests the strong role for local leadership to be deeply involved.

The city of San Francisco has had an ongoing battle with PG&E over municipal ownership of the electrical system for that city (for a summary see Bradshaw *et al.*, 2003). Since acquisition of the power from the Hetch Hetchy project, San Francisco has had some resources but has not been able to garner the necessary public support for public investment in the expensive transmission lines that would carry Hetch Hetchy power from the Sierra Nevada to the city.

Similarly, the city would have to purchase the distribution system from PG&E and provide additional generation resources. The scale of the project has not discouraged city public power leaders from trying six or more times to obtain voter approval for public power. Each proposal needed a majority vote in elections, and in each case public power has not received enough votes. Each time this has been proposed PG&E mounted a huge and well-funded public relations campaign to oppose the proposal, and in heated and contentious battles they have defeated public power.

However, leading to the current efforts in city involvement in public power, the same public power advocates with the city Public Utilities Commission leadership achieved part of their goal, a part that makes San Francisco the State's leading agile power community for those communities served by private-owned utilities. The ballot in November 2001 included four energy-related initiatives, and two passed that authorized the city to become a clean energy producer for city use and eventually the larger public. A recent report from the city described the initiatives this way:

> *In November 2001, the electorate of San Francisco voted on energy-related ballot initiatives that would provided financing for renewable energy and energy-efficiency projects. Proposition B authorized the issurance of $100 million for the acquisition, construction and installation of projects for City agencies, departments and enterprises. Proposition H simply authorized the San Francisco Board of Supervisors to issue revenue bonds for renewable energy and energy-efficiency projects for private sector or City projects without requiring a vote of the electorate.*

> *The SFPUC has already identified specific solar photovoltaic and wind projects that would qualify for financing under Proposition B. Both SFPUC and SFE will be working with the private sector and appropriate City agencies to facilitate the installation of renewable and energy-efficient technologies in commercial and residential properties. (SFPUC, 2002)*

One of the ways this leadership works out is to show that it has a positive economic benefit to the city. One of the proposals in San Francisco was to have extensive power development on the Moscone Center, the city's huge convention center that hosts millions of visitors each year. With its huge roof, and heavy use, energy conservation and photovoltaic power generation issues converged. It is interesting that the leadership of the city chose this project because it turns out to be a financially beneficial project.

The Moscone Center Energy-Efficiency Retrofit is an example of the energy measures that the city of San Francisco is doing after voters passed Proposition B, mandating that the City float a $100 million revenue bond to pay for energy-efficiency measures and solar photovoltaic installations on City buildings. The project nets the city $210,000 a year, even after paying the interest on the loans that it requires. Note that the savings accruing to the City of San Francisco start immediately even though the bond is for 20 years. This is a model and there are many other applications where this might work, such as on sports facilities, university buildings, or factories and shopping centers. The following Table 12.1 shows how the energy-efficiency measures and solar photovoltaic installation pay off the bond over time.

Another critical function for economic development is the role of leadership to remove real and perceived barriers in the way of development, often regulatory barriers. The classic example of this was the leadership role that the federal government played in promoting nuclear power where legislation was passed to limit liability of firms to disasters associated with their plants.

The leadership function is essential to economic development of emerging industries because perception can be everything. The Governor's statements about renewable energy standards, advocacy of the State signing on to greenhouse gas reduction standards, and continuing publicity about the State leadership in finding a new energy direction have all contributed to the perception that the State is on the right track for a potential investor and entrepreneurial leadership.

Governor Schwarzenegger in his first State of the State address (2004) made the same point with humor by noting that if he could sell his own "B" movies, then he "could sell anything." This self-confident and even bold leadership from the highest level of State (and national) government is critical for regions and communities. Thus the assignment of OPR senior staff to work with the BV/HP community was critical in bringing all the parties together under the tacit assumption that the Governor approved the collaborative work process and its outcome. This is civic markets in action.

At the local level, San Francisco saw a number of leaders who while outspoken fully recognized that they needed expert assistance. What the community activists knew from past experience, and what the Governor Davis' staff needed to know fast during the energy crisis, was that the market forces had all the data and experts to prove their case for whatever policy they needed (Clark, 2001). Hence in San Francisco, the Mayor spoke in favor of clean energy for BV/HP but also recognized the need for his own SFPUC staff to come up with a plan. Similarly, the local elected council members did the same. Even

Table 12.1.

Energy saving measures	kWh savings	$ saved/year
Energy-efficiency installation		
Conversion to variable frequency drive systems	3,035,768	$364,293
Energy management system recommissioning	896,336	$107,560
Occupancy sensors for selected zones	202,043	$24,245
Replace metal halide and incandescents with new fluorescent T-5 fixtures	2,346,303	$281,556
Replace magnetic ballasts with T-5 fixtures	172,900	$20,748
Metal halide to compact fluorescent conversion	14,964	$1796
Renewable energy installation		
Powerlight 688 kW photovoltaic installation	825,000	$99,000
Cumulative energy savings		
Annual energy-efficiency savings	6,668,314	$800,198
Annual solar PV savings	825,000	$99,000
Net reduction in utility electricity consumption	*7,493,314*	*$899,198*
Extremely conservative estimate of overall energy and cost savings	*5,325,000*	*$639,000*
Financing		
Cost of energy-efficiency measures		$3,200,000
Cost of solar PV system		$4,200,000
Gross project cost		$7,400,000
Estimated California Public Utilities Commission incentive		$2,100,000
Estimated California Energy Commission efficiency incentive		$175,000
	Net cost	*$5,125,000*
Annual debt service on 20-year bond at 5.5% interest		*$429,000.00*
Moscone annual savings		
Annual utility bill savings		$639,000
Annual debt service		$429,000
Annual net savings from project		$210,000

Source: Casper and Ross (2003).

the community activists worked with compatible thinking economic and energy experts.

In the end, the OPR staff convened the "large group" meetings as they were called, while cochairs were assigned to the sub groups who developed technical working papers. During the same time frame, the voters of San Francisco City and County supported a $100 million bond measure to "green the city," primarily through solar/PV systems. It was the SFPUC who took the lead on that effort and hence was asked to take on the burden of drafting a City and County Energy

Report (2002). The Report was to be put before the Mayor and elected officials in November/December 2002. The same Report went to the CAISO among others for approval. The Report team members had included representatives from all these groups, including the CASIO.

After many months of meetings, sub-meetings, field trips, side talks, many emails, draft position papers, arguments and compromises on all sides, a consensus emerged. The SFPUC The Electricity Resource Plan: Choosing San Francisco's Energy Future Report was issued in November 2002. However, it was ultimately (late Winter 2003) not accepted by the CAISO with whom it had been developed. The Recall campaign and election came, derailing OPR staff and the process by the end of 2003. The BV/HP community is threatening to sue the CAISO and the new Mayor of San Francisco and Governor of California must now face the issues anew.

12.5.2. Information for expanding industries

The collection of information that is needed for economic development in the agile energy system is becoming available. This information is collected by the public for private business or public–private partnerships that can expand energy development. Information about what can be done is the first step to assembling the resources to do it.

One of the most important functions of the Bay View projects is that the State and various outside agencies provided extensive information resources that both identified the problems, but more importantly identified positive social and economic programs that could work to solve the problems. The identification of local assets to be used in the area is critical.

Another example involves the role that resource planning plays for the potential development of alternative and local resources for the city. While many potential analyses are possible, the following chart was widely discussed in San Francisco, and it shows the elimination of the Hunters Point power plants and the reduction in the role of Potrero plants. The graph shows that there will be a short term increase in imported power followed by the rapid introduction of energy efficiency and cogeneration, both green applications and the lowest costs of power available. While new combustion turbines will be added in 2004, the remainder of the growth will be taken up by solar and distributed generation. The plan shows a blueprint for the planning of the city power resources for over a decade, during which time a greater role for hydrogen can be expected (Fig. 12.3).

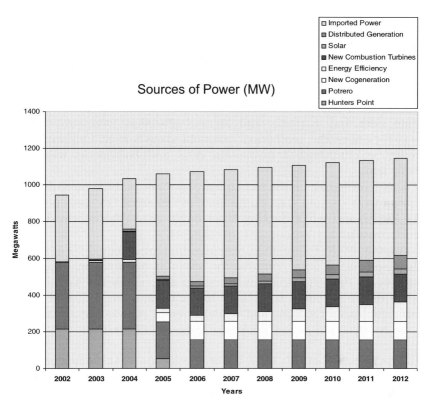

Fig. 12.3. Recommended San Francisco Electricity Resource Portfolio.
Source: SFPUC, 2002.

It is important to note that the role of conservation, cogeneration, solar and other renewable and clean generation projects are local and likely to generate more local jobs and economic activity. However, without the plan and resource assessments these projects cannot get started. And now into 2004, these have been delayed. Nonetheless, private industry sees great potential in San Francisco and the BV/HP area in particular. A number of large corporations are now placing advance technology equipment on loan or leased to the local government. An agile energy system has been started and is impacting the energy infrastructure in San Francisco.

Programs around all the available technologies have been very effective information sources for local action programs. The complexity of the technologies and the availability of resources means that local leaders can not really know what their options are without some authoritative assistance. In San Francisco, for example, the

State and San Francisco PUCs both assisted local planning groups with material on the most cost effective solar panels, estimates of wind potential on city watershed lands just South of the city, and the use of biomass and gas produced from sewage treatment (the city has a 2 MW plant that runs on gas that would have otherwise been wasted by flaring it off). Some estimates of the potential of marine energy from tides, bay currents, and thermal gradients were provided as was review of the geothermal potential elsewhere in California that could be purchased. Transmission costs and bottlenecks were also evaluated.

This information on the technological options and the more detailed assessments behind the summaries is essential to any potential developer, and while the developer might check the information, its public availability encourages investments.

Another of the information resources that are essential for economic development at local community levels is information about the sources of financing that investors can use. Clark (2004a) outlined some of the potential sources of financing assistance that can help build hydrogen facilities, and while different sources are available to solar construction in San Francisco, these are illustrative.

- US Department of Energy programs support innovative uses and applications of new technologies. The range of federal DOE programs is extensive, and innovative programs often have good luck in securing federal resources.
- The State Treasurers Office has a number of bond funds for application to local projects. The State Infrastructure Bank, for example, is a revenue bond that is issued by the State on behalf of selected projects with public benefit. The interest rate on these bonds is considerably lower because they are tax free to investors, and they are backed by the State. This makes lower cost financing available to selected projects. California Advanced Energy and Fuel Transportation Act (CAEFTA, authorized 1994) can provide over $200 million in financing. It is a special bond authority in the Treasurer's office (passed in 1994) allowing local funds to be raised for infrastructure and new advanced technologies (including energy).
- Local communities have various options to issue municipal bonds with lower rates.
- The CPUC can work to deliver funding through its various programs or by mandating utility compliance with certain programs.
- The California Energy Commission has a number of incentive programs for businesses that can help it meet its goals, such as those established in the Integrated Resource plan.

- The California Power Authority or a similar state agency has responsibility for encouraging investment in the power system.
- The highway and transportation agency, Cal Trans, has an increasing role with energy-efficiency and alternative fuels for cars, buses, and mass transportation.
- Tax incentives, such as rebates for investments or subsidies on fuels. These can be applied to stationary sources as well as vehicles.

12.5.3. Brokers create networks for business success

The third component of the economic development effort to increase economic development efforts involving agile energy systems is to serve as a broker in making the network viable and effective: for example, the establishment of public–private working groups involving key parties. In the competitive model, there were few roles for brokers but in the agile energy system there is so much cooperation and interdependence that brokers are essential. The broker acts as a catalyst in making links, solving problems, and identifying resources that are needed.

Economic development brokers often do not think of themselves as economic developers, as they may play this function as planners, regulators, or just administrators. However, they are typically marginally involved in the project being developed, at least over the long run. The broker function, however, is essential to making the connections that allow a renewable producer to identify and become a hybrid company, to finding appropriate markets, to adapting a technology such as biomass to the needs and resources of a particular area.

The local area works closely with all the state agencies and local government programs, and these partnerships have been discussed throughout the book. Economic development brokers essentially work to make sure that collaborations form when they are needed. Interestingly, these collaborations are widely needed and in the local energy field one of the key roles of energy program managers is to hold meetings, conferences, and negotiations where interested parties can find that they have a common interest and work together to solve it. The brokering role has had great success already. The facilitation of the State in setting standards for intermittent production is a state example. In addition, at the local level the key has been to help communities solve siting problems and to engage the community in setting standards and programs for conservation.

Another brokering function is helping to create markets for innovative programs and firms that build the local economy. One of the most important findings of economic development is that without a reliable and well-functioning market for what ever is being produced, the innovative companies have a hard time getting started.

The changing power system bridges community desires for reliable inexpensive energy that improves rather than degrades the environment and the community desire for economic stability and growth. This chapter has shown both that economic interests can be resolved at the local level and that the pursuit of advanced energy systems is a classic economic development challenge. The tools of economic development are parallel to the tools used to fashion good energy policy, and the good news is that this is something economic developers understand.

12.6. Conclusions

This chapter concludes our examination of the five key ideas that shape our understanding of the California energy crisis. In the first half of the book these ideas were examined in terms of the breakdown of the traditional vertically integrated utility and the energy crisis of 2000–2001. In the second half of the book we revisited these same ideas in terms of their role in creating an alternative future. While this theme covers the core issue of the electrical system, the implication is that energy has a central role to play in economic well being of the whole state. The energy crisis became an economic development disaster while the new agile energy system can become a new engine for sustainable economic development that will support the environment.

Economic development suffered a catastrophic hit from the energy crisis in California. The case has been made in this book that the energy crisis resulted from a misguided effort to deregulate the electric power sector under the neoclassical economic assumption that competition would reduce prices and resolve the tensions in the vertically integrated utilities regulated on a return on investment basis. The system was facing many challenges, including new technologies, growing importance and viability of independent power producers, high-cost nuclear plants, growing demand associated with economic growth, successful conservation efforts, and out-of-state competition with excess low-cost power.

Under the botched deregulation scheme that the State adopted, the utilities sold a majority of their generating capacity and the State established new agencies to collectively buy power and manage the grid. However, this scheme was subject to massive market manipulation by the generators who withheld enough power to cause prices to skyrocket and blackouts to cycle throughout the State during the winter which typically has the lowest power demand. The high prices caused the new state agency responsible for purchasing power to cease operations, the private utilities to enter bankruptcy or were on the verge of doing so, and the state Department of Water had to use state government credit to purchase power on behalf of the utilities. Retail rates were frozen which insulated consumers from these problems, for a while.

The energy crisis had at least a $40 billion cost to the consumers in California, and this will eventually be paid by electricity consumers over a number of years. However, the main point is that what initially was intended to reduce costs of electricity and to eliminate the regulatory presence has in fact resulted in the opposite result. The system is more expensive and there are more layers of state involvement than when the electricity system was run by regulated utilities. The result of these problems is that the economy suffered a deeper hit during the recession and has been somewhat slower to rebound than the rest of the country.

The good news is that economic development benefits are widespread from agile energy development. We have shown that sustainable energy systems are also good sources of employment and that local communities can take a larger role in tapping the benefits in terms of local employment and business activity. The tools of economic development include mobilizing local leadership, providing leadership, and brokering partnerships among participating groups.

The agile energy system also makes use of the five key ideas. We argue that new environmentally friendly technologies that make use of renewable resources not only are better for the air and global warming, but they are also cost effective. We note that the technological advantages of wind, geothermal, and especially conservation and cogeneration constitute a new economically advantageous opportunity as well. Furthermore distributed sources eliminate the reliance on ever-increasing grids that suffer breakdowns that were experienced across the United States and Europe. The agile technologies provide reliability and lower costs which will help rebuild economies.

The second core idea was that the agile energy system should not be either fully deregulated or reregulated based on the old model. The agile system is built on new rules of collaboration, oversight, and the civic good. This is achieved through public–private partnerships rather than adversarial regulation.

The third core idea is that the competitive economic model based on neoclassical economics needs to be replaced by economics that take the public interest into account. The new economics is a hybrid of public and private interests that give rise to the type of understanding of the new role that energy plays in the economy.

The fourth core idea is that complexity of planning needs to be turned from a liability into an asset. Whereas system complexity caused problems for system planners who could not know all options, in the agile energy system planners develop multiple options and strategies that will enable redundancy and reliability so that the lack of understanding of one part of the system will not lead to catastrophic problems throughout. This was demonstrated with a system in which agile components gradually replace the existing brittle components of large utility owned and grid interconnected entities that are successful just because they are parts of the dominant system.

This model leads to the realization that the whole agile system has enormous positive economic development benefits, in contrast to the catastrophic costs of the deregulated system. This can be illustrated by two concluding points. First, the agile energy system reflects models for sustainable economic development based on benefits of natural capitalism (Hawkin and Lovins, 1999). Environmentally sustainable business practices have substantial economic benefits as well. Second, the local community can be involved in pushing forward their new energy system which will also generate jobs and local well being. This economic development potential can be seen clearly in the emerging hydrogen economy which is the topic of the next chapter.

Concluding Chapters
Roadmap to the Future

Chapter 13
The Hydrogen Freeway: A Paradigm Change Today

13.1. Introduction

One of the clear pathways to achieve energy independence in California and the rest of the world is through a paradigm change (Kuhn, 1962)—"hydrogen." President Prodi (2002) and his advisors (Rifkin, 2002) had advocated policy makers to embrace an "hydrogen economy." But it took USA President Bush's State of the Union Address in January 2003 to accelerate the worldwide level of activity surrounding "hydrogen and fuel cells." Governor Schwarzenegger made reference to hydrogen in his fall 2003 campaign for Governor but was far more adamant in his State of the State Address (2004).

However, hydrogen has captured people's imaginations since the mid-1800s as a fuel for motors and industrial use. According to the excellent history of hydrogen included in Peter Hoffman's book, *Tomorrow's Energy* (2002: 29), Jules Verne wrote in 1874 of the possibility of using water broken down into hydrogen and oxygen by electrolysis as the "fuel for steamers and engines! Water to heat water." The future was clear but it took over a century to become real.

German and English engineers worked on using hydrogen along with gas or diesel in combustion engines during the 1930s. Applications were made to airplanes, submarines, torpedoes, trains, and other uses. It did not take much visionary thinking to see the value of hydrogen in producing weapons. Fuel cells increased interest in hydrogen in the 1950s after Francis Bacon, a British scientist, developed the first practical hydrogen-air fuel cell, a design that would be of interest to the USA space program.

By the mid-1990s, the Ballard fuel cell, and realization of the dangers of global warming, led to further popularization of hydrogen.

Several articles appeared in *The Economist* and *Science* that promoted hydrogen as the fuel of the future. Hydrogen, is plentiful, clean, and harmless. Moreover it is safe contrary to myths (Hoffman, 2002; Lovins, 2003; Clark, 2004b). A number of academic research units and corporations have invested considerable resources to document the safety of hydrogen, among them are Norsk Hydro (2003), Stuart Energy (2003), along with many government and nongovernment organizations (CFCP, 2003).

Jeremy Rifkin (2002) has perhaps done more than any other contemporary author to document and provide some definite direction too how hydrogen public policy could be developed. His book, *The Hydrogen Economy* (December 2002), provides the "translation" from science and technology into policy making language which allows decision makers to move far more rapidly into implementing "Hydrogen Economy(s)" globally.

Within a month of his book's release, it was translated into several languages. The impact was global. For example, President Prodi of the European Union, who had been aware of Rifkin's work in environmental and hydrogen policy, asked Rifkin to serve as an advisor to the EU (Rifkin, 2004).

California, meanwhile was addressing head-on its infrastructure future needs through the Commission for the 21st century (CCA, 2002), with hydrogen as one part of the solution in a distributed energy generation model. The proof will be California's ability to set a course for the future, which is both ubiquitous and responsible for all its citizens. Maintaining and increasing environmental goals will always be a cornerstone for California decision makers as the public consistently supports strong regulations and controls on the use of the State's natural resources. In that context, California continues to lead the world in providing a clean sustainable energy future.

13.1.1. Public–private partnership in civic markets

Partnerships can be meaningless if there is no overall purpose and vision. The leadership of State Government during the California energy crisis had often been criticized for lacking just that—vision and leadership. While there is some truth to that, it is not true in another fundamental way: state leaders needed to take action for the public good to deal with a major catastrophe that they inherited. Nonetheless, most of the Executive and Legislative branches of government never really understood the California energy system, let alone its relationship to the environment and climate. Most of these same leaders also participated in the bipartisan deregulation plans in the first instance.

Despite all, there was strong vision and leadership throughout the energy crisis of 2000–2002. The state leaders took a stand as to developing policies and programs that included conservation and new programs that included clean, renewable energy along with environmental justice, and statewide planning. However, key to long-term vision was a basic element found everywhere, which was on the surface of it bipartisan: hydrogen. The vision and the leadership within state government did not know much about hydrogen during the energy crisis, but soon moved ahead on it by late 2003 prodded along in part by President Bush.

Governor Schwarzenegger promises to aggressively pursue the hydrogen economy. The pivotal issue for hydrogen will be the kind or source of the hydrogen. Hydrogen is simply a carrier of energy. It requires fuel to be converted into hydrogen. As discussed in more detail below, hydrogen will be seen as produced from either renewable or fossil/nuclear fuels? At this point, suffice it to say that the technical and economic links between renewables and hydrogen are not only critical challenges, but also enormous opportunities.

Increasing numbers of studies are examining both the technical and economic relationships between renewable energy and hydrogen. Berry (1996) was one of the earliest to make the connection which was followed by the studies that he helped to lead at Lawrence Livermore National Laboratory in the mid-1990s (Berry *et al.*, 1999) followed by others (Isherwood *et al.*, 2000; Kammen and Lipman, 2003). Berry's conclusions about renewables and hydrogen are significant and since 1999, the economics have improved by several factors:

> *Hydrogen can be used to facilitate the introduction of renewable energy resources since it can be used as both an energy carrier and a storage medium to compensate for the intermittency of many renewable resources. Using renewable resources and hydrogen we can serve both the electric sector and the transportation sector. It has been suggested (Berry, 1996) that there may be a synergy between the transportation and electric sectors when renewable resources are used. This section investigates the possibility of such a synergy (1999: 4).*

Indeed, a hydrogen economy exists today. What a California Governor's Office Hydrogen Forum revealed in August 2003 (Clark, 2004a) was that while research and development is always desirable as part of public policy making, there are numerous companies and communities who want and can implement hydrogen infrastructures, vehicles, and stations now" (Clark, 2004a). Hydrogen is "apolitical," and the need to implement a hydrogen economy is neither political nor unattainable.

The Report from this Forum substantiates that a "consensus developed" among government officials and industry leaders whereby California in particular, but any nation-state, in order to achieve energy independence must commercialize innovations and technologies to serve its social, economic, and environmental goals. "Hydrogen is one such 'leveling' or bipartisan innovative technical advancement." (Clark, 2004a). While President Bush predicted in his January 2003 Sate of the Union Address that hydrogen and fuel cell vehicles would be available for his grandchildren to drive (20 years away), the "competition" globally is occurring today (Abrahams, 2003) as the EU responded to the International Ministers Conference called by Abrahams in Washington DC in November 2003 to plot a near-term global hydrogen economy (October 2003a,b).

President Prodi puts it more to the point. Either the EU "sinks or swims" (2003) in competing for hydrogen markets now. Hence, both one of the reasons that he personally has taken an interest in the hydrogen economy and the European Community has allocated billions of EUROs to funding research, deployment, and procurement of hydrogen-based commercial products and services. It is no accident either that Rifkin (2003) has been engaged in working with the European Union. Nor is it an accident that the group of over 50 representatives from academia, industry and government at the California Hydrogen Forum, during the summer of 2003, and many of the 200+ people attending the US Department of Energy and University of California, Davis, Institute of Transportation Summit in Asolimar, California, clearly acknowledged that hydrogen businesses are prepared today to advance the hydrogen economy into the marketplace in tandem with continued research, development, and standards. Much of the same conclusion came from a High Level Group report at the EU in June 2003 (June, 2003). Thus, the future for hydrogen is now and not in 20–30 years (Garvin, 2003).

Hydrogen is plentiful and businesses exist today that commercialize it. As the scientific community might phrase it, the research and development community proceeds in its linear scientific methods, but more nonlinear and hence parallel safe and clean hydrogen technologies exist today that avoid the "chicken and egg" syndrome. Hydrogen is ready. Society is ready. Public policy makers must act now for the future of society. Despite some skepticism and debate from academics (Tromp et al., 2003; Keith and Farrel, 2003) but with counter arguments from others (Kammen and Lipman, 2003), the hydrogen future is now.

13.2. The "Paradigm Shift"

As Clark (2003a,b, 2004a) summarized the hydrogen economy, it is the next "paradigm shift" now under way as a major change in the way California policy makers and industry are looking for clean fuels and energy for the State. Current volatile gasoline prices, growing demand especially for natural gas, and the national and international energy/environmental crises are motivating this shift. The Economist perhaps put it best in October 2003 with the front cover title "The end of the Oil Age" and article (Economist, October, 2003: 11). Here, the argument was made that for the developed or even developing world to continue its dependence on fossil fuels would be a continued source of world conflict. A new fuel-based world order was needed.

Indeed, fossil fuel supplies are decreasing in California and elsewhere to no more than 50 years of reserves even by conservative standards (Anderson, 2000). The entire country of Norway, now the second largest oil and gas producer in the world has national priorities to shift from fossil to other fuel sources in terms of both national usage as well as its basic revenue producing commodity with annual profits exceeding USD $25 billion. The future, however, for the hydrogen paradigm is also mired in conflict.

On the one hand are the "green hydrogen" advocates (GHC, 2003) argue that hydrogen must be derived and produced only from renewable energy sources. While the costs today for renewable hydrogen production are higher than fossil fuels, they are rapidly becoming cost competitive and market based as researchers over the last five years have successfully documented (Berry *et al.*, 1999; Ogden, 1999; Lipman and Kammen, 2003; Lamont *et al.*, 2004). Berry *et al.*, summarize the potential in the late 1990s as:

These analyses identify the most economic ways of serving a given set of energy demands (electricity and/or transportation fuels) from a given set of resources (renewable and conventional). In each case, the quantities of energy to be served every hour and the types of resources available are specified. The analysis then determines the most economical system configuration (sizing the various components of the system) and operation to meet these demands using the specified resources.

Correctly evaluating the costs of a case requires a two-stage optimization: the configuration of the system must be optimized and, for each configuration the

Agile Energy Systems

operation of the system must be optimized. We optimized the configurations by trial and error, altering the configuration until a minimum cost was found. (Berry et al. 1999: 4)

Since this study, one of the most effective ways to address the economic issue is through what has become know as "hybrid" technologies (Isherwood *et al.*, 2000) or where two technologies are combined and hence increase performance while saving on costs (Lagier, 2003). Hybrids are covered more thoroughly elsewhere in this volume. However, a number of both academic and practical examples document these advantages (Clark, 2003, 2004).

The other approach to hydrogen can be called "dirty" or "black." The US Government and many large oil producing countries and companies advocate fossil fuel or nuclear-based hydrogen production. The USA Government has allocated over USD $1.3 billion to hydrogen research, development and collaborations with almost USD $750 million in new funding. Most of these funds, however, are directed toward fossil fuels, nuclear, and clean coal technologies. The 2004–2005 Energy Bill in the US Congress is also skewed in this same direction.

What is important to note here is that the production of fossil fuels and now the production of hydrogen from natural gas have had a long history similar to the green hydrogen model. Historically gasoline and diesel fuels also cost more when first introduced in the market. Moreover, some of the most aggressive hydrogen producers today are the same oil and gas companies who also produce dirty hydrogen. They see, for example, natural gas through reforming technologies as the immediate future for producing hydrogen. As Berry *et al.* (1999) point out:

we consider a pathway to introducing hydrogen based electric generation to the power grid. We first consider a base case that is entirely powered by conventional technology: a natural gas turbine. Then we consider several variations. The first variation replaces 40% of the natural gas generation with a fuel cell. Hydrogen for the fuel cell is generated using a natural gas reformer. This case allows us to compare the costs of the two systems. (1999: 20)

The issue of dark or dirty hydrogen is significant for a number of reasons. Consider, however, only the economic and competitive ones. The EU is advocating a "dual" policy but heavily weighed toward the green hydrogen. The GHC makes the same point (November 2003b). In essence, hydrogen derived from natural gas is perhaps the best transition to an hydrogen economy. According to a study by the California Office of Planning and Research and the CA Fuel Cell

Partnership (2000), "Globally, proven natural gas reserves are estimated at 60 years or more of projected use, and even 100 million HFCVs (20% of the vehicle stock in all developed nations) would add only about 2% to projected consumption in 2025." (2000: 4–14).

The same Directed Technologies study cited earlier showed that over the next 40 years, if hydrogen were produced solely from natural gas and no other sources, there would be an 8–11% increase in demand. For example, Ogden's early study (1999) of the Los Angeles area reports:

> *Ample natural gas resources are available in (Los Angeles) area to produce hydrogen transportation fuel in the near term. Fueling a fleet of 200,000 fuel cell cars and light trucks plus 330 fuel cell buses would require about 26 million scf H2/day. This amount of hydrogen could be produced via steam reforming from about 8 million scf/day of natural gas or about 0.3% of the total natural gas flow through Southern California Gas's distribution system (which carries about 3 billion scf natural gas/day) (1999: 715).*

The bottom line issue is that in the Los Angeles area there already exists adequate resources and industrial capacity to produce enough hydrogen to start the hydrogen economy. In addition, the economics and investment required is well less than many other energy projects such as Liquefied Natural Gas (LNG) ports running between USD $3 and $5 billion. This does not include the costs for transportation either by pipeline, highway, or other means. The hydrogen paradigm allows a rethinking of priorities and investment in strategies that will have long-term benefits of agile energy.

13.3. Hydrogen Facts and Feasibility

Hydrogen is highly flammable and takes a small amount of energy to ignite it and make it burn. However, it has a wide flammability range, meaning it can burn when it makes up 4–74% of the air by volume. Studies from US Department of Energy and other research organizations compare the volatility of hydrogen to other fuel. The results demonstrate that hydrogen is much safer and controllable (Hexeberg, 2003). Hydrogen burns with a pale-blue, almost-invisible flame, making hydrogen fires difficult to see (Stuart, 2003). The combustion or production of hydrogen produces no carbon dioxide (CO_2), particulates, or sulfur emissions. It can produce nitrous oxide (NO_x) emissions under some conditions.

Hydrogen, as discussed, can be produced from renewable resources, such as by reforming ethanol or natural gas (this process emits some carbon dioxide) and by the electrolysis of water. Hydrogen is the most abundant element in the universe. As Rifkin (2003) put it,

Hydrogen—the lightest and most abundant element of the universe—is the next great energy revolution. Scientists call it the "forever fuel" because it never runs out. And when hydrogen is used to produce power, the only byproducts are pure water and heat (Rifkin, 2003: Commentary).

But perhaps even more importantly, Rifkin notes:

The real benefits of a hydrogen future can be realized only if renewable sources of energy are phased in and eventually become the primary source for extracting hydrogen. In the interim, the U.S. government should be supporting much tougher automobile fuel standards, hybrid cars, the overhaul of the nation's power grid with emphasis on smart technology, the Kyoto Protocol on global warming and benchmarks for renewable energy adoption (Rifkin, 2003: Commentary).

Among others, Freeman (2003) expresses similar sentiments about the need for security in terms of both energy but also in terms of national security and avoidance of terrorism and future foreign wars. The following Hydrogen Facts document why a hydrogen economy is present today. These facts are compiled from the US Department of Energy, EU High Level Group Commission Research, private industry, and nongovernmental organizations and dispel many of the myths surrounding hydrogen (Lovins, 2003). First, hydrogen is a colorless, odorless, tasteless, and nonpoisonous gas under normal conditions on Earth and

- Accounts for 90% of the universe by weight.
- Is not commonly found in its pure form since it readily combines with other elements.
- Is found in the water that covers 70% of the Earth's surface and in all organic matter.
- Is found in fossil sources such as oil, natural gas, and coal and can be derived from nuclear fuels.

Today, hydrogen is primarily used as a feedstock, intermediate chemical, or specialty chemical (Norsk Hydro, 2003). Many envision a hydrogen future which will use hydrogen as an energy carrier or fuel (USA, Japan, and EU among others). NASA in the USA is the primary user of hydrogen as an energy carrier.

The amount of energy produced by hydrogen, per unit weight of fuel, is about three times the energy contained in an equal weight of gasoline and nearly seven times that of coal. In launching space vehicles, NASA was just as concerned about the weight of vehicles fighting Earth's gravity as it was about power during and after a space launch. Hydrogen energy density per volume is quite low at standard temperature and pressure. Storing the hydrogen under increased pressure or storing it at extremely low temperatures as a liquid can increase volumetric energy density.

The US hydrogen industry currently produces 9 million tons of hydrogen per year (enough to power 20–30 million cars or 5–8 million homes) for use in:

- Chemicals production
- Petroleum refining
- Metals treating
- Clectrical applications (DOE).

Steam methane reforming accounts for 95% of the hydrogen produced in the US (DOE) Other methods of hydrogen production are

- Gasification of fossil fuels (e.g., coal)
- Splitting water using electricity (electrolysis), heat, or light
- Thermal or biological conversion of biomass (DOE)

The economics of hydrogen are closer than many believe. While any policy needs to be conservative and reasonable, as well as flexible if miscalculations are made, the range of numbers for hydrogen include cost effectiveness. This analysis can be done at several levels, with different uncertainties. For example, data in Hoffman (2002: 87) from studies done by Ogden *et al.* suggest that photovoltaic electricity can start to be competitive. For example, energy prices are equivalent for gasoline at $1.00 per gallon and hydrogen produced at $7.67 per gigajoule.

In the US gasoline prices are now nearly double that at near $2.00 per gallon as we write, and in Europe gasoline prices are at least $4–5 per gallon equivalent. This means that in the US hydrogen at around $15 per gigajoule or in Europe at around $30 per gigajoule is competitive. The Ogden data suggest that photovoltaic sources can produce hydrogen at $22–30 per gigajoule.

The use of hydrogen is most attractive economically when it can substitute for gasoline for transportation purposes, gradually being used for electricity in homes, businesses, or factories as the economies of production reduce prices further. Typically, a gasoline internal combustion engine (ICE) is 18–20% efficient in terms of converting energy from gasoline into motion. Much has been made recently in the conversion of vehicles to hydrogen-powered ICEs which are about 25% efficient (Freeman, 2003).

These vehicle uses probably are not economical without incentives for their positive environmental benefits. On the other hand, pure hydrogen fuel cell vehicles like Toyota's FCHV-4 are 60% efficient— three times better than today's gasoline-fueled engines. Some of the discussions of using methanol fuel cells are about 38% efficient which means that there are significant efficiency advantages to using hydrogen produced from renewable electricity.

Combining the efficiencies of producing hydrogen at scale from photovoltaic sources and using it in efficient fuel cell vehicles that are several times as efficient in the use of fuels is already cost effective. Ogden estimates that the cost of delivered hydrogen even including the cost of pipelines from distant desert locations would be the equivalent price, including tax, if gasoline sold at $1.29–1.60 per gallon, which is what American drivers are paying now.

In addition, the environmental costs are near zero with huge advantages economically and in terms of health and life style at no additional cost. Factor in as well the reasonable avoidance of international tensions and resulting defense costs needed to guarantee oil security, the benefits are overwhelming. In short, California realizes that if the nation does not work toward a hydrogen economy that is economically realistic and geopolitically wise, the State will do it anyway. This is the promise of the hydrogen future for California.

13.4. Hydrogen Energy Stations

The hydrogen freeway is now under construction and leads the world in the number of H_2 refueling stations. Southern California through the SCAQMD has aggressively taken the lead as the need and demand in Southern California are extraordinary. Hydrogen energy stations are the most economical and efficient approaches to get clean hydrogen into common use and therefore create new markets and businesses. SCAQMD and private corporations (Clark, 2004a) have all indicated that the "energy station" for power and fuel is the most viable and economic approach to commercializing hydrogen.

Hydrogen can be stored on-site in homes and businesses and then used during times of day when grid connection energy is expensive. Or hydrogen can be stored and simply used for all power needs. Stuart Energy (2003) introduced, in 2003, a small electrolyzer system for such applications. Other companies are certain to follow suit.

The transportation of hydrogen is currently by pipeline or by roadway via cylinders, tube trailers, and cryogenic tankers, with a small amount shipped by rail or barge. These pipelines, which are owned by merchant hydrogen producers, are limited to a few areas in the US where large hydrogen refineries and chemical plants are concentrated, such as Indiana, Southern California, especially near the ports of Long Beach, Los Angeles and San Pedro, Texas, and Louisiana.

The locations coincide with the oil and gas production, refining and storage facilities near ports. Hence, despite the official reports on the increase demand for natural gas and the future need for hydrogen (CEC, 2003) one of the major reasons for California being pressured to allow liquefied natural gas to be shipped, refined, stored, and transported is to accommodate the oil and gas companies.

Herein lies the next problem in the hydrogen economy. Hydrogen is distributed via high-pressure cylinders and tube trailers that have a range of 100–200 miles from the production facility. For longer distances of up to 1000 miles, hydrogen is usually transported as a liquid in super-insulated, cryogenic, over-the-road tankers, railcars, or barges, and then vaporized for use at the customer site. Hydrogen can be stored as a compressed gas or liquid, or in a chemical compound. The environmental dangers are apparent, but the safety and security risks are far more compelling.

Hydrogen refueling stations and the creation of a "hydrogen freeway" are essential to creating a cost-competitive hydrogen infrastructure. The statistics today eliminate the "chicken and egg" argument that hydrogen is not cost competitive due to its high operating and maintenance costs. Hence, hydrogen will be another 15–20 years in further research to bring down the costs to commercial and mass market levels.

Yet these H_2 stations can be operational in homes and businesses. They can be modeled after current retail fueling stations, but also supply power for the local community homes, stores, and businesses. Linking Los Angeles and San Francisco via a "hydrogen freeway" is an important symbol for showing the vitality of the hydrogen economy. But more importantly, it can be commercially done.

Cal Trans and SCAQMD have focused on the hydrogen energy station approach. Several industrial partners have done so likewise. Toyota has done cost planning analyses demonstrating the practical and economic benefits. ChevronTexaco has contracted for economic and business models studies as well.

To have a hydrogen economy and hence the concomitant infrastructure, one of the central elements is setting "standards, codes and protocols" for safety, security, fire, and even business case certainty. California did as much with the Zero Emission Vehicle (ZEV) requirements in the 1990s. Governor Davis did so again in 2002, by signing the "greenhouse gas" (parallel and even stronger than the Kyoto Accords) bills. When society sets "high" goals and standards, civic markets are both endorsing societal values and being economically competitive.

Building "Hydrogen Highways" across America which then supply fuel for the hydrogen vehicles now and those coming to the market soon should also provide power for homes, businesses, and public buildings. These new infrastructures are not far away in the future. Again the fuel source is important. For example in California, there is an abundance of renewable energy fuels like sunshine, wind, and geothermal. But in other parts of the USA there are other more abundant fuel sources such as clean coal, oil, and gas.

Nonetheless, renewable energy sources should be the primary policy goal for sources of hydrogen fuel production to be used for on-site and grid connected power. When one or more technologies like wind and hydrogen production are combined, the costs of these hybrid technologies are greatly reduced (Isherwood, 2000; Clark, 2003; Lagier, 2003). See below for further discussion and details from CEC on the potential of hybrid technologies (CEC, 2003 website: http://www.energy.ca.gov/reports/index.html). Renewable energy sources can be reliable and "firm load" when used as "hybrids" such as solar/PV with hydrogen fuel cells (Clark and Morris, 2002; Lagier, 2003). Clean energy is good for the environment and the health of human beings especially children. The California Power Authority "Clean Energy" report and program at website www.capowerauthority.ca gives further details on actual financial costs for renewables. Furthermore, hydrogen energy stations can be the solution to environmental justice issues.

For example, in San Francisco, a case has been made from the local community when it rallied around environmental justice issues to create clean power generation sources to replace dirty 40+ year old power plants. Community leaders embraced hydrogen energy stations and even advocated wind turbines off the south San Francisco former Naval Ship Yard as one source for renewable energy production.

Further, the San Francisco City and County as noted earlier had passed a $100 million bond measure to provide solar/PV systems to public and private buildings. Linked with the production of hydrogen, significant economic and technical issues will be solved. Honda, recognizing this strategy has offered two leased (at a discount) hydrogen fuel cell cars to the City Government.

The change and action that create "empowerment" at the local level such as San Francisco, Los Angeles, Santa Monica, Berkeley, Pleasanton to name only a few and through regional organizations like SCAQDM have taken the national led in creating a hydrogen infrastructure. The general public policy is known as distributed energy generation and needs to be seen as flexible energy systems with the "agile energy infrastructure systems" advocated in this volume. Basic information on distributed generation can be found with the CEC at website, among other places: http://www.energy.ca.gov/distgen/strategic/strategic_plan.html.

When energy systems are seen at the State or multistate level, they are "agile energy infrastructure systems" since they combine local on-site power generation http://www.cpuc.ca.gov/PUBLISHED/REPORT/13690.htm (e.g., solar power for hydrogen energy stations supplying both power and fuel) with grid energy and fuel resources (e.g., hydroelectric and wind for hydrogen storage). Note now that the California ISO, with its Tariff approvals from the FERC, were able to get the imbalance rules changed such that the storage of hydrogen for future peaking and as base load creates a new firm energy supply from renewable generated resources (FERC, 2002).

Government-led initiatives and programs greatly expedite the reality of the hydrogen economy. Government fleets should have specifications that require hydrogen conversion of internal combustion engines that set goal of hydrogen fuel cell vehicles. Livermore National Labs scientists (Clark, 2004a) estimate that it will take 100,000 vehicles for the hydrogen economy to become financially fueling self-sustainable.

Implementing the hydrogen economy can further help the State to achieve its RPS goals, such as California have set 2017 for 20%. Renewables but will be there at that goal by 2010. Several European countries have set goals higher, such as Denmark for 50% by 2020. And Governor Schwarzenegger with 20% by 2010. http://www.energy.ca.gov/renewables/documents/legislature.html

Berry *et al.* (1999) "address(es) the question of increases efficiencies from combining transportation and electric generation (when) we determined the sum of the costs of separate systems—one serving electric only and one serving transportation only—and compared it to the cost of a combined system." (1999: 11). Perhaps Rifkin (2003) put it best:

The real benefits of a hydrogen future can be realized only if renewable sources of energy are phased in and eventually become the primary source for extracting hydrogen. In the interim, the U.S. government should be supporting much

tougher automobile fuel standards, hybrid cars, the overhaul of the nation's power grid with emphasis on smart technology, the Kyoto Protocol on global warming and benchmarks for renewable energy adoption (Rifkin, 2003, Commentary)

Hydrogen is a good example of hybrid technologies (Lagier, 2003; Clark, 2003). Hydrogen can be supplied through either electrolysis or through reforming. Both compressed gas and liquid hydrogen storage have been included. The energy penalty for liquid hydrogen storage is 3–4 times that of compressed hydrogen, but its capital cost is only 5–10% as much. This makes liquid hydrogen storage the most useful for long-term storage when large amounts of material need to be stored in one season and released in the another.

13.5. Combining Renewables and Hydrogen

As noted above, early theoretical and modeling work (Berry, 1996; Berry *et al.*, 1999) demonstrated the links between renewable energy generation (grid connected or on-site). Hybrid technologies were later modeled as an avenue to be cost effective in developing an hydrogen economy (Isherwood *et al.*, 2000; Clark, 2003, 2004). As Berry *et al.* (1999) put it about the links or synergy between sectors in order to be more cost effective:

> *To be more concrete, a synergy implies that the cost of a combined electric and transportation system is less than the sum of the costs of two separate systems, one dedicated to serving electric demands and the other dedicated to serving transportation fuel demands. To make this analysis we compare two alternative ways of configuring the overall system. Under one approach, there will be separate systems for providing electricity and transportation fuel. Each system will have its own set of components: generators, electrolyzers, and storage. Each will be configured to meet its own demand at least total annual cost. The other approach combines the two systems. One set of each type of component is used. They are configured to serve the combined demand of electricity and hydrogen at least total annual cost.*
>
> *To address the question of increase[d] efficiencies from combining transportation and electric generation we determined the sum of the costs of separate systems—one serving electric only and one serving transportation only—and compared it to the cost of a combined system. (1999: 11)*

The Green Hydrogen Coalition (GHC) was formed in the fall of 2003 to advocate for renewable hydrogen generation. Today, most commercial hydrogen is harvested from natural gas via a steam reforming process. Yet the supply of natural gas is as finite as our oil supply, and therefore not a dependable feedstock for hydrogen. Petroleum, coal, and nuclear resources are all potential sources of hydrogen but are not clean, safe, and long-term solutions. Producing hydrogen from petroleum will not free the US from dependence on foreign oil. Coal extraction has significant impacts on the land and produces nearly twice the amount of carbon dioxide as natural gas, resulting in the emission of increased heat-trapping gases.

The US Department of Energy and the coal industry counter that extracting hydrogen from coal would be viable if a commercially effective and safe way can be found to sequester carbon dioxide (CO_2). The Bush administration is seeking more than one billion dollars for research and development to make CO_2 sequestration a reality. However, carbon sequestration, and the quest for "clean coal," is not the silver bullet solution for producing hydrogen that the Bush administration is portraying it to be.

Carbon sequestration is the process of permanently storing CO_2 gas in geologic or ocean reservoirs. If proven to be safe, permanent, and environmentally benign, sequestration could be used to reduce atmospheric CO_2 emissions from burning coal and other fossil fuels, potentially making them more acceptable sources of hydrogen or electricity in the short term.

However, producing hydrogen from coal can never be an option unless the carbon from coal can be stored safely for the long term without other adverse environmental impacts. The safety and long-term viability of storage is uncertain, and the adverse environmental and health impacts of coal mining, mountain top removal, and power plant waste disposal are still a problem with even the most advanced coal-fired power plant and carbon sequestration technology being considered.

Nuclear power could also be used to produce hydrogen, but there are unresolved safety and disposal issues that have not been adequately addressed. Nuclear power plants are also vulnerable to potential terrorist attacks. Still, the Bush administration in a short-sighted effort is seeking more than a billion dollars to develop a new nuclear power plant designed to produce hydrogen.

13.5.1. Renewable options

There is another way to produce hydrogen—one that uses no fossil fuels or nuclear power in the process. Renewable sources of energy—solar photovoltaic (PV), fuel cells, wind, small sustainable hydropower, geothermal, and even wave power—are technologies that are available today and are increasingly being used to produce electricity. That electricity, in turn, can be used through the electrolysis process to split water into hydrogen and oxygen. According to several analysts (Hoffman 2002; Rifkin 2002) the efficiency of electrolysis is around 75–80%, which means that nearly all the energy value of the electricity can be stored as hydrogen. Clearly this is a positive factor given the importance of finding a way to store electricity, since it must be used later or at peak hours once it is created.

Hydrogen generation with electrolysis allows storage of intermittent production of renewable energy, which solves one of the key problems of renewables discussed throughout the book. Since some of the electricity being generated can be used to extract hydrogen from water, which can then be stored for later use, society will have a more continuous supply of power. As Berry *et al.* put it (1999) in economic terms, the combination of solar/PV and hydrogen production leads to "savings in several areas and the results suggest that the SPV capacity would be cost justified in its own right. However, we also note that adding the SPV capacity changes the LDC for the fuel cell. Further savings could be obtained by adding a fuel cell that has low capital costs, even if its efficiency is quite low" (Berry *et al.*, 1999: 20). With the costs of fuel cell construction and operations rapidly declining annually by a factor of two (SFCC, 2003), the total costs for hydrogen and its low costs for the market will make it extremely competitive in a short time.

Clean biomass, which includes nongenetically modified sustainably grown energy crops and sustainably retrievable agricultural wastes, could also be an important near-term source of hydrogen for fuel cell vehicles and electricity generation. Clean biomass is a proven source of renewable energy that is utilized today for generating heat, electricity, and liquid transportation fuels.

Furthermore, clean biomass can be used to produce hydrogen through a process called gasification in which the biomass is converted to a gas and hydrogen is extracted. Virtually no net greenhouse gas emissions result from these biomass processes because a natural cycle is maintained in which carbon is extracted from the atmosphere during plant growth and is released during hydrogen production. Replanting and reforesting are prerequisite for maintaining a renewable hydrogen supply from biomass.

The potential of new technologies for storage also are promising. For example, the promise of the production of hydrogen from renewable, energy comes from wind developers themselves.

In personal discussions Romanwitz (2002), the CFO at Oak Creek in California, stated:

> *Conventional Pumped Storage has a capital cost of around $1,500 per KW and a turn around efficiency of around 72%. The concepts that I am working on are anticipated to provide a very substantial improvement to those numbers both in terms of Capital Cost and in terms of better efficiency....Other Storage technologies have costs and performance in that same range, such as Compressed Air and the Chemical Storage of Ionology... Ion exchange technologies may be more cost effective and efficient by a significant margin. (Romanwitz, 2002: 1)*

13.5.2. Using hydrogen for vehicles

Once produced, hydrogen can be stored and used, when needed, to generate electricity or be used directly as a fuel. Storage is the key to making renewable energy economically viable. It is worth noting that both Toyota and Honda in their North American Headquarters in Torrance, CA produce hydrogen from their solar/PV electricity systems and operate hydrogen refueling stations for their fleet of hydrogen vehicles. Most of the analysts feel that the best use of hydrogen produced from renewable sources now is to use it directly in applications where it can be delivered to the place needed, rather than installing utility scale generators that turn the hydrogen back into electricity for the grid. The most appealing use of hydrogen is in vehicles where the fuel cell gets higher efficiencies than gasoline combustion engines and delivers the power where it is needed on the highways.

One of the major challenges facing the world's urban areas is atmospheric pollution caused by the internal combustion engine. In recognition of this, the United States passed the Clean Air Act in 1990 requiring that 22 major metropolitan areas improve their air quality or lose federal funding. The Los Angeles basin area, with a population of over 10 million people and surrounded by a crescent formation of mountains at the edge of the Pacific Ocean, was the catalyst for the State taking some action to clean up the air.

Beginning in the late 1980s and for six years, the California Air Resources Board (CARB) sponsored a statewide inquiry into a proposed set of regulations that initially required car manufacturers to sell ten percent (10%) zero emission vehicles (ZEV) starting in 1998 with increasing percentages every two years thereafter. This series of regulations has since been adopted by 12 other states and the District of Columbia, and is expected to be adopted by 11 other states.

These regions represent 40% of the US automobile market. Now other countries in Europe and Asia are adopting similar regulations. While the regulations have been modified to adjust to industry concerns, the percentages of ZEV automobiles expected to be delivered to each category are: utilities 90%; Federal 70%; State 50%; businesses in nonattainment areas 50%; other businesses 22%. This totals 925,000 fleet vehicles in 2003. While CARB action over the summer of 1996 allowed the auto manufacturers some flexibility in meeting the deadlines, the basic regulations remain and will be enforced and not greatly compromised in the future.

Meanwhile in 1999, CARB initiated the formulation of the California Fuel Cell Partnership (CFCP) as a government and private sector association. The Partnership is located in West Sacramento with a facility for all international manufacturers. Its recent strategic plan called "Bringing Fuel Cell Vehicles to Market: scenarios and challenges with fuel alternatives" (2001) calls for a variety of perspectives for the commercial implementation of vehicle fuel cells in California (Bevilocqua, 2001). Since 1999, CFCP has:

- Put 24 fuel cell vehicles on California roads.
- Assisted transit agencies place orders for seven fuel cell buses
- Established two Hydrogen-fueling stations
- Built and maintained a state-of-the-art testing and demonstration station in West Sacramento, California
- Conducted a hydrogen vehicle facilities study "for housing and design of hydrogen fuel cell vehicles"
- Produced an emergency response guide by end of 2003 to train six fire departments
- Convened a worldwide forum in October 2002
- Reached over 500,000 people with information on fuel cells
- Allowed over 5000 people to drive fuel cell vehicles
- Helped to increase awareness of fuel cells in California from less than 25% in 2000 to four in ten by end of 2003.

Aside from environmental regulatory legislation, there is an inherent market demand for energy generation and storage devices. Pollution free power systems using fuel cells appear to be the best long-term solution (Isherwood *et al.*, 2000). A hydrogen refueling station will be installed, for example, at Los Angeles International Airport in 2003 under an aggressive South Coast Air Quality District (SCAQMSD) program, which provides almost 50% of the financing.

By the end of 2003, another six stations were awarded matching funds. The same technology push for hydrogen and fuel cells will assist shipping companies where their vessels docking and loading in port areas are also under local pressure to eliminate pollution arising from their idling engines while in port. Iceland is leading the world in developing demonstration sites for fishing vessels.

California is pioneering the way for fuel for vehicles operated in fleets but available for the public. The State with local communities is also advancing hydrogen energy stations that provide power for urban shopping business districts, at airports, and in public parks such as Yosemite. These hydrogen energy stations will provide power for local communities in anticipation for the growing demand from fleet vehicles and private citizens which is anticipated to grow in 2004 and beyond.

Additionally, these commercial applications favor the economics of electric propulsion in stop-and-go, high standby driving profiles. Ironically, in a parallel market demand, the military needs large, silent, low-thermal profile vehicles, with peak power supplied by high-rate batteries, ultra capacitors, or flywheels. The key is hybrid energy generation and fuel systems that rely upon renewable energy (Lamont *et al.*, 1999; Northern Power, 2002; Lagier, 2003; Clark, 2004b).

In spite of favorable market demands, large corporations and multi-national firms by themselves are reluctant to introduce new technologies; this process is often perceived as too risky and expensive. Instead, corporations appear to prefer a strategy that gives them a free ride in the marketplace, trying to "capture" profits from innovation introduced and developed elsewhere. Regulation may be necessary both to "force" firms to pursue innovation and social welfare, and to "coordinate technological research," according to government policy where competitive advantages in the form of standardization and market dominance can be achieved. Shnayerson (1996) confides in his inside look at GM's development of the electric vehicles or EV1 that:

> the mandate (in California for ZEVs), by forcing the world's largest carmakers to start the hard R&D march to electric vehicles at a time when no one but GM wished to do so, has been a triumph of social policy as important to the betterment of this country in its day as the Clean Air Act was a generation ago (Shnayerson, 1996: xv).

Regulations also significantly affected Federal Government funding for developing new technologies. Federal Government funded research in new technologies for substituting ICE with fuel cells (e.g., the case at Lawrence Livermore National Laboratory) demonstrates the role of such national laboratories as opposed to industry

R&D efforts. This is a very important role for federally funded R&D, since it solves some "market failures" (Nelson, 59) and increases investment returns in terms of social welfare. Nationally funded R&D provides new technologies in a longer-term perspective from 3 to 5 years as opposed to industries needs for 1–2 years and even less time in the software sector.

Nevertheless, in early January 2002, the US Department of Energy Secretary Abrahams announced in Detroit and again at special session of the EU in Brussels (2003) that the USA would invest over $1.3 billion in hydrogen and fuel cells technologies. While scholars and journalists who closely watch the American government (Rifkin, 2003) are skeptical about the intention of the US Government to focus research on the long-term future of these technologies so as to derail the current federal anti-pollution regulations, the initiative is significant and a dramatic shift in public policy which had been recommended by Partnership for New Generation Vehicles (PNGV) from the internal combustion engine development to new hydrogen infrastructure and fuel cell economy.

13.6. Hydrogen Today

It is not enough for government to fund innovation, since research investments become irrelevant if there is no market. Government funds have to be coordinated to speedup innovation and to reduce its costs. This means creating markets as well as products. Evidence is mounting that the markets are opening up now and can be part of today's agile energy solution.

Corporate leaders are "bullish" on hydrogen and fuel cells, a dramatic change from only a few years ago (Clark and Paolucci, 1997) when they either blocked or skeptical about hydrogen. Some cynics argue that the major corporations (oil, gas, automakers, energy generators, and others) are simply diverting attention from their real goal: maximize profits at all costs to society. Many environmental groups, for example, see the push for electric vehicles as a case in point, where the auto industry left both government regulators and consumers with public policies and guidelines unfulfilled.

However, others (Clark, 2004a) including former Chairman of General Motors, Robert Stempel (2002) who noted that:

> *The transformation to hydrogen power is underway. Major oil companies recognize this and have made significant investments in hydrogen systems, including better batteries using hydrogen (nickel-metal-hydride batteries), photovoltaics and fuel cells...*

The critics doubt such a sea change in the auto market can happen fast enough to make a difference. But Ford already has announced plans to launch a hybrid-electric SUV by the end of next year. Hybrid-electric-powered vehicles by GM and DaimlerChrysler are expected to follow suit. By 2005, some industry experts predict 3 million hybrid-electric vehicles on the road (Stemple, 2002: Editorial).

The American news program, "60-Minutes" (Stalh, 2003) ran a program in the fall of 2003 about the new GM "HY car" which operates with hydrogen on fuel cell power and is now in beta tests, but headed to the marketplace within the next five years (Brown, 2003).

Many policy makers, including President Bush in his 2003 State of the Union see a far nearer term, such as 2020, for the introduction of hydrogen into the economy. Others, such as S. David Freeman see "Hydrogen Now" rather than even a decade away (Garvin, 2003). Schwartz and Randall (2003) outline some of the basic steps that are leading to hydrogen development over the last decade in "10 Years of Energy Innovation":

1995

- General Motors rolls out an electric car, the Impact (later refined into the EV1), at the Greater LA Auto Show.
- GE introduces the H System, a natural gas-burning turbine that uses gas, steam, and heat-recovery technologies.

1997

- In Japan, Toyota unveils the Prius, the first mass-produced gas-electric hybrid.

1999

- Chicago spends $8 million installing solar panels in old industrial sites to light municipal buildings and parks.

2000

- The South African company Eskom begins construction on the first pebble-bed modular reactor, a safer kind of nuclear plant.
- Iceland declares itself the world's First Hydrogen Economy—major corporations (DiamlerChrysler, Shell, Norsk Hydro etc.) focus technological demonstration projects there.

2001

- Clean Energy Systems develops a power plant that runs on natural gas and releases steam and carbon dioxide.

- State of California signs a MOU with Iceland to collaborate on the Hydrogen Economy with geothermal, fuel cells, and other technologies.
- European Union announces its Clean Cities program—10 cities to have fuel cell (hopefully hydrogen) powered buses.

2002
- Honda leases the first of five fuel cell cars to Los Angeles. The 80-horsepower FCX's only emission: water.

2003
- Major car makers (now including GM) target California with new hybrid commercial (2004) and hydrogen-fueled vehicles (estimated to be in 2006).
- US DOE announces major RFP on hydrogen, based technologies ($250 million) on President's State of the Union Speech in January 2003.
- EU announces its plans on Hydrogen under direction of President Prodi with a number of High Level Reports and funds (over Euro 1 Billion)—focus more on "green hydrogen."
- Ireland approves the world's largest offshore wind park, 200 turbines on a sandbank 15 miles long and a mile wide.

2004
- Governor Schwarzenegger announces hydrogen freeway plans for California
- President Prodi initiates over EURO 700 million program
- President Bush announces USD $200+ million "winners" in hydrogen initiative
- Hybrid cars are in the mass market with hydrogen fuel cars expected in 2005

The move to hydrogen infrastructures is moving ahead on a global scale. The European Union, for example, has announced in late 2002 a multi-billion US Dollar program under President Prodi (EU, 2002). The program is primarily geared to "clean fuels" (e.g., renewables, not fossil or nuclear) for producing hydrogen. This approach is in total opposition to what President Bush announced in his State of the Union address in late January 2003. Rifkin (2003) and others have pointed out that the Bush Administration means by hydrogen, fuel sources that are "clean coal," nuclear, and natural gas. The vast majority of the USD $1.3 billion that Bush announced for creating an American hydrogen economy will go toward those fossil fuel sources.

Here we focus only upon the California case in part as a result of the need for California to provide solutions to its energy crisis in 2000–2002 (Clark, 2001). We used optimistic estimates of the costs and efficiencies of various technologies including natural gas technologies, since this should give a more useful and robust picture of the tradeoff between these technologies at the time that they may fully penetrate the market.

For example, both the California Power Authority's (CPA) Investment Plan and the Renewable Energy Plan for the Governor show that the costs for renewable energy technologies such as wind but also solar and fuel cells are cost competitive when seen in the aggregate, compared to fossil fuels, and purchased in large quantities. Similarly, Bolinger *et al.* (2001) analyzed the bids received by the CPA for wind and geothermal power facilities to find that both technologies were competitive with traditional power resources.

Additionally the IGAWG's Standard Practices Manual (Schultz *et al.*, 2001) showed that these technologies were competitive using a project financing life cycle analysis of new technologies as well as externalities such as health, climate, and environmental impact. What has yet to be considered are the fuel source costs for development. For example, what does it cost to drill for oil or mine for coal as compared to the use of the sun or wind (Weil, 91).

These cost analyses point out that the economic issue is closer than usually assumed. The technological innovations that will make hydrogen viable are not as far off as many critics think—no need to wait 10 or 20 years as is claimed by some. What these critics fail to recognize is both the fact that existing sources of energy are undervalued and the hydrogen economy is closer than most think to being cost effective even without subsidy. James and James (2001) show that electricity costs are undervalued in their research in the European Union's of "the true costs of electricity":

The results of a major EU-funded study undertaken over the last 10 years and released in Brussels in July show that the cost of producing electricity from coal or oil would double and the cost of electricity production from gas would increase by 30% if external costs, such as damage to the environment and health, were taken into account. These costs amount to up to 2% of the EU's gross domestic product, not including any costs associated with global warming, and are absorbed by society at large rather than through the cost of consuming energy. The study was conducted by researchers in all EU member states, and in the US. It is the first study to attempt to quantify the damage resulting from all different forms of electricity production across the EU. (James and James, 2001)

In sum, the options for taking positive steps to introduce hydrogen into the economy now seem feasible. The demonstration of its viability is not at question, and gradually the affordability of hydrogen strategies is becoming less of an issue. What is now most important is the need to mobilize public efforts to create the markets and the incentives for firms to go through the long process of investing and perfecting technologies that at scale will become beacons for an energy hungry world.

13.7. Conclusions

The hydrogen freeway is being built now. Hydrogen fuel has advantages due its being derived from a number of sources. It is important to determine how hydrogen will be produced on a large scale. USDOE estimates that large amounts of hydrogen are already in production in California and other regions in the USA, but primarily from reformulated natural gas. Hydrogen can also be made from fossil fuel sources such as oil, coal, and also nuclear, though each of these sources has both negative environmental impacts and serious waste problems.

Producing hydrogen from renewable sources is preferable from an environmental perspective but more costly than natural gas. Certainly other natural and renewable sources of hydrogen such as geothermal, solar, water, wind, biomass, and combinations thereof have been discussed above already. Hydrogen fuel sources can be leveraged from existing resources and areas such as State Water Projects. For example, the ability to store hydrogen in water-pumping stations in the Central Valley is staggering. Produce energy from wind or solar technologies and then store it. Furthermore, hydrogen can be produced from other abundant renewable resources like wastewater and biomass.

The role of government at all levels remains critical. It should be through a combination of policy, procurement, and transportation plans. State support of the hydrogen-powered vehicles can transform the nascent industry into a broad consumer market. Procurement of state vehicles is a critical first step in this process. Codes, standards and protocols are policy tools that will help the hydrogen economy grow.

Nonetheless, education and training of the workforce must be a central focus and concern. Beginning in the elementary but through community colleges for technical skills development and into the university for advanced training into the research institutions much needs to be done. Above all government can support the entrepreneurs who are turning ideas into new industries and businesses that are building the hydrogen economy.

Finally, continued development and advances in hydrogen appear to be ready to mimic the telecommunications and lifescience fields. That is, public–private partnerships in these fields, often with substantial government funding, have proven to help the creation of new companies, business sectors, and lower costs for all consumers. Hydrogen is about to launch onto the same pathway. And the commercial results will be even more dramatic.

Chapter 14
Conclusions: Implementing Agile Energy Infrastructures

14.1. Introduction

The key to a successful long-term energy strategy for all citizens in the 21st century is that it be reliable, cheap, clean, environmentally sound, and cause minimal climate change. In short, the road ahead must be based on hybrid renewable and distributed technologies. The political, social, and economic systems that are necessary to deliver these technologies should follow the "agile energy system" paradigm. A growing number of technologies are cost effective and reliable to be parts of the agile energy system. Certainly, such was the case whenever new technologies are introduced into the market place. However, without an engaged civic market framework at work, emerging technologies that facilitate flexible and diverse energy systems which create the agile energy infrastructure system(s) will not be optimized.

Unless the energy infrastructure of the future is civically responsible and forward thinking, consumers of power around the world will not be able to take advantage of such technological, economic, and social advances. Constant technological innovations are critical to the future health and well-being of any society, region, state, or nation. In short, as noted throughout the book, there is today a "paradigm" shift to change to hydrogen which meets the criteria for agile energy infrastructure systems on an international scale.

The commercialization of environmentally sound technologies in transition to reconfigured power systems serving regions and communities in the future makes socio-economic and political sense. The collateral sensitivity to the environment that goes with energy efficiency and renewable sources of power generation translates into public well-being and support of civic markets. The analytical reports that emerge from the current worldwide energy crises are that

443

advanced conservation, diverse fuel supplies, distributed (rather than grid) generation, and renewable technologies are cost effective and affordable. Yet the deregulated/privatized/liberalized[1] energy and regulated infrastructure systems have both interfered with and appear to be a large part of the energy crisis itself. To continue down either pathway is neither practical or prudent. The future energy infrastructure systems must be agile in that they reflect public–private partnerships, collaborations, or consortia such as those expounded and advanced within "civic markets" framework.

The thesis of this book is that the breakthrough in creating agile energy systems must be led by the civic sector where public benefit from private long-term investments and innovation takes precedence over private short-term greed and inertia. This is not a socialist agenda, but a realization that in energy policy because of techno-logical constraints (electricity cannot be stored), the conventional deregulated or privatized market does not work.

14.2. The Transition in Energy from Chaos to What Works

Internationally, there are no examples where a fully privatized and deregulated system has successfully provided a broad package of persistent political, social, or economic benefits to the public. The significant lessons from the California energy crisis from 2000 to 2002, the American and Canadian Northeast blackouts of 2003, and the regional blackouts throughout the EU, including a major section of London, most of Italy and France, are all evidence of the failure of deregulation models and the need for a major change in both public outlook and economic factors.

Historically, the pattern for most of the last hundred years of electricity has been government regulation and control of integrated monopoly utilities. In exchange for an "efficient" market (exclusive access to serve a city, region, or country), a combination of public and private entities were regulated to avoid excessive profits. This structure of public sector regulation of private (or sometimes publicly owned and operated) power companies is crumbling. This volume has argued that to replace the old system a new one is emerging. An agile

---

[1]These terms are often defined as being distinctly differently as noted earlier in the book. While acknowledging these subtle differences, they will be used interchangeably herein to exemplify the dynamics of the two extremes: deregulation (market forces) vs. regulation (government).

energy system offers different products combined to meet civic needs through private companies.

The public role in the agile energy infrastructure system is to assure that power utilities and their partners provide energy that is both reliable and fairly priced. The role of government is being redefined so that these companies are not only receiving the traditional return on investment model, but also overseeing the structured markets and stimulation of beneficial investments. In this oversight function through a civic market framework that will favor the introduction of new affordable technologies which (1) are environmentally favorable; (2) will restructure pricing systems; (3) will assure investment in conservation, demand side management, and peaking capacity; (4) will favor distributed sources of power that put less strain on the grid; and (5) will collaborate with public and private efforts to stimulate local economic development. These are the public goods that an agile energy infrastructure system can maximize.

Clearly the paradigm shift is international. Around the world most countries have started to restructure their electricity systems, and most developing countries are considering the issues of privatization and competition under pressure from the World Bank and International Monetary Fund. The new energy infrastructure system is not about "privatization" versus "deregulation/competition." The reality is that many countries are better off retaining their public investment in their power system; or at least these countries need to retain some significant parts of it, rather than selling to private (usually foreign) interests who have little civic interest or restraint on profiteering. The agile energy system builds on the "middle ground," which is a blend of private and public ownership as a combination of competition with regulation in the form of codes, standards, and protocols developed for the public good.

The new "Civic Core" model is outlined in Fig. 14.1. The conventional "Standard Prescription" model (Hunt, 2002) has been used internationally (see above Fig. 2.1). This well-established model suggested that energy sector reform was irreversibly going in the direction of privatization, deregulation, liberalization, and hence competitive markets. Internationally almost all countries were moving diagonally toward the upper-right corner to achieve this desired end state in large part due to regional pressures and multinational organizations (such as the World Bank, IMF, and Regional Finance Banks in Asia and Europe) forcing the privatization of public power companies. Based on the California energy crisis and subsequent experiences, this deregulation/privatization model has obtained the end goal and purpose all wrong.

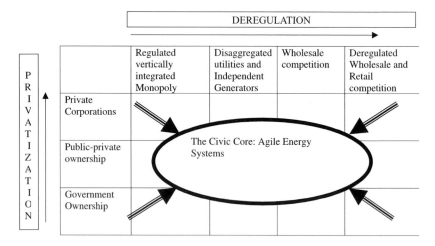

Fig. 14.1. Agile energy systems rather than the Standard Prescription.

Instead, the agile energy infrastructure systems rest in the center of the two extremes—regulation or deregulation, and public and private—not at either end. Agile energy systems reflect the framework of civic markets which combine in ownership, operation, or control over public and private power generation systems. Indeed, a key point in the deregulation debacle issue is that California has a largely private system which proved unworkable. Instead, the California municipal energy sector in the State (primarily Sacramento and Los Angeles) avoided the deregulated utilities problems and did rather well during the energy crisis.

Thus, deregulation or privatization are not the solution to the energy sector. In some countries, such public policies have led (throughout Nordic Countries, Germany, France in particular) to different and less extreme examples of privatization. In fact, these countries have really quasi-privatized in large part to break the hold of dysfunctional government agencies, policies, and political/union power that stand in the way of technological modernization and environmental change.

Agile energy systems within the overall power infrastructure and sector meet and exceed that challenge for change. The key to a successful future is partnerships between public sector organizations and the private sector companies that are part of the civic market framework. Private firms, both competitive and innovative, need the support of public funds, resources, and long-term contracts. Agile energy systems achieve the middle ground for the good of all consumers (every citizen as a private person or within a company).

These agile energy systems reflect the middle or compromise between the extreme political–economic public polices.

The middle range of options is what can be called the "Civic Core." It represents the realm of the agile solution, which is neither static nor linear. Instead, the new agile energy systems must be dynamic and changing to meet new regional energy needs and demands. The "Civic Core model" is nonlinear, multidimensional, and optimized to promote market competition as well as meeting the codes, standards, and protocols set in conjunction with the public sector.

The civic core is based on agility principles rather than simplistic models of neoclassical competition. The role of regulation is neither full regulatory control, nor no control, but civic oversight. Instead of privatization the civic model utilizes public–private partnerships. A future business environment, that is full of uncertainty and where systems and companies are developing at the edge of chaos, is naïve to think that a totally regulated system can best determine the future of any infrastructure. At the best, such thinking is wishful. Instead, regulation should be more like a public–private partnership where the good of the public is the highest goal. California's post-energy crisis policies have clearly moved in that direction.

When considering how change is portrayed, it is all too often seen in one-dimension. Throughout this volume, change has been seen as both dynamic and interactive. In short, it is a three-dimensional phenomena. Change occurs because in everyday business life and due to situations and people who act in them, simple one-dimensions are not reality. Instead, the application of civic markets to create, implement, and maintain agile energy systems, which themselves are rooted in the needs and constraints of local communities, must be dynamic and subject to change.

Thus, the international paradigm is not about whether to introduce competition through deregulation or not. In reality, the emerging technologies that allow firms and communities to self-generate and self-organize energy systems guarantees a certain amount of competition in any case. The international reality is that electric power is not evolving to a private deregulated competitive market, but rather that it is becoming a hybrid of public and private interests where public oversight assures that the system operates for the public good. Indeed, it is a shift to finding a new nonideological approach to public sectors now in order to leverage private company's ability to innovate and implement new ideas with the overall public interests of local citizens.

What is emerging, according to what some European scholars would label as "social constructionism" (Lund, 2000; also see Berger, 1965; Pool, 1997) related energy–environment–climate change issues, are public policies and programs in collaboration with business activities. Clearly the public has decided that it prefers the societal concern over the environment and climate to the profit-making only interests of the market. Repeated polls of every demographic among California citizens shows overwhelming support of environmental protection policies and programs.

There is little or no evidence that the promises of the deregulated market to reduce prices, provide better service and hence deliver more reliable services to customers, has occurred anywhere in the energy sector. Given this "nonvoting mandate" for a cleaner, greener, just environment along with the protection of the atmosphere from a variety of pollutants including the major cause, energy, the public interest in the energy, environmental, natural resources, water, climate, and waste sectors will continue to increase.

In order to accomplish these social constructionism goals, as has been argued here, a much more decentralized or distributed energy generation system must be pursued. Such agile energy systems rely on regional or local balances of energy supply with demand, reducing the need for transferring ever larger quantities of power over from a central grid that is transmitted to distant locations. These centralized energy generation systems have now become too complex to manage and costly to operate. With a distributed or localization model that includes both "micropower" useful for on-site generation and "sustainable buildings," the catastrophic consequences of grid failure will be eliminated by agile local energy delivery systems. The reliance on renewable sources directly leads to the implementation of an agile system based on the hydrogen paradigm derived from renewable energy generation.

Perhaps the best evidence that California did the right things in addressing its energy crisis of 2000–2002 was the "Great Blackout" in the eastern part of the USA in the summer of 2003. Over 50 million people lost power in almost a dozen states and large parts of Canada simultaneously on August 14, 2003. While all the reasons and causes for the blackout may not be known for some years, if ever, a consensus has grown that the American version of "privatization" or "deregulation" was largely responsible. Deregulation increased out of state or regional sales of energy generation. Yet, at the same time, it reduced any incentives for local transmission systems to invest in the capacity to handle much more complex and longer transmission paths (including employee training, technological advances, and backup systems).

The Wall Street Journal, soon after the Great Blackout, put it best in a leading front page story by David Wessel who stated in his headline

"A Lesson from the Blackout: Free Markets often need Rules—Visible Hand" (2003: 1). He then went on to note that "Federal Agencies Attack Mistakes in Electricity, Broadband and Others." The point that Wessel made so well was that markets are great ways to organize and in many ways compete to reduce costs but they need "adult supervision" (David, 2003: 1). In short, governments need to be actively involved in energy and other infrastructures. The reality of the California energy crisis is that this state is now at the cutting edge of the transition to this new energy future.

14.3. The Challenge of the Localization Model

Localization calls attention to the fact that the agile energy system is a hybrid between public and private ownership through partnerships, collaboratives, and consortia. It includes public oversight of flexible, but increasingly competitive open markets. Oversight is needed in order to assure that indeed competition takes place rather than private monopoly power which was a result of deregulation.

The danger in energy systems is being at any of the bipolar extremes of the classic ownership competition model. This is a significant revision of most mainstream thinking about energy infrastructures which assumed inevitable and irreversible progress toward a competitive private sector market. While this type of market might be ideal for steel or computers, the instantaneous quality of electricity supply and demand prevent that model from being applicable to electrons. The localization of energy is precisely the place where there is more flexibility and capacity to solve the supply and demand conundrum that is core to the modern reliable, advanced- and renewable-based energy system.

The localization model is not a typically exciting place for nation-state or federal policy makers and their initiatives. It is easier to explain that privatization or competition are good and therefore systems should seek either of these extreme goals. After all, so the argument goes "the pendulum must swing in another direction." Or for economists, the business cycle directs extremes in public policy making. In California, the strength in the energy system, however, is not at either end. Instead, it is in the middle, because that is exactly the place where there is the most system agility, long-term ability to be creative, democratic in response to unforeseen problems or changes, and when competitively aggregated purchases, cost effective. Localization is not a compromise or centrist position, but it is the source of agility in the market place.

As many experts agree, the deregulation approach did not work in California and in much of the northeast America and parts of Canada. Most experts have become revisionists in arguing that the energy sector was "restructured" rather than deregulated. Hence the energy sector did not go far enough in being "market driven." Yet almost all of these experts were either a part of the deregulation planning and policy making or advisors to those who were involved. Such "revisionist" history is clear and apparent.

The specific type of regulatory structure that is used to achieve public and societal goals depends on the political and socio-economic heritage of the State or country implementing it. Our goal here is not to suggest one model or an ideal structure, but to outline the broad objectives that can be reached by a number of different regulatory or oversight structures that ensure an agile energy system within a nation-state.

The core oversight issue is to find the right combination of incentive and mandate to enable the existing utilities to reach the objectives of becoming an agile power supplier. Utilities have one huge advantage to partner with providers of renewable and distributed power and that is that they have the ability to make long-term contracts and they can blend resources into their overall pool, providing backup and reliability for individual resources that may be intermittent. They can establish concise civic market rules, such as "intermittent" rules as was done in California for renewable energy resources such as wind and solar (Clark and Morris, 2002), thus promoting options that would be less viable without interconnections on a grid scale.

The primary concern looking into the future is to establish clear and user-friendly rules for industry and the public sector to follow. The private sector must have clear and consistent rules in order to do business. Otherwise, the risk and uncertainty in the market will cause businesses not to get involved or leave the sector.

Concerns over a range of rules are apparent from contracts, fees, and even workers' compensation to standards and goals set by the State. For example, in fashioning the public–private partnerships of the agile energy system the following questions need to be addressed:

- What is the role of local governments? How can their energy use and programs or regulations about local civic goals contribute to an agile energy system?
- Can local and state fees, rules, and incentives be standardized? The diversity of local rules and incentives undermines the ability of innovators to find standard markets, while local diversity is conducive to innovation.

- How much flexibility is optimal? In a developing system aiming to nurture diverse options, firms need long-term contracts assuring them of steady business (as well as debt payments). The ability to plan long term is essential in order to arrange financing and conduct viable business transactions, but each long-term commitment reduces short-term flexibility for new options that might come along.
- How can the State balance environmentally sound programs that are grid connected versus those that serve on-site demand? The balance between using the grid as a "one-way" source of power that is generated elsewhere and the grid as a "two-way" buffer and backup source is an unresolved issue. It is not much of an issue when very few solar panels pump power into the grid when the sun is shining and their owners draw from the system when it is not. However, the grid used this way becomes more of an unknown problem when large numbers of power consumers use the grid for reliability and backup when their on-site generation is not able to supply demand. (However, this seems an easier problem to solve because it is relatively local, compared to the complex interstate and international grid that failed in New York in the summer of 2003.)
- Who balances the different kinds of renewable energy generation? From a system balance perspective, how should incentives and resources achieving the Renewable Portfolio Standards be allocated? Should the State require that renewables should be balanced according to source (wind, geothermal, solar, biomass, etc.) so that each industry can achieve a viable market presence and the system is effectively diversified? Or should the State utilize price or proximity to demand, or some other factor. The CEC has an Integrated Energy Resource Plan (fall 2003) which covers some of these issues. However, one of the problems is that each industry "lobbies" for its own self-interest. Hence the wind industry will often be at odds and negatively compete with the solar industry.
- Who looks out for hybrid systems? As noted earlier, there is a need for renewable industry to combine or create "hybrid technologies" (Isherwood *et al.*, 2000; Clark, 2002; Lagier, 2003; Clark, 2004). Here, the idea of combing wind energy generation with storage devices such as "pumped storage" or fuel cells allows the renewable energy source to become "base load" and reliable. Such hybrid energy technologies can create a new base load and diversify the energy generation system away from fossil or nuclear power generation. The same kind of approach can be done with on-site

energy generation, for example. Solar can be combined with hydrogen production that can be stored for fuel cells on-peak usage. The same approach can be used for the storage of hydrogen for other uses such as vehicle fuel. The costs for each technological system are therefore substantially lowered.

- Can the public value provide funding for the indirect benefits of innovation? When public institutions like Community Colleges along with other university campuses, State Public Buildings, and local government building target new or retrofitted sustainable buildings, the costs for the renewable energy products will decrease as well as the costs for operating the buildings themselves, thus saving funds for future operations and maintenance. In November 2002, Californians approved over $20 billion in other bond measures for affordable housing, public school construction, and infrastructures (e.g., water and waste). Many of building codes, standards, and protocols for these facilities will include sustainable measures such as LEED and state sustainability requirements (Sowell *et al.*, 2002–2003).

The goal for modern and future energy systems around the world is now well established: to introduce renewable, clean, and hybrid technologies in rapid succession to diversify the energy sources so that price and reliability are not based on any one dominant set of fuels, as well as to promote the use of renewable power in order to protect and enhance the environment. But from a policy point of view, this goal is hard to enact let alone accomplish. That is partially why it has not been done anywhere before, and California is stepping out in front to provide leadership and applications.

14.4. Toward Worldwide Agile Energy Infrastructure Systems

What is apparent from the energy crisis in California is that regulatory debacles are not necessary and that the foundation for a better agile energy system is largely in place. A solution to the stagnation and unreliability of current energy systems lies not in the reckless pursuit of competition but in the blending of public and private interests in an agile system that develops the renewable and environmentally sound technologies that are capable of supplying energy for the future. This is neither a futuristic nor hopeless dream. California has rebounded from the world's worst energy crisis that blacked-out an otherwise functioning system and has implemented many of the steps that demonstrate the viability of an agile energy infrastructure system.

The foundation for an agile system is in many documents, but the interconnection of the parts is not yet recognized. For example, the California Energy Commission proposed a plan giving renewables more significance in June 2001, but it falls short of an integrated vision. Various organizations such as the California Bay Area (San Francisco) Economic Council hired consultants to make plans. Plans and potential solutions have been offered by the Union of Concerned Scientists, the Center for Energy Efficiency and Renewable Energy, the Energy Foundation, and the list goes on. All the plans made one basic assumption: the deregulated market would exist and be modified or adjusted to allow market rules to govern new energy generation.

The thesis of this book is that deregulation and privatization strategies that blindly institute free markets for electrical power are neither viable nor in the civic interest. While the previous vertically integrated utility subject to public utility commission regulation will not be likely reinstated in California or any other place where changes have been initiated; the theoretical limitations and practical dangers of deregulation are also clearly demonstrated.

On the other hand, we do not see any potential or advantage to return to the previous regulated system as it was too inflexible to adapt to the changing potentials of renewable and distributed resources. Vertically integrated monopolies which control all sources of power and their distribution are no longer viable in California and in most other countries because they are too rigid and lack the agility to meet civic needs. We would not argue against changes in the electric system in most countries, but the model of change cannot be the deregulation paradigm that was the cause of California's $40 billion crisis, the New York grid failure, and increasing problems in Europe and elsewhere.

Thus, while looking for change in the power system around the world, we see the need for an increasing role for governmental and civic participation in the power system rather than less. What is good for "the market" is not necessarily good for the general public. The agile power system can be implemented in most countries, depending on local circumstances and unique resources and needs. The advantages of making agility the goal rather than commercialization of public assets is that rich and poor countries alike will see civic benefits rather than private greed, and will see the maximization of both environmental and economic benefits.

Implementing an agile energy infrastructure system based on the five principles outlined earlier, requires decisiveness toward a new form and delivery systems for clean energy not just in California but worldwide. The development of the civic market frameworks in implementing such a clean energy pathway have benefits relating back to each of the chapters in the book. Consider these advantages again in brief.

14.4.1. Technological benefits

First, technology has opened many doors for the community or county seeking more civic benefit from their energy system. Whereas the old technology of choice around the world has been increasingly large centralized power stations connected by complex high-voltage grids, the disadvantages of this system are becoming clear. These systems are dirty, fragile, and increasingly expensive. They require large investments of capital which favor large corporations, and technology that comes from the largest developed countries.

The alternative technologies of an agile energy system not only utilize renewable sources of power that diversify the power sources for an area, but they are cleaner. The tension between more demand for power and the realization that producing that power will lead to global warming and other environmental changes necessitates finding less-invasive technologies.

Wherever they are first implemented, the systematic build-out of new-technology energy generation systems, for example in public buildings, can be distributed throughout the State, and will accelerate the public's awareness of these products for consideration in buildings owned and operated in the private sector. State and local agencies and their buildings will become "show places" for these alternative energy technologies and demonstrations of how these on-site generation systems work. Moreover, the costs for such products to the general public will be reduced due to increased manufacturing and supply. This is already happening in California and it comes through the public–private partnership that enables technology transfer to proceed efficiently.

14.4.2. Civic and social benefits

Society benefits through participation in the power system rather than simply as a regulator. The limits of regulation are that the utilities and the public utility regulators are in a win–loose game whereas the agile power system goes beyond preventing unfair and unreasonable profits to assisting utilities to be creative suppliers of a commodity that everyone needs. The agile power system is one in which there are as many winners as there are innovative ideas about how to provide power through renewable and distributed forms.

Often these benefits are ignored by conventional economics being outside the standard cost–benefit analyses. Known as externalities these are perhaps the most significant and cost-saving benefits. In California, the concern for environmental justice- impacts communities surrounding power plants as the sites emit particulates, toxic fumes, and other health endangering wastes (Salazar-Thompson *et al.*, 2003).

Increasingly, auditors and analysts see the benefits from considering externalities in both the costs for power generation and as the savings in health and social costs when they are implemented. By late 2003, the California Department of Finance had begun experimenting with these types of analytical models. Especially with severe budget crises, the used externalities appear to be even more attractive.

14.4.3. Economic benefits

Participating in the new "social capitalism" (Clark and Li, 2002) allows a rethinking of the role of utilities in the economy as well as the economic premises on which policy changes are made. The issue is not simply lower price through competition, but it is to provide maximum public good through cooperation. For example, in the civic market model, state and local governments can regain control of their energy bills through restoring their stability to on-going budgeting needs and focusing on improving the public services that they are expected to provide to their "clients"—their citizens.

By creating local and regional power generation, public and private customers can free themselves from the vulnerabilities of the central electric grid and its transmission lines. Thus they become more "secure" in terms of power supply and from attack or unwanted emergencies. Hence government services become more reliable. In addition, by installing environmentally sound localized generation systems in government buildings, state and local agencies can contribute to the amount of renewable electricity in the system with huge economic benefits to the local area.

By meeting the self-sufficiency challenge, government agencies can directly contribute to reducing the amount of electricity imported from out of state, hence contributing to a longer-term opportunity for the State as a whole to become self-sufficient. Renewable and clean energy contributes to efficiency as well as local or on-site generation.

14.4.4. Planning benefits

The promise of the agile system is that it is not so tightly coupled that it is vulnerable to massive failures such as gripped eastern US in 2003.

The grid failure that plunged New York and other eastern USA and Canadian cities into darkness could have been avoided. In reviewing the catastrophe the most common threads of argument were that the grid had become stressed because with deregulation there was both more power flowing longer distances as suppliers bid their power in markets increasingly distant from their source. Few localized companies had the incentive to invest what was necessary to make the physical grid capable of carrying the loads it was getting.

From a regional planning perspective, it would have been much more beneficial to society, if the policy direction over the last 10 years had been to promote distributed and locally generated power. Instead the emphasis was to expand the large centralized grid and its transmission lines to accommodate purchases of power hundreds or even thousands of miles from where it was being consumed. The 2004 USA Energy Bill, therefore, is on the wrong pathway as it essentially argues for expanding the grid and transmission lines for power and natural gas.

In addition, the 2003 Blackout Reports suggested that the ability of technicians to stabilize the grid was hampered by the complexity of both the physics of energy transmission and by the difficulty of not knowing fast enough about problems that were happening in other parts of the system. At the time of the crisis, regulators and others who still believe in deregulation were calling for investing more in the grid—American Vice President Richard Cheney said up to $500 billion was needed.

There is an easier, far more cost-effective way. By reducing the scale of dependence on the centralized grid through solar/PV and other renewable power generation, near where it is being used, capacity conservation and efficiency can be achieved. Power transfers for peak periods or security reasons that really matter, make the best use of the grid. This localization model approach not only will meet immediate challenges but also will contribute to surrounding states, regional, and local community goals such as air-quality improvements and environmental protection.

14.4.5. Economic development benefits

Implementation of the agile energy strategy by state and local agencies will signal manufacturers and vendors of these products that California represents a growing and secure market. With additional economic incentives and development plans, these firms will become a core part of business expansion plans for many years to come, thereby contributing to the growth of additional high-technology industries locating in California and bringing an expansion of job opportunities, training, and educational opportunities.

Finally, given the events of September 11, 2001, California like the entire country must address the issue of secure infrastructures. Energy is one of the key sectors. Governor Davis implemented such an emergency plan in January 2001 where none existed before as part of his plan to provide sustainable energy to the State.

In 2004 and beyond, the implementation of a secure energy infrastructure is imperative on the regional and local levels in order to provide dispersed energy supply, local power needs, and independence from central grids. Governor Schwarnegger is pursuing a similar pathway but at a far more rapid rate with a series of Executive Orders, initiatives, and public partnerships.

The economic benefits for the State are significant as public policies are the driver for an expanding environmentally sound and clean energy industries. Such new industries provide jobs and careers through new companies as well as through the State's public and private academic research institutions. California is ready to embark on the hydrogen economy paradigm. Moreover, it will soon be the first sustainable nation-state.

14.5. Toward an Agile Energy System

The creation agile energy systems has already occurred serendipitously, due to the historical expediency from local and state governments in California. The government sector is responsible for the public benefit from private long-term infrastructure investments and innovation which take precedence over private short-term corporate shareholder values, management, and executive greed, as well as business inertia due to cost-cutting needs. This is not a socialist ideological agenda, but a practical realization that in energy (and most likely in other infrastructure sectors) public policy that turns the energy sector over to competitive markets does not work because of the civic need for diverse, reliable, and clean energy.

The market will simply not invest on its own for the public good. Deregulated energy companies rarely provide and promote technological innovations. What is lost in a change to markets is that both the public and private sectors can benefit when they work in collaboration. This has been well-documented now in California with such regulatory initiatives as the "zero emissions vehicle" laws, clean air and water regulations, and even "nonsmoking" acts and programs. Aside from public benefits for the environment and health, more new industrial development and the conversion of older established industries (like the automotive industry) are seeing vast new and profitable markets.

Internationally, there are no fully privatized and deregulated systems which have successfully provided a broad package of persistent benefits to the public. What has worked historically is public regulation and oversight of integrated monopoly utilities, where in exchange for an efficient market, such as the regional exclusive access to serve a city, region, or country, has resulted in a combination of public and private entities. These new "civic markets" were regulated to avoid excessive profits and protect the interests (environmental, access or distribution of services) of the public.

The current structure of public regulation of private or sometimes publicly owned and operated power companies is crumbling. This book has advanced the case whereby an agile system is emerging where multiple private firms offering different products combine to meet civic needs. The public role in the agile energy system is to assure that power utilities and their partners provide energy that is both reliable and fairly priced.

The civic market framework is not accomplished through the traditional return on investment model, but based on oversight of structured economic markets, which are stimulated by beneficial investments that enhance the health, and environment of all citizens. In this public oversight function, civic markets favor the introduction of new affordable technologies that are environmentally favorable.

Civic markets have already been shown conducive to restructure pricing systems and market mechanisms which will assure investment in conservation, demand side management. Perhaps even more compelling is that civic markets are critical in providing peaking capacity that favor distributed sources of power, which put less strain on the transmission grid and more emphasis on renewable energy. Such agile energy systems when in collaboration with public and private efforts to stimulate local economic development mitigate system failures and provide for flexible systems. These are the public goods that through civic markets, an agile energy system can maximize.

The new localized energy market in California was in "transition" until 2003, when it embraced the civic market framework to develop agile energy systems and implemented the hydrogen paradigm in 2004. Pressures to either reregulate the power markets and to deregulate further only lead to more chaos and a dysfunctional for governments, citizens, and corporations alike. Most likely the future agile energy system will be the localization model which is a combination of both extremes.

The sustainable California will have clean, renewable local-distributed energy systems, through on-site and cogeneration, along with regional generation as well as clean fuels for vehicles. The basic core will be rapid implementation of the hydrogen economy paradigm. This new localized energy market place will redefine how integrated resource management is implemented in a public market where private companies can compete in a socially responsible manner.

References

Abraham, Spencer (January 14, 2002) Deregulation is working, LA Times, A17.

American Association for the Advancement of Science. Analysis of the projected effects of president's FY 1998 budget on federal R&D. Science & Technology in Congress, April 1997, 3.

American Public Power Association (eds.) (1996) *Competition and Restructuring in the Electric Utility Industry.* Washington DC, American Public Power Association (1996) *Payments of Taxes in Restructuring.* Washington DC, APPA; (1999) *Straight Answers to More False Charges Against Public Power.* Washington DC, American Public Power Association.

American Wind Energy Association FERC endorse fair treatment of wind in wholesale electricity markets. Washington DC, Press Release, March 28, 2002.

Anderson, D.V. (1985) *Illusions of Power: A History of the Washington Public Power Supply System.* New York, Praeger.

Andrews, S. (1994) Perry Bigelow: energy efficiency Maestro. *Home Energy* 11(2).

Angelides, Phil, A new era of environmental investment and responsibility. Institutional Investor Summit on Climate Risk. UN Headquarters, NY, NY (November 21, 2003a), unpublished, pp. 1–4.

Angelides, Phil (December 2003b) Acceptance speech for "Lifetime award for the environment", California League of Conservation Voters, Tenth Annual Meeting, Los Angeles, CA.

Arbnor, I. and Bjerke, B. (1997) *Methodology for Creating Business Knowledge.* USA, SAGE.

Asmus, Peter, (August 2002) Gone with the Wind: How California is Losing its Clean Power Edge to ... Texas?. The Energy Foundation, San Francisco, CA.www.ef.org and Palo Alto, CA. The Hewlett Foundation www.hewlett.org.

Associated Press (June 27, 2003) Energy market redesign, new power plants urged. Sacramento, CA, electronic.

Aston, Adam (March 3, 2003) A strong tailwind for wind power, GE's entry—and buy-green laws—have the industry racing ahead. Industrial Management, electronic.

Atwood, Ted, Clark Woodrow and Morris Gregg (2001) *State of the art, wood-biomass energy generation.* Government of Italy, ANPA (Department of Environment), Rome, Italy.

Aubrecht, Gordon, J. (1994) *Energy* (2nd Ed.). NJ, Englewood Cliffs.

Bachrach, Devra and Kathy Rosen (February 2002) Comparison of electric industry restructuring across the US States. University of California, Berkeley, Energy Resource Group (California Energy Commission Data Task, 2001) and published in Governor Gray Davis, Commission for the 21st Century, Infrastructure Report.

Bachrach, D., Ardema, M. and Leupp, A. (2003) *Energy Efficiency Leadership in California.* National Resource Defense Council and Silicon Valley Manufacturing Group, New York.

Ball, Jeffrey and Scott Miller (June 16, 2003) US to seek cooperation on hydrogen fuel-cells. *Wall Street Journal*, electronic.

Ballonoff, Paul (1997) *Energy, Ending the Never-ending Crisis*. Washington DC, Cato Institute.

Banerjee Neela, US and Europe in fuel cell pact, NY Times, March 7 2003, <http://www.nytimes.com/2003/03/07/business/worldbusiness/07ENER.html?ex=1048 037688&ei=1&en=8fdaa4de223332ed>.

BankBoston (March 1997) MIT: The impact of innovation. Boston, MA, pp. 1–14.

Banks, Ferdinand (October 2003) Economic theory and update on electricity deregulation failure in Sweden. Unpublished paper presented at Arne Ryde Memorial Conference on Nordic Electric Markets, Lund University, Sweden.

Banks, R.D. and Heaton, G.R. (Fall 1995) An innovation-driven environmental policy. Issues in Science and Technology, pp. 42–50.

Barnett, Andrew (1995) Do environmental imperatives present novel problems and opportunities for the international transfer of technology? New York and Geneva, Science and Technology Issues UNCTAD, pp. 21.

Barth, Fredrik (ed.) (1962) *The Role of the Entrepreneur in Social Change in Northern Norway*. Bergen, Norway, Universitetsforlaget.

Bashmakov, Igor (2002) Electricity sector restructuring in Russia: mismatched goals and strategies. Presentation at United Nations Environmental Program Brainstorming Session on Power Sector Reform and Sustainable Development, Paris.

Bay Area Economic Forum (April 2001) The Bay Area—A knowledge economy needs power: a report on California's energy crisis and its impact on the Bay Area Economy. McKinsey & Co., San Francisco, CA, pp. 1–74.

Bay Area Economic Forum (October 2001) California at a crossroads, options for the long-term reform of the power sector. McKinsey & Co., San Francisco, CA, pp. 1–56.

Bay Area Economic Forum (2002) *The Economics of Electric System Municipalization*. San Francisco, Mimeo.

Beamish, Thomas, D. (2002) *Silent Spill: The Organization of an Industrial Crisis*. Cambridge, MIT Press.

Beck, F., Hamrin, J., Brown, K., Sedano, R. and Singh, V. (2002) *Renewable Energy for California, Benefits, Status and Potential* (Research Report #15 ed.). Washington DC, Renewable Energy Policy Project.

Behr, Peter (June 16, 2003) US seeks hydrogen fuel partnership—energy chief to urge European support in developing clean source of power. Washington Post, electronic.

Benson, Mitchel (November 3, 2002) As problems mount for utilities, cities pull plug on deregulation: ballot measures across US attempt rollback of electricity deregulation. *Wall Street Journal* electronic, mitchel.benson@wsj.com.

Berg, David and Grant Ferrier DRAFT. Competitiveness of the U.S. Environmental Products and Services Industry. Office of Technology Policy. U.S. Department of Commerce, Washington, D.C. due 1997, pp. estimated 200+.

Berger, Brigitte (ed.) (1991) *The Culture of Entrepreneurship*. San Francisco, CA, Institute for Contemporary Study Press.

Berger, P.L. and Luckmann, T. (1966) The social construction of reality—a treatise in the sociology of knowledge. New York, Doubleday and Company.

Berman, D.M. and O'Connor, J.T. (1996) *Who Owns the Sun*. White River Junction, Vermont, Chelsea Green Publishing Co.

Bernstein, Mark (January 2001) California energy market report, Winter 2000–2001, unpublished paper presented to Staff in California State Legislature, Sacramento, CA, Santa Monica, CA, Rand Corporation.

Berry Gene (March 1996) *Hydrogen as a Transportation Fuel*. Lawrence Livermore National Laboratory, UCRL-ID-123465.

Berry, Gene, Alan Lamont and Jill Watz (1999) Modeling renewable energy system using hydrogen for energy storage and transportation fuels. Energy Program, Lawrence Livermore National Laboratory, Livermore, CA, unpublished research report.

Bevilocqua Knight, Inc. (October, 2001) Bringing Fuel Cell Vehicles to Market: scenarios and challenges with fuel alternatives. California Fuel Cell Partnership. Sacramento, CA, Chapters A-I, pp. 1–220.

Blakely, E.J. and Bradshaw, T.K. (2002) *Planning Local Economic Development, Third Edition*. California, Thousand Oaks, Sage.

Blinder, Alan (1998) *Asking about Prices*. Princeton Un. Press, Princeton, NJ.

Blumer, H. (1969) *Symbolic Interaction: Perspective and Method*. Englewood Cliffs, NJ, Prentice-Hall.

Blumer, H. (1976a) Qualitative methods. Berkeley, Institute for The Study of Social Change, University of Calif.

Blumer, H. (1976b) Social interaction. Berkeley, Institute for The Study of Social Change, University of Calif.

Blumstein, C. Goldman, C. and Barbose Galen (2003). *Who Should Administer Energy-Efficiency Programs?* Berkeley, University of California, Energy Institute.

Bolinger, Mark and Ryan Wiser (May 2002a) Utility-Scale renewable energy projects, A survey of clean energy fund support. Clean Energy Funds Network, Lawrence Berkeley National Laboratory, Berkeley, CA, pp. 1–16.

Bolinger, M. and Wiser, R. (2002a) Quantifying the value that wind power provides as a hedge against volatile natural gas prices. Portland, OR, American Wind Energy Association.

Bolinger, Mark and Ryan Wiser (May 2002b) Customer-sited PVs: A survey of clean energy fund support. Lawrence Berkeley National Laboratory, Berkeley, CA, pp. 1–16.

Bollman, Nicholas *et al.* (2002) Regionalism: Special report and Roundtable Briefings for California State Assembly, California Public Policy Institute, San Francisco, CA.

BoO1: a city within a City, Malmö, Sweden, 2001.

Borenstein, Severin, James Bushnell, Christopher R. Knittel and Catherine Wolfram (October 2001) Trading inefficiencies in California's electricity markets, University of California, Energy Institute, Power Working Papers Series.

Borenstein, Severin, James Bushnell and Frank Wozlak (June 2002) *Measuring Market Inefficiencies in California's Restructured Wholesale Electricity Market*. University of California Energy Institute, CSEM WP-102 website, http://www.ucei.org, CSEM Working Papers.

Bouille, D., Dubrovskyu, H. and Maurer, C. (2001) *Reform of the Electric Power Sector in Developing Countries: Case Study Argentina*. Washington DC, World Resources Institute, IEEBF.

Bradshaw, Ted (1996) *The Potential of Near Zero Peak Energy Housing in California Final Report to the California Institute for Energy Efficiency*. Unpublished.

Bradshaw, Ted K. (1985) Power from communities: The growth of municipal energy production in California. *Public Affairs Report* 26(2 and 3): 1–16.

Bradshaw, T.K. (1976) New Issues for California, The World's Most Advanced Industrial Society. *Public Affairs Report* 17(4).

Bradshaw, T.K. and Blakely, E.J. (1999). What Are Third Wave State Economic Development Efforts: From Incentives to Industrial Policy. *Economic Development Quarterly* 13(3): 229–244.

Bradshaw, T.K. King, J.R. and Wahlstrom, S. (1999) Catching on to Clusters. *Planning* 65(6): 18–21.

Bradshaw, T.K. and Winn, K. (2001) Gleaners, balers, and do-gooders: options for linking sustainability and economic development. *Journal of the Community Development Society* 112–129.

Bradshaw, T.K., Munroe, T., and Westwind, M. (2004) Economic Development via University-Based Technology Transfer: Strategies for Non-Elite Universities. *International Journal of Technology Transfer and Commercialisation* (forthcoming).

Bradshaw, T., Munroe, T. and Lee, R. (2003) *Public Power in California.* Philadelphia: X Libris.

Bradshaw, Ted and Woodrow W. Clark (May 2002) *The California experience, from deregulation disaster to flexible power.* UNEP and IEA Conference, Power Sector Reform and Sustainable Development, Brainstorming Meeting, Paris, FR.

Bradshaw, Ted and W.W. Clark (July 2002) Flexible power systems, civic markets and municipal utilities as alternative solutions to the electric crisis. Community Development Society Meeting, Cleveland, Mississippi, unpublished paper presented Community Development Society, Cleveland, pp. 1–20b.

Brennan, Tim (2001) Questioning the conventional "wisdom". *Regulation* 63–69.

Brennan, Timothy J., Karen L. Palmer, Raymond J. Koop, Alan J. Kurunick, Vito Stagliano, and Dallas Burtraw (1996) *A Shock to the System: Restructuring America's Electricity Industry.* Washington DC, Resources for the Future.

Brennan, Timothy J., Karen L. Palmer and Salvador A. Martinez (2002) *Alternating Currents: Electricity Markets and Public Policy.* Resources for the future, Washington DC.

Brigham, Jay (1998) *Empowering the West: Electrical Politics Before FDR.* Lawrence, Kansas, University Press of Kansas.

Broad, William J. (May 13, 1998) Study Finds Public Science is Pillar of Industry. Science Times, New York Times, pp. 1–2.

Brooks, Nancy Rivera (September 15 2002) Power Trade Slump may hit Consumers energy—lack of deals, possible shortages could mean higher prices as merchants struggle and plant-building slows. LA Times, C1+.

Brower, M. (1994) *Cool Energy: Renewable Solutions to Environmental Problems.* Cambridge, MIT Press.

Brown, Kathryn S. (1999) Bright future or brief flare for renewable energy? *Science* 285: 678–680.

Brown, Lester (2001) *Eco-Economy.* New York, WW Norton.

Brown, R.H. (Sept 1978) *Bureaucracy as praxis: towards a political phenomenology of formal organizations.* Administrative Science Quarterly.

Buchholz, Todd G. (1989) *New Ideas from Dead Economists.* Penguin Press, New York.

Bush, President George W. State of the Union Address (January 2003).

Bush, George W. (April 18, 2001) National Energy Plan. Vice President Richard Cheney as reported in Los Angeles Times.

Bushnell, James (June 2003) Looking for trouble competition policy in the U.S. electricity industry. University of California, Energy Institute, Berkeley, CA, unpublished, pp. 1–57.

Bushnell, J. (2003) California's Electricity Crisis; A Market Apart (Center for the Study of Energy Markets Working Paper 119 ed.). University of California Energy Institute: Berkeley.

Business for Social Responsibility Education Fund. Moving Toward Sustainability, A.

Bryce, R. (2002) *Pipe Dreams: Greed, Ego and the Death of Enron.* New York, Public Affairs Publisher.

Byrne, J. and Mun, Y.-M. (2003) Toward a New Political Economy of Energy Commons; Lessons from US Electricity Restructuring. in N. Wamukonya?

Byrne, John A. (November 25, 1996) The Best and Worst Boards: Our new report card on corporate governance, Business Week, pp. 82–120.

California Air Resources Board (CARB) Secondary benefits of zero emission vehicle rules. Sacramento, CA, Sept 01.

California Commission for the 21st Century, Infrastructure Report, *Building Better Buildings: A Blueprint for Sustainable State Facilities* (*Blueprint*), -chairs, Maria Contreras-Sweet (Secretary of Business, Housing and Trade Agency) and Guy Bustemonte (Lt. Governor of California), Governor in Executive Order D-16-00, Feb 02, http://www.ciwmb.ca. gov/GreenBuilding/TaskForce. http://www.bth.ca.gov/invest4ca/FullReport.pdf

California Consumer Affairs Agency (CCA) (April 2001) Flex Your Power Programs. Sacramento, CA.

California Consumer Affairs Agency (CAA) (December 2001) Building Better Buildings: A Blueprint for Sustainable State Facilities, Sustainable Building Task Force and the State of Consumer Services Agency. http://www.ciwmb.ca.gov/GreenBuilding/Blueprint/Blueprint.pdf.

California Consumer Power and Conservation Financing Authority (2002) *Clean Growth: Clean Energy for California's Economic Future.* Sacramento, Mimeo, March 2002, www.capowerauthority.ca.

California Consumer Power and Conservation Financing Authority (CPA) (June 2002), PULSE program, http://www.capowerauthority.ca.gov/financing/PULSE.htm.

California Department of Finance (2002) *Statistical Abstract.* Sacramento, Department of Finance.

California Department of Finance, Demographic R.U. (2002) *Population Projections by County.* Sacramento, Department of Finance.

California Energy Commission (CEC) (2003–2004) Natural Gas Working Group: Liquefied Natural Gas Team, monthly reports, Sacramento, CA.

California Energy Commission (CEC) (December 2003) Integrated Energy Resource Plan.

California Energy Commission (CEC) (September 2003) Climate Change and California. From Integrated energy Policy Report Proceeding. (02-IEP-01) #100-03-17D. Sacramento, CA.

California Energy Commission (January 2003) Distributed Generation Strategic Plan (Final Report), Electronic at: http://www.energy.ca.gov/distgen/strategic/strategic_plan.html

California Energy Commission (CEC) (February 2002) Summer 2001 conservation report, Sacramento, CA.

California Energy Commission (CEC) (2002) Renewable Energy Program, Annual Project Activity Report to the Legislature (pub # 500-02-068) and Report Appendix, (pub # 500-02-068A) http://www.energy.ca.gov/reports/index.html.

California Energy Commission (June 2001) Investing in California. Sacramento, CA.

California Energy Commission (2001) Future Energy Plans for California Report, Sacramento, CA.

California Energy Commission (September 2001) Natural Gas Infrastructure Issues: Committee Revised Final Report, Sacramento, CA, pp. 1–122.

California Energy Commission (2000) *Guidebook for Combined Heat and Power.* P700-00-011. Sacramento, California Energy Commission.

California Energy Commission (2000) *The Role of Energy Efficiency and Distributed Generation in Grid Planning.* Sacramento, State of California, Report P300 00 003.

California Energy Commission (CEC) (1994) Bi-annual Electricity Report. Sacramento, CA.

California Fuel Cell Partnership (CFCP) (2003) Annual Reports, Data, Information and Web Site, Sacramento, CA. www.fuelcellpartnership.org.

California Fuel Cell Partnership (CFCP) (December, 2001) Bringing Fuel Cell Vehicles to Market. Sacramento, CA. www.cafcp.org/recent_event.html.

California Fuel Cell Partnership (CFCP) (Summer 2003) Hydrogen Programs. Sacramento, CA. www.cafcp.org.

California Independent System Operator (CAISO) (2002) (March 28, 2002) Intermittent Resources Report. Folsom, CA. Website: http://www.caiso.com/docs/2002/02/01/200202011116576547.html.

California Independent System Operator (CAISO), Report Series from Intermittent resources working group, board resolution on imbalance rules, consensus proposal and tariff revision filing, and wind generation forecasting (January 2002). Tariff reform for Intermittent Energy Resources (wind and solar) before the Federal Energy Regulatory Commission (FERC) which accepted the reform on 28 March 02 and is listed on: http://www.caiso.com/docs/2002/02/01/200202011116576547.html.

California Interagency Green Accounting Working Group (IGAWG) (March 2002) A Five Year Energy Efficiency and Renewable Investment Plant for Public Buildings, Governor's Office of Planning and Research, Sacramento, CA.

California Lawyer (October 2001) In the next year California wants to build as many as 50 new power plants. Not if residents of San Francisco's Potrero Hill get their way, pp. 29–33.

California Public Utilities Commission (CPUC) (2002) Rebate Program for on-site power generation, San Francisco, CA. The CPUC program provides $4.5 per peak watt (or 50%, whichever is less) for photovoltaic systems between 30 kW and 1 MW. For more information contact John Galloway (jhg@cpuc.ca.gov).

California Public Utilities Commission (2002) *Report on Wholesale Electric Generation Investigation*. San Francisco, CPUC.

California Public Utilities Commission (CPUC) (September 1999) Definition of distributed generation, Decision #99-10-065.

California Stationary Fuel Cell Collaborative (CSFCC) (2002) Governor's Office of Research and Planning; California Air Resources Board and the University of California, Irvine. National Center for Fuel Cells Sacramento, CA. www.stationary fuelcells.org.

California Stationary Fuel Cell Collaborative, (August 28, 2002) Mission Statement.

CalPirg June (2002) Renewables Work: Job growth from Renewable Energy Development in California. Sacramento, CA.

Cantwell, J. and Barrera, P. (1996) The localization of technological development in firms with inter-company cooperation, Evidence of the inter-war cartels. *Economics of Innovation and New Technology*.

Caporaso, James A. and David P. Levine (1992) *Theories of Political Economy*. Cambridge Un. Press, Cambridge

Casazza, J.A. (2001). Electricity choice, pick your poison. *Public Utilities Fortnightly* 139(5): 42–49.

Casson, M. (1996) Economics and anthropology—reluctant partners. *Human Relations* 49(9): 1151–1180.

Casper, Kristin and Ross, J.R. (2003) Greenpeace, Program Data, San Francisco, CA.

Castells, Manuel and Peter Hall (1994) Technopoles of the world, the making of 21st century industrial complexes. Routledge, London and NY.

Casti, J.L. (1994) *Complexification*. New York, Harper.

Cavanagh, Ralph (March 5, 2001) Revisiting 'the genius of the marketplace': Cures for the Western electricity and natural gas crisis, unpublished paper, Natural Resource Defense Council, San Francisco, CA.

Cavazos, R.J. and Buss, T.F. (2003) Electric industry restructuring: An overview of Policy Issues. *Review of Policy Research* 20(2): 203–217.

Chapman, R.N. (September 1996) Hybrid power technology for remote military facilities. Power Quality Solutions/Alternative Energy Proceedings, pp. 415–427.

Christopher Coburn (ed.) and Dan Berglund (1995) Partnerships: A compendium of state and federal cooperative technology programs. Battelle Memorial Institute, Battelle Press.

Chomsky, N. (1957) *Syntactic Structures*. The Hague, Mouton and Co.

Chomsky, N. (1966) *Cartesian Linguistics*. NY, Harper & Row.

Chomsky, N. (1968) *Language and Mind*. Berkeley, Un. of Calif. Press.

Chomsky, N. (1980) *Rules and Representations*. NY, Columbia Un. Press.

Chomsky, Noam (1988) *Language and Problems of Knowledge*. Boston, MA, MIT Press.

Chomsky, N. (November 1997) Market democracy in a neo-liberal order: doctrines and reality, Z-Magazine (electronic version).

Chomsky, N. (1998) Free Market Fantasies: Capitalism in the Real World. AK Press, CD Audio, San Francisco, California.

Cicourel, A.V. (1974) *Cognitive Sociology*. NY, Free Press.

Clark, Woodrow W. (2004) Distributed generation public policy. Energy Policy, London, UK, Elsevier, Fall 2004.

Clark, Woodrow W. (2004) Qualitative Economics to be published in 2004.

Clark, Woodrow W. (August 2004) The California Hydrogen Economy: meeting summary and CD presentation data, Hydrogen Forum, Los Angeles, CA.

Clark, Woodrow W., William Isherwood, Ray Smith, Salvador Aceves and Gene Berry (2004) Distributed generation: remote power systems with advanced technologies. Energy Policy, Elsevier, London, UK, Fall 2004.

Clark, Woodrow W. (2003–2004) Personal communications with Major AutoMakers and Oil-Gas Companies, not published or confidential.

Clark, Woodrow W. and Istemi Demrig (2003) Journal of Corporate Governance.

Clark, Woodrow W. and Michael Fast, *Interactionism: Toward a Science of Business and Economics*. London, UK, Inderscience Press, forthcoming fall 2004.

Clark, Woodrow W., Todd Feinberg *et al.* (January 2003) California's next economy. Governor's Office of Planning and Research.

Clark, Woodrow. (fall, 2003) W. Distributed Generation Public Policy. Energy Policy, London, UK, Elsevier.

Clark, Woodrow W. II and Xing Li (Fall 2003) Social Capitalism: an economic paradigm for the transfer and commercialization of technology. *International Journal of Technology Transfer and Commercialisation*, Vol. No., electronic.

Clark, Woodrow W., Lund, T. Atwood and Jenkins, B. (eds.) (2003) Energy and Environmental Planning: toward a more sustainable world. To be published by Elsevier Press.

Clark, Woodrow W. and Arnie Sowell (Nov 2002) Standard Practices Manual: life cycle analysis for project/program finance. International Journal of Revenue Management, London, UK, Interscience Press.

Clark, Woodrow W. (2002) Greening Technology. International Journal of Environmental Innovation Management, Interscience, London, UK.

Clark, Woodrow W. (2002) Entrepreneurship in the commercialization of environmentally sound technologies: the American experience in developing nations, in John Kuada (ed.), *Culture and Technological Transformation in the South: Transfer or Local Development*. Denmark, Samfundslitteratur Press, Copenhagen.

Clark, Woodrow W. (Nov 2002) The California Challenge, energy and environmental consequences for public utilities. Utilities Policy, Elsevier, UK.

Clark, Woodrow W., Andrea Kune, Todd Feinberg and Adam Kaplan (October 2003) Sustainable environmentally sound technologies (EST); the role of public policy, California Labor and Workforce Development Agency, unpublished.

Clark, Woodrow W. and Gregg Morris (Dec 2002) Public–Private Partnerships: the case of intermittent resources. Energy Policy, Elsevier.

Clark, W.W. and Morris, G. (August 2002) Policy making and implementation process: the case of intermittent power. International Energy Electrical Engineers (IEEE). http://grouper.ieee.org/groups/scc21/1547/index.html.

Clark, Woodrow W. and Dan Jensen, J. (2002) Capitalisation of Environmental Technologies in Companies: economic schemes in a business perspective. *International Journal of Energy Technology and Policy,* Vol. 1, Nos. 1/2. Interscience, London, UK.

Clark, Woodrow W. and Emilio Paolucci (Dec 2002) Fuel cells in the energy sector, from R&D to commercialization. *Journal of Clean Production.* Special Issue.

Clark, Woodrow W. and Istemi Demirag (Dec 2002) Corporate Governance: the Enron fiasco in America, Special Issue. *Journal of Corporate Governance.*

Clark, Woodrow W. and Jensen, J.D. (2001) The role of government in privatization: an economic model for Denmark. *International Journal of Technology Management* 21(5/6).

Clark, Woodrow W. and Henrik Lund (2001) Civic Markets: the case of the California energy crisis. International Journal of Global Energy Issues, Inderscience, London, UK.

Clark, Woodrow W. and Jensen, J.D. (2001) The role of government in privatization: an economic model for Denmark *International Journal of Technology Management* 21(5/6).

Clark, Woodrow W. and Olav Jull Sorensen (Dec 2001) Entrepeneurship, theoretical considerations. International Journal of Entrepreneurship. UK, Interscience Press.

Clark, Woodrow W. (2000) Developing and Diffusing clean Technologies: experience and practical issues, OECD Conference, Seoul, Korea.

Clark, Woodrow W. and Jensen, J.D. (Nov 2000) Public Partnerships: privatization in the public sector. *Journal of International Management* 540–568.

Clark, Woodrow, W. and RaeKwon Chung (Co-Directors) (Nov 2000) Transfer of Publicly funded R&D programs in the field of climate change for environmentally sound technologies (ESTs). From Developed to Developing Countries: A summary of six country studies. Framework Convention for Climate Change, United Nations.

Clark, Woodrow W. and Henrik Lund (1999) Energy and environmental planning. unpublished edited volume of papers from two international conferences. Aalborg, Denmark, 1998 and Sacramento, CA.

Clark, Woodrow W. and Emilio Paolucci (Nov 2000) Commercial development of Environmental Technologies for the Automobile. *International Journal of Technology Management.*

Clark, Woodrow W. (1997) Transfer of Publicly Funded R&D Programs in the field of Climate Change for Environmentally Sounds Technologies (ESTs): From Developed to Developing Countries—A summary of six country studies, UN Framework Convention for Climate Change.

Clark, Woodrow W. and Emilio Paolucci (1997) Environmental Regulation and Product Development: issues for a new model of innovation. *Journal of International Product Development Management.*

Clark, Woodrow W. and Joyce Jensch (1995) Turning Swords into Plowshares: Lawrence Livermore National Lab. *Channels.* Vol. 8, No. 6. SEMI Publication, Mountain View, CA, pp. 14–15.

Clark, Woodrow W. (Fall 1994). Defense Conversion: Lessons from the American and European Cases. *Journal of Business and Industrial Marketing,* Vol. 9, No. 4. England, MCB, University Press, pp. 54–68.

References 469

Clark, Woodrow W. and Dan Jensen, J. (1994). The IO fund: international alliances for developing SMEs. Paper on the Danish Government Fund for business development in transitional economies.

Clark, Woodrow W. (Fall 1993). Revitalization of Silicon Valley. *Technology Transfer Magazine*, Washington DC, pp. 20–28.

Clemmer, Steven, Deborah Donovan, Alan Nogee, and Jeff Deyette (2001) *Clean Energy Blueprint: A Smarter National Energy Policy for Today and the Future.* Union of Concerned Scientists with American Council for an Energy-Efficient Economy, Tellus Institute, Cambridge, MA, pp. 1–39.

Coase, R.H. (1987) The Nature of the firm. *Economica* 4(Nov): 386–405.

Coase, R.H. (1988) *The Firm, the Market, and the Law.* Chicago, Un. of Chicago Press.

Coase, R.H. (1993) The Nature of the firm: influence, in Williamson, Oliver E. and Sidney G. Winter (eds.), *The Nature of the Firm: Origins, Evolution, and Development.* Oxford Un. Press.

Collins, James C. and Jerry Porras (1994) *Built to Last.* Successful habits of Visionary Companies. NY, HarperBusiness.

Congressional Budget Office (CBO) (September 01) Causes and lessons of the California electricity crisis.

Congressional Budget Office, Summary "The California Energy Debacle, A Perspective on the Lessons Learned." Metro Investment Report, Los Angeles, CA, 2001, p. 4, 8 and 15.

Congressional Research Service (CRS) (May 6, 1997) #85031: Technology Transfer: Use of federally funded research and development, Committee for the National Institute for the Environment, Washington DC, pp. 1–13.

Cooper, John F., Dennis Fleming, Douglas Hargrove, Ronald Koopman and Keith Peterman (1995), A refuelable zinc/air battery for fleet electric vehicle propulsion. Paper presented to SAE Future Transportation Technology Conference and Exposition in Costa Mesa CA; Lawrence Livermore National Laboratory, Livermore, CA, August 7–10.

Cooper, John F. and Woodrow, W. Clark Jr. (1996) Zinc Air Fuel Cell: an alternative to clean fuels in fleet electric vehicle applications. *International Journal of Environmentally Conscious Design and Manufacturing* 5(3–4): 49–54.

Corbett, Judy and Corbett (October 1995). *Village Homes.* Council of Economic Advisors, Supporting Research and Development to promote economic growth: the Federal Government's Role. Washington DC, pp. 1–16.

Courtney, H. (2001) *20/20 Foresight; Crafting Strategy in an Uncertain World.* Boston, Harvard Business School Press.

Courtney, H. (2001) *20/20 Hindsight: Crafting Strategy in an Uncertain World.* Cambridge, Harvard Business School Press.

Crew, M.A. (1989) *Deregulation and Diversification of Utilites.* Boston, Kluwer Academic Publishers.

Crow, R.T. (2002) What works and what does not in restructuring electricity markets. *Business Economics* 41–56.

Cruver, Brian (2002) *Anatomy of Greed.* New York, Carroll and Graf Publishers.

Dalton, Donald H. and Manuel G. Serapio Jr. (1995) Globalizing industrial research and development. Washington DC, Office of Technology Policy, US Dept. of Commerce, pp. 1–87.

Dalton, M. (1950) Conflict between staff and line managerial officers. Reprinted in A. Etzioni (ed.), *A Sociological Reader on Complex Organizations.* pp. 266–274.

Darmstadter, J. (2002) Whistling in the wind; toward a realistic pursuit of renewable energy. *Brookings Review* 20(2): 36–39.

Danish Innovation Centre (January 1994) Innovative entrepreneurs: Experiences from the scholarship scheme. Taastrup, DK, Danish Technological Institute, pp. 1–36.

Demirag, Istemi, Clark, Woodrow W. and Dennis Bline (1998) Financial Markets, Corporate Governance and Management of Research and Development: Reflections on US Managers' Perspectives, in I. Demirag, *Corporate Governance, Accountability and Pressures to Perform: An International Study.* Oxford, UK Oxford Un. Press.

Dickerson, M. (April 2001) Tennessee using California power crisis as recruiting beacon. *Los Angeles Times*, 1.

Dorf, R.C. (1982) *The Energy Answer, 1982–2000.* Andover, MA: Brick House Publishing Co.

Dcouglas, J. (ed.) (1970) *Understanding Everyday Life.* Chicago, Aldine.

Dowlatabadi, Hadi and Michael A. Toman (1991) *Technology Options for Electricity Generation.* Washington DC, Resources for the Future.

Drucker, Peter (1993) *Post-Capitalist Society.* Oxford, UK, Butterworth-Heinemann, Ltd.

Dubash, Navroz K. and Sudhir C. Rajan (2001) Power politics: process of power sector reform in India. *Economic and Political Weekly* 3367–3390.

Dunn, J. (2002). Eye of the Hurricane: California's Energy Crisis: An Interview with Senator Joseph Dunn. *Verdict* 8(4): 3–29.

Economist (2002) The ship that sank quietly, February 16, pp. 57–58.

Economist (February–March, 2002) RE Enron.

Economist (March 23, 2002) It's good for you: energy liberalization. pp. 13–14.

Economist (March 4, 2002) Social Science comes of age. pp. 42–43.

Economist (January 19, 2002) The Real Scandal.

Economist (August 17, 2002) Economics Focus: the fruits of fieldwork. p. 60.

Economist (December 6, 2001) The Amazing disintegrating firm.

Economist (July 01) How to keep the Fans turning.

Economist (August 2001) California Economy, the real trouble. Electronic version.

Economist (September 01) Economic Man, cleaner planet. Electronic version.

Economist (October 25, 1997) Science and Technology Section: At last, the fuel cell. London, UK, pp. 89–92.

Economist (September 20, 1997) Editorial: The visible hand. p. 17.

Economist (August 23, 1997) The puzzling failure of economics. p. 11.

Editorial. San Francisco Business Times, Vol. #10, No. #20, January 5–11, 1996, p. 33.

Electric Power Research Institute (EPRI) (November 2001) California Renewable Technology Market and Benefits Assessment, Final Report to the California Energy Commission.

Ellis, Virginia and Nancy Vogel (September 30, 2001) 8 State Power contracts seen as Bad Deals. Los Angeles, Times, pp. 1 and 14.

Energy Info Source, Green Power Tags Report, 2003, electronically.

Envirogen Inc. (1996) Annual Report. Princeton Research Center. 4100 Quakerbridge Road, Lawrenceville, NJ. 1997. Environmental Company of the Year (November 1996).

Environmental Protection Agency (February 1997) Environmental technology Verification Program: Verification Strategy. EPA. Office of Research & Development. Washington DC, pp. 1–18.

Environmental Goals and Policy Report (EGPR) (November, 2003) Governor's Office of Planning and Research, Sacramento, CA. Available on Local Government Commission Web Site; www.localgovernment.org.

Esselman, Walter H., Jack M. Hollander and Thomas R. Schneider (February 15–17, 1994) The Electricity-Society Connection: A Forum of the Electric Power Research Institute. Carmel, CA.

Etzioni, A. (ed.) (1964) *A Sociological Reader on Complex Organizations*. N.Y., Holt, Rinehart & Winston.

Etzkowitz Henry (August 14–21, 1994) The Triple Helix: A North American Innovation Environment, NAFTA Conference, British Columbia, Canada, pp. 1–22.

European Commission (1997) *Energy for the Future: Renewable Sources of Energy*. Report COM (97)599 Final ed.

Faruqui, Ahmed, Hung-po Chao, Vic Niemeyer, Jeremy Platt and Karl Stahlkopf (2001) California syndrome. *Power Economics* 24–27; (2001) Getting out of the dark. *Regulation* 58–62.

Federal Energy Regulatory Commission (FERC) (March 28, 2002) California Independent System Operators, Intermittent Resources Ruling. Docket Nos. ER02-922-000 and EL02-51-000 <htttp://cips.ferc.fed.us/cips/default.htm>.

Ferguson, R. Wilkinson, W. and Hill, R. (2000) Electricity use and economic development. *Energy Policy* 28: 923–934.

Fisher, Jolanka V. and Timothy P. Duane (2001) *Trends in Electricity Consumption, Peak Demand and Generating Capacity in California and the Western Grid, 1977–2000*. Program on Workable Energy Regulation Working Paper PWP 085 ed. Berkeley, University of California, Energy Institute.

Fitzgerald, Garrett, Mark Bolinger and Ryan Wiser (September 2003) Green Buildings: the expanding role of State Clean Energy Funds. Lawrence Berkeley National Laboratory, US Department of Energy, pp. 1–11.

Flavin, Christopher and Nicholas Lenssen (1994) *Power Surge: Guide to the Coming Energy Revolution*. New York, W. W. Norton.

Fortune, The Letter to Ken Lay, (January 16, 2002).

Freeman, Christopher and Carlota Perez (1989) Structural Crisis of adjustment, business cycles and investment behaviour. in Giovanni Dosi, Christopher Freeman, Richard Nelson, Gerald Silverberg and Luc Soete (eds.), *Technological Change and Economic Theory*. Pinters Publ., London, pp. 38–66.

Freeman, C. and Hagedoorn, J. (1995) Convergence and divergence in the interantonalizaton of technology, in J. Hagedoorn (ed.), *Technical Change and the World Economy: Convergence and Divergence in technology Strategies*. UK, Edward Elgar, Aldershot.

Friedman, Thomas L. (2000) The Lexus and the Olive Tree. Anchor Books. New York, NY.

Fry, Paul R. (1996) The Record of Community-Owned Electric Utilities. *Competition and Restrucuring in the Electric Utility Industry*. American Public Power Association, Washington DC, APPA.

Fusaro, Peter C. and Ross, M. Miller (2002) *What Went Wrong at Enron*. Hoboken, NJ, John Wiley and Sons.

Garbesi, Karina and Alan Ramo (2002) *Electricity Industry Deregulation in California: The Erosion of Public Goods*. Hayward, California, Department of Geography, California State University.

Garvin, Cosmo (2003) Hydrogen Now. Sacramento, Sacramento News & Review, April, 17. Front page plus.

Gates, Robert (2001–2002) Personal discussions. GE Wind.

Gavin, Robert (September 17, 2001) Think Small: distributed generation may be the key to making deregulation work. *The Wall Street Journal* 17–18.

Gechill, Lynda (October 24, 2003) Davis energy expert resigns before new governor forces him out, San Francisco Chronicle, pp. 1+.

Geddes, David (Summer 1993) Economic Development in the 1990s: Toward a Sustainable Future. *Economic Development Review* 71–74.

Gehl, Steven (2004) Energy Roadmap for the Future, five year strategies. Energy Producers Research Institute (EPRI), Palo Alto, CA.

Geller, Howard (2003) *Energy Revolution: Policies for a Sustainable Future.* Covelo Island Press.

Geller, Howard and Goldstein, D.B. (1998) *Equipment Efficiency Standards: Mitigating Global Change at a Profit.* Washington DC, American council for an energy efficient economy.

General Accounting Office (2002) *California Market Design Enabled Exercise of Market Power.* Washington DC, US General Accounting Office.

General Electric (GE) Wind, Tehachapi, California, 2004. (http://www.gepower.com/corporate/en_us/aboutgeps/2003releases/022703.pdf), http://www.gepower.com/dhtml/wind/en_us/index.jsp

Gibson, Rowan (ed.) *Rethinking the Future*: rethinking business, principles, competition, control and complexity, leadership, markets and the world. London, Nicholas Brealey.

Giddens, Anthony (1998) *The Third Way.* London, UK, Polity Press.

Gilbert, Richard J. and David M. Newbery (1994) The dynamic efficiency of regulatory constitutions. *Rand Journal of Economics* 25(4): 538–554.

Givoni, Baruch (1972) Alternatives to Compressor Cooling in California Transitional Climates. *Program of the 1994 Annual Conference, Institute for Energy Efficiency.*

Global Change Research (1999) Our Changing Plant: An investment in Science for the Nation's Future. The FY 1999 US Global Change Research Program, Washington, DC, US Government Printing Office.

Goldman, C.A., Eto, J.H. and Barbose, G.L. (2002) *California Customer Load Reductions During the Electricity Crisis.* Berleley, Environmental Energy Technologies Division, Lawrence Berkeley Laboratory.

Gore, Albert (1993) Technology for a Sustainable Future: A Framework for Action. Washington, DC, US Government.

Gotch, Mike and Elvia Diaz (revised from 1998) How often do governors say 'No', Non-confidential internal working document, October 2001, pp. 1–5.

Governor Gray Davis (January 9, 2001) State of the state. Sacramento, CA.

Governor Gray Davis (January 8, 2002) State of the state Sacramento, CA.

Governor Gray Davis (September 2003a) Office of Planning & Research (OPR). Environmental Justice Report, www.lgc.org.

Governor Gray Davis (September 2003b) Office of Planning & Research (OPR). LifeSciences Regional Strategic Plans, San Francisco, Los Angeles, San Diego, and Statewide. Sacramento, CA, www.monitorgroup.com. Governor Gray Davis Office of Planning & Research (OPR). Energy and Environmental Programs and Policies. September 2002. http://test-www.opr.ca.gov/redesign/energy/RenewableEnergy.html. Revised and published, 2003c at website: www.lgc.org.

Governor Gray Davis, The One Stop Shop for the State of California funds for Renewable and Energy Efficiency Programs. Updated (last 2001) www.governor.ca.gov.

Governor Gray Davis (January 9, 2001) State of the state. Sacramento.

Governor Gray Davis (September 21, 2001) California Power Plant Pollution down 25 Percent, Press release, pp. 1–2.

Governor Gray Davis (January 24, 2002a) How California Got into the Energy Crisis, Talking Points, pp. 1–3.

Governor Gray Davis (January 31, 2002b) Press Release, Letter to FERC Chairman Wood.

Governor Gray Davis (January 31, 2002c) *Talking Points.* Sacramento, Ca.

Governor Gray Davis (January 31, 2002d) Governor Davis calls for Federal Investigation of Enron's role on California Energy Crisis.

Governor Gray Davis, Climate Change Legislation (Greenhouse Gas)—Pavley Bill AB #1493 Signed by Governor Davis, 22 July 2002e, http://www.leginfo.ca.gov/bilinfo.html.

Governor Gray Davis (March 18, 2002e) Support for Renewable Energy, Press Release, Potrero Hill Neighborhood Community House, SF.

Governor Gray Davis (April 2002f) Renewable Portfolio Standard. Press Release and news conference in San Francisco.

Governor Pete Wilson (September 23, 1996) Press Release, Energy Deregulation, Governor's Office, Sacramento, CA.

Governor Arnold Schwarzenegger (2004) State of the State. Sacramento, CA.

Governor's Web Site (1993) Special Finance Assistance for Energy Efficiency and Renewable Programs. Sacramento, CA, August 2001–2002. Website: http://www.governor.ca.gov.

CGraedel, T.E. and Allenby, B.R. (1995). *Industrial Ecology.* Englewood Cliffs, NJ,

Prentice Hall.

Grandy, Doug *et al.* (Lead Editor) (July 2002) Renewable Energy Strategic Investment Plan, Governor's Office of Planning and Research, Interagency Working Group, Sacramento, CA.

Greene, Andrew (July 1, 2002) What Color is Your Electricity: What Color is Energy Age? Public Utilities, Fortnightly, Navigant, Burlington, MA, pp. 1–12.

Griffin, K. (2001) *California's Current Electricity Situation.* Sacramento, California Energy Commission.

Griliches, Z. (1990) Patent statistics as economic indicators. *Journal of Economic Literature* 28: 1661–1707.

Grindley, P. Mowery, D.C. and Silverman, B. (1994) SEMATECH and collaborative research: lessons in the design of high-tech consortia. *Journal of Policy Analysis and Management* 13(4): 723–758.

Gulati, R. (1995a) Does familiarity breed trust? The implications of repeated ties for contractual choice in alliances. *Academy of Management Journal* 38(1): 85–112.

Gulati, R. (1995b) Social structure and alliance formation patterns: a longitudinal analysis. *Administrative Science Quarterly* 40: 619–652.

Gullestrup, H. (August 1994) Evaluating Social Consequences of Social Change in the Third World Countries. Development Research Series, Working Paper No. 30, Department of Development and Planning, Aalborg University, Aalborg, DK.

Hakansson, Hakan and Ivan Snehota (March 1995) Developing Relationships in Business Networks. Sweden, University of Uppsala.

Hakansson, Hakan (April 1994) Lecture, Network theory. Aalborg, Denmark, Aalborg University Center.

Hampton, H. (2003) *Public Power: The Fight for Publicly Owned Power.* Toronto, Insomniac Press.

HarvardWatch (May 21, 2002) Deregulation deception: Harvard, Enron, and the Alliance to Deregulate Electricity markets in California and Beyond. Cambridge, MA, pp. 1–25. <http://www.harvardwatch.org/>

Hawken, Paul, Amory Lovins, and Lovins, L.H. (1999). *Natural Capitalism: Creating the Next Industrial Revolution.* Boston, Little Brown and Co.

Hawken, P., Lovins, A. and Lovins, L.H. (1999). *Natural Capitalism: Creating the Next Industrial Revolution.* Boston, Little Brown and Co.

Hawkins, David (2003) California Wind Generation Program, California Independent Systems Operator. Folsom, CA. unpublished paper.

Hayek, F. von (1942–1943), Scientism and the study of society. *Economica* 8–11.

Heaton, George R., R. Darryl Banks, Daryl W. Ditz (1994) Missing Links: Technology and Environmental Improvement in the Industrializing World. Washington, DC, World Resources Institute, pp. 1–54.

Hebert, Josef (June 16, 2003), *Role of Fossil Fuels, Nuclear Power Complicate Talks on Hydrogen's Future.* Associated Press, Boston Globe, electronic.

Heilbroner, Robert (1989) *The Making of Economic Society,* revised for the 1990s. London, UK, Prentice-Hall International.

Heiman, Michael (2002) *Renewable Energy Under Deregulation: A View From the States.* Carlisle, PA, Envirnomental Studies Dept, Dickinson College.

Henton, Doug (December 2001) Next Silicon Valley: Riding the Waves of Innovation. Silicon Valley Network, Palo Alto, CA.

Henton, Douglas (1999) Civic Entrepeneurs.

Henton, Doug and Kim Walesh (April 1998) Linking the New Economy to the Livable Community. Irvine Foundation, Irvine, CA, pp. 1–29.cc

Hexeberg, Ivan (May 23, 2003) Key barriers and challenges for a change to hydrogen— Norsk Hydro, Norway. EU Hydrogen Roundtable, Brussels.

Hicks, Kathleen H. and Stephen Daggett (March 6, 1996) DOD Environmental Programs: Background and Issues for Congress, Congressional Research Service, Committee for the National Institute for the Environment, Washington DC, pp. 1–29.

Hoffman, Peter (2002) *Tomorrow's Energy; Hydrogen, Fuel Cells, and the Prospects for a Cleaner Planet.* Cambridge, MIT Press.

Hofrichter, Richard (2000) *Reclaiming the Environmental Debate.* Cambridge, MIT Press.

Hogan, William W. (1992) Contract Networks for Electric Power Transmission. *Journal of Regulatory Economics* 4: 221–242.

Hohensmser, Christoph, Robert L. Goble and Paul Slovic (1992) Nuclear power, in Jack M. Hollander (ed.), *The Energy-Environment Connection.* Covelo, CA, Island Press, pp. 133–75.

Holdren, John P. (1992) Energy Agenda for the 1990s, in Jack M. Hollander (ed.), *The Energy-Environment Connection.* Covolo CA, Island Press, pp. 378–391.

Holland, J.H. (1992) *Adaptation in Natural and Artificial Systems.* Cambridge, MA, MIT Press.

Hollander, Jack M. and Thomas, R. Schneider (April 17, 1995) Energy Efficiency, How Far, How Fast? Palo Alto, CA, EPRI, pp. 1–45

Hughes, Thomas (1983) *Networks of Power: Electrification in Western Society, 1880–1930.* Baltimore, Johns Hopkins University Press.

Hunt, Sally and Graham Shuttleworth (1996) *Competition and Choice in Electricity.* New York, John Wiley.

Hunt, S. (2002) *Making Competition Work in Electricity.* New York, Wiley.

Hvelplund, Frede (1999a) Political and economic liberalisation and renewable energy— Price or quota markets? The Danish wind power example. unpublished paper, Aalborg University, Denmark, First International Conference on Energy and Environmental Planning.

Hvelplund, Frede (1999b) Technological Change and Public Regulation at the Energy Scene. unpublished paper, Aalborg University, Denmark, First International Conference on Energy and Environmental Planning.

Hvelplund, Frede (1997) Energy Efficiency and the Political Economy of the Danish Electricity System, in Atle Midttun (ed.), *European Electricity Systems in Transition.* Oxford, Elsevier, pp. 133–166.

Hwang, David (February 2002) UC Initiative of High Energy Density Storage Systems for leveling of power usage demands in California. Collaborative Proposal from Engineering Colleges of the University of California.

Interagency Renewable Energy (grid connected) Finance Working Group (IREF), Renewable Energy Finance Plan. Unofficial/internal State of California, Sacramento, CA, Draft September 2002.

International Energy Agency (September 21, 2002) Energy and Poverty, Chapter #13, World Energy Outlook 2002, Ministerial Meeting, Osaka, Japan.

Isherwood, William (1998) Distributed Power Options for remote Sites. University of California, Lawrence Livermore National Laboratory, unpublished paper.

Isherwood, William, J. Ray Smith, Salvador Aceves, Gene Berry and Woodrow W. Clark, II with Ronald Johnson, Deben Das, Douglas Goering and Richard Seifert (Fall 2000) Economic Impact on Remote Village Energy Systems of Advanced Technologies. University of Calif., Lawrence Livermore National Laboratory, UCRL-ID-129289, January 1998. Published in Energy Policy.

Jawetz, Placus *et al.* (2003) Renewable Energy Technology Diffusion. Final Report. San Francisco, CA, pp. 1–32.

Jenkins, Bryan M. (September 20, 2002) A resource replacement strategy in the context of sustainability and energy, the cost of oxygen and the intrinsic rationalization of fuel taxes. Draft paper from University of California, Davis.

Johnson, R.J. and Scicchitano, M.J. (2000) Uncertainty, Risk, Trust, and Information: Public Perceptions of Environmental Issues and Willlingness to Take Action. *Policy Studies Journal* 28(3): 633–647.

Joskow, Paul (2000) *Deregulation of Network Utilities, What's Next?* Peltzman and Winston.

Joskow, Paul L. (1996) Introducing competition into regulated network industries, from hierarchies to markets in electricity. *Industrial and Corporate Change* 5(2): 341–382.

Joskow, Paul L. and Richard Schmalensee (1983). *Markets for Power: An Analysis of Electric Utility Deregulation*. Cambridge, MIT Press.

Kammen, Daniel and Timothy Lipman (June 16, 2003) Letter to the Editor, Science, RE: Tromp *et al.* On Potential Environmental Impact of a Hydrogen Economy on the Stratosphere, to be published in fall 2004.

Kapner, Suzanne (August 29, 2002) British Reopening the Debate over Privatization. NY, NY, NY Times, p. 1+

Katz, M.E. and Ordover, J.A. (1990) R&D cooperation and competition. *Brookings Papers on Economic Activity.* pp. 137–203.

Kenidi, Ron (April 2003) Personal communications. Huntington Beach, CA.

Krugman, P. (2003) *The Great Unraveling.* New York, W. W. Norton and Co.

Kuhn, T. (1970 (1962)) *The Structure of Scientific Revolution.* Chicago, University of Chicago Press.

Kuttner, Robert (March 25, 2002) The Road to Enron: The American Prospect, Vol. 13, No. 6.

Kuttner, Robert, The Enron Economy. The American Prospect, Vol. 13, No. 1, January 1–14, 2001.

Kuttner, Robert (April 15, 2002) Where's the outrage?: the unfortunate dwindling of the Enron scandal. The American Prospect.

Kwoka Jr., John, E. (1996) Public Versus Private Ownership of Electric Utilities: A Comparison of Price Performance. *Competition and Restructuring in the Electric Utility Industry,* ed American Public Power Association. Washington DC, APPA.

Lagier, Christian (May 2003) Overcoming the technical challenges of hybrid systems: commercial examples. Distributed Generation Annual Conference, San Diego, CA.

Lakoff, G. (1970a) Linguistics and natural language. *Synthese* 22: 151–271.

Lakoff, G. (1970b) Global rules. *Language* 46, 3 (Sept.): 627–639.

Lamont, Alan (1999) Equilibrium Modeling Applied to Market Penetration and Systems Operations. unpublished paper, Aalborg University, Denmark, First International Conference on Energy & Environmental Planning.

Lamont, Alan and Clark, W.W. Jr. (August 1997) The LLNL China Energy Model, Paper presented at USDOE Conference on Energy Models and Systems, Washington, DC (published, 2001).

Lamont, Alan and Gene Berry (1999) Coupling Carbonless Utilities And Hydrogen Transportation, unpublished paper, Aalborg University, Denmark, First International Conference on Energy & Environmental Planning.

Landau, M. (1969) Redundancy, Rationality and Problems of Duplication and Overlap. *Public Administration Review* 29(4): 346–358.

LaPorte, T. (ed.) (1991) Responding to large technical systems: control or anticipation. Boston, Kluwer academic publishers.

Lash, Jonathan and David T. Buzzelli (March 1997) The Road to Sustainable Development: A snapshot of activities in the United States, President's Council on Sustainable Development, pp. 1–50.

Lawrence Livermore National Laboratory (February 2002) High Performance Solid Oxide Fuel Cells for clean efficient power generation. USDOE Contract Number # W-7405-ENG-48. Livermore, CA.

Lehmann, Peter, C.E. Chamberlin, G.S. Chapman, N.T. Coleman, R.A. Engle, D.A. McKay, M.W. Marshall, A.M. Reis and J.I. Zoellick (2000) Field Testing of a PEM Fuel Cell in an Integrated Power System, Schartz Research Center, Humboldt State University, Arcata, CA.

Lenneberg, E. (1970) *Biological Foundations of Language.* The Hague, Mouton and Co.

Lior, Norm (2001) What went wrong in California's electricity market. *Energy* 26: 747–758.

Lloyd, Alan (March 5, 2003) Chair of California Air Resources Board and CA Fuel Cell Partnership, The Path to a Hydrogen Economy, Testimony to Committee of US House of Representatives, Washington, DC.

Loomis, Carol J., … (April 15, 2002) And the Revenue Games People (like Enron) Play: got energy trading contracts. Fortune, pp. 190–191.

Lovins, Amory B. (1976) Energy strategy: the road not taken. *Foreign Affairs* 65–96.

Lund, Henrik (2001) Flexible energy system data in Denmark. draft report for Danish Energy Ministry.

Lund, H. (2000) Choice Awareness: The Development of Technological and Institutional Choice in the Public Debate of Danish Energy Planning. *Journal of Environmental Policy Planning* 2: 249–259.

Lund, Henrik (1996) *Elements of a Green Energy Plan which can create job opportunities. General Workers Union in Denmark.* København, DK.

Lund, Henrik (1997) Economic Development and CO2 Reduction Policies, Proceedings of International Conference on Urban Regional Environmental Planning in an Era of Transition, Athens, Greece, pp. 570–579.

Lund, Henrik (1998) Environmental Accounts for Households: a method for improving public awareness and participation. *Local Environment* 3(1): 43–54.

Lund, Henrik and Frede Hvelplund (September 1997) Does Environmental impact assessment really support technological change? Analyzing alternative to coal-fired power stations in Denmark. *Environmental Impact Assessment Review* 17(5): 357–370.

Lund, Henrik and Woodrow W. Clark II (November 2002) Management of fluctuations in wind power and CHP: comparing two possible Danish strategies, *Energy Policy.*

Lutzenhiser, Loren (1994) Innovation and Organizational Networks; Barriers to Energy Efficiency in the US housing industry. *Energy Policy* 22(10): 867–877.

Lynch, Loretta (December 25, 2002) Energy Future, beyond the deregulation debacle. San Francisco Chronicle, electronic.

Maddox, Ed, personal discussion, SeaWest, Spring 2001.

Manifesto on the California Electricity Crisis, Institute of management, Innovation, and Organization, University of California, Berkeley, January 26, 2001.

Marcus, W.B. (2003) *Clean and Affordable Power: How Los Angeles can reach 20% renewables without raising rates*. West Sacramento, CA. West Sacramento, Environmental California research and Policy Center and The Center for Energy Efficiency & Renewable Technologies, JBS Energy, Inc.

Marcus, William and Jan Hamrin (2001) How we Got into the California Energy Crisis. (Paper given at National Renewable Laboratory, March 01). San Francisco, CA, Center for Resource Solutions.

Markels, Alex (2002) Prevailing Winds. *Mother Jones* 27(4): 38–43.

Marshall, Jonathan (May 7, 1997) Electricity Monopoly Ends Jan. 1 (1998), *San Francisco Chronicle*, Headline Story, pp. 1 and 11.

Martin, Mark (February 3, 2002) California system was easy pickings: Enron helped build market, then exploited weaknesses. San Francisco Chronicle, San Francisco, CA, p. 1.

Martin, M. (November 2001) Power glut may doom new plants. *San Francisco Chronicle* 15.

Martinot, Eric (2002) Power Sector Restructuring and Environment: Trends, Policies and GEF Experience.

Martinot, Eric, Akanksha Chjaurey, Debra Lew, Jose Moreira and Njeri Wamukonya (2002) Renewable Energy Markets in Developing Countries. *Annual Review of Energy* 27: forthcoming in 2004.

Matteson, Gary (June 2002a) Comments on The California Energy Commission on Distributed Generation Strategic Plan.

Matteson, Gary, Anna Ferrera and Michael Theoreau (August 12, 2002) Report on Distributed Generation. Renewable Energy Workshop.

Mazmanian, Daniel A. and Michael, E. Kraft (1999) *Toward Sustainable Communities*. Cambridge, MIT Press.

McClosky, Deirdre, N. (1998) *The Rhetoric of Economics* (2nd Ed.). University of Wisconsin Press.

McGraw Hill (2002) PowerWeb, Entrepreneurship, http://register.dushkin.com.

McNamera, W. (2002) *The California Energy Crisis: Lessons for a Deregulating Industry.* Tulsa, Oklahoma, PennWell Corp.

McNeill, D. and Freiberger, P. (1993) Fuzzy Logic, the discovery of a revolutionary computer technology—and how it is changing our world. New York, Simon & Schuster.

McWilliams, C. (1949) *California: The Great Exception*. New York, Current Books; Mead, G.H. Mind, Self, and Society—from the standpoint of a Social Behaviorist. The University of Chicago Press, Chicago, 1962 (1934).

Meller, Paul (June 17, 2003) Europe and US will share research on hydrogen fuel. NY Times, electronic.

Meyer, Niels (June 2000) Renewable Energy in Liberalised Energy Markets: EuroSun Conference, Copenhagen, pp. 1–10.

Mez, Lutz, Atle Midttun and Steve Thomas (1997) Restructuring Electricity Systems in Transition, in Atle Midttun (ed.), *European Electricity Systems in Transition*. Oxford, Elsevier, pp. 3–12.

Midttun, Atle (2001) *European Electricity Systems in Transition*. Oxford, Elsevier.

Moen, Jan (2002) "Transfer of Power Sector Reforms", Presentation at the United Nations Brainstorming Session on Power Sector Reform and Sustainable Development, Paris.

Mooz, W.E. *et al.* (1972) *California's Electric Quandry*. Santa Monica, Rand Corporation.

Morris, D. (2001) *Seeing the Light*. Washington DC, Institute for Local Self-Reliance.

Morris, Gregg (2003) An economic model for renewable energy investments: internal draft model for the Interagency Renewable Agency Working Group, Governor's Office of Planning and Research, State of California, unpublished. Sacramento, CA.

Mowery, D.C. and Oxley, J.E. (1995) Inward technology transfer and competitiveness: the role of national innovation systems. *Cambridge Journal of Economics* 19(1).

Mowery, D.C., Oxley, J.E. and Silverman, B.S. (1997). Technological Overlap and Interfirm Cooperation: Implications for the Resource-Based View of the Firm. Research Policy.

Munroe, Tapan and Leslie Baroody (2001) *Lessons From California's Electricity Crisis*. Occasional Paper 34 ed. Boulder, Colorado, International Research Center for Energy and Economic Development.

Münster, Ebbe (2 June 2001) Combined Heat and Power: Nord Pool Exchange. PlanEnergi. Denmark, nord@planenergi.dk www.planenergi.dk

Narin, Francis, Kimberly S. Hamilton and Dominic Olivastro (March 17, 1997a) The Increasing Linkage between U.S. Technology and Public Science. Research Policy (1998), pp. 1–17.

Narin, Francis (1997b) Patent citations by Environmental Categories: personal communication and analysis for Dr. W.W. Clark for The role of publicly-funded research and publicly-owned technologies in the transfer and diffusion of environmentally sound technologies (ESTs): The Case of the United States of America.

NASA (1996) Acquisition of transferable technologies. Office of Technology Commercialization, Washington DC.

National Academy of Science (November 29, 1995) Recommendations for Federal Science and Technological Funding. Washington DC.

National Science Foundation (1997) Science and Engineering Indicators, Appendix A, pp. 136–139, 150–153, 172–175.

Navarro, Peter (May 5, 2002) Opinion Editorial, Los Angeles Times.

Nelson, R.R. (1994) Why do firms differ, and does it matter? in R.P. Rumelt, D.E. Schendel and D.J. Teece (eds.), *Fundamental Issues in Strategy*. Boston, Harvard Business School Press.

Nelson, R.R. and Winter, S.G. (1982) *An Evolutionary Theory of Economic Change*. Cambridge, MA, Harvard University Press.

Nelson, Richard, R. (1990) Capitalism as an Engine of Progress. *Research Policy*. Elsevier Science Publishers B.V., North Holland, pp. 193–214.

Newbery, David, M. (1999) *Privatization, Restructuring, and Regulation of Network Utilities*. Cambridge, MIT Press.

Newbery, David M. and Michael G. Pollitt (1997) The restructuring and privatisation of Britain's CEGB—was it worth it? *Journal of Industrial Economics* 45(3): 269–303.

NIST Public & Business Affairs Division: Technology Administration, FY 1997 Appropriations Summary, personal communication, August 1996.

Nobel Laureates (NL) (2001) Energy Manifesto. University of California, Berkeley.

Norsk Hydro (2003) Guide to Hydrogen safety codes and standards, Oslo, Norway.

Northern California Power Agency (2000) *NCPA Annual Report, 1999–2000*. Roseville, CA, NCPA.

Northern Power Systems (NPS) (Spring 2002) Newsletter, Hybrid Energy Systems, Vermont.

Office of Technology Policy (Summer 1997) The Global Context for U.S. Technology Policy. U.S. Department of Commerce. Washington, D.C., pp. 1–11.

Ogden, Joan, Developing an infrastructure for hydrogen vehicles: a Southern California case study. Un. of California, Davis, Institute for Transportation Studies 1999. http://www.princeton.edu/~energy/publications/pdf/1999/Developing_infrastructure_hydrogen.pdf.

Organization for Economic Co-operation Development (1997) Enhancing the Market Deployment of Energy Technology: A survey of eight technologies. Paris, France, International Energy Agency.

O'Toole, J. (1976) *Energy and Social Change*. Cambridge, MIT Press.

Patel, Visu and Tim Haines with Woodrow W. Clark (May, 2001) Notes on Base and Resource Load Management, unpublished, California Department of Water Resources, Integrated Resources Management Plans.

Peltzman, S. and Winston, C. (2000) *Deregulation of Network Industries, What's Next*. Washington DC, AEI-Brookings Joint Center for Regulatory Studies.

Penn, David W. (1999) *Public Power: Better Than Ever and a Great Investment for the Future*. Washington DC, American Public Power Association.

Perkins, L. John (1996) What is Physics and Why is it a "Science"? Lecture presented at Graduate Physics Seminar: Senior Physicist, Lawrence Livermore National Laboratory, University of California, at University of California, Berkeley.

Perkins, John (1997) Alan Lamont and Woodrow Clark, Global Sustainability though SUPERCODE Optimization and Meta*Net Economic Equilibrium Codes. LLNL, LDRD Project Proposal and Report.

Peyton, Carrie (January 26, 2002) Audit urges new leadership for power grid. *Sacramento Bee*, Sacramento, CA, p. 1.

Philipson, L. and Willis, H.L. (1999) *Understanding Electric Utilities and De-Regulation*. New York, Marcel Dekker.

Pickhardt, M. and Niederprum, M. (2002) Welfare Effects of Electricity Market Deregulation in Germany. Western Economic Association International Annual Meeting, Seattle, July 2002.

Pineau, P.-O. (2002) Electricity sector reform in Cameroon, is privatization the solution? *Energy Policy* 30: 999–1012.

Ponder, Steve (Spring, 2001) Personal discussion, FPL Energy.

Pool, Robert (1997) *Beyond Engineering: How Society Shapes Technology*. Oxford, UK, Oxford University Press.

Porter, Michael E. (1980) *Competitive Strategy: Techniques for Analyzing Industries and Competitors*. New York, Free Press.

Porter, M.E. (2000) Location, competition, and economic development: local clusters in a global economy. *Economic Development Quarterly* 14(1): 15–34.

Porter, M.E. and van der Linde, C. (1995) Green and Competitive: Ending the Stalemate. Harvard Business Review 73.5 (September/October 1995), pp. 120–133.

Porter, Michael E. (1990) *The Competitive Advantage of Nations*. NY, NY Free Press.

Porter, M.E. (1998) Clusters and the New Economics of Competition. *Harvard Business Review*.

Rambach, Glenn (December 14, 1999) Integrated renewable Hydrogen/Utility Systems USDOE Contract number #DE-FC36-98GO10842, Desert research Institute, Reno, NV, pp. 1–64.

Rand Corporation (Winter 2000–2001) California Energy Market Report, Santa Monica, CA.

Rastler, Dan (December 2002) Distributed resources: year 2002 Highlights. Energy Research Producers Institute, Palo Alto, CA.

Redwood-Seyer, Jonas (2002) Widening Access in the Context of Power Sector Reform— an Overview of the Institutional Challenges in Africa.

Reinert, Erik (1998) Raw materials in the history of economic policy, in Gary Cook (ed.), *The Economics and Politics of International Trade*. London and NY, Routledge, pp. 275–300.

Reinert, Erik (1997) The Role of the State in Economic Growth. Working Paper #1997.5, University of Oslo, Centre for Development and the Environment, pp. 1–58.

Reinert, Erik (1996) Economics, 'the dismal Science' or 'The Never-ending Frontier of Knowledge? On technology, Energy, and Economic Welfare, Norwegian Oil Review, No. 7, pp. 18–31.

Reinert, Erik (1995) Competitiveness and its predecessors—a 500 year cross-national perspective. *Structure Change and Economic Dynamics* 6: 23–42.

Reinhart, William (March 2003) Personal Communication, Torrance, California.

Renewable Energy Policy Project. *Job Creation from Solar Energy in Brookline*. Washington DC, Renewable Energy Policy Project.

Revkin, Andrew, C. (November 3, 2002) Climate talks shift focus on how to deal with changes. New York Times, Electronic.

Richlin, E. and Del Chiaro, B. (2002) *Clean Energy at the Crossroads: Charting the Potential for Renewable Energy in Los Angeles*. Los Angeles, CA, California Public Interest Research Group.

Ridley, Scott (1996) *Profile of Power*. Washington DC, American Public Power Association.

Rifkin, Jeremy (2003–2004) The European Union Hydrogen Economy. Series of papers and articles. http://www.foet.org/JeremyRifkin.htm

Rifkin, Jeremy, (June 16, 2003) The Dawn of the Hydrogen Economy Keynote Address to the European Union Hydrogen Conference, Brussels. http://europa.eu.int/comm/research/energy/nn/nn_rt_hy3_en.htm.

Rifkin, Jeremy (2002) The Hydrogen Economy, 2003. New York, NY. Penguin. http://www.foet.org/JeremyRifkin.htm

Romanwitz, Hal, The Economic Case for Wind and Pumped Storage. unpublished business plan, Winter 2002 and presented at Mountain States Public Utility Conference, Westminster, CO, Jan 2003.

Romm, Joseph, J. (1993) *Lean and Clean Management*. New York, NY, Kodansha International.

Rose, Craig, D. (January 17, 2003) FERC rules against state, power contracts are valid. Bloomberg Business News, Staff and news Services, Washington, DC, electronic.

Rosen, Christine (1997) Noisome, Noxious, and Offensive Vapors, fumes and stenches in American Towns and Cities: 1840–1865. *Historical Geography* 25.

Rosen, Christine Meisner, Janet Bercovitz and Sara Beckman, Implementing Environment Programs across dispersed supply chains: a transaction costs analysis of exchange hazards in Green Supplier relations in the Computer Industry, to be published.

Rosenfeld, Arthur, Tina Kaarsberg and Joseph Romm (November 2000) Technologies to reduce carbon dioxide emissions in the next decade. *Physics Today* 29–34.

Rosser, M. (2002) Experiences of economic transtion in complex contexts. *International Journal of Social Economics* 29(5/6): 436–452.

Rudnick, H. and Monter, J.-P. (2002) Second Generation Electricity Reforms in Latin America and the California Paradigm. *Journal of Industry, Competition, and Trade* 2(1–2): 159.

Rudolph, Suzanne and Robert (1973) *The Modernity of Tradition*. Chicago, University of Chicago Press.

Sacramento Bee (April 2001) Gorging Profits. Sacramento, CA, from California Energy Commission.

San Francisco Public Utilities Commission and Department of Environment (SFPUC), The Electricity Resource Plan: Choosing San Francisco's Energy Future. San Francisco, CA, November 2002.

Sarbanes-Oxley (2002) Finance and Corporate Governance in American Firms, Washington DC. Signed into law by President G.W. Bush, 30 July 2002.

Savage, Paul (March 11, 2003) Hybrid Cars Today, Hybrid Buildings Tomorrow. Nextek Power Systems.

Savitski, David W. (Winter 2003) Ownership selection in the Electric Utility Industry, to be published in *Utility Policy Journal*.

Sawyer, Stephen (1986) *Renewable Energy: Progress, Prospects*. Washington DC, Association of American Geographers.

Saxenian, AnnaLee (2002) Local and Global Networks of Immigrant Professionals in Silicon Valley. San Francisco, CA, Public Policy Institute of California.

Saxenian, AnnaLee (1999) Silicon Valley's New Immigrant Entrepreneurs. San Francisco, CA, Public Policy Institute of California.

Saxenian, AnnaLee (1994) *Regional Advantage: Culture and Competition in Silicon Valley and Route 128*. Cambridge, MA, Harvard Un. Press.

Schipper, L. Meyers, S. and Kelly, H. (1985) *Coming in From the Cold, Energy Wise Housing in Sweden*. Washington DC, Severn Locks Press.

Schultz, Don *et al.* (Lead Editor) (October 2001) Standard Practices Manual: revision. Governor's Office of Planning and Research, Interagency Working Group, Sacramento, CA.

Schumpeter, J. (1934) *The Theory of Economic Development*. Cambridge, MA, Harvard Un. Press.

Schumpeter, J. Capitalism (1942) *Socialism and Democracy*. New York, NY, Harper and Brothers.

Schwartz, Peter and Doug Randall (March/April 2003) How Hydrogen can save America. Wired Magazine, electronic.

Science, Special Section, Who Finances Research and Development. Vol. 275, 1729, March 21, 1997.

Sclar, E.D. (2000) *You Don't Always Get What You Pay for: The Economics of Privatization*. Ithaca, New York, Cornell University Press.

Scott, J.C. (1998) *Seeing Like a State, How Certain Schemes to Improve the Human Condition Have Failed*. New Haven, Yale University Press.

Shelton, George (2002) Smoking Gun Shoots Down Bush View of Power Crisis. Los Angeles Times, B5.

Shilling, John D. (August 14, 2002) Financial Markets do Impact the Environment, Overview for New America Foundation Project: the Environment and International Finance, unpublished paper.

Shnayerson, Michael (1996) The Car that Could, the inside story of GMs Revolutionary Electric Vehicle. New York, NY, Random House.

Silverman, B.S. (1996) *Technical Assets and the Logic of Corporate Diversification*, University of California, Berkeley, Haas School of Business, unpublished doctoral Dissertation.

Singh, V. (2001) *The Work that Goes into Renewable Energy*. Washington DC, Renewal Energy Policy Project.

Sioshansi, F.P. (2001) California's dysfunctional electrictiy market, policy lessons on market restructuring. *Energy Policy* 29: 735–742.

Smeloff, Ed and Peter Asmus (1997) *Reinventing Electric Utilities*. Covelo, CA, Island Press.

Smil, Vaclav (2000) Energy in the Twentieth Century: Resources Conversions, Costs, Uses, and Consequences, in *Annual Review of Energy 2000*, Vol. 25, Annual Reviews, pp. 21–51.

Smith, Adam (1937) *The Wealth of Nations*. New York, NY, Modern Library, reprint.

Smith, J. Ray, S. Aceves, Clark, W.W. Jr. and Perkins, L.J. with Gehl, S., Maulbetsch J., Vemuri V.R. and T. Nakata (1997) Optimization for Power Utility Applications. University of Calif., Lawrence Livermore National Laboratory, internal R&D project proposal.

Solar Catalyst Group and Clean Edge Inc. Solar Opportunity Assessment Report. Berkeley, CA, 2003, pp. 1–67.

Sorensen, Olav Jull (1996) "The Network Theory: an introduction to its Conceptual World", International Business Economics, Aalborg, DK: No. 8, pp. 1–18.

South Coast Air Quality Management District (SCAQMD) (2003–2004) Requests for Bids, Fall 2003—Results 2004. Dimond Bar, California, www.scagmd.org.

Southern California Edison (2003) Economic and Development, Rosemead, CA. www.sce.com/ebd.

Southern California Edison (2003a) Selecting the Right Technology for your business: a small business guide. Economic and Development, Rosemead, CA. www.sce.com/ebd; (2003b) Financial Resources Manual: a guide to capital access and financial information. Economic and Development, Rosemead, CA. www.sce.com/ebd.

Southern California Public Power Authority. *2000 Annual Report*. www.scppa.org.

Sowell, Arnie *et al.* (2002–2003) Sustainable Building Task Force; codes and standards, Department of General Services, Consumer Affairs Agency, Sacramento, CA.

Stanton, S. (May 2001) Special Report: How Californians got burned—The state electricity system is in shambles, and the worst may be ahead. *Sacramento Bee*.

State of California (December 22, 2001) Strategies for a Climate change Initiative. Draft internal document Climate Change Interagency Task Force, pp. 1–25.

Steiner, F. (2000) *Regulation, industry structure and performance in the electricity supply industry* (Working Papers No. 238 ed.) Organization for Economic Cooperation and Development.

Stempel, Robert C. (April 4, 2002) UAS Hydrogen Economy Here and Now, editorial.

Stipp, David (November 12, 2001) The Coming Hydrogen Economy: fuel cells powered by hydrogen are about to hit the market, Fortune, Electronic.

Summerton, Jane (1994) *Changing Large Technical Systems*. Boulder, Westview.

Summerton, Jane and Ted K. Bradshaw (Jan–Feb 1991) Toward a dispersed electrical system. *Energy Policy* 24–34.

Sweeney, James L. (2002) *The California Electricity Crisis*. Stanford, CA, Hoover Institution Press.

Tansey, B. (2003 July) Power giant files for bankruptcy. *San Francisco Chronicle*.

Tatum, Jesse S. (1995) *Energy Possibilities*. Albany, State university of New York Press.

Tatum, Jesse S. and Ted K. Bradshaw (1986) Energy Production by Local Governments: An Expanding Role. *Annual Review of Energy* 11: 471–512.

Teece, David J. (Spring 1998) Capturing value from Knowledge Assets, the new economy, markets for know-how, and the intangible assets. *California Management Review* 40(3): 55–79.

Teece, D.J., Rumelt, R.P. Dosi, G. and Winter, S.F. (1995) Understanding corporate cohence, theory and evidence. *Jounral of Economic Behavior and Organization* 23(1): 1–30.

Teece, D.J., Bercovitz, J.E.L. and De Figueiredo, J.M. (1994) Firm Capabilities and Managerial Decision-making: A theory of Innovation Biases. Unpublished, University of California, Berkeley, USA. Haas School of Business.

Thomas, Steve (1997) The British market reform: a centralistic capitalist approach, in Atle Midttun (ed.), *European Electricity Systems in Transition*. Oxford, Elsevier, pp. 41–87.

Thurow, Lester, C. (1996) *The Future of Capitalism, How Today's Economic Forces Shape Tomorrow's World*. New York, NY, William Morrow & Comp.

Toffler, Alvin and Heidi Toffler. *The Third Wave*.

References483

Tromp, Tracey K., Run-Lie Shia, Mark Allen, John M. Eller and Yung, Y.L. (June 2003) Potential environmental impact of a hydrogen economy on the stratosphere. *Science* 300: 1740–1742.

Turner, J.A. (1999) A realizable renewable energy future. *Science* 285(5427): 687–689.

Turner, Rob (June 2, 2003) Fortune Small Business: The Next Big Thing—solar power from Powerlight, Tom Dinwoodie, Fortune Magazine, electronic.

United Nations (1994) Report of the Workshop (Oslo, 13–15 October, 1993) on the Transfer and Development of Environmentally Sound Technologies (ESTs). New York and Geneva, UNCTAD, pp. 1–51.

United Nations (1997) Promoting the transfer and use of Environmentally Sound Technology, A Review of Policies. New York and Geneva, Science and Technology Issues, UNCTAD, pp. 1–53.

US Department of Commerce (1997) The Global context for US Technology Policy, Washington, DC, pp. 6–7.

US Department of Energy (DOE) (2001) *Subsequent Events, California's Energy Crisis.* Washington DC. http:/www.eia.doe.gov/eneaf/electricity/california/subsequentevents.html.

US Department of Energy (1996) Industrial Partnership Office, viewgraph slide on number of CRADAs, Lawrence Livermore National Laboratory.

US Department of Energy (1994) Principal Investigator's Information Protection Guide— definitions, Lawrence Livermore National Laboratory.

US Department of Energy (1994) Progress through Industrial Partnerships. Lawrence Livermore National Laboratory.

US Environmental Protection Agency (USEPA) (February 1997) Environmental technology Verification Program, Verification Strategy. EPA. Office of Research and Development, Washington DC, pp. 1–18.

van Est, Rinie (1999) *Winds of Change: A Comparative Study of the Politics of Wind Energy Innovation in California and Denmark.* Utrecht, Netherlands, International Books.

Varnamo Demonstration Plant Report, 1996–2000, Malmö, Sweden, Sydkraft AB, 2001.

Vesper, Karl H. (1990) *New Venture Strategies* (Rev. Ed.). Englewood Cliffs, NJ, Prentice Hall.

Vogel, David (1995) *Trading Up: Consumer and Environmental Regulation in a Global Economy.* Cambridge, MA, Harvard University Press.

Waldorp, M.M. (1992) *Complexity: The Emerging Science at the Edge of Order and Chaos.* New York, Simon and Schuster.

Walsh, James (2002) *The $10 Billion Jolt, California's Energy Crisis: Cowardice, Greed, Stupidity, and the Death of Deregulation.* Los Angeles, Silver Lake Publishing.

Walshok, Mary Lindenstein (March 1994) *Rethinking the Role of Research Universities in Economic Development.* Industry & Higher Education, pp. 8–18.

Wamukonya, Njeri (2003) "Power Sector Reform in Developing Countries. Mismatched Agendas". In Njeri Wamukonya, ed., Electricity Reform: Social and Environmental Challenges. United Nations Environment Program, Riso Center, Roskilde, Denmark, pp. 7–47.

Watkins, James D. (August 1, 1997) Science and technology in foreign affairs. *Science* 277: 650–651.

Weare Christopher (2003) The California Electricity Crisis: Causes and Policy Options. San Francisco, CA, Public Policy Institute of California.

Weber, M. (1964) *Social and Economic Organization.* The Free Press, New York.

Weick, K.E. (1979) Cognitive proccesses in organizations. *Research in Organizational Behavior* 1.

Williams, J.C. (1997) *Energy and the Making of Modern California*. Akron, Akron University Press.

Williamson, Oliver E. and Sidney G. Winter (eds.) (1993) *The Nature of the Firm: Origins, Evolution, and Development*. Oxford Un. Press.

Williamson, Oliver E. (1996) *The Mechanisms of Governance*. Oxford Un. Press.

Wiser, Ryan, Meredith Fowlie and Edward Holt (November 2001) Public goods and private interests: understanding non-residential demand for green power. *Energy Policy* 29(13): 1085–1097.

Wiser, Ryan and Mark Bollinger (2003) Lawrence Berkeley National Laboratory, Berkeley, CA.

Woo, Chi-Keung (2001) What went wrong in California's electricity market? *Energy* 26(8): 747–758.

Wood, A.R. (July 2003) Utilities save big as towns lose out. *Philadelphia Inquirer*.

World Alliance for Decentralized Energy (WADE) (October 2002) Conference Summary, 3rd International CHP and Decentralization Conference and USAID International Conference on Bagasse Cogeneration, New Delhi, India, pp. 1–2.

World Commission on Environment and Development (WCED) (1987) *Our Common Future* ('The Brundtland Report'). Oxford, Oxford University Press.

Younger, Dana (2000) Renewable Energy and Energy Efficiency Fund for Emerging Markets, Ltd. From IFC—World Bank, Washington, DC.

Ziman, Richard (December 2003) Acceptance speech for Sustainable Business Award. California League of Conservation Voters, Tenth Annual Meeting, Los Angeles, CA.

Index

Index